HELL OR HIGH WATER

HELL OR HIGH WATER

— MY LIFE IN AND OUT OF POLITICS —

PAUL MARTIN

⟦A DOUGLAS GIBSON BOOK⟧

McCLELLAND & STEWART

Library and Archives Canada Cataloguing in Publication

Martin, Paul, 1938–
Hell or high water / Paul Martin.

"Douglas Gibson books".
ISBN 978-0-7710-5692-5

1. Martin, Paul, 1938–. 2. Canada – Politics and government – 1993–.
3. Cabinet ministers – Canada – Biography. 4. Prime ministers – Canada –
Biography. 5. Politicians – Canada – Biography. 6. Businessmen – Canada –
Biography. I. Title.

FC636.M37A3 2008   971.07'2092   C2008-901949-0

We acknowledge the financial support of the Government of Canada through the
Book Publishing Industry Development Program and that of the Government of
Ontario through the Ontario Media Development Corporation's Ontario Book
Initiative. We further acknowledge the support of the Canada Council for the Arts
and the Ontario Arts Council for our publishing program.

A Douglas Gibson Book

Typeset in Sabon by M&S, Toronto
Printed and bound in Canada

ANCIENT FOREST
FRIENDLY
This book was produced using ancient-forest friendly papers.

McClelland & Stewart Ltd.
75 Sherbourne Street
Toronto, Ontario
M5A 2P9
www.mcclelland.com

1 2 3 4 5   12 11 10 09 08

To Sheila

Contents

CHAPTER ONE

An Ordinary Childhood

My mother was born Eleanor Alice Adams in the village of McGregor about ten miles southeast of Windsor, Ontario. There were fewer than fifty people in McGregor, which was not much more than the place where the highway crossed the railway tracks. There were a couple of dozen houses, a church, and a general store that belonged to my grandparents.

I guess McGregor was too small to be fussy about social distinctions, because my mother was the product of what in those days they called a "mixed marriage." Her mother, Amelia, had been born a McManamy, from Irish-Catholic stock. Her father, Edgar, was a Protestant. Now, Edgar was a wonderful man, but it was Amelia who was the dynamo in the family. At some point before the Depression, she moved the family business to Windsor, where she established a small pharmacy and eventually a second. With hard work and determination, my grandmother managed to lift the Adams family out of poverty and give it a tenuous grip on the middle class, which somehow survived the 1930s. In time she was able to buy a farm near McGregor and a cottage in the village of Colchester, which is where I spent my summers as a child and is the place I still remember as my childhood home.

The cottage was shared by my mother and my Aunt Mame and their families. It was not a grand place at all. I still remember when the outhouse was replaced with indoor plumbing. Originally, there was just one big bedroom upstairs, which was later divided in two.

An addition downstairs created another bedroom. Church benches once belonging to a great-uncle who had been a Methodist circuit rider sat in the living room, a constant reminder of the Protestant side of the family. We had an icebox, and I remember Clyde Scott, who brought the ice wagon around to refill it. All my life I have referred to the refrigerator as the icebox, and long before the age of Google and the BlackBerry, my sons would look at me and say, "My god, what century are you from?"

Behind the cottage was a potato patch my Uncle Vince had ploughed under and rolled by hand to create a makeshift tennis court soon after the cottage was built in the 1920s. This was not a fancy clay court; when it rained, it turned to mud, and it was my job to take the hand roller and restore the court to playable condition and mark out the lines again with lime.

The cottage was on a street perpendicular to the main road, on the other side of which was a field we called "the park," running to the cliff overlooking Lake Erie. During the day, the calm waters lapped at the shore, as the giant lake freighters passed five or six miles off in the shipping channel. By night, there were often huge winds and lightning storms the likes of which I've never seen again. For me, it was a magical place. Many years later, I took Sheila back there and asked her to marry me.

During my childhood, there was no beach. In fact, high water was causing cliff erosion. My mother used to tell us that when she was a young girl, they could go through the park and down some stairs to a beach and walk along the sand and rock about a quarter-mile to the Colchester dock, which seemed miraculous to me. Later, when I was at Canada Steamship Lines (CSL), and I happened to be in the area, I looked out and saw to my astonishment that the beach had reappeared, recreating the fabled scene from my mother's childhood. One of the captains at CSL said that the low water was unprecedented, and I told him that no, actually, this was untrue; it is a cycle that recurs every three or four decades. He challenged me, and we went back and checked the records, and sure enough I was right.

Besides me and my sister, Mary Anne, who was born when I was five, there was a large cast of cousins who populated the cottage and with whom we grew up almost as a single family. Mame's son, Michael, was a few years older than I was, and I still regard him as a brother. My Uncle Vince's daughters – Jane, Ann, Pat, and Amy – were fixtures at Colchester as well. My mother was often the main parental presence at the cottage because Dad was usually away in Ottawa, Aunt Mame had inherited responsibility for the drugstores, and Uncle Vince ran the farm. Even back then, farming was a precarious profession, so Vince also worked as a shipper at Chrysler, while his brother, my Uncle Clare, worked at Ford and sold eggs on the side.

Many people assume that because my father was a cabinet minister, my early life was saturated in politics and cosseted by privilege – far from it. Throughout my childhood, for Mary Anne and me our mother was the dominating presence in our lives. Even after we moved to Ottawa and started school, she was the constant presence that made our childhoods ordinary in the best sense, protected from the crosswinds of politics and from the temptation to think we were something special just because we had slid down the banisters in the Parliament Buildings. She was in so many ways the free-spirited complement to my dad's buttoned-down world of achievement and ambition. She had studied at the Royal Conservatory of Music, and it was she who gathered the family around the piano in Colchester, accompanied by my Uncle Clare on violin, while Mary Anne and my cousins drowned out my own reedy voice in a sing-song of Stephen Foster tunes. And it was the fear of her wrath that set me on a short-lived attempt to run away from Colchester to China after hitting Roseanne Cole on the arm with a stone and making her cry. It was my mother's presence that created the glow of good fortune around my childhood that I still feel today.

My mother was the more easygoing of my parents, and the one many people said I took after. My sister, Mary Anne, was deeper than I was, more sensitive, more introspective, then as now. She took after Dad, which meant that on those occasions when he was around and playing his walk-on part as family disciplinarian, there were bound to be clashes.

Our neighbours in Colchester were not politicians or public servants, as they might have been in Ottawa. This was the age when a working man at an American auto plant could afford a summer home. Many of the people on our street were autoworkers or other working people from Windsor and Detroit. The cottages were jammed close together, and when the Detroit Tigers were playing, the game would be on everyone's radio. You could walk right down the street without missing a pitch.

Our American neighbours seemed wealthy by Canadian standards, and it was through their eyes that I had my introduction to the American way of life. – not only the prosperity but also some of the social conflicts. These were the families that felt squeezed at work and in their Detroit neighbourhoods by the great Afro-American migration from the South to the industrial heartland, and as a result they sometimes gave vent to racial attitudes that were foreign to us. It was those rising tensions that eventually led Detroit to explode – like many other American cities – in racial violence during the 1960s. In my high school and college years, I marched for civil rights in Detroit and elsewhere in Michigan, often alongside the sons and daughters of our Colchester neighbours who did not share their parents' views. Once, I attended a rally where Martin Luther King, Jr., spoke – though he was just a tiny figure in the distance from where I stood, the crowd was so large. More frequently, I marched with small groups of a hundred or two hundred through working-class suburbs such as Flint and Lansing, where we were often outnumbered by angry crowds flinging racist catcalls – and worse – our way.

My father, as I have said, was often away, and as a result, I have been asked many times how it was that we came to be so close. The answer is that it is not always the quantity but the quality of the time you spend together that binds son to father and father to son. When he was in Colchester, Dad and I would often go off into Lake Erie, or to Lake St. Clair, and laze away hours together with nothing more to disturb us than the nibbling fish. When Dad put down his fishing rod and went back to business, I was usually delighted to go along for the ride.

Sunday, for example, was seldom a day of rest in the home of Paul Martin, Member of Parliament for Essex East. No, Sunday was a day for meeting and greeting constituents. The area around Windsor, with its booming auto industry, was a magnet for workers of every background: Croatian, Italian, Polish, Serbian, German, Estonian, and Lithuanian. Many were European refugees who had arrived after 1945. One of the first things they did upon settling was to form churches, and, luckily for my father, many of those were Catholic. Add that to the French-Canadian population in the area, which was also quite large, and my father had a wealth of choice when deciding where to attend Mass on a Sunday morning. One week it would be St. Anne's in Windsor, the next week Annunciation in Stoney Point, and so on throughout the riding, as we distributed our public prayers as broadly as possible.

For me, these summer Sundays were a chance to spend time with my dad. In the winter, in Ottawa, where we moved when I was eight, I was busy with school and he was busy with parliamentary and government business. In those days, the House of Commons often sat in the evening, and MPs had to remain within the sound of the division bells in case there was a vote. On weekends, my father usually took the long train ride down to Windsor, leaving me, Mary Anne, and my mother behind in Ottawa while he tended to his constituency. And since my father was also a minister in the government of William Lyon Mackenzie King, and later of Louis St. Laurent, he often had to travel across the country and abroad.

But a Sunday in the summer – that was special. My father was not a formal man, but there were certain expectations of an MP in those days. So, even in the sweltering summer heat around Windsor, he wore a suit and tie, and donned a hat – a Homburg, I think. He and I got into the large grey Buick with running boards that jutted out beneath the car doors and headed out on the road. My father was a terrible driver, because the driving was less important than spying a familiar constituent by the roadside and waving. Or picking up a hitchhiker, and engaging him in a discussion, not so much about politics as about who the fellow was and to whom he was related. Adding to the danger was his deep and abiding belief that you should look at someone when you talked to them. This habit was even more alarming than his passengers realized, since it was not obvious to everyone that he had sight only in one eye. When he looked politely at his passenger, the responsibility for avoiding collisions had really defaulted to others using the road.

In those days, the Catholic Mass was in Latin, so the service was quite familiar whatever the ethnic association of the church. The sermon might sometimes be in a language I did not understand, though I do not remember that being a cause of great sorrow to me. The only complaint I had was about some of the Eastern European churches, whose services seemed to go on and on; I thought Dad should pick churches with shorter Masses. After the Mass, Dad would join the priest in greeting the parishioners as they filed out.

My father was a voracious reader, mostly philosophy, history, and biography; but he was also extremely sociable – an unusual combination. He was outgoing and loved being with people, but his meanderings around the constituency were also motivated by political necessity. Essex East was extremely diverse and by no means a safe Liberal seat. He won it from a Conservative, and although it remained in Liberal hands for several decades after he retired, it eventually passed to the New Democratic Party (NDP). Thus, political uncertainty made him one of the first MPs to develop sophisticated riding organizations, getting letters of congratulations out to newlyweds and notes of condolence to the bereaved. Not everyone in his era did these things, but he felt it was necessary. He often said that without the support of the people of Essex East, he would never have had the opportunity to play on the national and the world stage, and he never took that for granted. In his travels around the country and the world, he became famous for asking: "Is there anyone here from Windsor?" He loved it, but he had no choice.

In that way, I later realized, I was like my dad: I often had to push myself to get up and go to the many social occasions that politics demands, but once I got there I almost always enjoyed it. Being with your constituents is the greatest tonic against the cynicism that sometimes infects the common portrayal of politicians. Most people really do appreciate the work of those they elect. Folks would come up and say, "Oh, it's so good to see you!" They didn't know what you had been doing, but they knew you had been working for them. My dad took huge strength from this, as I did later on.

My father was legendary for his ability to recollect the names of constituents, which arose out of his affection for people. But everyone's memory has its limits, and no one can recall sixty thousand names. So he developed some tricks to get around the awkward moments. "Paul, you remember our friend," he would say, which by so obviously dumbfounding me would usually provoke the constituent to introduce himself, saving the occasion for all concerned – except me, of course. From time to time, Dad also suffered one of those embarrassing encounters that afflict all political figures, when they approach someone who hasn't the faintest idea who the great person is. He had a trick for this situation too. "Well, Paul," he would say, "I think we should go now, don't you, Mr. Martin?" I often wondered whether that wasn't the reason I was named after him.

After church, there was usually a picnic or a summer fair to attend. We'd head off in the car to one of the nearby villages – St. Joachim, Stoney Point, or Belle River. It was no imposition to be taken to a country fair. Much of the time, I was expected to hang around close to my father, though I could also sneak away for a while to watch a horse-pull or a ploughing match. Every politician will tell you that one of the challenges of political life is that while there are very few occasions for exercise, there are many, many opportunities to eat. My father faced an internal struggle at practically every social event, at which there were tables of fresh-baked treats hot from the kitchens of the local ladies.

As we left one event, my father would ask directions to whatever was the next. This was another opportunity to talk with a constituent, but it did not, so far as I could see, involve an actual exchange of information. Back in the car, we would launch off once again into the unknown, exploring obscure nooks and crannies of the riding not because of my father's desire to track down even the most remote voter but because even after decades of plying the roads of Essex East, he still had no idea where most of them led.

Later in my life, people often said to me: "You grew up in such a political family; you must have understood all about politics." But that wasn't the way it was. A doctor's child doesn't necessarily know all about medicine just because he accompanies his father on hospital rounds. My only political involvement as a child was touring around the riding with my dad. I wasn't interested in politics; I was interested in being with him. And if I was playing baseball when he set out, well, I would stay and play baseball, like any kid would. As I grew a little older, politics began to have a different significance in my life. Most parents have their own ways of keeping their kids in line. In my house, it was: "If you get in trouble, it is going to be in the headlines in the *Windsor Star* and your father's going to lose the next election." Unfortunately, there would be a couple of occasions when I would test this proposition.

Politics also impinged on my childhood in that I was forever being told by my father before meeting someone new: "You're about to meet a great man; this is someone who has done great things." And paradoxically, as a result I have never been much impressed with important people. There were so many of them in my childhood, and to tell the truth, not all of them lived up to their advance billings, certainly not in the eyes of a kid.

One occasion when this attitude of mine surfaced later became part of family lore. When I was about sixteen years old, my father took me to the opening of the new post office in Belle River. Dad had worked hard to get the post office, and so there were a lot of speeches about how important this building was – the greatest human achievement since St. Peter's in Rome, it was generally agreed. And for this, my father's praises were properly sung. A day or two later, I went with him to New York, to the United Nations, where he had been instrumental in the first breakthrough in the admission of new member-nations. There had been a rapid increase in the number of countries in the world after the Second World War as the former European colonies gained statehood. However, their entry into the United Nations was often blocked by one or the other of the great powers – principally the United States and the Soviet Union – who did not want to see the voting balance in the General Assembly tilted one way or another. For the new member-states ushered into the world assembly in considerable part through my father's efforts, it was a great day. I sat with the Canadian delegation and heard my father praised by country after country in speeches from the podium. When it was all over, someone asked me what I thought of all these people saying what a great man Dad was, to which I was heard to reply: "Well, it wasn't bad, but the speeches were better in Belle River."

Years later, it was a thrilling moment for me when I mounted that same UN podium for the first time to give a speech myself. The childhood memories came flooding back. And the same is true, I am happy to report, when I have had occasion to speak at Belle River.

While my mom was everything you could want in a mother, she was not entirely a conventional political wife. She was a beautiful woman with a great sense of humour, both of which allowed her to take politics on her own terms and participate in her own way. My father recounted the story of her first social encounter with the prime minister – a luncheon at Laurier House in Ottawa. Dad was still a young member and quite nervous about any encounter with the man who would determine his political future.

"My husband thinks you're a very great man," she told Mackenzie King as they arrived.

"And what do you think, Mrs. Martin?" Mackenzie King asked.

"I'm going to take some convincing," my mother replied – not exactly the response Dad had coached her to give before they left home. To my father's astonishment, the very next day Mackenzie King dropped by their apartment in the Sandy Hill district of Ottawa, which was only a couple of blocks away from his, and invited my mother to join him on his afternoon stroll.

In the riding, my mother was also a considerable political asset to my father because of her vivacity and natural grace. While my father was in and out of the constituency because of his parliamentary and government duties, she was a much more regular presence. During campaigns, when my father could be something of a thorn in the side of the local organizers – like many candidates, somebody to be managed and handled – they could always turn to my mother, knowing they would have a sympathetic ear. While my father might race through a social or political gathering, my mother had a tendency to linger, because there was always someone there who didn't want to let her go. Sheila had a very similar experience after I entered political life. As the MP or the candidate, my job at an event was usually to shake the hand of every person in the room, which made real conversation impossible. There were many occasions when I had done my duty and was ready to cut out of one event to get to the next but had trouble pulling Sheila away from a group with whom she had become engrossed in conversation. The view of all my supporters in my constituency of LaSalle-Émard was that Sheila was my greatest political asset. I did not disagree.

For her part, my mother was never keen on sitting on the podium with her hands crossed in her lap while my father sang the praises of the Liberal government, so her campaign appearances were selective, and grew less frequent over the years. She used to tell a story of canvassing during an election in the early years with one of my father's organizers, Blackie Quenneville. The Quenneville family were stalwarts of my father's campaigns and later became great supporters of mine. Blackie's father, Alfred, had been one of my father's organizers, as were his daughters Izzy and Ramona. In the next generation, Fred Quenneville and his wife, Barbara, who had been close to my father, also worked for me in the 1990 leadership campaign, as did their children, Camille and Carl, in 2003. Four generations of Quennevilles working to help two generations of Martins! Anyway, it seems that while Blackie and my mom were going door to door during one campaign sortie, a fair number of posters for the Conservative candidate went missing along their route. My mother would laugh as she recalled the scene of Conservative workers showing up in a car and discovering what they were up to. There followed a wild car chase through Windsor, because my mother realized that while it was one thing for Blackie Quenneville to get caught ripping down Tory posters, it was something quite different for Nell Martin, wife of the Liberal MP, to be caught dead to rights. In later years when her children raised her "outrageous" behaviour, she always claimed that the Tories had started it. I'm inclined to believe her.

There were undoubtedly moments of delight for my mother during my father's long political career. But it was not a world she had chosen or would have chosen if it had not been for my father, which may lie behind some of my own ambivalence to the profession. The demands of politics on the life of the family are vividly illustrated by the circumstances of my own birth. My father, still a backbencher, had been asked by Mackenzie King to join the Canadian delegation to the League of Nations Assembly in Geneva in September 1938. Unfortunately, the departure date more or less coincided with the expected day of my arrival in the world. And so, on August 28, at the Hôtel-Dieu Hospital in Windsor, my mother's physician induced my birth in time for Dad to catch the train for Montreal and connect with *The Empress of Australia*, which was steaming for Britain September 2. "It was not easy to leave them," my father later wrote, "but after a wrenching goodbye, I went on a mission of which my wife fully approved."

It was typical of my mother that while she was capable of great patience where her family was concerned, she also had limits that could reveal themselves in spectacular fashion. The most famous story about her is when she was walking along Ouellette Street in Windsor with my father, who was smoking a cigar and in full rhetorical flight, no doubt about some great accomplishment of his. It was all too much for Mom, who did not have much time for my father in his moments of pomposity. She sat down on the curb and refused to move until my father agreed to come down to earth. The sight of the Honourable Paul Martin on a street corner with his wife sitting stubbornly on the curb attracted a few gawkers, then a few more, until there were perhaps twenty or thirty witnessing the embarrassing scene. In the years since, I have personally met all three thousand of them, who each describe it to me with the vividness and relish that only an eyewitness can bring to the job.

After a lifetime of political demands that she had not chosen for herself, who can blame my mother for looking forward to a day when they would subside? To be honest, I think the happiest time of her life may have been at the end of my dad's career, when he was High Commissioner in London and no longer had the responsibilities of a politician.

When my father was appointed to the cabinet in 1945, the decision was made to move the family home to Ottawa. As it happened, this coincided with the most dramatic incident of my childhood. Among my best friends in Colchester were the Coles – Mike, Vince, and Roseanne – whose father was a milkman in Detroit. Theirs was a traditional Irish-American Catholic family. Both Mike and Vince later became Maryknoll missionaries, and Roseanne joined the convent for a time. One day when I was seven years old, I was playing with my cousin Mike and the Coles and began feeling strange – as if I had a huge plate filling a void in my stomach – and I went and sat down on some swings at the McPhersons' next door. I guess it caught the attention of the adults when I suddenly fell quiet. I remember going home and telling my mother that I was feeling sick. I don't recall experiencing the alarm that my mother obviously did as she rushed me to the hospital. Like every parent in this era, she lived in dread of one disease above all: polio.

It was an age of polio epidemics, of children paralyzed or brought to an early grave. What I remember is being dressed in a white hospital robe and sharing a room with twenty or thirty other kids my age. I do not remember any pain. I still have an image of my parents standing at the door, watching me, presumably from behind glass, not allowed to enter the sickroom. It was only later that I was told my parents believed I would likely die or spend my days in an iron lung.

My father learned of my illness when a note was passed to him during a cabinet meeting. C.D. Howe immediately offered him the use of a government plane to fly home to Windsor, saving him the day-long train trip. I can only imagine what this news meant to my father, whose own life had been blighted by polio, though a different strain. His family, which was clustered around Pembroke, Ontario, were great athletes. My grandfather was a keen organizer of sporting events, and my grandmother's youngest brother, Jean, played hockey for the New York Americans. When he was four, my father fell seriously ill. For a year or two after he survived the immediate crisis, he was pulled around town in a wagon or sleigh by his father and brother because he remained paralyzed on the left side and could not walk. Although he had a partial recovery, Dad permanently lost the use of his left arm and he always had a bit of a limp in one leg. The illness also cost him the sight in his left eye. It was one of his great regrets that his handicaps prevented him from being the "sportsman" he wished he could be. When he was a student at St. Mike's at the University of Toronto, he coached the hockey team because that was the closest he could come to the actual game. Later he enlisted in the army reserves, but suffered the regret that only those who have lived through wartime can understand when he was judged not physically fit to serve. This is not to mention the financial strain my father's illness placed on his family in the early years. His father, a millworker and later a grocery store clerk, struggled to make ends meet at the best of times, the more so with a sickly child. This searing childhood experience explained my father's later passion for universal medical care.

A few years after my illness, I had a startling encounter with my dad as he worked in his study. When I interrupted him, he was uncharacteristically short with me, and my mother hustled me out of the room. I only later learned what it was all about. At the time, the recently invented polio vaccines that eventually proved so effective in suppressing the disease were being administered in North America on a mass scale for the first time. However, a number of children in the United States had apparently contracted polio from the vaccinations themselves. The American government had decided to halt its vaccination program while it figured out what had gone wrong. As minister of health at the time, Dad needed to decide whether to follow the Americans in declaring a moratorium on vaccinations. The Canadian vaccine was not from the suspect American lab, but from a different one here in Canada – the Connaught Laboratory. Still, no one could be perfectly sure whether there had just been a bad batch of vaccine or if something more fundamental was amiss. It was as he pondered this decision – loaded with personal and public significance – that I had interrupted him. He eventually allowed the vaccination program to go ahead – a decision that ultimately saved many lives and rescued many others from a terrible blight.

What I remember about my own recovery from polio was that it delayed my entry into grade three at École Garneau, a French-language separate school on Cumberland Street in Ottawa. Even after I started attending classes, I was supposed to take it easy – for two years, my mother later told me. I wasn't supposed to play baseball or football, for example, though it was a rule I pretty much ignored when I was out of my parents' sight. Also, I wasn't supposed to be upset. I remember that while out with friends several miles from home I lost a softball without a cover, which for some reason was precious to me. A few days later, I came home to the upper-floor duplex where we were living on Goulburn Street and was stunned to find the cover-less softball lying there. Much later, my mother told me that she had bought a new softball and removed the cover, thus resolving the mystery. A prohibition against upsetting an eight- or nine-year-old is not likely to improve his temperament or character, however, and apparently it did not improve mine. After seven or eight months of being coddled, I did something – I don't remember what – that led my mother to blow her stack, and I remember catching it like no one had ever caught it before. At that point, things returned to normal.

Ottawa in my youth, in contrast to Windsor, was Old Canada: riven by linguistic divisions. In Ottawa, I had a unique perspective on the linguistic divide. My father's family was originally Irish, and had come to Canada in the 1840s, fleeing the potato famine. They settled around Thurso in Quebec and were assimilated, as many Catholic immigrants were at the time, into the francophone population. My dad was born after the family moved to LeBreton Flats in Ottawa. Soon after that, they moved to Pembroke, where the family remained part of the francophone community and my father grew up. My father always considered himself a Franco-Ontarian and was schooled in French until university, though interestingly enough my aunts, who were a few years younger, considered English their first language, which may have had to do with their own schooling or perhaps even the ethnicity of the archbishop in later years.

My father's extended family in Pembroke played the same role in my Ottawa life as my mother's did in Colchester. Pembroke in my childhood memory is perpetually winter, just as Colchester is perpetually summer. My Aunt Lucille would take me for walks in the snow or out toboganing. I called her "Ceo," but she was known in the family as "Blackie" because of her dark complexion – according to legend, a legacy of Indian blood somewhere in the family line. There was also my Uncle Émile and Aunts Marie, Aline, Claire, and Anita. Aunt Anita was more than an aunt, in fact. A public servant who lived in Ottawa, she eventually moved in with my family, parenting us whenever my parents had to be away. She was also a great Ottawa Rough Riders fan, which no doubt contributed greatly to my own interest in professional football.

The French-English divide in Ottawa extended to the Catholic Church. When I was old enough to be an altar boy, I remember being questioned by the French Oblates at École Garneau about serving Mass at the Irish Oblate provincial house near my home – a crime second only to consorting with Jesuits! A little more important for me as a boy was the fact that to get to École Garneau, I needed to fight my way past Osgoode, the English public school. And then, if I made it that far without a bloody nose, I had to navigate by St. Joseph's, the Irish-Catholic school, where my Irish-Canadian heritage and my still-nascent grasp of French counted for nothing.

My best friend at school was Dick Robillard. I was a guest during many discussions around their dinner table about the fact that there were harsh limits on how high Dick's dad, who was a public servant, could rise in his career because he was French-speaking. There was also the lingering aftertaste of Regulation 17 – which had banned French-language instruction in Ontario's schools for a time. My grandfather had been an outspoken opponent of Regulation 17, and it remained very much a part of the recent history of Franco-Ontarian society in general and their schools in particular. I remember the teachers telling us about the St-Jean-Baptiste Society and the need to preserve the French language. For me as a boy, these experiences revealed something about Canada – the Old Canada at least – and the need to recognize the value of our two linguistic traditions. Later on, I realized how this also opened me up to the "multiculturalism," as we would come to call it, in places such as Windsor.

But these experiences of the Old Canada were not as deeply stitched into my personality as they had been for my father. My dad grew up as a member of a francophone Catholic minority in Ontario, and never lost the sense of being an outsider that it fostered in him. His family was also poor, as was often the case with Franco-Ontarians. That having been said, the long climb of the lame little boy from Pembroke to Collège St-Alexandre to the University of Toronto, Harvard, Cambridge, then to the House of Commons and ultimately minister of the Crown would have been impossible without the early patronage of a friendly Irish-Catholic archbishop.

My father eventually settled in Windsor, half a province away from where he had grown up. Although he was a lawyer, that meant something very different in a town such as Windsor than it did in the great commercial centres of Montreal and Toronto. The clients and eventually the constituency he came to represent there had many of the features of the outsider as well: a population heavy with newly minted Canadians as well as francophones, filled with people who made their living with their hands and with their sweat, in the great new industries then developing. Windsor was a multi-ethnic industrial boomtown in the shadow of the United States. It was a place where New Canadians were getting on with making new lives for themselves in new industries and were too busy to worry about Canada's traditional preoccupations. The dominant relationship was not between English and French, as it was in Ottawa, but between us and the United States – a rivalry that was usually friendly but also very intense.

In contrast with sedate and proper Ottawa, Windsor was a border town that was proud of its racy legacy from the era of Prohibition. I remember my mother pointing out a house near the cottage that had once been a "blind pig" – or speakeasy – and I remember the implication that she had been an occasional customer. According to legend, freighters would show up at the Hiram Walker distillery on Monday to be loaded for Cuba only to be back two days later to reload. When we moved back to the riding after the Liberal defeat by John Diefenbaker in 1957, Dad bought a house in Walkerville that had once belonged to a notorious rum-runner named Harry Low. There was also a story that the house we had bought had a secret tunnel to the Detroit River, three miles away. Mary Anne and her best friend, Sheila Cowan, spent a good portion of their adolescence looking for it, without success.

My father often said that it was important that you represent a constituency that reflects your own political goals, something I remembered many years later when I chose the ethnically and socially mixed riding of LaSalle-Émard in which to run. As the advocate of the little guy, the working man, the immigrant, and the francophone, my dad made himself the principal proponent in his generation of the socially progressive strain of Liberalism. Although he was a great friend of C.D. Howe, and said in later years that Louis St. Laurent was the greatest of the four prime ministers in whose cabinets he served, he represented a very different perspective than their fiscally conservative, business-oriented Liberalism and would often butt heads with them in order to enlarge the social responsibilities of the government in the postwar years.

The college my father had attended – a junior seminary, really – was St-Alexandre's on the east bank of the Gatineau River. On a clear day, you could see down the Gatineau, across the junction with the Ottawa River, to the Peace Tower on Parliament Hill. When Sir Wilfrid Laurier died in February 1919, Dad sneaked away from school and walked the ten miles into Ottawa to watch the funeral procession. The deep emotional connection with Laurier and his vision of Liberalism never left him. It was in part about identification with a great francophone who was also a great Canadian, a Catholic of anti-clerical views. But it was also about a particular kind of politics: the politics of inclusion, and the use of the state to address the worries of the common people – education, health care, and financial security. It was about providing people with the material foundations with which to enjoy the freedoms our society could afford.

As a matter of practical politics, these ideas fused with the sentiments and ambitions of the constituency my father represented. Windsor was in the process of becoming the classic union town during my father's period as MP, and he was proud to walk with union leaders at the head of the Labour Day parade. This was not as simple and straightforward as it may seem today. Just south of the border, the American labour leader, Walter Reuther, who was a friend of my father, was leading the charge to unionize the auto industry. The United Auto Workers were militant, as they had to be to take on the auto giants, while also being anti-communist and supportive of the war effort during the Second World War. The union movement of the time advocated not just better wages, benefits, and conditions but also a larger, more secure, and dignified role for the working man in North American life. It inspired great passions. I remember that Walkerville, where many of the auto industry executives lived, was for many years a wasteland for my father. I remember as well my father's pleasure late in his parliamentary career when he finally wrested the area from the Tories.

My father's battles for public pensions, employment insurance, and health care addressed the needs and desires of his constituents and arose from a vision of a very substantially reformed capitalism. If it was a struggle sometimes to convince his cabinet colleagues to come up with the cash for what must have seemed extravagant ideas, he could always come home to the riding and have it driven home to him that it was the right thing to do. In my own career, I have tried to be faithful to my father's legacy. True, I am a fiscal conservative, but I have always coupled that to a belief that sound finances are the underpinning, the way to pay for the social Liberalism I also believe in and that I inherited from my father. This brand of Liberalism begins with Laurier – a deep respect for individual freedom and a belief that the state has the responsibility to open up the social, educational, and economic opportunities that will enable the poor to achieve that freedom. No trickle-down economics there!

It says something about the bond my father forged with his constituents that, much later, when he stepped down as High Commissioner to Britain, he didn't retire to Ottawa but headed back to Essex East to be with "his people," as he liked to call them.

One time in the late 1940s, my father drove Mary Anne and me to a church picnic. On the way, Mary Anne asked, "Daddy, what is Essex East?"

"Don't you know," I interjected. "Essex East is the Promised Land."

CHAPTER TWO

Young Man and the Sea

Father Edmund McCorkell was a Basilian priest who was registrar of St. Michael's College at the University of Toronto when my father was a student there and who later became Superior of the college. My father greatly admired his lectures in political philosophy, and they became lifelong friends, with Father McCorkell officiating at my parents' wedding in Windsor in 1937. He was a gentle and generous man. So I am sure that when Father McCorkell, in the course of a visit to our place in Colchester, asked about my studies in the last year of high school, he didn't mean to ruin my summer.

There was an unquestioned assumption in my family – certainly unquestioned by me – that once I finished first year at the University of Ottawa, which was the equivalent of grade thirteen in the rest of the province, I would follow in my parents' footsteps by going to the University of Toronto: St. Michael's College, to be precise. My mother was a graduate in pharmacy from the U of T. My father had completed a degree in philosophy at St. Mike's, the Catholic college on campus, before going on to Harvard and Cambridge.

In general, my high school studies weren't going at all badly, despite the fact that I was not an avid student. My preoccupations in those years were always sports. I played baseball in Windsor's warmer climes and hockey in Ottawa. I played high school football when the season was on and swam and played basketball for the university team. The record showed that I could spend my spare time as I pleased and still get through school with a minimum of effort at exam time. There was really only one unhappy exception: algebra. Later in life, in business and in government, I had a knack for numbers. But this did not come from a mastery of the intricacies of quadratic equations. In fact, while I had received firsts in most of my other subjects in the weeks before Father McCorkell posed his question, I had failed algebra. No need to worry, I explained to him, because as I understood it, algebra was not required in light of my other marks. I was not prepared for his response.

Not long after my conversation with Father McCorkell, Dad and I headed out onto the placid waters of Lake Erie. Fishing was one of those rare occasions in my father's life that did not, in his opinion, require him to wear a shirt and tie. Usually it was a time for the two of us to relax together without any distractions and we both enjoyed it.

"Well," he said once we had muscled the little steel rowboat out into the lake and were arranging our fishing tackle. "Now, what about St. Mike's?"

"Well, I've got a problem. I didn't get algebra. Father McCorkell says that means I won't be able to get into St. Mike's. It looks like I'll be staying at the University of Ottawa for at least another year."

When I was finance minister, and later prime minister, I developed a reputation for a volcanic temper – exaggerated perhaps, but not entirely undeserved. Let me just say that I was not the first member of the Martin clan to exhibit this characteristic. My father's temper was not the slow, simmering kind. It was more the sort that blows the top off some great mountain, darkens the skies, and drapes the landscape in ash before settling back, almost as suddenly, to a quiet, looming presence.

The fishing excursion did not last as long as originally planned. Before I knew it, I found myself working with a tutor for hours each day through the long, hot summer, studying for my algebra "sup." Perhaps through the intercession of the clergy, if not an even higher power, I arrived at St. Mike's late that fall, but arrived nonetheless.

It must be hard for those of any other generation to understand the extraordinarily lucky timing enjoyed by pre–baby-boomers like me. Our parents had lived through two world wars that had depleted their generation and scarred those who survived. They had also weathered a devastating Depression. For my father's family – who struggled financially at the best of times – the Depression had been a period of real suffering, insecurity, and want. It left its lifelong mark on my father. Even once he enjoyed political success and national renown, he was haunted by a lingering fear of financial ruin. It was not until his very latest days that the fear bred in him by the Depression loosened its grip. Even for my mother's family, which weathered the Thirties better than my father's, there was a real prospect of being pitched back into the poverty they had escaped by dint of enormous effort over many years.

But for us, the pre–baby-boomers, all that was literally history. Our experience was of universities yawning with places waiting for us, law firms and medical schools yearning for bright young people, and businesses with too much to do and not enough capable people to do it. The unprecedented economic growth of the 1950s and 1960s pulled us up the ladder of success. It never occurred to us that if we wanted to go to university or to law school, or to get a job in business, there would be any problem. For the generation after us, who faced stiffer competition in a weaker economy, that was not the case. This was one of the reasons that in later life I felt so strongly that it was unfair for my generation to ask our children to pay for the financial and pension deficits we had created.

I had some of Canada's greatest scholars teaching me at the U of T – the historians C.P. Stacey and Tom Symons, among others. I was also just as likely to audit a course I had never enrolled in as attend those where I was supposed to be. Marshall McLuhan, for example, lectured in a backroom of House #2 (now called McCorkell House, after my father's friend), where I was quartered at St. Mike's. His class was handier, and much more interesting, than some of the philosophy courses in which I was actually enrolled.

At the time, my principal objective in life was to play in the Canadian Football League (CFL). My friend from Colchester, Jerry Philp, who remains a good friend to this day, was the best athlete I ever knew and went on to have a long career as an end with the Toronto Argonauts. (His wife, Joanne, was also a tremendous cook, and in my years at the University of Toronto she gave me much needed respite from the residence cafeteria.) I had been a reasonably good high school football player. However, I did not have the size to make up for my lack of talent, or the talent to make up for my lack of size. When I tried out for the University of Toronto Blues, my grandmother had died and I showed up late for training camp, and was rocked when I didn't make the team. It taught me a hard lesson about being prepared if you really want something. In the meantime, I swam and played water polo and basketball. I played tennis in the summer and skied in the winter.

A lot of my attention and enthusiasm in these early years went into my summer jobs. I had begun working when I was quite young. The story my father used to tell of us driving by a tobacco farm in the riding when I was about thirteen or fourteen is well known, and quite true.

"Boy. Thank god I don't have to do that," I said. "Look at those people working in the hot sun."

For my father this was an alarm bell, and the next day I found myself picking tobacco in the fields of Essex County. It was the most backbreaking job I ever had. It meant reaching down thousands of times a day to the base of a plant to sever the tobacco leaves as the dry, dusty air filled your nose and eyes and the searing sun beat down on your back and neck. It certainly gave me the incentive to find my own work the next summer. At the time, there was a thriving fishery on Lake Erie. Mance Campbell had a fishing business and his boat was moored just off the Colchester dock. So, when I was contemplating my escape from the tobacco fields, I went over and asked whether I could get a job on his boat and he said yes – as simple as that. I loved the idea that I could get up at four in the morning, head to the dock in the pre-dawn light, jump on the fishing boat, and we were away. I did the grunt work: helping to pull in the nets filled with bass, perch, and – the big prize – Lake Erie pickerel, the best-tasting fish that ever swam. We packed the fish on ice and then cleaned them at the dock when we returned. It was not exactly the deep sea, but I loved it. It was the beginning of my lifelong romance with boats, ships, water, and anything nautical.

Unfortunately, perhaps because of a downturn in the fishery, I had the job for only one summer. My father was determined that I keep working and next year landed me a place at the Hiram Walker distillery. It should have been a dream job, I suppose, but it was office work and I chafed at it, like a big dog locked in the house all day, looking out the window at real life. As soon as I could, I found other work, in construction, and quit Hiram Walker. That was the beginning of a series of similar jobs over the next few years, working for Eastern Construction in Windsor. I am sure my dad, who was friends with the owners, Bud and Ed Odette, got me in, though I put it about that they had hired me as a ringer for their fastball team. Fastball was a fast-pitch variation of softball, and Windsor's fastball league was one of the best in the country. I was sure I was about to write a historic page in the annals of the company team. This little bit of myth building came crashing down when I struck out almost every time at bat, and I was soon back in the Essex County baseball league where I belonged.

So I worked in construction, and worked hard, though that is not what the Odettes would remember me for, any more than for my prowess on the fastball field. Ed Odette had a brand-new Chrysler Imperial, a very fine automobile, which had some kind of a problem and needed to be taken to the shop. It took about two weeks to get fixed, and I was dispatched to get the car, which Ed Odette had only driven once before. By this time, I was an experienced driver for a teenager, having driven pickup trucks and even a cement mixer. On the way home from the garage, somebody had evidently misplaced a stop sign, because I didn't see it, and I hit another car at the intersection. Luckily no one was seriously hurt, but the Imperial was totalled. If I needed further proof that the Odettes were family friends, let me just say that I wasn't fired.

Later on, I was hired by Coca-Cola. I considered it a great inequity that my friend Ed Lumley (who later became a cabinet minister under Pierre Trudeau and John Turner) was allowed to drive a truck while I was relegated to a secondary role as his helper, something he has never let me forget. It has since been pointed out to me that my experience with the Odettes, and a later one during a summer job in Alberta that I landed through Maurice Strong, did not recommend me to any job involving holding the driver's wheel.

Maurice Strong was president of a company called Canadian Industrial Gas and Oil when I was in university. He gave me a job near Morinville, in the oil patch just north of Edmonton. My assignment was to drive around to the wellheads checking gauges. Being a clever young fellow with lots of initiative, over the course of a few weeks I noticed two things: the gauges never changed and the Calgary Stampede was going on just 190 miles south. It seemed to me that it would be an important part of my education to see the Calgary Stampede. Naturally, I took the company pickup as my means of transport, though I neglected to tell anyone. After a merry day taking in calf-roping and the like, I headed back to Morinville. It started to rain hard while I was negotiating the back roads. The roads were clay – gumbo really – a substance that was new to this Eastern city-boy. I hit a slippery patch and flipped the truck into the ditch many miles away from any place I could reasonably have been if I had actually been doing my job. Maurice has always insisted that he did not fire me, and I don't recall that we had a face-to-face confrontation. I am nonetheless pretty sure my employment was terminated, whatever he says, because I soon found myself hitchhiking north to Hay River on the south shore of Great Slave Lake in the Northwest Territories.

In Hay River, I was excited to land a job with the Yellowknife Transportation Company, which plied the Mackenzie River north to the Beaufort Sea with several tugboats and dozens of barges. I was hired for one of the tugs because they needed extra crew for a salvage job they were planning to undertake once they unloaded up north – or rather "down north" as the expression was, because the Arctic was downriver. After the Second World War, someone had bought a military surplus Landing Ship Tank (LST), designed to run aground and release troops and equipment on enemy shores. After being brought to the Beaufort Sea for use as a barge, the LST had broken free of its moorings and drifted ashore on an island, where it had been abandoned. The people running Yellowknife Transportation had decided that it was worth trying to salvage the LST for use on the Mackenzie.

One day, while were waiting at Tuktoyaktuk to mount the salvage expedition, I had some free time and decided to take a walk on the tundra. People don't realize this, but it can get extremely hot in the North in the summertime and after walking for an hour or so, I was tired and decided to lie down for a nap. I slept for maybe half an hour. When I woke, I sat up and looked across the Arctic landscape, virtually featureless in every direction. I simply had no idea where I was or how to get back to camp. I could have set out in any one of four directions, and maybe walked for hundreds of miles without finding anybody. As I stumbled about, lost, I heard the sound of water and was elated: the Mackenzie! I walked for half an hour toward the sound, but when I got there, it was nothing: just a tiny stream whose sound had been magnified in the windless air suspended over the treeless landscape. I continued to wander for several hours before, by the grace of God, I came to a place I recognized and was able to make my way back.

Later, the mate on the tug, who had befriended me, took me back to where I had been and showed me how I had gone wrong. He was Métis, well acquainted with the tundra. He demonstrated how, if I looked carefully, it was possible to see the imprints of my boots on the spongy ground. Had I understood that, I could have followed my own tracks back to camp from where I had slept. It struck me how well he knew and understood his environment. And it occurred to me that many Aboriginal people from the North, coming to our cities in the South, must feel at least a little like I had when I was stumbling around on the tundra.

After that, I stayed close to the tug but not out of trouble. A few days later we headed out into the Beaufort Sea and managed to free the LST. We lashed it to our tug with a steel cable and towed it back toward the mouth of the Mackenzie. But as we chugged along, a storm blew up, slapping our faces with sleet and churning up the sea. Huge plates of pack ice began to squeeze in on us, and I was sent up the radio antenna tower to keep watch. When the wind shifted again, all of a sudden a chunk of pack ice slammed into the tug and threatened to overturn it. I was still high on the antenna, which had swung out over the heaving water and ice at an ugly tilt. Our ship and our lives were now in the balance, and the captain decided the only way to save the situation was to cut the LST loose. The crew waved and shouted for me to come down from my perch, but I didn't listen because I was enjoying the show. Thinking that I had descended as I had been ordered to, they went ahead and took an axe to the tow cable. When it snapped, the tug swung violently back and forth with me up top being flipped around like a rag doll and hanging on for my life.

We left the LST behind us at the mercy of the storm, and for all I know it is still up there somewhere. I am lucky that I am not still up there with it. By the time we made it back to port, the summer was almost over, and I made the long trip back to Toronto and to university.

My experience on the Mackenzie was part of a lifelong romance with the North. I had already visited the First Nations settlement of Winisk on Hudson Bay one summer while working on construction of the Mid-Canada Line – a series of Cold War defence installations similar to the better-known DEW line but strung south of the Arctic Circle. And, of course, every time I was near the sea, I was reluctant to leave. Another summer, I shipped out from Arvida, Quebec, on a Canadian vessel called the *Sun Rhea*, whose primary job was carrying bauxite between Jamaica and Norway. I was made a cadet officer rather than an ordinary seaman, an honour I later learned meant getting less pay for doing the same work: mostly scraping paint.

It was another aspect of the good fortune of the pre–baby-boomers that I was able to range so freely around the country. My father's name may have helped get some of the jobs, but most of them I got just by walking in and asking, and that was important to me. The desire to be master of my own fate – my own boss, if you like – was one that would often serve me well in my career, particularly in business, where I took some big gambles that luckily for me paid off. But that same aspect of my character could sometimes rankle when I was not in charge, or if I was in charge but was hemmed in by constraints imposed by others.

University, sports, and summer jobs. In later years, people had difficulty believing that amid all this, politics was not a priority for me in my youth. But it was not. A few political incidents jump out at me from the early and mid-1950s, mainly because they were isolated in my consciousness. I remember having a Coca-Cola with Louis St. Laurent at 24 Sussex, for example, and meeting Vincent Massey at Rideau Hall, probably because my dad was so insistent that "you will remember this for the rest of your life." I remember the 1953 election when I campaigned door to door as a kid for my dad and the Liberals won a huge majority. I have almost no political recollections from then until – bang – it was election night 1957. We watched the local and national results at my dad's campaign headquarters in Windsor and then returned to Aunt Mame's house, where I recall the family sitting around the table in disbelief. Although the Liberals had won a plurality of the votes, they had fewer seats than John Diefenbaker's Progressive Conservatives. Dad, however, had hung on to Essex East.

But if politics was not a preoccupation or priority of mine, my father's career continued to be. My first semester at the U of T began in the fall of 1957, just a few months after the Liberals' defeat. Although Mr. St. Laurent briefly considered forming a coalition with the Cooperative Commonwealth Federation (CCF) and some independents in the House of Commons to stay in power, he soon decided to resign as prime minister and announced his intention to retire from politics: he was seventy-five years old at the time. A leadership convention was arranged for January 1958, and it was clear from the start that my father would be a candidate. Still, it was always a long shot. C.D. Howe represented the right wing of the party and my father the left. The party establishment, including Mr. St. Laurent himself, cleaved closer to Howe's fiscally conservative politics.

Lester Pearson had been both a friend and rival to my father over many years. They had had many common experiences, especially on the international stage, and they held similar views on issues both international and domestic. But Pearson had entered politics only in 1948, and he had gone straight from being undersecretary of state for External Affairs (what we would call deputy minister nowadays) to leading the department in cabinet. Although he was a true social reformer and later brought in medicare as prime minister, Pearson had not participated in many of the party's social reform debates of the early 1950s, in which my father, as minister of health and welfare, had been at the centre. To the party establishment, my father looked like he would take the party further left than they wanted to go. And it didn't hurt Pearson's prospects one bit when he was awarded the Nobel Peace Prize in 1957 for his work on the Suez crisis, which had been a source of considerable national pride.

When I arrived at the U of T, I became a member of the campus Liberals, mainly because it was expected of me as the son of a prominent Liberal and prospective leadership candidate. My actual involvement in the leadership race was pretty limited. It is important to understand that there has been an enormous evolution in the organization and sophistication of leadership contests over the last half-century. The race that culminated in the convention in 1958 would seem primitive (and relatively cheap!) in comparison with the 1968 race that chose Pierre Trudeau. And the evolution continued through to the conventions that selected Jean Chrétien in 1990 and me in 2003. My involvement in the 1958 convention was mainly limited to helping organize the floor demonstration. The convention was in Ottawa, and I used my University of Ottawa connections to put together a group of university and high school students who donned the Martin colours and paraded through the hall at the designated moment waving Martin signs and chanting to the sound of the obligatory brass band. We were the hoopla. I remember great resentment that the chairman of the convention cut off our floor demonstration prematurely, though I am not sure that a little more "spontaneous enthusiasm" from us would have made much difference to the result.

Maybe it was the relative intimacy of the leadership process in 1958, without the massive organizations and the riding-by-riding grudge matches that were featured in later contests, that explains why the ties between the two candidates stayed so strong. Maybe it was the fact that, by the time the delegates gathered in Ottawa, everyone could already clearly see what was coming. For his part, once he became leader, Mr. Pearson continued to treat my father with the utmost respect and friendship, and my father was happy to reciprocate.

Soon after the Liberal leadership convention, Canadians were heading back to the polls with John Diefenbaker's Tories feeling the wind in their sails. During the campaign, there was a major rally at Massey Hall in Toronto, where both Pearson and my father were featured. Naturally, I teamed up with the campus Liberals and we made the noise that helped make it a very successful meeting. When it was over, we spilled out of the hall, full of enthusiasm, and gathered on Yonge Street without any very specific plan other than maybe to head to a pub. A policeman came along and said: "All right, break this up. No demonstrations here. No congregating here."

I stepped forward and in a moment of stirring street oratory declared that this was a free country, and that we had the right to free speech, and that there were a couple hundred university students standing courageously behind me in defence of our liberties.

"Well, I'm telling you to move along," the policeman repeated.

"By god, we're not moving," I answered. "We're staying right here. You can't make us go."

"Well, that's fine," he replied. "We're bringing the paddy wagons and you can all come downtown and explain it to the judge."

And at that moment I realized that the massed forces of the University of Toronto Young Liberals had melted away, perhaps looking for that beer. The next thing you know I was in a jail cell. At six o'clock the next morning, a captain from the Salvation Army, God bless him, showed up and chatted with me to keep my spirits up, commiserating with my outrage at the attack on my civil liberties. Not long afterwards, I was standing in front of a judge who was asking me what happened. When I started to explain the injustice of my incarceration, he cut me off and said, "Why don't you just get out of here, go home, and stop causing trouble?"

My father happened to be listening to CBC Radio and caught an item about his son being arrested – the first he had heard about it. I got home in time to receive his call. Let's just say it was reminiscent of our fishing expedition a few years before. It was not the last time he would have reason to excoriate his son for getting mixed up with the law during an election campaign.

After graduating from the U of T and starting law school, I became reacquainted with Sheila Cowan, a girl from Windsor. Sheila's father, Bill, was a partner in the law firm of Martin, Laird, Easton, and Cowan. The firm was perfectly balanced politically, with two Liberals and two Tories, and Cowan was one of the latter. Despite having his name prominent on the firm's masthead, my father was not in active legal practice, of course, when he was a cabinet minister. After the 1957 election, although he retained his seat, he was out of government and therefore temporarily returned to practising law part-time in Windsor. He purchased the Low home in Walkerville. As it happened, the Cowan family lived two doors away. Sheila, who was named after her mother, became a close friend of my sister, Mary Anne, whose convent-school background, fluent French, and flamboyant personality made her an exotic addition to Walkerville High. I first met Sheila on a trip home from university when she was still in high school, but as she will tell you, the vast difference in our ages precluded our encounter from turning into anything more. Some years later, when Sheila turned up at the U of T herself, she called me to see if a friend could get a ride with me down to Windsor one weekend. It didn't work out, but I used the occasion to ask her whether she'd like to come bowling (although I had never bowled before) with my friend Bob Fung and his girlfriend (and eventually his wife), Enid. That began a romance that has lasted now for more than forty years. At the U of T, we went to the movies together and occasionally to the theatre; most frequently we just met up on campus for a Danish and coffee, which was about all I could afford.

One incident early in our courtship that is all too clear in my memory happened on a skiing trip we took to Blue Mountain near Collingwood, Ontario. I had invited Sheila to come up with me and the Wendling twins, Peter and Paul, whom I lived with in university and who are still close friends. She was not an experienced skier, and on about the third run she took a terrible tumble that resulted in a fractured ankle. I drove her to the Collingwood Hospital, where she spent the night in a hospital bed and I tried to sleep as best I could in the corridor. The next day, we drove back to Toronto with Sheila in a cast. Not long afterwards, when we were both back in Windsor, Sheila's father took me aside and gave me what-for because I had taken his little girl away with me on a romantic weekend tryst. Some romance. Some tryst.

Over Christmas in 1964 – the year Sheila graduated from the U of T and I finished law school – we went down to the cottage in Colchester and I asked her to marry me at the water's edge. Sheila tells me that she and her mother snickered in the next room as I stammered out the news to her father, who did not give his consent without first subjecting me to a vigorous grilling. It wasn't just that I was a Catholic and the Cowans were United Church. More problematically, my father was a Liberal MP and Bill Cowan's father had been a Tory MP.

Coming from a Protestant family, Sheila was required to take a pre-nuptial course. Fortunately, Father Bellyea, who was a wonderful priest and had been at St. Mike's when I was there, agreed to take on the task of schooling her in the Catholic ways. They ended up spending most of their time discussing Jane Austen. The wedding was originally planned for June but was delayed to September because my dad was expecting a spring election. As it turned out, the election wasn't till November, so our wedding, which took place on September 11, actually occurred during the run-up to the campaign. It was a tremendous party, made all the more satisfying for the Martins because my dad invited all his election workers and Bill Cowan had to foot the bill. The ceremony was held at Assumption Church near the university, and the reception afterwards was at Beach Grove Golf Club. Our honeymoon consisted of one day across the river in Detroit, and then we headed back to Toronto, where I started the bar admission course. We had found a basement flat near the Mount Pleasant Cemetery in Toronto. But because of the election, we spent many of the early weekends of married life doing family political duty back in Windsor – Sheila's first experience of a campaign.

My friends and family will tell you that I have always found it hard to talk about my emotions – even those I feel most deeply – perhaps I should say *especially* those I feel most deeply. Unlike my father, whose joys and sorrows were often visible on his face and in his eyes, I have a tendency to change the topic when something comes too close to home. Sheila likes to recall my speech at the wedding, in part because it was easy for me to make jokes and impossible, as it turned out, to say the familiar, and important things, such as thanking the Cowans for raising Sheila, telling my parents how much they meant to me, and proclaiming with all the friends and family there that I loved Sheila and why.

The truth is that in a life blessed with luck, my greatest good fortune was to meet Sheila. I loved her when she was in her twenties. I love her even more now. She has been a wonderful mother. The fact that Paul, Jamie, and David have all turned out so well is due entirely to her. How she put up with four men in the house I will never know. After David and his wife, Laurence, gave us Ethan, our first grand-son, and now Liam, our second, when I watch them all at the farm in the Eastern Townships, it reminds me once again what Sheila has given me.

Sheila is in some ways my opposite. Where I can be impatient and impetuous, she is calm and considered. But we also share a love of people as well as a need from time to time to withdraw. We enjoy the same company at dinner, and as likely as not, we are also ready to head home at the same time. But most important, Sheila has been a friend and companion as well as a wonderful wife. Whether it involved family, business, or politics, when I was down, there was never a more powerful tonic for me than just being with Sheila. When my career took its unexpected – and from her perspective, unwelcome – turn from business into politics, Sheila never wavered in her support. As it turned out, she took to the political life more than she expected, though she was clearly happy when it was over. I have had and continue to have a life that would have been impossi-ble without her, a life that is never happier than when she is with me.

CHAPTER THREE

Down to Work

From the moment I flipped his truck on the road home to Morinville, I did not see Maurice Strong again until my wedding day. I had finished law school, and my dreams for the future had begun to gel around the idea of an international career. I had managed to get a stint in the legal branch of the European Coal and Steel Community in Luxembourg, and was thinking that I might want to work as a field officer with the World Bank or a United Nations agency. It was more of an impulse than a plan. Like many young people of my generation, I wanted to make the world a better place and was searching for a way to do it. Maurice had by that time already established a fine reputation with his unusual combination of business and development work; so naturally I turned to him for advice. He pointed out that the developing world was not really crying out for fledgling lawyers like me. He suggested that I should go into business, acquire some experience that would be helpful in the Third World, build up a bit of wealth for myself and my family, and then launch into my more far-flung ambitions. I didn't know the first thing about business or have an interest in it for that matter, and I said so. But Maurice wasn't troubled by that and invited me to join him as his executive assistant at Montreal-based Power Corporation, where he was chief executive. Here, instead of a pipe-dream, was a plan, and an offer of a job at a salary of $9,000 a year. Could life get any better?

Maurice Strong was born in 1929 in Oak Lake, an agricultural town in southern Manitoba with a population of just a few hundred.

He completed only grade ten before quitting school but managed to make his way in the world with a combination of ambition, drive, and intelligence, becoming by turn a businessman, social activist, environmentalist, and diplomat of international standing and impact.

By the time Maurice came into my life, he had already had a business career that took him from the Arctic to Africa and back to Canada. In the 1950s, he had been hired by the Winnipeg-based Richardson family to become an oil and gas analyst, one of the first ever in Canada. Later on, he managed to get control of a firm called Ajax Petroleum, which eventually became Canadian Industrial Gas and Oil. A friend of his named Bill Richardson (no relation to the Winnipeg Richardsons) had an idea based on his knowledge of mining history. The ancient Romans had been great miners, and the locations of many of their mines were well known. Most of them had been abandoned once they had been mined out. But Richardson's notion was that with modern technology they could be brought back into production. In particular, the friends fixed their sights on a mine in Anglesey in North Wales. At the time, as I have already mentioned, my father had lost his ministerial job in the Diefenbaker victory and was supplementing his modest MP's salary by practising law part-time. Maurice approached him to manage the purchase of the Anglesey mine. While nothing ever came of it, Maurice and my father became good friends, and I met someone who would eventually become one of the greatest influences on my life.

Maurice not only gave me a summer job but he launched my business career, and continuously led by example, organizing the historic United Nations Rio Summit on the environment in 1992 (to pick one of his many accomplishments), which I attended as the opposition environment critic. In early years, he was more of a friend of my father's than of mine, and more of a mentor to me. But his significance in my life went beyond our direct contact. His career would be remarkable anywhere but especially here in Canada.

For some reason that I have never been able to fathom, Canadian business people, unlike their counterparts in the United States and the

United Kingdom, are suspicious of any mixture of business and public service. A business person who decides to enter public life is seen as having lost his or her bearings or perhaps suffering from a strange psychological disability. As for public servants having risen through long years of hard work and commitment to the public good, how could they have anything to contribute to the hard edge, stand-on-your-own-two-feet world of business? These wrong-headed attitudes not only deprive Canadian companies of a wealth of useful experience, but they also have a pernicious effect on the public service. When I was prime minister, one of the first speeches I gave was to the senior leaders of the public service, in which I recalled the story of Gordon Sinclair, a gifted public servant who resigned as head of the Coast Guard when I was in business because he was tired of being accused of living off the public teat. I concluded by saying, "Can anyone tell me why someone who spends his or her whole life building a better health-care system, or strengthening the public finances so that we can secure our social programs, is deemed to be making a lesser contribution than someone who makes hula-hoops?" It is an attitude that does Canada little credit.

Maurice Strong cut a different path: a career that travelled through both business and public service. He was an early developer of the Canadian oil patch and also an early exponent of global environmentalism. He was a titan of industry and one of the builders of what has become the Canadian International Development Agency (CIDA). He has served Canada and the world, primarily through the United Nations. He has sometimes been criticized for his restless movement from job to job. But that flows naturally from his visionary nature. For me, what he offered was a pathway that honoured both business and public service for their unique contributions. He also gave me an insight into the challenges of the environment and of development in the Third World, which has stayed with me all my life.

If all this seems terribly idealistic, remember the times. The security we felt, the growth we experienced, and the limitless possibilities that opened up in the postwar years fuelled an optimism and sense of hope that is only beginning to re-emerge. In the United States, it produced the aura of "Camelot" around John F. Kennedy's brief presidency. But everywhere in North America among people of my generation it inspired the dream of a better world.

Many years later, when I was well established in business, I was invited to speak to a class at the U of T law school. As a student, I had been taught at this same law school by some of the giants of Canadian legal thinking, including Caesar Wright, Ronald St. John MacDonald, and Bora Laskin (who later became chief justice of Canada). They were men who very much believed that the law was an enterprise devoted to the improvement of the human condition. I was introduced to the class as someone who had been waylaid by a business career on his way to working on the problems of the developing world.

When I was finished my talk, one of the students stood up and said, "This stuff about you wanting to go and help in the Third World sounds like a load of bull. Come on, why wouldn't you just want to get your law degree and get a job and get on with life?"

I went back at him pretty hard. "There's a real problem with your question," I said, "and it is symptomatic of what I know a lot of you think. The fact is, among my peers, it was very much the norm to be concerned about the wider world. I have to wonder what the matter is with your generation. Don't you have any sense of duty to others?"

He came back at me even harder. "Mr. Martin, when you went to law school, did you have any doubt that you'd get in?"

"No," I replied.

"Well, I did. And when you went looking for an articling position, did you have any doubt you'd get one?"

"No, there were all kinds of jobs."

"Well, it is different for us. Half of us don't know if there will be jobs for us when we graduate."

It underscored for me once again how privileged my generation had been because we had had the luxury to pursue an idealism that some other generations did not. More recently, I have been struck in talking to university audiences by the extent to which this idealism has returned, perhaps the product of a strong economy similar to that of the 1950s and 1960s.

But all this was in the future for me when I moved to Montreal and joined Power Corporation in spring of 1966 immediately after being admitted to the Bar of Ontario. Power Corporation opened up a world of action, decision, and results, for which I quickly learned I had something of a knack. For Sheila and me, it was a time of transition from our student years. I still remember my first business lunch and realizing that the bill was about what Sheila and I normally spent on groceries for a month!

The move also meant that Sheila and I were parachuted into Montreal at a time when Quebec was in a wonderful turmoil – what we now know as the Quiet Revolution. This "revolution," the rapid modernization of Quebec society, was led by nationalists such as Jean Lesage, the former federal Cabinet Minister and then Premier of Quebec, who also believed deeply in both Quebec and Canada. They were engaged in a process of fundamental reform that permeated every aspect of life and made us want to live at the centre of this exciting swirl of events. The fact that Power Corporation was head-quartered in Montreal clinched my decision to take the job. I was an Ontarian of mostly Irish descent, but I was very aware of my francophone roots. I had been educated in French and had grown up with francophone friends. The Quiet Revolution resonated deeply with me. The changes were taking place not only in culture, education, and the arts but also in business, as Quebecers found the confidence to take their destiny into their own hands. It was a very exciting time and I wanted to be part of it.

Power Corporation got its name as a holding company from two investment dealers, Arthur Nesbitt and Peter Thomson, who traded in the bonds of Shawinigan Power and B.C. Power and in the process acquired much of their common stock, eventually securing control of each. Along the way, Power Corporation had also acquired an oil company called White Rose, which it sold to British-American Oil in 1962. The next year it sold Shawinigan Power to the Province of

Quebec, which was creating Hydro-Québec; similarly, the Province of British Columbia acquired B.C. Power as it formed its provincial utility, B.C. Hydro. The fact is, both companies were acquired under the hammer of a threat to nationalize them. As a result, Power found itself sitting on a great pile of cash. It used that cash to build a huge holding company. This was very much the business fad of the time: a hierarchy of subsidiaries, often doing business in completely unrelated fields, held by controlling minority stakes to create a kind of corporate pyramid. That's how Power Corporation initially worked. Of course, eventually many of these far-flung investments got into trouble; and Maurice Strong was hired to sort it all out. I entered the corporation at what I later realized was a pretty rarified level. There was an enormous amount to do as the company reorganized, so despite the fact that I was the most junior person in the executive office by a long stretch, I was given a tremendous amount of leeway.

I had only begun to get my sea legs, however, when Maurice abruptly left Power, much to the disappointment of the board of directors. My dad was deemed the culprit. As minister of external affairs, he lured Maurice away to become head of Canada's External Aid Office (later to become CIDA). As a protégé of Maurice Strong's, I figured I was a goner, and would have been if the new CEO, Bill Turner, had not stared the naysayers down and asked me to stay on as his executive assistant. Bill Turner, one of Canada's best business leaders, eventually became one of my most significant tutors in learning what business was all about. However, when Lester Pearson announced he was stepping down some months later in 1967, I took a leave of absence to support my father's bid for the leadership. The leave of absence was no more than a precaution in my mind, because I actually intended to use the natural break in my relationship with Power Corporation to reorient myself toward the promised international career.

By the time the leadership campaign was over, Paul Desmarais, whom I did not know, had engineered a reverse takeover of Power. At our first meeting, he asked me what I did at the company, and

With my mother. (All photos in this section courtesy of the Martin family, except where otherwise noted.)

My mother (right) takes tea with her husband's boss, Mackenzie King. When he asked if she considered him a great man she replied, "I'm going to take some convincing."

Me (in pugnacious pose) with my cousin Mike and the Coles
at our summer place in Colchester, on Lake Erie.

Facing off in winter with Michael in Windsor.

In Colchester, with my cousin Michael,
whom I still regard as a brother.

My parents Paul and Nell, in summer and winter.

With my mother and sister, Mary Anne.

Visiting my father at the
United Nations in New York.
"The speeches were better in
Belle River."

Wearing 32, I took my high school football seriously, and my principal objective in life was to play in the CFL.

Growing up, once again at Colchester with my cousin Mike.

Back from the North at the University of Toronto.

Windsor, September 11, 1965. "In a life blessed with luck, my greatest good fortune was to meet Sheila."

I enjoyed the excitement of the business world in Montreal, first as a "corporate firefighter" for Power Corporation, then as the head of Canada Steamship Lines. "I own the company, I thought. I've done it." (Deborah Samuel, *Vista* Magazine)

The whole family celebrates the launch of a CSL ship at Collingwood in November 1984 (from left) my father-in-law, Bill Cowan; my son Jamie; Sheila; my mother; David; my father; my mother-in-law, Sheila Cowan; me; and Paul. (Schuller Fotography)

A typical pose at home. (Deborah Samuel, *Vista* Magazine)

With my father, very late in his life.
(Deborah Samuel, *Vista* Magazine)

Sheila and I at home in the Eastern Townships with (from left) Jamie, David, and Paul.

The head of Canadian Steamship Lines.

I told him. Then he asked me what I wanted to do, and I told him I wanted to quit and go abroad. "I don't know you," I said, "and it has nothing to do with that. I've done my thing here and I want to see what I can do in the developing world." Somewhat taken aback, he made a pitch for me to stay for a year. I did stay: for thirteen. Throughout this period, I always imagined that at some point I would quit and pursue my ambition to work for the World Bank or the United Nations, but whenever that point seemed to have arrived, a new and compelling challenge would arise at Power. Furthermore, our first son, Paul, was born on our first wedding anniversary in 1966. Jamie came along in 1969 and then David in 1974. I was a family man now, and I wanted to secure my family's financial future – something that had worried my father most of his life.

When Sheila and I first arrived in Montreal, we had lived in a small duplex near Côte-Vertu until we were able to afford a house in Mount Royal, which reminded us of the Walkerville area of Windsor where our families had lived. Eventually we were able to move to a larger house in Mount Royal and then bought a house in Westmount. In the late 1970s, Sheila and I started to look for a place to get away from the city on weekends and in the summer. At first we tried to find a house on the water but discovered that everything was out of our price range. Eventually, we chose a 150-year-old farmhouse in a little valley near Knowlton in the Eastern Townships, about an hour outside Montreal. Several farms in the valley, including the one we bought, had belonged to a family called Moffat – early British settlers. We don't know exactly when they put down stakes in the area, but there is a diary entry from an Anglican minister in the 1840s saying that it was the Moffat brothers who came to greet him when he first arrived. Much of the little valley had been cleared by the Moffats to create farmland, but it always was quite marginal land. The steep hillsides must have been difficult enough to plough with a horse-drawn rig. When tractors replaced horses in the 1940s, they couldn't work on them without flipping and so the farm was abandoned – and eventually naturally reforested. Today, there is sheep pasture along the narrow valley floor, and Sheila and I are now sheep farmers. Basil Moffat, who was born a few hundred metres away and is descended from the original family of settlers, works the farm and lives on a house near our own. He is a fixture in our home as well as on the land. To my great good fortune, he likes to get up at an ungodly hour and have coffee with friends in town before stopping by for an early morning chat, where he provides me with all the local news and we both complain about the weather.

In the early years, the farm was the place where we could get away and spend what people nowadays call "quality time" together. Back then, it was just being with the family. The old farmhouse was not quite as romantic as it may sound. They were able to make rickety houses in the nineteenth century too. Ours had been partially renovated when we got it, but it has taken thirty years of incremental changes designed by Sheila to make it the relaxed country home it is today – big enough to accommodate the changing cast of family who inundate the place. It has gradually replaced the cottage in Colchester as my sentimental home.

As many people do after their kids come along, in the 1970s Sheila and I were settling into the rhythms and routines of family life. We started the boys off in a local French school, St. Clement's, but then, because of the frequent strikes in the public school system at the time, moved them to Collège Stanislas and eventually to Lower Canada College. When the boys were young, I worked late almost every night and travelled frequently. Sheila says I never changed a diaper, which is libellous. She also recalls that in those years she wasn't particularly keen on having me around the house while she tended to their meals, baths, and homework. I tended to come home after all that and spend a little time with the boys before putting them to bed. We were together more on weekends at the farm, the house a chaotic scene with the boys and their friends mingling and generally raising Cain.

The boys learned to ski in nearby Knowlton. Most weekends we would take them to the hills along with our neighbours, Brian and Nancy Gallery and their daughters. The Gallerys became very close friends, despite the fact that he was an active Tory and an early backer of Brian Mulroney. I'm glad to say he helped me later on, for which I'm sure he will earn bonus points in heaven.

By this time I had stopped skiing due to an injury I had suffered some years earlier. Sheila and I had gone with some friends to a summer cottage they had rented in Muskoka. Given my world-famous modesty in later years, you may be surprised to discover that I could be a bit of a show-off back then. I was a pretty good water skier, and one day with everyone sitting on the dock enjoying the sun and some refreshments, I had the idea that I would get up on one ski and zing by at top speed, spraying Sheila and her friends. What I didn't realize was that there was a boat docked there with a very short anchor-rope. When I came roaring by, my ankle hit the rope, and I spun into the dock, ramming my knee with full force; then I flipped into the air before landing with an unpleasant thud. The vacation ended in Bracebridge hospital, and I ended up three to four months a year in a cast for several years afterwards as the doctors did reconstructive work. Thus ended the elite sports career of Paul Martin. It also meant in later years that the boys needed to snow ski without benefit of their father's technical advice. Amazingly, they all became good skiers.

My sons couldn't be more different. Paul, the eldest, is like his mother: quiet and happy to be on his own. Jamie can be quiet but is mostly very sociable. What sets him apart is that the musical ability that ran in both my family and Sheila's, but somehow skipped us and the two other boys, has landed with him. David is more like me: seldom quiet and feeding off the company of·others. As kids, the boys had the common experiences of many Canadian children, such as music lessons (for two of them – hopeless), team sports, and summer camps. Later on, they found summer jobs, often working in places that allowed them to see a bit more of our country. One summer, young Paul worked in the Arctic, for example, not far from where I had once taken my walk on the tundra.

Eventually, two of the boys went to the University of Toronto, while David went to McGill – all of them initially in arts. Subsequently, Paul completed an MBA in shipping at the City University of London and eventually moved to Singapore with Canada Steamship Lines (CSL) for several years before returning to make his home in Canada. Jamie had a band and later studied at the American Film Institute; he now lives in Los Angeles and runs his own film production company. David completed an MBA at Cambridge and worked with my friend Laurence (Ladi) Pathy's shipping company for a time, where he, too, learned the shipping business, and then spent time with Merrill Lynch. Now he runs a private equity fund and is active with CSL but is also very involved in projects involving Aboriginal Canadians. In fact, David and Paul were both well along in forging other business careers before getting involved in CSL (about which, more later).

It has been a great blessing for Sheila and me that my departure from politics coincided with the arrival of our first grandson, Ethan, and that his parents, David and Laurence, live in Montreal. Our good fortune grew when two years later (indeed, just before I wrote this) Ethan's younger brother, Liam, appeared on the scene. As a grandfather, I have discovered that I am in an intense competition for Ethan's and Liam's time, which I often seem to lose to Sheila. My birthday and Ethan's fall close together, and as it happened we each gave the other a tent as a gift the last time round. One of them has become a semi-permanent part of the furniture in our living room. When I see how involved David is with his two sons' daily care, I realize how much about parenting has changed, and perhaps how much I missed out on. Like a lot of fathers of my generation, I regret that I did not spend more time with my boys when they were young. I greatly admire – and perhaps even envy – David's involvement with his sons. I will admit, though, that I have exercised a grandfather's prerogative not to change diapers. Laurence has also told me that in the interest of historical accuracy I should not exaggerate David's domestic involvement.

Apart from family, my preoccupation in the 1970s was my business career. After rejoining Power, I had become a corporate firefighter, going into a troubled business, fixing the place up, and getting out again. This shaped my decision-making style, which later served me well in politics, though it opened me up to a great deal of criticism as well. My job was to go into a company – whether it was a glass manufacturer or a shipyard – and either make it profitable or sell it off. As a thirty-something lawyer, I was acquiring business experience as I went along, but obviously did not have detailed knowledge of any of the industries into which I was plunged. When I started, Paul Desmarais would sometimes suggest I go in with someone else, but I always refused. "Send someone else if you want, but if I go in, I want to know I am in charge – that I have full authority."

The first big deal I ever did concerned a company called Congoleum Nairn, the inventor and marketer of linoleum, in which Power had a large stake. For a long time Power and the other major owner, the Nairn family, had been looking to sell, but nothing had ever happened. Somehow, I got the assignment to divest Congoleum Nairn. I got hold of Brian Aune and Tom Kierans at Nesbitt Thomson. Eventually, we worked out a sale to Bath Industries, which planned to merge the two companies. It was a huge transaction by Canadian standards, and some of the senior people at Power balked because I had done the deal on a handshake. The fact was I was able to sell an investment for much more than the board had originally expected, and in the end, to my amazement, all these senior people got out of the way and let me execute my plan. When it came time to sell, though, it was politic to get the approval of the head of the Nairn family, Sir William Nairn, who was in Scotland at the time, and we only had a week to do so. Although the sale was critical to the family fortune, when I phoned him to explain the situation, he told me that it was impossible for him to deal with this at the moment because it was the opening of the grouse-shooting season, an almost sacred time. I explained the urgency, but he made it clear that the grouse shooting came first. So I told him: "Fine, I am going ahead – we're selling now. What you do is up to you." So he came on board, which taught me a lesson about setting an objective, getting the authority, and going for it. That was my start as a corporate troubleshooter.

What I discovered in the coming years, as I moved from company to company, was that somewhere in senior management there were almost always people who knew what the problems were – and, more importantly, what the solutions were. It was just that they didn't have the authority to make the hard decisions, they couldn't convince the shareholders, or they were split among themselves about how to go about it. So my first job was simply to listen. Massive debates would break out around the table. I'd poke and prod, and I'd gradually come to a conclusion about what had to be done.

I extracted three simple rules from this experience. First, listen. Second, act. And third, don't get distracted by non-essentials; get the core issues right and the rest will take care of itself. Occasionally, as a result of impetuosity to get to a decision, which was my natural inclination, I made a mistake and got myself in a hole. But not too often. When I became prime minister, I was accused of taking too long to make a decision, which gets me exactly wrong. I believe that you should take all the time available because it leads to a better outcome; but my weakness was and is to rush to a decision, not to worry it. There is a larger point to be made, though, about modern decision making, whether it is in business or government. There is a view that strong leaders in both fields make decisions and impose them from on high through a well-established hierarchy. There may have been a time when this worked, but rigid hierarchies don't function so well in the information age, when lines of communication are no longer strictly vertical: they are horizontal and diagonal and every which way. Whether in business or in government, rigid now also means brittle. A leader needs to know where he or she wants to go but needs to consult widely before forging a path – both for what can be learned and to rally support. Consultation works not just because it gives the folks at the top a fuller picture of the information and ideas available; it also helps get buy-in where it is most needed. Some see listening and discussing as signs of weakness. I don't! The way we shaped our budgets at Finance when I was minister and the way we got Aboriginal groups and the provinces and territories onside with the Kelowna

Accord when I was prime minister are good examples of where reaching out worked superbly. If we learned anything from the experience of the Meech Lake and Charlottetown accords, it has to be that the old model of leaders deciding and citizens meekly following along needs to be junked.

When I joined the Department of Finance and sat round the table with my officials, they didn't need to hear from me; they were the experts. I wanted to hear from them, and I wanted to challenge them to refine their positions – or change them if that was appropriate. At Finance, we had meetings where there would be long, bruising debates about policy direction, where everyone would argue like hell. Sometimes if I wasn't getting the advice I thought I needed, I got mad. But by the end of it, I had heard all the arguments, probed all the weak spots, listened to all the advice, and was ready to take up my responsibility to make a decision. Just as in business, I usually found at the end that I had complete loyalty from the people around the table – not just to me but to the decision I had made.

When I was prime minister, some people said this style was too consultative: that my job was to lead, not to listen. I don't believe that. Of course, the job is to lead, but listening is part of leading effectively. Throughout most of my life, in whatever position I've held, I've been lucky enough to have the final decision. I know what I think, but I have never believed myself to be an expert on everything, and I have always appreciated hearing what the best minds had to offer before making a decision.

CHAPTER FOUR

My Own Boss

Some of the most important lessons I learned at Power early in my career were about corporate vision and corporate responsibility, and I learned them in significant part because of the example of Paul Desmarais. He was very much at the centre of Quebec's Quiet Revolution, an immensely successful businessman at a time when francophones in the province were only beginning to take their place in the corporate boardrooms. But it is important to remember that he was originally a Franco-Ontarian. I believe that this had something to do with his confidence in taking on the anglophone business establishment and also his willingness to look beyond Quebec's, and Canada's, borders for opportunities.

I remember one occasion when he told me over a drink that his biggest challenge as a businessman in Quebec was not penetrating the anglo establishment: it was breaking out of the psychology of the francophone business community, whose inclination was to work within their own closed circuit of friends and business partners. "Don't take on the English" was the implicit message: "they'll eat you up." Desmarais was ready to take on not just anglo Montreal but Canada and the world. He was among the first Canadian businesspeople to recognize the rise of Japan, for example.

It was in Japan that I was able to demonstrate my own incisive grip on managing global business negotiations. Desmarais and I were there to meet with the huge investment house, Nomura Securities. The negotiations between the Nomura people and our group were conducted through a translator. When we were discussing our respective positions internally, however, we rarely felt the need to leave the room. They would speak among themselves in Japanese – which of course we could not understand – and we would speak in English. At one point, it occurred to me that they might actually be able to understand our internal conversations, so I suggested we switch to French. Desmarais thought that was a great idea, and that's how we proceeded. That evening, there was the usual lavish dinner thrown for us, and our Japanese host began by toasting us in perfect English. I looked at my fellow Power Corporation executives and acknowledged their silent applause. Then, with a twinkle in his eye, our host turned toward me and concluded his toast in flawless French.

Desmarais was also quick to recognize the significance of the avalanche of petro-dollars in the 1970s, establishing a relationship with Saudi Arabia's oil minister, Sheik Ahmed Zaki Yamani. I did not play any role in his business dealings with the Saudis, but I do remember one related incident worth recounting. Consolidated Bathurst, which was a subsidiary of Power Corporation, leased a fishing lodge on Anticosti Island in the mouth of the St. Lawrence. Several of us, including John Robarts, the retired Ontario premier who was then on Power's board, went up to the lodge for a few days of fishing just before an important Saudi visitor was being hosted there by Paul Desmarais. We were given one simple instruction: to stay away from a crate of especially fine French wine that was being held for the visit. That wasn't a particular problem since there was another case of perfectly splendid wine that we made our way through. Except . . . As we were preparing to leave, someone realized we had emptied the wrong crate. The next couple of hours were spent in panic, rummaging through the garbage cans for the discarded bottles, into which we decanted the cheaper wine that had been intended for us. We never heard any complaints so I guess it passed muster, but I will never forget the sight of the former premier of Ontario piling into the Dumpster with the rest of us.

In 1971, Bill Turner left Power Corporation to become president of Consolidated Bathurst, in which Power had a 35 per cent stake.

"Connie Bathurst," as it was known, was one of Canada's most important pulp and paper companies and, like the industry as a whole, was in the doldrums. Turner asked me to help him work on the turn-around – an offer I gladly accepted. He was one of the giants of the Canadian business community and working with him was going to be worth several MBAS. I was put in charge of five tissue mills in New York state and California, which were not part of Connie Bathurst's core business, with the object of making them profitable and then selling them. It was heavy sledding against the more well-established brands such as Scott and Kleenex, but in the end we got the mills onto a better footing and sold them off. Turner, who was very much a modern business manager, then asked me to establish a planning department along the lines of one that had been pioneered at General Electric. It was a learning experience for me, but I must admit I pre-ferred the crisis-filled days of managing the tissue plants.

Turner had a rare insight into the workings of the Canadian as well as the global economy, and I learned an enormous amount from him. Looking back over my business career, I realize how lucky I was to have mentors such as Maurice Strong, Paul Desmarais, and Bill Turner as well as friends such as Ladi Pathy, who later became my business partner. It is no accident that I've wanted my sons, early on, to meet people such as Wallace McCain, Jimmy Pattison, Murray Edwards, and Gerry Schwartz – successful entrepreneurs with strong social con-sciences and a healthy pride in their own country. This is also one of the reasons that in my post-political career I have devoted so much energy to encouraging a sense of entrepreneurship in Africa and among Aboriginal Canadians here at home, giving promising young business people the chance to learn from the experience of others.

In 1973, Paul Desmarais asked me to take over as president of Canada Steamship Lines. CSL was a Power subsidiary at the time, and its chairman was Paul Desmarais's brother, Louis, who later became an MP under Pierre Trudeau. Once again I jumped at the opportunity, this time because it was not just a fix-and-sell job but rather a chance to guide and build a company that I believed Power intended to hold on to over the long term. For me, with my passion for everything marine, it was love at first sight.

My first challenge was to deal with the troubled Davie Shipyard on the south side of the St. Lawrence River within sight of Quebec City's walls. Among its many problems, the shipyard had a history of bad labour relations. So I hired a new labour lawyer by the name of Brian Mulroney.

My experience with the Davie Shipyard also gave me new insight into Paul Desmarais. He never forgot where he came from. Soon after I arrived at CSL, I toured the shipyard and discovered that an expensive new ventilation system that was supposed to suck fumes out of the paint shop didn't work. Unless we ripped out the system and put in a new one, the workers were going to be breathing toxic fumes. The tricky thing was that as the new president of CSL who just been hired to turn the Davie Shipyard into a money-making operation, my first order of business was going to be to ask the board for money to dismantle a costly new system and make another huge investment to replace it.

Sure enough, the issue blew up at a board meeting. As I knew they would, some of the board members asked: "What is the return on investment?" My answer was: "There is a financial return, but the main return on investment is the health of the employees; this is the right thing to do."

The discussion was not going well. In the midst of this debate, Desmarais arrived at the meeting late and asked for a summary. I explained my proposal, and that it was an issue of the health of the workers. "Good enough for me," he said. And that was Paul Desmarais.

Canada Steamship Lines is the oldest shipping company in Canada, with a historic legacy. It is an amalgam of several predecessors, one of which had its origins in the mid-nineteenth century, when farmers on the Richelieu River in Quebec banded together to get their produce down the river and along the St. Lawrence to Montreal. By the time I took over, the company had sprawled into many areas. In addition to its shipyards, it owned one of Canada's largest trucking companies, Kingsway Transports; the Voyageur bus line, which was the main passenger carrier in and out of the province of Quebec; and shipyards in Quebec and Ontario. But the core business was the transport of grain from what is now Thunder Bay to the elevators in Montreal, Quebec City, and Trois Rivières and the carriage of iron-ore back from Sept-Îles to the steel mills of Hamilton and the American industrial cities on the Great Lakes.

There were two kinds of ships on the lakes at the time: the conventional bulker, which was essentially just a very long box, and the self-unloader, which, as the name implies, contained a series of conveyor belts and a long boom that enabled it to discharge its cargo without extensive port facilities. Although they were used elsewhere in the world, self-unloaders were particularly important on the Great Lakes. The reason for this was that although they could load and unload much more quickly than a bulker, the self-unloading apparatus took a big chunk of the cargo space. For ocean-faring vessels that sometimes travelled weeks between ports, it wasn't worth sacrificing the carrying capacity. But on the Great Lakes where the distances between ports weren't as great, it made economic sense to load and unload quickly so as not to tie up valuable shipping and port capacity sitting dockside.

When I became president of CSL, the company's core Great Lakes shipping business was coming under a terrible squeeze. The American steel industry was being smothered by international competition, mainly from Japan. Every day, it seemed, another American steel giant was declaring Chapter 11, or bankruptcy. At the same time as our steel customers were going broke, changes in the customer destination meant that more Canadian grain was heading west through Vancouver instead of east through Thunder Bay. In the meantime, our trucking business was facing increasing competition from much larger American companies, as Canadian trade patterns shifted more north-south. The whole thing was a mess, and now it was my mess to clean up, beginning with its most important division, shipping. CSL's decline was steady and relatively fast, but it still allowed time for adjustment. Through the 1970s, we continued to turn a profit but at a declining rate of return. It was clear to me that we needed to do two challenging things: upgrade the workforce and build new and more efficient ships.

The Seafarers International Union (SIU), which organized much of the CSL workforce, had a colourful and contentious history. It had been built by Hal Banks, an American labour leader later accused of being mob-connected, who had been brought to Canada by the government at the end of the 1940s to keep communist-led unions off the waterfront and who had forged a relationship, albeit a tense one, with the president of CSL, T. Rodgie McLagan. By the time Banks fled back to the United States in 1964 to escape charges of beating up another union leader, he had established a tradition of rough-and-tough unionism. When I arrived at CSL, some of this was history but not the troubled labour relations that were part of Banks's legacy. The leader of the SIU was (and still is as I write) Roman Gralewicz. He is a huge man with gruff manners that belie a shrewd and subtle mind. He is smart and honest and totally dedicated to his membership, but dealing with him is not for the faint of heart. We fought like hell, but over time I acquired great respect for him. His members were lucky to have him, but the truth is, so was the industry, whether it realized it or not.

It was a difficult time in labour relations more generally. Inflation was running wild and workers started falling behind from the moment they voted to accept a new contract. Gralewicz came to the table with some outrageous demands, using even more outrageous rhetoric. We clashed and we went through several strikes. But he always understood something important, which was that the technology of the industry was changing, and that his members needed training in order to keep up with it. In one of the rounds of bargaining in the late 1970s, Gralewicz came to the table demanding, among other things, an extra cent an hour to be devoted to the training and upgrading of seamen's skills. The ship owners association, or at least the majority of its members, said no. I thought Gralewicz was right, and though it took some doing, we eventually got the training fund in place. In retrospect, who would deny that it was Gralewicz and the SIU, not the owners, who were the visionaries?

At the same time, it was clear that CSL was not going to survive, let alone thrive, if it remained wedded to its declining core market. I believed that as markets developed globally, CSL was going to have to launch out beyond the Great Lakes and into the world. While we were a very small player from an international perspective, there was one area in which we could claim to be a world leader, and that was in self-unloading technology. I was convinced that this technology was applicable in niche markets around the world. The difficulty was that the conventional "lakers," including our self-unloaders, were very much engineered for their environment on the Great Lakes: they were long, thin, matchsticklike craft designed to pass through the locks of the Great Lakes and St. Lawrence Seaway. Seagoing vessels, in contrast, were short, wide, and stumpy, which allowed them to withstand the buffeting of ocean waves. It was too risky for us to build dedicated ocean-craft right away, so we decided to develop an "ocean-laker," which was a hybrid capable of going to sea but also narrow enough to operate on the Great Lakes. This meant a loss in cargo capacity. However, it would allow us to test new markets without gambling the company's future.

The idea didn't have much attraction to Power Corporation, which was shifting its focus toward the acquisition of companies in the financial sector. So every time I came looking for $20 million or $30 million to build a new ship, they balked. It meant $20 million or $30 million less for building up holdings in which Power Corporation wanted to grow. Moreover, the board was understandably dubious about sinking vast sums into Paul Martin's vision of taking CSL global when the company clearly had difficulties maintaining profitability in its historic Great Lakes market. For them it was all a gamble and a distraction. The tension between my plans and Power Corporation's came to a head in the early 1980s when

Paul Desmarais decided he wanted to make a takeover bid for Canadian Pacific (CP). Like CSL, CP was in both shipping and trucking, and he was concerned that his bid would be held up because of competition legislation.

So, in June 1981, Desmarais called me into his office on the top floor of the CSL building, as he had done many times before. He told me that he wanted me to sell another company: this time it was CSL.

"Fine," I said, "except that I don't want to sell it. I want to buy it."

He pointed out that I didn't have the money. However, recognizing that I was an important part of any sale because of my knowledge of the company, he said he was willing to give me a chance.

"I'll make you a deal," he said. "I don't want you shopping the company around while you try to find a partner. So I'll give you one shot at it and a few weeks to find a partner and a bank, but if it doesn't work out, then I want you to sell the company to the best available buyer."

I said, "Deal."

Then he asked me about the bank, and I said I wanted to work with the Royal Bank, which had always been CSL's banker as well as Power Corporation's, but I knew that they would not deal without his okay. Desmarais phoned a vice-president at the Royal Bank and told him: "Paul Martin wants to buy Canada Steamship Lines. It's up to you whether you want to lend him the money, but I want you to know that he has my permission to talk to you."

Ten minutes later, I was walking across the street to see Ladi Pathy, who was the president of Fednav, the largest Canadian deep-sea shipping company. Pathy is one of the most successful but least known of Canada's business leaders. He has quite a story. He was born of Hungarian parents in Alexandria in Egypt, where his father, Ladislas Pathy, was Hungarian consul general prior to the Second World War. Those who have read Michael Ondaatje's novel *The English Patient* may remember that there was another Hungarian expatriate in the region at the time, Count Almasy – who is portrayed in the novel as a dashing, romantic figure. In truth, he was a Nazi double-agent.

Ladi has given me permission to quote the following passage from an oral history dictated by his father, which provides some insight into the adventures of the sinister count. "It would appear that at the time of El Alamein at the end of June 1942, Almasy – who by then was an A.D.C. [Aide-de-Camp] to Rommel – came over from the German lines in a British jeep and British uniform to the British lines. The British followed him, and he spent some ten days at the Shepheard's Hotel in Cairo. At the end of his stay the British permitted him to return to the German lines, which he did, except that he lost his briefcase. In other words, the briefcase was taken by the British. In that briefcase a number of interesting documents were discovered, including a list of some 90 people who were to be the first to be arrested – whenever the Germans would enter Cairo or Alexandria. One of the names in this list was mine."

Of course, the British eventually threw Rommel's army back without ever giving him the chance to round anybody up in Egypt's great cities. The Pathy family continued to live in Egypt for the remainder of the war, and afterwards Ladislas Pathy continued his business career in shipping and insurance. He and his three brothers also acquired the Egyptian franchise for Coca-Cola, which was an instant sensation there. A *Time* magazine article in 1950, about Coca-Cola's "conquest" of the globe, described the Pathy brothers as "Egypt's shrewdest businessmen." However, the Pathys left Egypt after King Farouk was deposed in 1952 by a coup that brought Gamel Abdel Nasser to power and a wave of nationalization of industry. Ladi's family then moved to the United States, where he had already gone to attend boarding school. After graduating from Princeton University and NYU law school, he ended up in Montreal with his wife, Constance, who is Dutch, but as a young girl lived all over the world. He joined Fednav, which at that time was a small family-owned shipping business founded by one of his uncles in 1944. He later bought out his father and his uncle and built Fednav into a great international shipping company with headquarters in Montreal.

Ladi and I had become acquainted during my early years at CSL. When the opportunity arose to buy the company, he happened to be sitting on a lot of cash from an unsuccessful run he had taken at acquiring Abitibi Paper but that had nonetheless yielded him a significant profit. In the ten minutes it took to walk from Paul Desmarais's office to Ladi's, I worked out the elements of a leveraged buyout in my head. I didn't have much money personally, but I knew the company inside out and I controlled the deal. My idea was that Ladi and I would each put up an amount equal to my (modest) total net worth for the common shares of CSL, which would give us equal control over the company. However, Ladi was also going to have to come up with an investment many times larger, in order to provide the equity base, which he would take in the form of preferred shares. Although they wouldn't confer any control over the company, these shares would put him first in line to get his money back if things went wrong. The rest of the money – the lion's share, in fact – would have to come from the bank, which would loan us money secured by CSL's assets. It took perhaps twenty minutes to lay out my plan and another twenty minutes for us to discuss it. Then Ladi and I shook hands, and that was it.

The next day, I flew to Toronto to speak to the bank. I had enough equity investment from Ladi to convince the Royal Bank to come in behind the deal. Within a week, I was back in Power's offices, ready to offer something in the order of $160 million for the company. But, to my shock, Paul Desmarais balked. He had concluded the CP deal wasn't going to come through and had decided to hold on to CSL. You can imagine how I felt. Luckily for me, a week later, he phoned me to say that the CP deal was back on[1] and that we could start talking again.

The negotiations over the buyout lasted several months, and they transformed my relationship with Paul Desmarais. Up until then, I had always been an employee – one with ideas of his own but still an

---

[1] The CP deal eventually fell through, as it happened.

employee. I needed to bargain hard if I was to have any chance of success, however, and Desmarais was an equally tough negotiator, as was Power's president, Jim Burns. Many times John Rae, later the organizer of Jean Chrétien's campaigns, who was and is an executive at Power, kept the bargaining rolling by pushing both sides back to the table. At one point, I became quite discouraged about my chances of getting a deal, whose failure I increasingly realized would have huge negative implications for my career. My relationship with Desmarais had been so completely transformed in the previous weeks that it seemed unlikely he would want me to stay on as a subordinate. Though I enjoyed a good salary at Power, I had not really accumulated much wealth, and Sheila and I had a young family. Sheila had been very supportive from the beginning, but if the takeover fell through, in my own heart I knew I was gone from Power.

It was in this period that by chance I bumped into Maurice Strong on an airplane. We arranged to sit together, and I opened up to him about the state of the negotiations and my fears about their possible failure.

"Don't worry about that," he told me. "I'm working on several deals at the moment, and I could fit you easily into any one of them."

To this day I have no idea what he had on the go, but that conversation restored my certainty that I wanted to be my own man and that if the CSL deal fell through, I had options. I knew that I had crossed my Rubicon, and I went back to the bargaining table. We launched into a marathon thirty-six-hour negotiating session with me, my team, and Ladi's team on one side and a succession of Power executives on the other. Something that served me well in my business career (and later in politics) was my ability with numbers in a negotiation. I was no mathematician, as my schoolday travails with algebra bear witness, but just as some people can just sit down at a piano and play, I always had a feel for the numbers. In any business deal, the central issue is the "present value" of the future cash flows stemming from an asset about to change hands. I don't know how, but even with complex configurations under discussion, I could intuit what the value was. After the accountants had been sent off to do their calculations, they'd often come back with a result just minute decimal points off the figure I had been working with.

The negotiations were held in the offices of a law firm, and we would shuttle back and forth between our respective meeting rooms and the main table in the firm's boardroom. Ladi recalls that at one point in the discussions, he came over to the law offices to see how things were going but was having trouble finding me. When he got to the firm's library, he saw some feet sticking out from between the stacks. It was me, catnapping, a talent that always led me to try to conclude a negotiation in one marathon session if I could – a practice I continued when I went into politics. Finally, on August 8, 1981, we reached a deal with Power and the company was ours.

I remember walking into CSL the next morning and sitting down behind my desk. I own the company, I thought. I've done it. Never before or since do I remember having a moment quite like that.

In the end, Ladi and I paid about $180 million for CSL: the largest leveraged buyout in Canadian history to that point. Perhaps I should say "overpaid," because that is what we most certainly did. But I have always taken the view that if a company is worthwhile, overpaying is the least of your problems – if it isn't worthwhile, underpaying isn't going to get you out of a mess.

From our perspective, the deal was a gamble on four counts. Our goal was to build a global shipping company focusing on self-unloading technology. First: In order to do so we had to sell the trucking and bus companies for a reasonable price, so that we had the money to reinvest in new ships. We did! Second: We had to re-invest heavily in new lakers in order to increase efficiency and market share pending a turnaround in the Great Lakes market. The problem was, we were doing so at a time when most experts thought the turnaround would never happen. This worked out. Third: We had to build ocean-going self-unloaders at huge cost on the hope we could convince customers in certain niche international markets who had never used self-unloaders to give them a try. This worked out. Fourth, and this was the biggest risk of all, the deal was really an enormous gamble on interest rates.

This was the period of high inflation and skyrocketing interest rates. We negotiated on an assumption of 20 per cent rates, and on the day we signed the agreement, they hit 22 per cent, the highest ever interest rates in Canadian history. At the time, Henry Kaufman, the leading Wall Street prognosticator of interest rates, was predicting they would top out in the 30 per cent range. If they did that, we were dead. But I had the feeling that if they rose that quickly, they were likely to come down quickly too. We structured the deal to give ourselves a couple of years' breathing room whatever happened, and instead of rising, in the months after the deal rates eased to around 14 per cent and our gamble paid off. People sometimes said to me later: "What an enormous chance you took." Well, I have an answer for that. If you don't take the opportunity when it is there for you, don't expect it to return a second time. When I look back on it now, it was the same spirit that inspired my first bid for the Liberal leadership in 1990: the opportunity was there, so why not?

Ladi's experience in the international shipping markets was crucial to making the CSL deal go through. We needed to sell some of the company's ships offshore to raise cash and then lease them back so that our business would not be affected – something he was able to manage because of his knowledge of the global industry, which certainly exceeded mine. Once we acquired the company, I was able to pursue my vision of taking CSL global. My goal was to see CSL become the biggest self-unloader operator in the world, which it eventually did thanks largely to the management team that succeeded me when I went on to other things.

Hard as it may be to believe now, Ladi and I did this all on the original handshake. It wasn't until five or six years into our partnership that it occurred to us that if one of us died, it was going to be a mess for the families to sort out, and we committed our arrangement to paper. I was also beginning to think about whether my sons might want to play a role in CSL one day and about my own desire to be my own boss. To this end, in 1987, I approached Ladi, whose shipping interests were vast in comparison with my own, and asked him if he would sell his shares. He understood why I wanted him to do this – and agreed.

In my view, Ladi Pathy is one of Canada's unrecognized treasures – an extraordinary Canadian almost unknown to his fellow citizens. He owns and manages a business that operates all over the world and could live anywhere he wants to. He came to Canada relatively late in life but has chosen to put down roots here. When I asked him about that once, he had a straightforward answer, which is the measure of the man. He and his wife, Constance, love Canada. They both grew up in several countries, none of which they could ever call home. They wanted something different for their two sons, Paul and Mark. They wanted a country they could call their own.

When I first read the passage I quoted above from Ladi's father's wartime reminiscences, in which he describes the danger the family would have been in had Rommel overrun Egypt as he planned, I thought about how different Ladi's life might have been. I mentioned this to Sheila and she said, "Yes, but think how different yours would have been too."

Ladi's farm is near to ours in the Eastern Townships, and we continue to this day to be good friends. Along with Brian Gallery, Paul Echenberg, who worked with me at Connie Bathurst, and Huck Henry (a close friend who introduced me to much of the Toronto business community), we play golf regularly. The fact that they are the only people I can reliably beat is no coincidence.

My experience with CSL was closely linked with my political and economic ideas, both before and since. While many of the political elites were consumed with constitutional issues in the 1970s and early 1980s, my thoughts were going in a different direction. Growing up in Windsor in the shadow of America's industrial might, I had always felt the rivalry with the United States. As a young man, I was a "Walter Gordon nationalist." Walter Gordon had been finance minister for a time under Lester Pearson, and later went on to become one of the founders of an influential group called the Committee for an Independent Canada. In later years, although my dad and Mr. Gordon were anything but close, he was kind enough to meet with me every year to discuss the state of the country and the economy. However, my experience in business eventually convinced me that his formula of requiring Canadian minority ownership of companies operating in Canada was not going to work. Canada suffers from substantial diseconomies of scale in comparison with the United States. I was also convinced that with the inevitable rise of Asia and the strength of an increasingly integrated Europe, an inward-looking Canada would never succeed. I became convinced that Canada needed to meet world competition with its own economic muscle. The solution to the invasion of foreign transnationals was to create powerful international companies of our own – my ambition for CSL. I believed that our preoccupation with Canada's internal difficulties, and our impulse to meet international competition by trying to wall it out, flirted with danger – the danger that we would lose out in the world. Indeed it was these beliefs that drove one of the themes of my first leadership run in 1990: "Nationalism without walls."

When you understand how closely my ambitions for CSL were tied up with these ideals, you can appreciate my reluctance to divest my ownership of the company when I became finance minister and later prime minister. CSL was not only the result of the most audacious gamble of my life, it was also the incarnation of a vision I had for Canadian business. I believed that we had to succeed globally, both individually and as a country, if we were going to survive the transformation and increasing integration of the world economy.

My friend and close adviser, Terrie O'Leary (about whom, more later), warned me that CSL could be a political millstone, with the minister of finance's family owning a major Canadian business. And how could I be involved with a company that had ships flying foreign flags? The answer is that if Canadians are going to succeed in an international business such as shipping, they will have to be involved with foreign markets and foreign unions. Our ships always had the highest safety standards. But if you are operating in the coastal waters off Australia or Indonesia, it makes no sense to be a Canadian-flagged ship. The majority of CSL's ships do fly the Canadian flag and the Canadian fleet is growing. Most CSL employees are Canadians; the company has its headquarters in Montreal and is taxable right here in Canada. Maybe some people are not bothered when Canadian companies are bought up by foreign interests. I'd rather see us doing the buying than the selling. I understood exactly what Terrie was telling me, but selling CSL meant betraying the vision that had guided me from the beginning – and probably meant another Canadian asset eventually falling into foreign hands. In the end, just before I became prime minister, I transferred the remaining vestiges of ownership to my sons.

The disappearances of Canadian head offices as major Canadian companies are taken over by their international competitors has led to an important debate. I am among those who feel that these losses have deep consequences, ranging from decreased support for Canadian universities to the reduced exercise of Canadian sovereignty.

For example, when Doug Young, the minister of transport, masterfully piloted through the privatization of Canadian National Railway (CNR), as minister of finance I insisted that the legislation ensure, as much as possible, that the company would remain Canadian, with a head office based in Canada.

For the same reason I resisted the pressure to free Petro-Canada from similar restrictions when the government sold its remaining shares in the company.

On the other hand, as anyone who has watched the French or the Americans at work knows very well, it is not always necessary to proceed by legislation. I played that game too. Once, when Alberta Energy and PanCanadian Energy were contemplating the merger that eventually created EnCana, the two CEOs, Gwyn Morgan and David O'Brien, came to see the natural resources minister, Ralph Goodale, and me. They told us of their fear that a foreign bid was possible that could prevent a new Canadian energy giant being created. They felt if I expressed my support for the merger this might send an important signal that might be picked up where it would do the most good.

As it happened, I had an interview scheduled with David Crane of the *Toronto Star*, whose views on this general issue were well known. The interview took place soon thereafter, and the signal was sent, and duly published.

Whether it was received, we'll never know, but the merger of the two Canadian companies took place and EnCana was born. I hope it stays Canadian.

To those who say that Canadian companies benefit when they are part of a great international network, I'd say that I agree. No argument there. But why can't some of these great international networks have their head offices here?

To those who say that an open season on Canadian companies is a necessary step toward nirvana in the global marketplace, I'd simply respond with the question: "How come that's not true for the multitude of American, French, Japanese, Indian, and Chinese companies that are off-limits to foreigners?"

To those who say that the answer lies in reciprocity, again I'd say, fine. Except that by the time those other companies get around to offering us reciprocity, we'll have nothing left to be reciprocal with.

Finally, to those who say that people who share my opinions are afraid of globalization, I say, "You couldn't be more wrong! This has nothing to do with fleeing from globalization. It has everything to do with taking advantage of it – and you can't do that if you don't have the tools of the trade."

Now these are views that will not make me popular in some quarters. So be it!

In August 2006, a few months after I stepped down as prime minister, I was out in Vancouver for a meeting of the Liberal caucus. One evening, Belinda Stronach arranged for me to have dinner with some of the MPs that had been closest to me over the years. It was a wonderful event, with plenty of sentimental speeches and lots of wine.

After it was over, though, I had something left to do that evening. I had heard that there was a newly commissioned ship in harbour: the *Baldock*, which was 50 per cent owned by CSL and carried the company logo. For eighteen years I had not stepped foot on a CSL ship. At about ten that night, my executive assistant, Jim Pimblett, and I boarded a water taxi and rode out into the harbour. It was a beautiful evening, with the glittering lights of Vancouver all around us. The Mounties didn't like it, but I stood outside the cabin of the water-taxi on the flat stern section, supporting myself by grasping a thin metal pole, and took in the sea air. They liked it less when I raced up the *Baldock*'s ladder maybe four storeys in height. The *Baldock* is a seventy-five-thousand-tonne ocean vessel. It is a hybrid, whose front end, equipped with the most modern self-unloading technology in the world, was grafted onto a back end salvaged from an earlier ship. With Mounties in tow, Jim and I explored the bridge, the sailor's quarters, and state-of-the-art computer room with the Ukrainian captain, who knew only a little English and may not have had any idea who I was or what my connection to CSL might be. In the engine room, we scrambled over the enormous boilers and the propeller shaft on catwalks suspended above. Then we walked the length of the ship – almost two and a half football fields long – all below deck as I inspected the conveyer system that makes the guts of a self-unloader. It was the kind of ship I had dreamed of when I was building CSL in the 1980s – the kind that could range the world from Vancouver to Singapore. I had never seen one before. And it is part of a large fleet that is controlled by Canadians.

CHAPTER FIVE

Drawn to the Flame

For better or for worse, I have always lived my life intensely engaged in the challenge of the moment. There has never been a time when I dabbled in a little of this and a little of that. Since I stepped down as prime minister, many people have remarked on how completely my new preoccupations have taken over my life. When I do have dinner with an old political colleague, instead of trading old war stories I want to talk about the new projects I have launched with Aboriginal Canadians, in Africa, or perhaps about this book. Except when I am asked to give a speech or take on a particular task, I maintain only a passing interest in the current political scene.

This tendency to focus narrowly on the task immediately at hand has always been there, whether I was in business, or at the Department of Finance, or in 24 Sussex. There are always outside obligations, distractions, and pleasures, of course, that connect me to the other strands of my life and my career. But I tend to push them to the fringes of my consciousness. The same was true during my years at Power Corporation and at CSL. Given my background, politics inevitably intruded into my life during this period to some extent. It is only in retrospect, however, that my political involvement of the 1960s and 1970s, which was intermittent, episodic, and peripheral to my life, seems to have acquired some significance – and even then, the significance seems greater to others than it does to me.

Before I moved to Montreal, my involvement with the Liberal Party had always been in connection with my father's political career.

Still, I had made some friends among the Young Liberals, including Robert Demers. He later became known as the lawyer who negotiated with the Front de libération du Québec (FLQ) for the release of James Cross on behalf of the federal and provincial governments during the October Crisis in 1970. In 1966, shortly after I had moved to Montreal, the Liberal government of Quebec led by Jean Lesage called an election. Bob Demers was working for a young lawyer by the name of Robert Bourassa, who was running for the first time for the Quebec National Assembly in the riding of Mercier in the East Island of Montreal. Demers recruited me as the "warm-up man" at kitchen parties held for Bourassa. I would arrive at a home where there was to be a meet and greet with Bourassa before he got there and get the crowd warmed up. Then Bourassa would come along, and I would leave to do the same job at the next event. That way the candidate's time could be used to maximum advantage.

There was another Liberal candidate in the nearby riding of Dorion, named François Aquin, who later went on to become a key figure in the sovereigntist Rassemblement pour l'Indépendance Nationale (RIN), a predecessor to the Parti Québécois. Because of Aquin's obvious sympathies, some federal Liberals supported a rival, independent Liberal candidate, the well-known Quebec wrestler, Johnny Rougeau.

One day on our way back from a kitchen party for Bourassa, Bob wanted to drop by Aquin's headquarters. Not a lot was going on, and after about fifteen minutes, feeling restless, I decided to check out what was happening at Rougeau's campaign office, which was just a block away. The door was open, but there was no one around. I picked up some campaign literature and headed back to Aquin's office, where I hoped to persuade Bob it was time to go home. About fifteen minutes later, I heard a commotion in the front room and went out to see what was happening. There were two men the size of the Empire State Building – workers for Rougeau – shouting at the Aquin people: "You guys sent a spy into our headquarters and he took some of our stuff and we want it back."

It took me a couple of seconds to realize that I was the "spy." All hell was about to break loose, and even though Aquin's supporters greatly outnumbered the intruders, they were not about to take on the wrestler's buddies. Clearly it was up to me to straighten everything out. Unfortunately, while my French is good, I may have been a little weak on the street argot that day. I took them by the shoulders and said, "Come on, let's go outside and settle this." Not the perfect choice of words. As we stepped onto the street, from nowhere, it seemed, a clenched fist came crunching into the middle of my face. I don't remember much more of the moment, except that when I went back into Aquin's headquarters I had a broken nose.

It didn't end there, though. Aquin's people saw obvious political opportunity in my disjointed nose. You can imagine the headline the next day: Johnny Rougeau's Workers Beat Up Paul Martin's Son. The next thing I know, I get a call from my dad: "What have you done now?" Five minutes later, Guy Favreau, the Quebec lieutenant of the federal Liberal Party, phoned: "Rougeau is our candidate, and now you've given this coup to Aquin's campaign. The police are pressing charges. What were you thinking?"

Favreau's call was the first I had heard of criminal charges, which had apparently been pressed on Aquin's insistence. When I phoned the police, they refused to drop them on my say-so. So I phoned Aquin directly. "You've got to call the police and tell them it was all a mistake," I said, "and that they shouldn't worry about it." But Aquin said, "To hell with you." So I hung up and spent the next fifteen minutes trying to figure how I was going to get myself out of this jam. Then I phoned Aquin back and said, "Look, go ahead. Press charges. But I want you to know what my testimony will be. These guys came into your headquarters and all your supporters, who outnumbered them ten to one, went running for cover and left me to go out into the street with them alone. In fact, I may just phone up the papers and tell my side of the story this afternoon." Mysteriously, the charges were dropped. This was my last foray into the more muscular political arts – "muscular from the neck up," my father would have said.

The next year – the year of the leadership contest to replace Lester Pearson – would prove to be my last period of political activity for a decade and a half. At the outset, my dad appeared to be the front-runner. He was the most popular with the public among the likeliest contenders. As a Franco-Ontarian, my father had an obvious appeal to Quebec delegates, one he shared in varying degrees with Jean Marchand and Eric Kierans, of course. But unlike them, he had considerable support in the rest of Canada too.

There was a great deal of speculation about whether Marchand would run, in part because of the Liberal tradition of alternating between anglophone and francophone leaders. Marchand had always been regarded as the most senior of the so-called "wise men" recruited from Quebec by Pearson, who also included Gérard Pelletier and Pierre Trudeau. To this day, I think my father would likely have won had Marchand entered the race. Dad would have held his vote in English Canada and made inroads in Quebec. And Marchand's supporters would likely have stood behind my father once their candidate was eliminated. But it was not to be. Marchand decided not to run. Trudeau jumped into the race late and Marchand threw his considerable weight behind him.

As I mentioned earlier, I took a leave of absence from Power Corporation to work on my father's campaign. My job was to be a surrogate speaker at meetings Dad couldn't attend – a role my sons would later play in my own leadership campaigns. Although I went to events across the country, I concentrated on Quebec. My father's campaign was organized by Duncan Edmonds, with active involvement from Maurice Strong, Jack Austin, Hugh Faulkner, and Jimmy Pattison, among others. The campaign was run in much the same fashion as his 1958 leadership attempt. Paul Hellyer, in contrast, mounted a highly coordinated riding-by-riding campaign, which foreshadowed the organizations that would dominate future contests in the Liberal Party. But it turned out that neither approach could compete with the Trudeau phenomenon. Trudeau's campaign owed as much to John F. Kennedy's as it did to anything we had ever seen in

Canada before. It was about a change of generations; it was about sweeping out the old with the charisma of the new. Suddenly, all my father's advantages – his seniority, his experience, his diligent working of the party over decades – were disadvantages, as Liberals were mesmerized with the novelty and promise of Trudeau's candidacy.

By the day of the convention, April 6, 1968, we knew it would not happen for us. For the Liberals, it was the first true television convention. My father sat in the stands under the glare of TV lights while I buttonholed delegates on the convention floor. My concern wasn't so much winning as what the loss would mean to him. That evening, my father scrambled onto a table in a backroom at the convention centre at Lansdowne Park to speak to his supporters. He told them he would not be running again. "In years to come, I will walk along Wellington Street and point at the Parliament Buildings and say I used to work there," he told them. He knew that his long career in the House of Commons was nearing its end, though in my mind I did not see why he wouldn't run again and continue as external affairs minister under Trudeau as he had been under Pearson.

It is my strong memory, and Sheila confirms this, that neither my dad nor I seemed devastated by the loss. The day after the convention, in a gesture that I have never forgotten, John Turner, who had run a strong campaign, invited our family to his home for breakfast. Sheila still vividly recalls how placid my father was in contrast to John, who was still furious at what he saw as the "backroom deals" that determined the convention. I never did find out how my dad voted after he chose to drop off the first ballot. He never said, and I never asked.

Pierre Trudeau treated my father very well after the 1968 convention. The new prime minister had spoken out about Senate reform during the campaign. Although my father had decided that eleven elections were enough for him, he accepted an appointment to the Senate as government leader, given the challenge of reforming the institution. Later when it became clear that the prime minister was not able to follow through on plans for Senate reform, he

appointed my father High Commissioner to the Court of St. James –
in effect, the ambassador to Britain. My father accepted this post with
enthusiasm, though he worried that it would delay the writing of his
memoirs, which had become an important project for him. The time
in London turned out to be one of the happiest periods of my parents'
lives, and so I had every reason to feel grateful to Trudeau – and did.
In 1979, Joe Clark was elected as the Progressive Conservative prime
minister. He told my dad: "You can stay in London as long as you
would like. I am not going to ask you to step down." My father told
him that he wanted to come home to write his memoirs, however.
Prime Minister Clark's gesture was a gracious one for which both
my father and I were very grateful.

From the time my father left politics, my active interest in the
Liberal Party waned. I continued to have Liberal friends, of course,
including Ed Lumley and Jim Coutts, who were very involved in the
Trudeau government. But I focused almost exclusively on building
my business career. Frankly, I didn't pay much attention to politics.
When they needed warm bodies at a rally, I was happy enough to
show up. But if I thought about government at all, it was from the
perspective of a businessman.

Everyone in Quebec was affected by the October Crisis in 1970,
of course. We were all in shock after the kidnappings of James Cross
and Pierre Laporte. There were some provincial cabinet ministers
living in our neighbourhood in Mont Royal, and Andrée Bourassa,
the premier's sister, lived just down the street. So there were literally
soldiers and police in the streets. Sheila remembers the eeriness of
Halloween night, when she walked young Paul from house to house
in a neighbourhood bristling with military vehicles and armed men.
There were frequent bomb threats, but like many people we drove
the police crazy by ignoring the threats and refusing to vacate buildings. As for us, we installed our first-ever alarm system in the house
at the urging of the company. I was told not to park the car nearby,
for fear that it might be booby-trapped, and not to take a taxi because
it might be used in a kidnapping. But these were no more than minor

inconveniences. What was far more gripping for Sheila and me was the human and historical drama unfolding around us. We were stunned and deeply saddened when Pierre Laporte was found dead and enormously relieved when James Cross was finally released after his ordeal.

As the 1970s progressed, I found myself slowly growing out of sync with the economic policies of the Trudeau government. From my vantage point, it was clear that the global economy was changing fundamentally. The days of easy economic growth, abundant job creation, and low inflation were behind us. But like a lot of governments around the world, Canada's was slow to recognize what was happening. The economy was stalled but inflation continued apace, and a new term – "stagflation" – was coined. Many people in power apparently still believed that Ottawa could spend its way out of economic difficulties, and all that borrowed money would be easily handled in the next upturn. But of course it was nothing like that. And while failure to recognize the new economic reality may have been understandable for two, three, four years, even the passage of time did not seem to change the government's course. I still remained a strong Liberal, but a political career could not have been further from my mind at the time.

I remember having lunch sometime in the 1970s with Brian Mulroney. Sitting in the restaurant atop Place Ville Marie, Brian calmly told me of his plan to become prime minister one day. His accomplishments were considerable as a lawyer in the high-profile Cliche Commission investigating organized crime in Quebec's construction industry and later as a businessman. Still, I remember thinking he must be smoking something to imagine that a Quebec Tory was going to become prime minister any time soon. Nor did it occur to me that our career paths might intersect or even clash. If Brian had asked me that day what my ultimate ambition might be – which he did not – I probably would have replied that I would like to be president of the World Bank or the head of the United Nations environmental program. I was making my way in business then, hoping to reach the financial independence that Maurice Strong had talked to me about, and then, I thought, I would pursue an international career.

Brian has a somewhat different recollection, which he recounts in his memoirs, of what could be the same discussion, though I can't be sure. He locates it at the Power Corporation fishing lodge on Anticosti Island. I do remember that day, though not for any political conversation. It was extremely – and unusually – hot, so the salmon were not rising to the fly. In the circumstances, we both stripped down to what God gave us and plunged into the water to cool off – something that was absolutely forbidden in a salmon pool. Then we sunned ourselves on a rock. Someone snapped a picture: two future prime ministers in this exposed state. (Insert your own joke about "naked ambition" here.) That the photograph has never surfaced publicly is a matter of considerable relief to both of us.

During the campaign for the February 1980 election, which ended with Trudeau's surprise return to office after the Clark government, Jim Coutts called me up to help pack a hall for Trudeau in Montreal. I remember telling him: "I hope he's going to talk about the economy, and I hope he realizes how difficult Canada's position is becoming." I went and heard the prime minister talk once more about the Constitution, and I thought, My god, this is crazy. I was frustrated that he ignored the economy and what I saw as the sorry state of government finances.

I was also unhappy about the National Energy Program (NEP). It was not that I disagreed that the government had a role in shaping the oil and gas industry. I supported the creation of Petro-Canada, for example, because I believed there needed to be a major Canadian presence in the oil patch. In fact, one of my regrets as prime minister is that I did not create a bio-tech Crown corporation that could have helped aggregate and build Canada's strength in that field before being sold back into the private sector as Petro-Canada ultimately was. But I believed that the NEP was bad policy. It threatened Western Canada's economic development and isolated Canada from global currents. In the long run I was sure this would harm us.

At the time I was involved in a couple of Liberal policy talk-shops: most notably, Grindstone and the Faulkner Group. Grindstone, which was named after the Ontario resort south of Ottawa where it met, was an annual gathering of youngish, reform-minded Liberals to talk policy and have a few drinks. That's where I met Mike Robinson, who would later play an important role in all my national political campaigns. The Faulkner Group was a similar gathering that attracted a slightly older, more established crowd assembled by former Trudeau minister Hugh Faulkner. It was there that I met Peter Nicholson, the businessman, public servant, economist, and intellectual who would later advise me in many capacities during my time in government, and whose wife, Jane, became one of Sheila's closest friends. Because of my involvement in these groups – and perhaps also because my father has written that in these years I had already begun to consider my entry into politics – many people think this was the unofficial beginning to my political career.

Not so. In fact, to the extent that I was engaged in policy debates, I was more active in the international arena, as a founding board member of the North-South Institute, for example, and frequently attended meetings of the international branch of the Conference Board. I had also developed an interest in Aboriginal entrepreneurship – a domestic issue, to be sure, but hardly the express ticket to high political office.

As Sheila has said, if I was planning a political career at this time, she certainly didn't know about it. For the moment, I was immersed in the takeover of CSL, an adventure that not only required most of my time and energy but also had me gambling all of our relatively modest personal wealth.

In the fall of 1981, a matter of weeks after Ladi Pathy and I bought CSL, I did get a visit from three young Liberals: Peter Donolo, Alf Apps, and Terrie O'Leary. Like many young Liberals at the time, my visitors had two preoccupations: party reform and economic policy. Their concerns about economic issues were closest to my own. We had a long, free-ranging talk – much longer than they had imagined possible, as I later learned. I agreed to give a speech on economic policy at a Young Liberals convention that was to be held right before the party's annual conference. As it happened, my economic speech was overshadowed by an open challenge to Trudeau's management of the party at the convention. No one remembered much of what I had to say. However, the personal contacts I made with the Young Liberals had an enduring impact on my political life – though I did not recognize this at the time – and the economic principles I espoused formed the bedrock of my politics throughout my later career.

During this period I was also invited to speak to an audience of Saskatchewan Liberals. Afterwards, I was approached by an awkwardly dressed young man with a bad haircut. He introduced himself as David Herle and said that if I ever wanted to run for the leadership of the Liberal Party, he was going to be there for me. It seemed an unlikely offer and a slender foundation on which to build any such ambition. I had no idea at the time of the importance David would assume in my political career. And I had no way of knowing that he would develop into one of the shrewdest policy and political minds in the country. He came to work for me at CSL prior to going to law school and later played a prominent role in every national campaign I had anything to do with. He has been a great friend and a sound adviser over more than two decades, though I have not changed my views about his style of dress.

Notwithstanding David's surprising suggestion, my preoccupation at the time remained business. After all, having engineered Canada's largest-ever leveraged buyout a few months before (which is a polite way of saying I had borrowed an awful lot of money), I needed to drill down on my plans for refashioning CSL into a world player. When Pierre Trudeau stepped down in 1984, I was on a few journalists' speculative lists of potential candidates to succeed him, but that was just talk and certainly didn't amount to much in my mind. I took the much more modest role of chairman of the leadership debates, for which I was qualified mainly by virtue of my bilingualism and my gilt-plate Liberal name. I was personally (though not publicly) a supporter of Mark McGuigan, largely because of Windsor connections, which was just about as good as being completely neutral in the race since his prospects were so slender. Many of the young people who would eventually form the core of my organization, such as Terrie, David, and Richard Mahoney, were cutting their political teeth with John Roberts's campaign, though I was only dimly aware of this at the time.

Although the task of chairing the debates gave me an opportunity to see both the frontrunners, Jean Chrétien and John Turner, up close, I didn't know either man well. Ironically, at the time I knew Brian Mulroney much better. Sheila and I were among the legion of Montrealers who watched his courtship of Mila – and urged him to hurry up and marry her. Brian and Mila had continued to be friends after he became Leader of the Opposition, though we had almost no contact once he became prime minister.

Possibly because of this earlier friendship I was the lone Liberal appointee to the board of the Canadian Development Investment Corporation (CDIC) not to be fired after the Tories took office. I was horrified when I learned about this, but some of CDIC's managers urged me to stay on, embarrassing as the situation was, in the hope that I could ease the transition. CDIC's role was to make investments in key sectors of the Canadian economy – a task more suited to small-l liberal traditions than to those of the small-c conservatives just arriving on the board. At the first meeting I attended, the new chairman let loose with a crude blast at the previous Liberal government, saying in essence that everything that it had done was wrong. I counter-attacked and we got into a nasty row. I realized that my position on the board was hopeless and that to stay any longer would be a betrayal of everything we had done at CDIC during my four-year tenure, so I resigned.

By the mid-1980s, I had consolidated CSL's financial position as well as my own, and my mind was starting to turn to the possibility of the second career I had always assumed would be mine. It was time to fish or cut bait. Like many people in their mid-forties, I knew that if I did not make a break soon, I would probably never do so. Although my ambition had always been to work internationally, I now had to face the fact that I had not built a firm foundation abroad. After all, I had lived all my life, save for a few months, here in Canada. It was a little too late to go work for the World Bank as a field officer. In contrast, because of my pedigree perhaps, as well as my business career, I was actually in demand here in Canada. In 1986, Raymond Garneau, who was involved in recruiting candidates for the federal Liberals in Quebec, started to pressure me hard. When I said that I would think about it, he replied, "Don't think about it. If you do that you'll never run." I did think about it, but it didn't take me long to make up my mind.

There was one major obstacle, however: Senator Pietro Rizzuto, who headed the Liberal organization in Quebec. Unlike the rest of the country, where most candidates had to get nominated through a democratic exercise of party members at the local level, in Quebec the party machine designated the candidates, and nomination meetings were often no more than a formality. Rizzuto wanted me to run in Laval, which would have put me firmly under his thumb since he so completely controlled the organization there.

Jean Chrétien urged me to run in Windsor, which my father had represented. He was, of course, positioning himself to run for the leadership again and may have regarded me as a potential candidate at some point as well – preferably not against him. He argued that as a member from an anglophone Ontario seat such as Windsor, I would be in a better position to succeed a francophone Quebecer like him. Although I retained many friendships in Windsor, it had been a very long time since I had lived there, and I would clearly have been a "parachute" candidate. Besides, I did not see any particular reason at that point to tie my future to the tradition of *l'alternance*, which cuts both ways, of course.

In the end, I narrowed my own list of possibilities to three ridings: Rosemont in the East Island of Montreal, Brome in the Eastern Townships where Sheila and I had our farm, and LaSalle-Émard. I wanted a seat where I could win the nomination on my own and not be indebted to the party organizers. I settled on LaSalle-Émard in part because of what my father had always said about the importance of your constituency reflecting the objectives you have at the national level. It was a middle-class riding, about half francophone with the rest a mixture of allophones and anglophones. In 1984, the Conservative candidate, Claude Lanthier, had won the seat by a comfortable margin of almost four thousand votes. By the national party I was seen as something of a "star" candidate; however, this meant absolutely nothing to the voters of Lasalle-Émard. It has been my experience that apart from hockey players, most "star candidates" are stars only within a narrow segment of the population. This was certainly the case with me. The Liberal Party constituency executive was distinctly unimpressed at our first meeting. I got to know the members one by one, though, and over time they warmed to me. There had been talk that the riding might be contested, but in the end I took it by acclamation.

In preparation for my entry into political life, I had reorganized CSL under professional management and bought out Ladi Pathy's share. Given my feelings of responsibility to Ladi, if I had not been able to do this I might never have made the jump.

I also had to begin to prepare the company for my departure. This was finally completed when I asked a close friend, Tony Chesterman, who did not have a shipping background but who had a wonderful way with people, to come in as chairman. He eventually named Sam Hayes as president and Rod Jones as head of international business. While CFO Gerry Carter eventually headed the domestic operation, Pierre Prefontaine and David Tarr were confirmed as vice-president legal and head of CSL Equities, the real estate company in which Ladi and I remained partners. In short, I was gone, and the company has never looked back.

By the beginning of 1987, I was pounding the pavement in LaSalle-Émard. I plunged into the world of retail politics in a way I never had before and, I guess it would be true to say, never did again, since I always had national responsibilities in campaigns after that. Of course I had campaigned with my dad in Windsor many times, but this was different. He would walk down the street and people would shout out "Hi, Paul" and "Good luck." I would go into a supermarket or a mall and say, "How are you, ma'am? I'm Paul Martin, the Liberal candidate" and receive looks that would make "so what" appear welcoming. My dad only had to appear; I had to campaign. Believe you me – there is a difference.

On the other hand, I did have some small advantages. First of all, some of the people voting for me seemed to think I *was* my dad, and some others were under the impression that I was Pol Martin, a TV chef well known around Montreal at the time. I didn't spend much time trying to dissuade anyone that I was neither.

I was naive enough to be convinced I would win the seat even though more experienced Liberals thought it was a long shot. What only slowly dawned on me was that my opponent had been tremendously effective at working the riding. There wasn't a church basement or senior citizens' home Lanthier hadn't visited; he was a household name as well as a ubiquitous presence in the riding. We actually got to know each other quite well in the course of the campaign. His wife, Violeta, became great friends with Sheila – each hoping the other's husband would win, I suspect.

Despite my background, not all the subtleties of campaigning came naturally to me. At one service club luncheon, I shook the hands of people at every table, except the one populated by some of my most active supporters, figuring they already knew me. Before the day was over, I was working hard to keep them from deserting my campaign en masse over the snub. On another occasion, in a crowded restaurant, I shook hands with all the patrons and most of the people waiting on tables but didn't want to disturb one particularly overworked waitress. Later in the day, I received a call at my headquarters from her furious husband. I ended up going to their house to apologize.

I also got my first personal lesson in spin during the campaign. Brian Mulroney was planning a swing through the West Island, and into Verdun, and the Tories were spinning that I did not want him to come into my riding. The truth is that after the CDIC incident, the last thing I wanted was for the prime minister to pass through every constituency in the neighbourhood but mine. I should have challenged him to a debate as he passed through and made a big thing of it. But the Tories were quicker off the mark than I was, and got their story out first.

As a strong supporter of free trade, I was something of an anomaly in the Liberal Party in the 1988 election, though my position was that of the party since Laurier's time. However, LaSalle-Émard was not immune from the tides of the national campaign, in which John Turner's opposition to free trade played a major role. There were two big subway stations in the riding, and after the election was called at the beginning of October, I used to go down to one of them every morning at about six-thirty. I stood at the top of the escalator and snagged reluctant handshakes from commuters. I had some supporters standing behind me with big "Paul Martin" signs so that people had an idea of who I was. Maybe one in three would take my hand, or I'd be able to grab it as they'd whip by and whip by and whip by. And then the famous debate occurred, when Turner electrified the campaign with his dramatic attack on the Free Trade Agreement. The day after, people were stopping and coming back to shake my hand. In the first few weeks, I couldn't wait to get away from the subway station in the morning, and then suddenly I could have stayed all day.

The burst of public enthusiasm I had felt after the leaders' debate waned in my riding as it did across the country in the final days of the campaign. By election day, everyone but me was convinced that I had slipped behind Lanthier. I won by fourteen hundred votes. It was one of just two gains by the Liberals in Quebec that election.

CHAPTER SIX

Run for the Top

I had not entered politics with the intention of becoming prime minister. If I had a political role model, it was C.D. Howe, a businessman who had brought his private sector experience to bear in a brilliant, constructive, and influential political career. Howe was a cabinet colleague and often jousting partner with my father, and I had met him often as a boy. Perhaps surprisingly, given the difference in ages, Mrs. Howe and my mother were very good friends. (Coincidentally, Sheila's grandfather Donald James Cowan, a Tory, was Howe's predecessor as the MP for Port Arthur before being appointed to the bench.) I wanted to be the C.D. Howe of my generation, using my understanding of business and the larger economy to build a Canada that could take on the economic giants outside our borders. It was that dream that initially led me to fix on becoming minister of industry.

The aftermath of the 1988 election created a different dynamic, however. While the Liberal Party had entered that election campaign with a reasonable prospect of beating an unpopular Tory government, and we had eclipsed the Tories and a resurgent NDP in the polls for a time in mid-campaign, in the end Brian Mulroney succeeded in polarizing the electorate around free trade and secured himself a second majority. Although John Turner took some time to announce that he was stepping down as Liberal leader, it quickly became apparent that a leadership race to succeed him was underway. The hundred-to-one favourite was Jean Chrétien, who had lost to John Turner in 1984 but had been preparing for a second run from the moment the first had ended. Iona Campagnolo had famously remarked from the podium of the 1984 convention after John Turner's victory that Jean Chrétien was first in Liberals' hearts if not in their votes. He clearly did not intend that this would happen again. When he suggested in 1988, somewhat offhandedly, that I run in Windsor, I am certain he did not consider me a serious rival to his ambition. He was just clearing brush from the path. He thought the job was his. Still, there were issues. The trench warfare between the Chrétien and Turner camps, which never really stopped during Turner's leadership, meant that there were a lot of Liberals for whom Jean Chrétien was a hard sell. As for me, I had the virtue of novelty on the political scene, which could be a considerable political asset, as I had learned the hard way in the 1968 convention.

There is always room for more than one candidate in any race, and sometimes with a combination of luck and pluck, the underdog actually wins. Was it hubris for a barely elected rookie MP to begin thinking about the leadership of the Liberal Party? I like to think of it differently. It has been said that anyone who runs for Parliament can imagine himself an MP, and if you can imagine yourself an MP, you can imagine being a minister. If you can conjure up images of yourself as a minister, you can certainly picture yourself as prime minister. I had never been one to dally over taking an opportunity when it presented itself, for they rarely re-occur. And after the 1988 election, there was an opportunity – and I took it.

For all that our political careers eventually became entwined, for good as well as for ill, Jean Chrétien and I never really knew each other very well. I cannot clearly recall the first time I met him, but I imagine it would have been through John Rae, who, before he came to Power Corporation, had been Jean Chrétien's executive assistant when he was minister of Indian and northern affairs. Certainly, when Jean Chrétien became minister of finance in 1977 and his adviser Eddie Goldenberg asked me to speak with him about the economy, we were already acquaintances. During the 1970s and early 1980s, we often connected socially through mutual friends, sometimes golfing in a foursome with Rae and Ed Lumley or on fishing trips organized through Paul Desmarais (whose son, André, eventually married Jean Chrétien's daughter, France). I thought he was a nice guy.

When I appeared in Ottawa in late 1988 as the newly minted member from LaSalle-Émard, the media wasted no time in speculating about my potential candidacy to succeed John Turner. I was in the spotlight from the start. What made this somewhat burdensome was the assumption that as my father's son, I would be like a fish at home in the political sea. In fact, while I could undoubtedly find my way around the corridors of the Parliament Buildings better than any other rookie MP, I had less political *savoir faire* than many of the former city councillors, mayors, and MLAs who were sworn in for the first time along with me. At our first caucus meeting, John Turner asked each of the novice MPs to introduce themselves. When it came to my turn, I stood up and said "Paul Martin" with an English pronunciation, then repeated "Paul Martin" with a French pronunciation. There was a reaction in the room. I sat down and thought, What a rube.

In retrospect, I can see that I had not yet acquired many of the basic political skills that a leadership campaign would demand of me. A couple of years on the Opposition benches learning the issues, dealing with the media, and acquiring small political crafts such as speaking extemporaneously would have prepared me much better for what lay ahead. On the other hand, one of my greatest assets as a potential leadership candidate was that I was able to offer a fresh face and a fresh vision. I had begun to slip a line into my speeches to the effect that I wasn't sure which was more difficult, being introduced as a Liberal to a business audience or as a businessman to a Liberal audience. But of course it was that very novelty that was part of my political appeal.

In the last few weeks of 1988, while I was wrapping up my affairs at CSL, I invited Mike Robinson to Montreal for a chat. Mike was a former CFO for the Liberal Party who had an encyclopedic knowledge of its inner workings and a shrewd strategic mind. We knew each other from Grindstone but not particularly well. I think he was taken aback a little when I asked him whether he would become my campaign manager for a leadership bid. We had a very good discussion about my ideas and my goals in public life. Once he was convinced we were of a similar mind on the big issues, he quickly accepted. What obviously compounded his surprise that day was that he suddenly found himself in a meeting with David Herle, Dennis Dawson, Jim de Wilde, and a number of others, who showed him a campaign organization chart they had worked out with his name already pencilled in at the top. Since I first met him that day after my speech in Saskatchewan, David had continued as a very active Liberal. Along with John Webster and others, he had organized to defend John Turner's leadership during a bitter challenge by Jean Chrétien supporters in 1986. Dennis was a former Liberal MP who, after being defeated in 1984, had eventually come to work for CSL to help manage some of the regulatory issues facing the Voyageur bus lines. What this group unveiled for Mike was a fantasy organization, existing only on paper. But it was a start.

Mike likes to recount a story about a cocktail party he arranged for me at his home in Toronto a couple of months later. There were about a hundred people there to meet me. Mike asked me to say a few words, which I did. But while doing so I absent-mindedly bent down once or twice – maybe a hundred times according to subsequent legend – and picked up pieces of lint from the carpet, which I proceeded to roll around in my hand as I spoke. This horrified Mike's wife, known universally as M.L., who had not met me before and was unconvinced that this was a guy to whom it was worth her husband committing the next year of his life. Not ready for prime time, as they say. (M.L. and Sheila soon became great friends, as are Mike and I. I have long suspected that the friendship between the two wives was based, in part at least, on mutual sympathy.) Nor had I yet learned that as a candidate, or a presumed candidate, you aren't just on stage when you take the stage but from the moment you enter the room. A few weeks later, at a conference at Montebello organized by a number of Grindstone people, I headed to the micro-phone several times, only to abandon the speakers' line when someone else pre-empted the point I was going to make. Mike was among a number of my supporters who were flabbergasted at my failure to seize the platform offered to me.

I was more focused on developing my program, which eventually was summed up in the phrase "nationalism without walls." It was much more than a slogan. A young Liberal named John Duffy, who would continue to be a valuable supporter over the years, helped pen a booklet that laid out my political philosophy. I was arguing for a robust nationalism that set its sights on taking on the world, develop-ing competitive, Canadian-based multinationals, enhancing research and development, giving our businesses access to capital, and reduc-ing taxes, debt, and interest rates. I also put an emphasis on keeping our population healthy, educated, and secure through a greater empha-sis on innovative and expanded social programs. This was the era of the *Exxon Valdez* and its devastating oil spill in the delicate environ-ment off the Alaska coast. I argued that we should go beyond merely cleaning up our industrial messes and build an environmental indus-try in Canada that could develop and export new technologies.

At the time, I was not as focused, as I would later be, on the threat that deficits and mounting debt were posing to every other social, economic, and governmental objective we might have. It was not until I had been minister of finance and went through the depart-ment's numbers that I realized we would not be able simply to restrain spending to the level of inflation and grow ourselves out of the deficit. Still, looking back on the speeches and campaign materi-als I developed for the 1990 campaign, much of it with John Duffy's help, I am struck by how consistent they were with the speeches I had given to the Young Liberals in Halifax years earlier, and how clearly I set out the objectives that guided my political career for the next sixteen years – and, as a matter of fact, the projects I have taken up in Africa and here at home with Aboriginal Canadians – since election night 2006.

All very fine, Mike, David, Dennis, and John would tell me. Very inspiring stuff. But when John Turner announced his resignation in May 1989, I was still on the steepest slope of the learning curve. The night of his announcement, Barbara Frum had me as a guest on *The Journal*, the premier TV current affairs program of the time. I was nervous, the chair seemed to tip forward so I felt as if I was going to slide off at any moment, and I had prepared myself to rebuff direct questions about the leadership by insisting that "this is John Turner's day." Of course, the preamble to her first question was to the effect that we should skip past all the stuff about how it was John Turner's day. I will always be grateful to Mary Clancy and George Rideout, both Atlantic Canadian MPs, and Zoë Rideout, who bare-faced lied to me afterwards by insisting I had done well.

A few days later, while I was recording an interview with Eric Malling for CTV, he generously stopped the tape and told me that I should cool down and stop responding to every question as if it were an attack. They rolled tape again – and I was right back at it! What did come more naturally to me, and which my campaign team used to good effect as the campaign unfolded, was the question-and-answer session in meetings with Liberals. I loved the give-and-take on policy, which was usually the order of the day, and although I probably said too much on occasion from the point of view of my campaign team, they knew that this was one of the most effective venues for me to persuade party members and eventually delegates that I had the capacity to lead.

By the spring, Mike and David had assembled a small campaign team based in Ottawa, which included Kaz Flynn, the president of the Young Liberals, Daniel Despins, Mark Resnick, Jamie Deacey, Charles Bird, and Jonathan Schneiderman. I asked Richard Mahoney, a former president of the Young Liberals with a great knowledge of the party, who shared my interest in the developing world, to join me as my executive assistant.

Throughout my political career, and certainly in my two leadership campaigns, Young Liberals have been at the core of operations.

This started early on. Karl Littler, for example, became involved when he was a Dalhousie law student in the late 1980s; quite simply, he has as fine a mind as you will find anywhere. Michele Cadario is a woman whose strong social conscience has been her driving force, as it continues to be to this day. Bruce Young, Veronique de Passillé, David Brodie, Mark Watton, Sayla Nordin, Melissa McInnes, Marlene Floyd, Janice Nicholson, and Monica Masciantonio are all former Young Liberals who rose to senior positions on my staff.

I have never had much taste for the tasks of party organization, though I recognized from witnessing Paul Hellyer's campaign in 1968 how fundamentally important they were. My idea was to get the right people in place and concentrate on the campaign elements I could handle best myself: developing policy and speaking to Liberals. I was fortunate to get two fine campaign co-chairs – Iona Campagnolo, whose progressive views on Aboriginal issues were an inspiration for many of us and who had attained legendary status in the party, and Jean Lapierre, one of the youngest cabinet ministers ever appointed, and who symbolized the party's renewal in Quebec.

There was one early hurdle, however, that was crucial to my decision to run: the timing of the convention. This was a decision of the party executive. And I needed a long campaign. Having the experience of 1984, the Chrétien organization was already well developed, and Jean Chrétien himself was probably the best known Liberal in the country. Fortunately for me, one of the few niches of the party in which I had a foothold was the executive, many of whose members had been allies of John Turner during the insurgent Chrétien campaign for the leadership in the mid-1980s. Still, we needed to pull out all the stops. Gerry Schwartz, the brilliant Winnipeg-born, Toronto-based entrepreneur, was a member of the executive, though he made it a habit never to attend the meetings. On this occasion, however, he flew in from Toronto and stayed just long enough to cast a crucial vote for the convention to be held more than a year later.

The precise date was determined by the availability of convention facilities in Calgary – a location the party had set its heart on as a symbol of renewal. The executive was aware, of course, that June 23, 1990, also happened to be the deadline for adopting the Meech Lake Accord. But no one could have known that the struggle to pass the accord would come down to the last twenty-four hours or that we would be plunged into a full-fledged national unity crisis on convention weekend. I was a supporter of Meech Lake because I believed it strengthened Canada. It incorporated a fundamental recognition of Quebec's place in our country and it remedied a flaw in the 1981 patriation of the Constitution: the absence of Quebec's endorsement. I hoped that Meech Lake would put to rest many of the ghosts that have continued to bedevil us. As I have said before, I was not an enthusiast for the "neverendum" the constitutional debate had become, and I fervently hoped that the passage of Meech Lake would put an end to it. Nor did I want to see it become a divisive issue in the campaign. For the good of the party and the country, Mike sent out feelers to the Chrétien organization to keep it on a low burner – to no avail. Of course, it was not particularly to my advantage to make Meech an issue, since it badly split my own supporters. On the other hand, Jean Chrétien clearly believed that it was to his advantage, and he played the issue up till almost the end, when he had secured his support in English Canada. Then, suddenly, he decided that the debate was not working to his advantage, particularly in Quebec, and that it should stop.

Before the leadership race was even underway, Mike suggested I have lunch with Pierre Trudeau. "You can't go through the whole leadership campaign and not talk to the former prime minister," he said. So it was arranged that Trudeau and I would meet at the Mount Royal Club on Sherbrooke Street in Montreal.

Although I was often a critic of the Trudeau government's economic policies, I was a great admirer of his accomplishments. The Charter of Rights and Freedoms, which was his initiative, was an act of statesmanship and an enduring gift to Canadians. Although we took opposite views of the Meech Lake Accord, we had plenty of other things to talk about and the lunch went along amicably for a while. But then, inevitably, the subject of Meech Lake came up. He expressed his strong opposition to it, as he had done before many times in public. I replied that I believed that his portrait of Meech Lake was overdrawn. I said that the clause describing Quebec as a distinct society simply reflected reality, that it conferred no increase in powers to the province.

At the end of our discussion, referring to Meech Lake generally, he simply said, "Mr. Martin, you are wrong."

I replied, "No, Mr. Trudeau, you are wrong."

At which point he said, "I believe this luncheon is over."

And he knew what he was talking about, because at that moment he stood up and walked out of the dining room!

In my subsequent encounters with the former prime minister, neither of us ever mentioned that lunch; it was as if it had never happened. I later valued his advice on matters of common interest, particularly our foreign policy with respect to China. But we never spoke of Meech again.

At the time of the 1990 leadership, my organizers were divided on Meech Lake, as was the Liberal Party. To oversimplify, but not by much, it was my Quebec supporters and Mike Robinson on one side, backing the accord, and my supporters from the rest of the country on the other. David Herle, among others, told me that Meech was hurting me badly outside Quebec. When I announced in early 1990 that I was "unequivocally" behind the accord, removing any remaining wiggle room, Saskatchewan's Ralph Goodale phoned David and asked, "Did he really say 'unequivocally'?" I lost considerable ground in English Canada as a result of my position, and was unable to consolidate the support of John Turner's organization in Western Canada, which otherwise would almost certainly have fallen to me.

In the case of Jean Chrétien, I disagreed with him about the Meech Lake Accord on substantive grounds as well as on tactics. After all, he had a better than fifty-fifty chance of becoming the next Liberal leader. By stoking the fire of opposition to Meech Lake in English Canada, he was compounding the difficulties the Liberal Party already had in confronting the separatist push in Quebec in the coming election. This is why I wanted him to agree to a non-aggression pact over the issue, if not to change his opposition to the accord. Instead, he ratcheted up the volume. All the Liberal candidates – Sheila Copps, John Nunziata, Clifford Lincoln, Tom Wappel, Jean Chrétien, and me – participated in a series of debates across the country. Manitoba was a crucible in the Meech Lake controversy because it had a minority Conservative government wavering in its support for the accord and a Liberal Leader of the Opposition, Sharon Carstairs, who was a close ally of Jean Chrétien's and a fierce opponent of the accord. The province also had a charged history in matters related to language and Quebec. It was at the Winnipeg debate that Jean Chrétien decided to make his opposition to Meech Lake the sharp edge of his campaign. And it was there that I responded by saying that Pierre Trudeau was no longer leader of the Liberal Party and it was time to start looking to the future.

As I later learned, despite his public opposition, some of Jean Chrétien's closest aides were negotiating with Brian Mulroney's government over the accord behind the scenes. Mulroney could not bring Manitoba onside without Carstairs, and Carstairs would not come without the okay from Jean Chrétien. Much to their embarrassment, Eddie Goldenberg, Eric Maldoff, and John Rae were all discovered by the CBC in the Château Laurier, right across the street from the old train station where Mulroney and the premiers were negotiating over the accord. This backstairs negotiation obviously played a part in Carstairs's short-lived support for the accord during May and June of 1990, which briefly revived hope that it would be adopted nationally. Meanwhile, in public, after skewering me on Meech Lake in Manitoba and having attacked Meech all through the campaign to date, just prior to the Quebec debate Jean Chrétien made a speech at the University of Ottawa in which he signalled for the first time his flexibility on the issue.

All this set the scene for the Montreal leaders' debate, which would come to have an iconic significance for the Chrétien people in the history of the rivalry between our camps. I suspect that by this point in the contest, Jean Chrétien believed it was obvious he was going to win and the rest of us should just step out of the way. His very recent *volte-face* on Meech seemed to be motivated by the idea that having wrapped up the race, he could now turn his eyes to mollifying Quebec and winning the next election against the Tories. In other words, the other candidates should just roll over and accept that the prize was his. Of course, this seldom happens in politics. Every candidate gets into the race to win, and most of them – and certainly their supporters – can construct a scenario, however exotic, in which they can see a pathway to victory. My campaign was no different. We knew that Chrétien's supporters would pack the hall in Montreal and we did the same. Some of the Quebec delegates, including some of my supporters, shouted, "Vendu, vendu" (sell-out) at Jean Chrétien, and some of the young Liberals who had come in from elsewhere for the debate joined them. One of them, Bruce Young, who was a huge supporter of mine from British Columbia, joined in by shouting, "Fondue, fondue," not quite realizing what the others were saying.

None of us thought at the time that this was anything other than the continuation of a pretty rough-and-tumble campaign that had started long before we got to Montreal. The high-stakes negotiations going on in Ottawa at the same time to save Meech Lake totally overshadowed the leadership debate in the media. However, after the debate, some of Jean Chrétien's senior organizers called Mike Robinson in for a tongue-lashing. Recently, it has become clear that Eddie Goldenberg and Jean Chrétien allowed the memory of this event to turn into a bitter shrine in their minds – a moment never to be forgotten or forgiven.

There was a time early in 1990 when, despite the increasingly acid debate over Meech Lake, we strongly believed that I could win the convention. After a rocky start organizationally in English Canada we found our legs, especially in Ontario, where we had a strong campaign team, including John Webster, Tim Murphy, Joe Volpe, Albina Guarnieri, Pat Sorbara, Pam Gutteridge, and Jim Peterson. We also had Earl Provost, who, as a Young Liberal, was the first Paul Martin delegate elected in Canada.

In Quebec, we thought we were competitive in many ridings. In the first few days of delegate selection in mid-February, there were some hopeful signs. We had some initial wins in Ontario, where delegate selection started earlier than the rest of the country, including a hard-fought battle in Windsor St. Clair – the successor to my father's riding of Essex East. The media began to take our campaign more seriously. But the early optimism was short-lived. In English Canada, there were many delegate selection meetings where both Chrétien's campaign and my own turned out hundreds of supporters. We often lost by agonizingly narrow margins and, because of the winner-take-all system then in effect, came up empty even where we had considerable support. In Quebec, it was a different story. The party had decayed considerably, and delegate selection meetings were often poorly attended. But we underestimated Pietro Rizzuto's ability to turn out just enough supporters to beat us in these small meetings.

By the time we headed to Calgary, we knew it was a long shot, but we still had not given up hope. If Sheila Copps did well enough to force a second ballot, I was told that some of her organizers had agreed to help swing much of her support to me. In the days leading up to the vote I was performing well, and we had some success in moving Chrétien delegates to our side. Candidates always imagine that their convention speech can make a difference, though it seldom does. I laboured over my speech, and the general view in the media was that I bested Jean Chrétien that night. Sheila Copps gave a terrific speech, to the point that when her teleprompter broke down she carried on extemporaneously so well that no one in the audience noticed. In the end Jean Chrétien's victory on the first ballot came as a disappointment but hardly a shock. The night before, Sheila and I gathered our sons, who had worked hard on the campaign, and gave them the bad news that I was not going to win. I knew from my own experience that defeat can sometimes hit family members hardest.

Besides being the expiration date for the Meech Lake Accord and voting day for the Liberal Party leadership, June 23, 1990, was my father's eighty-seventh birthday. Out of the blue my supporters organized a celebration on the convention floor. A birthday cake appeared, and the whole convention burst into a chorus of "Happy Birthday to You," followed by a round of "For He's a Jolly Good Fellow." It was a special moment. Our situations were reversed from the two earlier conventions, and I knew my father's concern was solely about my well-being. But once again, others were to feel the sting of defeat much more bitterly than either of us did.

I knew that my Quebec supporters would be tormented by the victory of a man who had gone beyond criticizing Meech Lake to very publicly embracing one of its most ardent opponents, Newfoundland's premier Clyde Wells, at the convention. But I had no inkling that Jean Lapierre and Gilles Rocheleau, both Quebec MPs, would leave the party to help form Lucien Bouchard's Bloc Québécois. If I had known, I would have done everything in my power to dissuade them, which may be the reason they never spoke to me about it.

That night we had a tremendous party for my supporters. In politics, it is sometimes difficult to express how deeply you feel about the people who devote their time, energy, and enthusiasm to help you achieve your goals. They give up so much for you. I did my best to thank them as a group and as individuals. In the years that followed, the media often remarked at how extraordinarily deep the bonds were among my aides and supporters. Much of that was forged in the course of that first leadership campaign. Many of the people in the room that night went on to play significant roles in shaping the economic and social policies that they deeply believed would make Canada a better place. In an era when politics has lost its allure for many Canadians, it is worthwhile to stop once in a while and honour the efforts of those who do commit themselves.

For me, there was no anguish after the leadership race was over, only a slight feeling of disequilibrium. After all, I had never really been a regular MP. I had gone virtually directly from the corporate headquarters of CSL into a leadership campaign. How strange it was walking into the caucus meeting Jean Chrétien called the next day right there in Calgary. It was a very businesslike meeting, in which he assumed the role that he had successfully won, and I was another member of caucus. I had run for leader and lost. In the process, a lot of harsh things had been said and done. And the caucus had largely been united around him. You had to wonder, how was all this going to work?

CHAPTER SEVEN

Opposition

It is only natural after losing a leadership race to feel some uncertainty about your relationship with the winner. It was no
different for me. My dream of becoming the C.D. Howe of my
generation was undimmed, but what I could not be certain of at first
was whether that door would remain open. Within a few weeks,
however, Eddie Goldenberg came down to the farm in the Eastern
Townships and we discussed my future role in the Liberal Party.
Eddie's father, Carl, who had been appointed to the Senate by Pierre
Trudeau, had been a friend of my father. I had always liked Eddie,
and given his long association with Jean Chrétien, I certainly had no
quarrel with his decision to back Chrétien's leadership bid in 1990.
The most important thing for me was that I have meaningful work
within the party and eventually in government, and Eddie was clear
that this would be the case. Over the next decade, Eddie, along with
Chaviva Hošek, who was Jean Chrétien's policy adviser, would play
an important role in lubricating the political and governmental relationship between him and me.

Much of the day-to-day interaction between Chrétien's office and
mine was channelled through Terrie O'Leary, who had replaced
Richard Mahoney as my executive assistant after the leadership and
continued in that role for many of my most important years at
Finance. Terrie would be at my side through many political battles
and we would become the closest of friends. She has an extraordinary combination of gifts. She shares my interest and enthusiasm for

the details of public policy. But her political antennae are more acute than mine, and her understanding of political communications is formidable. She is an indefatigable worker when she commits herself to something, and a superb organizer and leader of people. Equally important, she is a thoroughly decent person, delightful and funny. I suppose that is part of the reason that I have never minded that she will take me apart when she disagrees with me, not only in private but in a room full of others, if she thinks it is time to give me what-for.

Jean Chrétien and I had a personal relationship that ran the gamut from cool to non-existent, so it was in large part due to Terrie's relationships with Chrétien's people that we found a way to make the governmental partnership work. At times, when Jean Chrétien would cut Eddie out of the loop, she would bring him back in, knowing this was important if we were to bridge the frigid river between me and the prime minister. Whatever reservations Eddie had about me and my role in the party and government – deep ones, apparently – he disguised them completely from me during more than a decade that we worked together under Jean Chrétien's leadership. I took him at face value and we got on with business.

My main concern in the summer and fall of 1990 was to carve out a set of tasks that would occupy me intellectually and politically. I was unprepared for the routine of Opposition life, which I had been spared in my rookie years by the leadership race. I wouldn't "troll" for media attention, as opposition MPs are supposed to do after question period at the House of Commons. Although I deeply disagreed with many of the Mulroney government's policies, I also understood, perhaps in part through my father, the complexities of governing and for that reason disliked the ritual denunciation of government actions that our system seems to demand of opposition MPs.

In retrospect, I can say that asking questions in the House of Commons is much more difficult than answering them. In government, if you are any good, you know your issues better than anyone else, and little, if any, preparation for question period is required. In Opposition it is very different. In thirty-five seconds, you need to blast the government, give context to the issue you are raising, and then let loose with a cleverly constructed question that will put the government on the spot. Terrie recalls that I once declined an invitation to have lunch at the American Embassy with Katherine Graham, the legendary publisher of the *Washington Post*, because I had to ask a question in the House in the afternoon and wanted to prepare. Terrie, who has a passion for John F. Kennedy, told me in no uncertain terms that I was going, and gave me a list of questions for Ms. Graham, who had been a friend of JFK's. She was not at all mollified when I came back to the office having gleaned nothing because I could not concentrate on anything else over lunch but my upcoming half-minute performance in the House.

There are a number of real problems with question period. The first is that it has little to do with the eliciting of information and contributes little to needed debate. Second, the first point might be tolerable if it was good theatre. It's not. Third, question period has two different audiences with two different perspectives. How many times did I leave the House of Commons with my caucus colleagues cheering because of some "brilliant" put-down, only to have a senior citizen (they are the ones who watch question period on TV) ask me on the weekend, "When are you and the rest of those hyenas in Parliament going to grow up?"

I asked for, and received, the role of environment critic. I already had a deep interest in the environment. In the beginning, my interest had been rooted in the conservation of Canada's wilderness. I thought preservation of the environment was a moral value, whether it was to have a decent and healthy country for children to grow up in or quite simply to be able to fish in rivers where there were actually fish. As I have said, the environment was an important part of my leadership platform. My political ambition remained to go into government as industry and trade minister, in the footsteps of C.D. Howe, but one of the things that had changed since his time was the clear link that had now been established between sound environmental policy and a nation's economic success. I also knew I already had the bona fides for the industry job from my business background. The environment critic's job would broaden my experience and deepen my knowledge on a vital issue.

Above and beyond the specific critic's job, however, I asked to be entrusted with the development of the party's overall election platform – an idea that met with indifference from my closest advisers, with the exception of Terrie. For twenty years, beginning with Pearson's defeat of Diefenbaker, the Liberal Party had been the party of government, and so its election platforms tended to be based on policies developed through the mechanisms of government. The specifically political gloss and the day-to-day campaign announcements – the "Gainesburgers," as the media called them – were drafted by party strategists. They did not reflect a medium- or long-term vision of where the Liberals wanted to take Canada. They were strategies for the campaign, but they were no more than that. As a result, the Liberals had failed to develop a comprehensive vision for the future. The most significant policy position the party had taken during the 1980s – opposition to the Free Trade Agreement[1] – had proven politically popular, but it was not grounded in a comprehensive economic or social strategy. The time had come to rethink many of the party's policies.

Jean Chrétien had run a classic front-runner's campaign during the leadership, which meant that he had never fully developed a policy platform. He was also cautious by nature, unwilling to be tied down to promises that might come to haunt him in government, which meant he would sometimes resist some of our more ambitious and specific ideas. But he was shrewd enough to see the political value of constructing a more elaborate platform, in part because he understood it would address public concerns about our readiness to

---

[1] It is important to remember that John Turner was not opposed to free trade per se. He was opposed to the particular agreement negotiated by the Mulroney government. I supported free trade, and while I felt the FTA was deficient in important areas I also felt it was the best we could get in the circumstances.

govern after nearly a decade out of power. Indeed, he ultimately made the platform we constructed into a defining document of his career as prime minister.

To get the process underway, Jean Chrétien appointed Chaviva Hošek and me as platform co-chairs. I knew Chaviva from the time she had been Ontario's housing minister and I was the Liberals' housing critic (during the leadership race) and we had hit it off. Later she became head of the federal party's research office. She brought with her the resources of her office and, more importantly, her deep convictions on a wide variety of policy issues. She had a profound understanding of how policy might affect the lives of individual Canadians, particularly women. I do not think that when she took on the job, however, she fully understood how ambitious my plans were.

Over the course of 1991, we organized dozens of meetings with Liberals across the country. Often tons of invitations were dispatched, and hundreds of people showed up. Chaviva and I both thoroughly enjoyed the experience of interacting with rank-and-file Liberals as we wrestled with the formulas we might devise for our social well-being and economic prosperity as a country. In addition, we organized many meetings with experts and organizations that had specialized knowledge of specific fields. It was during this period that I met Fraser Mustard, the brilliant Canadian physician and academic, whose pioneering work on early childhood learning deeply influenced me.

In my opinion, the modern Liberal believes in the freedom of the individual and is wary of an all-seeing state attempting to restrict that freedom. That's why Pierre Trudeau brought in the Charter of Rights and Freedoms and why I later sought to abolish its notwithstanding clause. At the same time, the modern Liberal is also a descendant of Sir Wilfrid Laurier, who championed the role of the state in providing the means by which individual freedoms are guaranteed for everyone. The dichotomy leads us to continually re-evaluate the role of the state to make it more progressive, for example, by bringing in health insurance and medicare, as my father and Monique Begin did, or by seeking to do the same with child care, as I was to do.

Of course, we could not develop a new platform in a political vacuum. It was crucial to free the party from the grip of the accumulated ideology of the party and set it on a new path. In the fall of 1991, the party held a conference in Aylmer, Quebec. The media at the time, and often since, portrayed the Aylmer meeting as a contest between "business Liberals," such as Roy MacLaren and me, and "social Liberals" such as Lloyd Axworthy, with victory going to the former. In reality, there were many divergent voices heard at the conference, but a common theme emerged: that globalization was not the property of the left or right but a fact of life with which Canadians had to come to grips. The conference opened the door to rethinking many of the party's traditional positions.

The Red Book, as the platform ultimately came to be called, was a collective effort involving thousands of Liberals and hundreds of hours of negotiation and discussion among Terrie, Chaviva, Eddie, and me. The language was crafted in part by John Godfrey, a Liberal MP and former journalist whose graceful pen added both poetry and seriousness to the end product. Although I had always understood the gravity of the problem posed by the mounting deficits run by the federal government from Pierre Trudeau's time through Brian Mulroney's, it was not until I became finance minister that I fully understood the difficulty of solving it. I still believed, as I think most of my colleagues in the party did, that the main engine of deficit reduction would be economic growth, and not a fundamental reorganization and reduction in the size of government. Everyone understood, however, that we needed a credible policy on the issue. Jean Chrétien suggested that we adopt the approach of the recently signed Maastricht Treaty, which created the European Union (EU) by tightening the economic relations between the countries of the predecessor European Community. It stipulated that members of the EU should not run deficits greater than 3 per cent of their gross domestic product. Ironically, it was a standard that two of the dominant players in the EU, France and Germany, did not achieve in the years to come. Although once in office I pushed well beyond that mark, reaching a balanced budget and ultimately running surpluses, its importance in the Red Book was to establish a credible goal with a specific timeline that had not just been plucked from thin air.

Meanwhile, I proposed that the Red Book be fully costed. Unlike election platforms since time immemorial, which promised the sky without seriously considering the consequences of implementation, ours would state plainly what we thought a proposal would cost, and how we would finance it while still achieving our goal of reducing the deficit. Demonstrating once again his natural caution, Jean Chrétien was reluctant to be pinned down so specifically. Ultimately, however, he, too, recognized the value of precise costing, as well as its implicit acknowledgement of the trade-offs necessary once we achieved power. We commissioned economist Patrick Grady to develop an economic model to reconcile the numbers and give the document the look, feel, and intellectual heft of a budget as much as of an election platform. I like to think that it embedded our specific campaign commitments in a clear expression of our party's economic philosophy that included job creation, responsible management of monetary policy as well as decisive action toward reducing deficits, and a careful enhancement of social programs as fiscal circumstances permitted.

I thought at the time that it would set a standard for party election platforms in Canada, and it did for a while. When I look at the 2006 election, however, when the Conservatives were able to take power on the basis of a series of uncosted promises (most of them broken early on), it is clear that I was overly optimistic.

In the midst of this process, in 1992, I also attended the Earth Summit in Rio as opposition environment critic. Prior to leaving, I conducted a round of intensive consultations with non-governmental environmental groups. This was when I met some of the leading activists in the environmental movement, such as Elizabeth May, Louise Comeau, David Runnalls, and Stephanie Cairns, who continued to be friends and advisers for many years. In government, you have a huge bureaucracy on which to rely for advice, but in opposition you find that it is often the non-governmental organizations (NGOs) that have the most readily available expertise. My contact with these groups convinced me of their enduring value, and even as finance minister and later prime minister, I made it a habit to consult with NGOs before embarking on a foreign trip whenever the subject was the environment or international development.

My companion on the Rio trip was the NDP's environment critic, Jim Fulton, who is a deeply committed environmentalist. Our role was to be observers and little else. Jean Charest, who was Canada's environment minister at the time, would meet with us each morning and listen to what we had to say. But naturally it was he and his bureaucrats who went off to the meetings where the actual discussions were held or, as often happens at such meetings, the communiqués previously negotiated were ratified. Of course, there was an extra dimension of interest in the summit for me because Maurice Strong chaired the meeting and had been the driving force behind creating the assembly.

The Earth Summit was in some ways a heady experience and in others a sobering one. Heady in that this was the first time the international community had come together to treat the issues of pollution, biodiversity, deforestation, desertification, water scarcity, and global warming as the common problems of humanity they had become. Yet, as was apparent to a degree at the time and became more obvious in the sobering aftermath, like many international meetings it produced much less than it promised. Media attention was focused on whether George Bush Senior, then president of the United States, would attend the meeting. He did, but to what end? Despite Maurice Strong's valiant efforts in the years that followed, there was little or no follow-through by world leaders to the high-flown rhetoric in which they indulged at Rio.

This gap between rhetoric and commitment angered and frustrated me, and influenced some of my strong views about global governance. In domestic politics, politicians who fail to keep their promises face the discipline of the electorate if the promise is important enough. No such discipline exists in international forums. Leaders who make international commitments, which in the modern world may be just as important as any domestic promises they will ever make, have little compunction about abandoning them once they've smiled for the leaders' "family photo" and headed home. These broken commitments at the international level bring the whole system of international governance into disrepute, paralyzing the world's attempts to deal with the hard edges of globalization.

My distaste for this practice later led me to adopt some controversial positions in government. While inside the cabinet, I was critical of Jean Chrétien's commitment to the Kyoto Accord without any plan to implement it. He did not expect to meet the goals to which the government had agreed, as Eddie Goldenberg has subsequently confirmed. It was in a similar spirit that I resisted pressure from my friend Bono, among others, to join other governments in a pledge to devote 0.7 per cent of gross domestic product to foreign aid. Even the supporters of the pledge understood that most of the leaders who made it had no intention of carrying it out, but they hoped that grand public declarations would put political pressure on George Bush. I believed strongly in the objectives of both the Kyoto Accord and the 0.7 per cent pledge. I just didn't like the cynicism of promising the earth and delivering nothing more than dust in the eyes.

A few weeks after I returned from the Rio summit, my father's health deteriorated sharply. He had been frail for several years. Still, he had kept up many of his regular activities, such as attending an annual conference of Canadian and British lawyers and judges at Cambridge University that he had helped to establish as High Commissioner. But we suspected he may have suffered from a series of small strokes because he had developed a tendency to trip unexpectedly, which worried us enormously. I had always maintained close contact with my parents, speaking with them by phone almost every day, and swinging by Windsor to see them whenever I was within an hour or two of their home. But that summer, when Dad was hospitalized after a major stroke, Sheila and I began making the trip to see them even more regularly. Early in September, Dad slipped into unconsciousness and several days later, on September 14, 1992, he passed away. At least we had had time to prepare ourselves and to say goodbye.

My father had been an MP for Windsor for thirty-three years, and had returned there in his retirement years. His funeral was an occasion not only for the family but for all of south-western Ontario. Outside Assumption Church, there was an honour guard of more than seventy Knights of Columbus in their regalia – black suits with red capes. The funeral mass was concelebrated by the bishop of London, John Sherlock, three other bishops, and perhaps a dozen priests. It was delayed a few minutes to accommodate several dozen MPs travelling from Ottawa on an Armed Forces plane that had been kindly arranged by Prime Minister Mulroney. Despite the many political dignitaries, and the crowd of about a thousand people, the funeral had an intimate quality arising from the fact that almost everyone in the room felt they knew my father and had been touched by him in some particular way. I gave the eulogy. I spoke about his French-Canadian upbringing, his Catholic faith, and his dedication to the people of Windsor and of Canada. I spoke about some of his accomplishments at home and abroad: as a father of medicare and of the Canadian Citizenship Act. But mostly I recounted the stories – the many funny stories – that reflected his lack of navigational skills, his exuberant love of politics, and his impish sense of humour. There was a lot of laughter in the church that day, which was what helped me get through it. Later, though, at the cemetery, when his casket was lowered into the ground, I wept.

The *Windsor Star* published what may have been my father's most eloquent epitaph. It was an editorial cartoon. It pictured Dad sporting angels' wings in heaven with St. Peter behind him. He looks around and utters his immortal line: "Is there anyone here from

Windsor?" Dad would have laughed. I still have that cartoon framed and hanging in my office.

For my mother, the public display of affection for my dad was a huge comfort at a devastating moment.

When I returned to Ottawa, the prime minister presented me with the flag that had flown at half-mast over the Peace Tower on Parliament Hill the day my dad passed away. For many years after, the flag, mounted on a pole, decorated my parliamentary office. It is now at my home.

I don't believe that my father's illness and death affected my political life except in the narrow sense that, absorbed as I was with my family on the one hand and the development of the Red Book on the other, I was aloof from the turmoil that gripped some of my fellow Liberal MPs during this time. Jean Chrétien faced a challenge from some of those within the caucus who wanted the party to take advantage of the public's outrage over the GST and promise to abolish it. Ultimately, the Red Book contained a commitment to *replace* – not abolish – the tax, whatever others might have said when ad-libbing their way through the 1993 campaign.

I watched with great interest, as did all of us, Brian Mulroney's belated resignation as party leader and the ascendance of Kim Campbell, first in the media and then for a time in public popularity. I was not one of those "Nervous Nellies" in the caucus who Jean Chrétien so famously castigated in the spring of 1993 because they feared another Tory victory. Maybe because of my involvement in developing the Red Book, I felt that we were extremely well prepared for the campaign once it came.

In early September 1993, Kim Campbell finally dropped the writ for the election. There was an eerie period at the beginning of the seven-week campaign when the Progressive Conservatives maintained a lead over us in the polls, seemingly defying the laws of political gravity. A week and a half into the campaign, on September 19, we released the Red Book. On Terrie's suggestion we had arranged the release to the media as a "lock-up" similar to what accompanies a budget. That is, the reporters were given the document but were sealed off from the world for a couple of hours while they read and absorbed the text and began preparing their stories. This is done for a budget so that a superficial read by reporters pressed to get their stories out doesn't adversely affect the markets. Of course, our platform was unlikely to do that, but the adoption of the lock-up mechanism added to the weight and seriousness of the document and helped ensure that it got more than a quick skim before being consigned to the wastebasket by the press corps.

It worked brilliantly. When the lock-up was over, we held a press conference at which Jean Chrétien was flanked by Chaviva and me. It emphasized party unity as well as the idea that the leader was backed up by a strong Liberal team, an important theme of the campaign. For the most part, reporters took the document seriously and Jean Chrétien used the opportunity to emphasize that the Red Book would create a new form of accountability to voters by giving a specific measure of success once in office.

Unlike in 1988, I had national responsibilities to campaign outside my own riding in 1993. That, perhaps along with a dose of realism, made me more nervous about my own seat than I had been the previous election, even though this time the conventional wisdom was that I would easily win. In 1993 and in subsequent campaigns, I was helped tremendously by Sheila's grace and skill as a door-to-door campaigner on my behalf, as well as a superb local campaign team that included my sons. Meanwhile, Terrie joined the Chrétien tour. With her detailed knowledge of the Red Book, she was ideally cast as a media contact on the plane and bus tour, where she spent long hours with reporters, answering their questions and stick-handling the issues they raised. No one disputed the enormous value she brought to the campaign tour. Some of the relationships she developed with reporters at the time continued to serve us well for years to come.

Unfortunately, however, she was an uneasy fit with the Chrétien people, some of whom continued to regard anyone with a Martin connection with deep suspicion. At one point, because of this, she was ready to quit the tour, and I had to go down to the bus station in Montreal, where the campaign bus was parked, to meet her and persuade her to stick with it. As the campaign neared its end, she phoned me and asked whether I would cover for her if she told the tour organizers she wanted to spend election night with Sheila and me. She had no intention of doing so, and spent the evening in Ottawa with David Herle and Richard Mahoney. But no matter, there was more than enough for Liberals to celebrate on election night, wherever they were and whoever they were with.

CHAPTER EIGHT

"Good Morning, Minister"

On November 4, 1993, I was sworn in as finance minister, along with the rest of Jean Chrétien's new cabinet, at the Governor General's residence at Rideau Hall. After the swearing-in, there was a reception for the freshly minted ministers and their families. It was an intoxicating moment, poised as we were between the satisfaction of electoral victory and the responsibilities of governing. Yet, it was there that Jean Pelletier, the prime minister's chief of staff, took me aside to tell me that my mother had been taken to the hospital. When I spoke with my mother's physician, he reassured me that her situation had stabilized and that I had time to attend that afternoon's cabinet meeting and meet briefly with the department the next morning before catching the plane for Windsor.

Right after the swearing-in, I stopped by the apartment building on Bay Street in downtown Ottawa where I was staying. David Dodge, who would be my deputy and was coming to meet me, stepped out of his own car at the same moment as I stepped out of mine. "Good morning, minister," he said in his inimitable nails-on-chalkboard voice. "Welcome aboard." I suspect I must have looked around to see who he was talking to, because it was the first time anyone had called me minister. After a brief meeting with David, I made my first visit to the departmental offices on O'Connor Street. Terrie O'Leary and I had a quick tour of the ministerial suite, and she immediately declared that the washroom in the corridor separating our offices would be a joint one. In fact, since my staff ended up being predominantly female, and the room filled up with hairspray and hand lotion, I don't think it would be true to say that it ever was a joint space at all.

The department had given me a huge stack of briefing books. One of the first things that caught my eye was David Dodge's biography, in which I discovered he had been responsible for managing the GST file – the target of many a Liberal attack when we had been in Opposition. When I went out to share this with Terrie, she was coming the other way, having just stumbled across the same information.

The next day, there was the planned briefing with David and the assistant deputy ministers, and I was off to the airport with a stack of briefing books in tow. By the time Sheila and I arrived in Windsor on the evening of November 5, it was well after dark, and I was uncertain whether we should go to the hospital so late. Sheila insisted, and I am glad that she did, because my mother's condition had worsened. Indeed, it was one of the last times that we were able to talk to her as she slipped in and out of consciousness. Throughout her life, my mother had always suffered from frailer health than my father. In the latter years, hers was a slower, steadier decline than my dad's. I am certain she knew he would have found it impossible to get through a day without her, and so she clung to life by sheer force of will. After he passed away, it was clear she felt she was now free to go, and it was just a matter of time. Increasingly, she suffered the symptoms of angina, including shortness of breath. She had been very ill before the campaign began, then rallied, then slumped again just before voting day. I had made a number of quick trips to Windsor during the election campaign and during the transition before we took office.

My sister lives in St. Paul, Minnesota, where her husband, Michael, was head of the English Department at St. Thomas University. They have two daughters, Katie and Julie.

Shortly after I had arrived at my mother's bedside on that eventful first day in government, she looked up and saw Sheila and our boys and Mary Anne and her family all gathered around her. She said only one word: "Why?" Thinking she was wondering why we were all at her bedside, Mary Anne told her that we had come because she was ill, and then she slipped back to sleep. A few minutes later she, she woke up and asked again, "Why?"

I told her, "Mother, we've explained to you. You've been sick and we're all here to make sure you get better." And then she said, "No, no. I don't mean that. I mean, why Finance? Why would you want to be minister of finance?"

My mother had a very deep faith, and was at peace with the idea of her own passing. When she got very ill, the medical staff put breathing tubes down her throat. On one occasion when they did this, Mom told Mary Anne and me that she didn't want to go through that again, and said that when it was her time to go, she wanted to be left to it. At the very end, I had a hard time accepting that wish; I would have done anything to keep her with us a little longer. My sister was more compassionate and willing to see the physicians step back and let nature run its course. Mary Anne was a great rock at a time when I found it hard to deal with my grief.

It was a tough week in which to have to plunge into the new job I had just taken on. The Hôtel-Dieu Hospital was the place I had been born, where my father had died, and where my mother would spend her last days. Now it was also the scene of my initiation into my responsibilities as minister of finance. With my mother slipping in and out of a coma and the family gathered around her bed, I suppose I resented the time I needed to spend learning my new job. But I had just three and a half months to prepare a budget, the first Liberal budget in a decade. As my mother's question implied, Finance was never the portfolio I had sought, so it was not as if I had the framework of a budget already sketched in my mind. My first preference was to be minister of industry. It took the energetic intervention of people such as Ed Lumley, the late Arthur Kroeger, and others, including Terrie O'Leary and David Herle, to persuade me to go for Finance. "If you want to be the modern C.D. Howe, you have got to be minister of finance," they told me. "The minister of finance is the most powerful minister in the government. In any other job, you'll have to depend on the finance minister to support whatever you want to get done." They were right, of course, which I soon saw. When I went to Jean Chrétien and told him that I would like Finance, he graciously consented, although my change of heart undoubtedly complicated his cabinet planning.

In that difficult week, David Dodge made a generous gesture by decamping to Windsor with some of the department's most senior officials. That way I could be briefed while still being able to keep vigil at my mother's bedside. For the most part, we met in the chaplain's room at the hospital, which effectively became my ministerial office. Subsequently I remember joking to a friend of mine who was a priest that I could feel the church's guidance as I prepared the budget. His reply did not miss a beat: "You can blame the church for a lot of things," he said, "but I suspect your budget is beyond saving."

A legend has grown up that at some point I threw all the briefing books into the garbage in disgust. I have no recollection of this, nor do any of the principals who would have been there had it actually happened. Like a lot of legends, though, it conveys a whiff of the truth. The briefing books had clearly been prepared with the idea that the new Liberal government was not going to place a priority on addressing our dire fiscal situation. I made it very clear from the start that I was serious, though I did not yet fully understand what that implied.

David and I also discussed an even more urgent decision I had to make. John Crow's term as governor of the Bank of Canada was about to expire in January, and the government would have to decide whether to reappoint him. Crow was a controversial figure in Canada, both because of his rigid focus on inflation and because of his testy personality and a take-no-prisoners rhetorical style. At the same time, he was a top-ranked central bank governor and was highly respected by the markets, which would be looking to us to prove our monetary bona fides by keeping him in place. Like any new government, we were treated with caution, if not suspicion, by the financial community. Although I had a business background, the meticulous fiscal reputation of Liberal prime ministers such as Louis St. Laurent had long been displaced, and I knew this was an obstacle

I had to overcome. John Crow symbolized monetary probity to the markets, so I wanted him to stay. Jean Chrétien wanted him to stay for the same reason, despite having been very critical of him when we were in Opposition. If we let him go, we thought, it was going to be a major blot on our economic copybook before we even got started.

I very much appreciated that Crow, like Dodge, came down to Windsor and met with me in the chaplain's office at the Hôtel-Dieu and later over dinner. I told him that I supported his fight against inflation and I understood the need to preserve the independence of the central bank. Under the law in Canada, the government can give directives to the bank, and the governor of the bank can resign if he or she deems them unacceptable. But that would be a calamitous political and economic crisis, similar to the one that rocked the Diefenbaker government in 1961 when it tried to fire the governor, James Coyne, who was pursuing a "tight money" policy. I wanted to make sure that Crow and I could work together. I was worried that raising interest rates at the wrong time could injure the fragile Canadian economy. It was still adjusting to free trade with the United States, and we had not yet felt the upturn that was taking place south of the border. At that initial meeting, we did not discuss precise details, but I was hopeful that Crow would prove to be someone with whom I would be able to work.

As the days passed, with me shuffling back and forth between meetings in the chaplain's office and my mother's bedside, her periods of consciousness grew fewer and fewer. More and more of the extended family gathered, bidding her farewell in the hospital room. For her, it was an agonizing week before she finally gave up her last breath. Once again, not much more than a year after my father's funeral, it fell to me to give the eulogy. Perhaps because my father was a public person and my mother was much more private, I found it a more difficult eulogy to give. Or perhaps it was because, as family tradition would have it, I take after my mother more than I do after my father. But it was not hard that day to fill the church with love and laughter.

"My mother just simply had a tremendous effect on anybody," I told the congregation. "Those of you who have been in our house and have seen the pictures know that many of them show my father with the great people of the world; and they're engaged in sober conversation, barely smiling. And then you see other pictures of the same great people, and they're smiling. Inevitably it's because my mother is in that picture."

I finished the eulogy with the story of a dream that my mother had recounted to Mary Anne and me just a few weeks before her death. In the dream, my dad was calling to her and saying, "Nell, come." Naturally we had lumps in our throats as she told us this, and we asked her what she had replied in the dream. She told us she answered, "Paul, I'm not coming. I'm not ready yet. Somebody else can get your coffee." The story created a great wave of laughter through the church. And then I told them what I truly believed, which was that she had been ready, and her time had truly come.

Hundreds of people came to my parents' home for a reception that turned out to be a great celebration of her life. Soon after, Dwight Duncan, then on the city council and later a provincial cabinet minister, proposed that a new variety of rose that had been developed in Windsor be named the "Nell Rose." What a touching tribute that was!

Soon after, I returned to Ottawa. I was beginning to wrap my head around some of the crucial issues I faced, the most urgent of which was whether to reappoint John Crow. Under Michael Wilson, one of my Conservative predecessors, the government had agreed with the Bank of Canada on a five-year plan to reduce inflation. There was one year left on the agreement, which at that point called for an inflation target of 1 to 3 per cent. I talked with David Dodge and said that we needed to establish an understanding with Crow on what the future target would be before reappointing him.

In my view, we were only going to dig ourselves out of our economic difficulties if the fiscal policies we adopted worked hand in hand with the monetary policies pursued by the bank. I didn't want to reappoint Crow only to find out later that we could not agree on our inflation target. His definition of price stability was widely interpreted to mean zero inflation. I fundamentally disagreed with that, because only a small slippage would tip us into deflation, which would have huge negative economic implications. My fear was that he might view the next round of target setting as an opportunity to make a major downward move. I believed in setting low inflation targets, but if the bank drove interest rates up too high with the goal of lowering inflation, that could send the economy into a downward spiral at a time when it was already vulnerable by raising to prohibitive levels the costs that businesses pay for borrowing or people pay for mortgages. If that happened, my only resort then would be to dismiss Crow – or live with the consequences.

So my idea was to settle on the targets, then reappoint him. Within the department, we decided that the inflation target should continue to be a range of 1 to 3 per cent, with the midpoint – 2 per cent – being the critical number.

It was clear from very early on that Crow was unwilling to accept the 2 per cent midpoint. His position was that the inflation band should be lowered and reset as 0 to 2 per cent. On the face of it, while the gap was significant, it did not seem insurmountable, and I wanted to find a compromise if we could. Not the least of my worries was that if we did not reach an accord, and I decided not to reappoint Crow, the financial markets would see this as a signal that we were not serious about inflation. Crow's deputy at the bank, Gordon Thiessen, who was just as adamant in his belief in wrestling inflation to the mat, shared our concerns about the dire consequences of losing Crow. He became a crucial intermediary, along with David Dodge, between Crow and me. One suggestion they discussed was keeping the top of the band at 3 per cent but lowering the bottom to 0.5 per cent. Endless versions of a one-page statement were faxed back and forth between Don Drummond, a key assistant deputy minister, and the bank. The text was pretty much agreed, but there was an unceasing tinkering with the numbers. It soon became an infuriating negotiation because of Crow's unwillingness to budge even a fraction of a percentage point.

Still, as the relationship deteriorated behind the scenes, the pressure continued to mount to keep Crow on board. Doug Peters, a highly respected former chief economist with the TD Bank who had just been elected as a Liberal and was secretary of state for financial institutions, fiercely opposed Crow's policies but nonetheless urged us to keep him on for fear that the dollar would tank if we did not. That rocked us. Meanwhile, most Bay Street analysts were outspoken in public about the need for Crow to stay. On December 2, when I held a televised meeting with a group of economists at the Conference Centre in Ottawa as part of my budget consultations, someone did an informal poll and announced, live on *Newsworld*, that the group favoured Crow's reappointment by a margin of roughly four to one.

I understood the argument for keeping Crow, yet I came to believe if we could find a credible alternative candidate to take the job, and agree on the inflation targets in a public declaration, the warnings of the market analysts might prove to be overdrawn. Even as my budget meeting with the economists took place, Dodge and Drummond were popping out to exchange faxes with the Bank of Canada. Increasingly, though, Dodge was looking at Thiessen's reaction rather than Crow's. Eventually, Dodge asked me if he could sound Thiessen out about taking the top job. I said yes. Thiessen, who was very loyal to Crow, indicated that he would consider it if necessary, and he and Dodge were able to agree on an extension of the existing inflation formula.

Finally, a meeting was arranged between me and Crow at my departmental office in Ottawa. I was determined to see, one last time, if I could reach a zone of comfort with him. The meeting went on for hours, with David Dodge waiting in Terrie's office for word, and then Terrie waiting in David's office. Crow was absolutely stuck on 2 per cent as the top of the range, with a target lower than that. In truth, I would have been willing to tinker further with the numbers to keep him on board. But in the end it was Crow's absolute intransigence that disturbed me. My god, I thought, if we can't agree on something like this in which our objectives are similar and we have no crisis in front of us, what's going to happen when there is a crisis? As the meeting wore on, I found myself coming to the conclusion that this game was over. I asked him point-blank whether he was saying that he could not live with anything but his precise demands, and he said yes.

"Well," I replied, "if that's the case, we're not going to be able to work together and we might as well deal with that."

He asked me whether I was saying that I did not intend to reappoint him, and I said yes. He agreed that he would step down without comment from either of us to ensure that there was no unnecessary roiling of the markets. And for several years the agreement held. Privately, he may have vented a bit, but in public he comported himself just as he promised, as I did.

The prime minister had been clear from the start that this was to be my decision, and so I arranged a meeting at his office to inform him of my intention. Like me, he had been critical of Crow's policies in Opposition and uncomfortable with his prickly personality. Still, my impression was that he shared my initial view that it might be better for the government if Crow were reappointed. Certainly he had every reason to expect that I would come back to him with just such a recommendation. He was surprised and clearly somewhat unnerved by what I had to say. "That's fine," he said at the time, but he later told me he had trouble sleeping that night.

The announcement to cabinet elicited a quite different reaction, the result of long-nurtured and deeply felt antagonism to Crow. Despite my confidence that the markets would accept Crow's replacement so long as it was clear that the institution remained sound and independent, we were all nervous the day of the announcement. In the event, Gordon Thiessen handled himself with the public skill that we all came to admire, and did so, to my relief, both in his native English and in French – which turned out to be much better than we had been told. The dollar actually rose slightly on the news of his appointment.

The choice of Gordon Thiessen turned out to be even more inspired than we understood at the time. His commitment to a sound monetary policy was no less adamant than Crow's had been. But in the place of Crow's astringent personality, we had a governor who blunted much of the criticism of the bank simply by his willingness to listen and his readiness to explain. He also proved to be a very effective and highly regarded voice for Canada on the world stage (though I have to say that every year at the World Bank/International Monetary Fund meetings in Washington, he would enthusiastically suggest a stroll back to the hotel, knowing I have no sense of direction, and, claiming to know the way, get us hopelessly lost). Seven years later, when Thiessen attended his last G7 meeting as head of the Bank of Canada in Prague, Alan Greenspan, one of the most respected central bankers of our generation, insisted on giving the farewell speech on behalf of his colleagues.

CHAPTER NINE

Three and a Half Months

As important as the decision on the governor of the Bank of Canada was, it was only one of many that a new minister with a new budget looming would face in the first few weeks in office. Although in retrospect it is obvious that I was able to forge a strong positive relationship with the ministry, which proved crucial to my success at Finance, that was by no means certain at the outset.

In Opposition, we had been very critical of the department's repeated failure to meet its deficit targets. On the other hand, we came to power with a very different approach to the public service than the Conservatives, who were traditionally suspicious of bureaucrats. They had huge ministerial staffs, so that meetings with the department, I am told, were like those of rival clans ranged against each other across the table. In contrast, we had been forced by an election promise to trim ministerial staffs to the bone, so that we were necessarily more reliant on the public service. Not only did I appreciate David Dodge's willingness to bring the leadership of the department to Windsor in the early days, but I also liked the fact that he made a point of including Terrie in departmental meetings – and later on Karl Littler, Ruth Thorkelson, and other members of my political staff – helping to build a relationship of trust.

The basic mechanism for preparing our first budget, starting from scratch with a deadline just three and a half months away, were rolling meetings that went on for weeks, often late into the night and through the weekends. It was referred to as a CMO – pronounced "see-mo" – which stood for "Cohen, Minister and others," a relic from the days of a deputy minister of finance from the early 1980s, Mickey Cohen. The meetings usually included me, Terrie, David Dodge, and an assortment of senior, and sometimes more junior, officials that changed according to the topic. My parliamentary secretary, David Walker, from Winnipeg, was a frequent participant. Some of the political staffers would also attend the meetings where they had some direct interest or responsibility. Karl Littler, for example, developed an expertise on taxes, while Ruth Thorkelson specialized in social policy. Michele Cadario attended on issues affecting Western Canada or where there were special caucus sensitivities.

We also made a point of including our communications people because we believed that, given the difficult decisions we were about to make, understanding the public's state of mind and speaking to it was not something to be done after we had shaped our policy. This was not just a political issue, it was also a democratic one. Remember, we were living in the shadow of the failed Meech Lake and Charlottetown accords, which had won broad support among the political elites in the country but had failed to rally the public or even earn their acquiescence. Meanwhile, Preston Manning, who led the Reform Party from just one seat to fifty-two in the 1993 election, correctly pointed out that although we discussed reducing the deficit in the Red Book, we had not created a public mandate for some of the difficult decisions it would require – far more difficult indeed than we had imagined before taking office and seeing the scale of the problem.

These were the same issues that led me to bring Elly Alboim to the table. Elly was at Earnscliffe, a consulting firm that had been hired by the previous government to help with budget communications. Prior to this time I had not known Elly, who was a former CBC bureau chief on Parliament Hill, but we were lucky to have inherited him. He provided a penetrating intellect not only on issues of communications but also of policy substance. He had the knack of waiting in a meeting until everyone else had said their piece, then jumping in with an analysis that took the discussion in a very different direction. Sometimes, I'd try to get him to speak first, but it usually didn't work.

Eventually, Elly was joined at the table by David Herle, by that time one of his colleagues at Earnscliffe. David brought an important perspective as a Westerner and as a close observer of national public opinion. He has a shrewd and sensitive policy mind, which was very important to me. I think it was sometimes a frustration to David that I valued his policy advice more than the polling he conducted. He would respond that the research he did into public opinion was the basis for giving the advice that he did.

The CMOs, which were generally held in the ministerial boardroom near my office, shattered some of the cautious traditions of the public service. I made it clear from the start that everyone was equal around the table. "When you come up here," I told them, "everyone has the right to speak, and anyone can tell me or the deputy or anyone else where to get off." It took a while for this to penetrate.

I have a temper. And I warned everyone that I was going to "lose it" from time to time. But I said I wanted them to come right back at me. Of course, the first couple of meetings, this didn't work at all. I'd raise hell and say, "That's the worst idea I have ever heard," and embarrassed departmental officials would sit around in dumbfounded silence.

There were two incidents that broke that pattern and allowed the CMOs to become the no-holds-barred discussions they had to be if we were to succeed. The first was an occasion when Terrie was having trouble coming to terms with some numbers we were discussing, and I told her that she couldn't count and to stop slowing us down if she couldn't keep up. Well, she went up one side of me and down the other, fourteen ways to Sunday. You could see that everyone else in the room was stunned: "My god, how is he going to react?" Here was the minister of finance being taken apart by his executive assistant in front of the department. The next day, I brought a little abacus someone had given me and announced

I had a presentation to make before the CMO began. "Terrie, in recognition of your difficulties with numbers, I want to present you with this abacus," I said – and everyone laughed.

The other incident involved David Dodge, whose temper was similar to my own. I was, especially in the early days, frustrated at what I saw as the rigidities in some parts of the department. I certainly did not like the fact that on their watch the country had piled up deficits that were invariably larger than their own projections. Although I appreciated that they had read the Red Book, I did not think that it should be treated like holy writ, which was their inclination at first. One day, on an issue I now forget, I told David that I didn't need him to quote the Red Book at me, and then I used words that graphically conveyed my opinion that he was way off base. He came barrelling right back at me and we had a huge battle.

After that, even relatively junior officials realized that they could take me or David on over issues they felt passionately about, and that their views would be taken seriously, and as a result, the CMOs became very productive exercises in policy making. They were similar in many ways to the meetings I had once chaired as an executive at Power Corporation and Canada Steamship Lines, but here they dealt with some of the most crucial issues facing our nation. Many of the participants have since said that these meetings were among the most intellectually stimulating hours and days of their lives. They certainly were for me, as we worked through everything from the fine points of tax policy to federal-provincial transfers, and occasionally how many angels actually do dance on the head of a pin.

After a debate had unfolded at a CMO, David Dodge would regroup with his officials while I usually met with Terrie. Later Terrie, David Herle, Elly, and I would also meet to discuss where we'd go from here. Finally David Dodge and I might meet. What was truly interesting in all this, however, is that while there were often strong views all round, the disagreements rarely broke down along political-departmental lines. There was a true intellectual melting pot.

The people who attended the CMOs soon learned that they might hear from me at any time. At first, it caused a bit of a surprise in the department when I wandered down to someone's office and started talking about whatever issue I was turning over in my mind, but the department got used to it. Because I am not someone who needs a lot of sleep at night, I also had the habit of phoning people at what they considered ungodly hours. This would hardly come as a shock to those I had worked with over the years, but it did to many of the Finance officials who hadn't known me before. I have no doubt these calls inconvenienced some people – even discombobulated a few at first. But I later found that they also became fodder for cocktail party conversation. Some people didn't mind telling their friends that we sometimes chatted at hours when most people were in bed. In later years, I was sometimes criticized for my decision-making process. That's fair game, but let me just say that, after thirty years of trying, it was this process that eliminated the deficit over the course of just four budgets.

David Dodge, as he proved many times when we worked together and subsequently in his career, is one of the great public servants of our era. He was absolutely committed to the ideals of the public service. His work ethic matched anyone's, while his intellect and institutional memory brought a perspective that proved fundamental to our success again and again. He was also a skilful manager of bureaucratic politics. On the fundamental issue of the deficit, the department and I forged a common view very quickly. In the early going, the leaders of the department may have been inclined to regard the deficit with more urgency than I did, though they had despaired of any politician ever dealing with it. Then our roles reversed, as I became seized with the immediate threat the deficit posed to the country and made it clear I was not backing away from this fight.

When we began, the initial problem we had to deal with was the consistent use of projections understating the deficit. For example, one of the first pieces of news I received as minister was that the deficit in the current fiscal year, originally projected at $32 billion, was going to come in at closer to $36 billion. Then, within a matter of days, the number rose to the $40 billion to $42 billion range. It was clear to me from the start that we needed a break from the past. I was determined to make sure we never again understated the deficit, and in fact I said that I believed overoptimistic projections were simply used as a cover for not dealing with the underlying issues that caused the deficits in the first place.

In late November, my speech at the Université de Montréal gave the public a stark look at the balance sheet that we had inherited from the Conservatives. We had already revealed that the 1992–93 deficit would come in higher than the previous government had projected. Because every time I asked, the number would go up, I predicted, over the objections of the department, that the deficit for the 1993–94 fiscal year then nearing its end would likely fall in the $44 billion to $46 billion range. That was higher than the department was predicting internally at the time and, to be fair, higher than the final result, which was $42 billion. But given the continual escalation in the deficit estimate as time went on, who was to know what it would end up being! I made the public commitment, however, that this was never going to happen again. In the future, I said, we would use the average of private sector economic forecasts and work those numbers through our fiscal models when producing our budget projections, rather than having the Department of Finance do all this internally as in the past. This was what many other countries did, but it was embarrassing to the department – although it sent the strongest possible message to the public and the bureaucracy that things were about to change.

We also challenged those who challenged us, particularly business groups, who had long been committed to aggressive deficit-cutting. I would usually begin with a presentation in which I described the various departments of government, explaining what they did and how much they spent, and would then open up the discussion. We had one such encounter with the Business Council on National Issues (BCNI) at the Rideau Club in Ottawa. I had been a BCNI member and had (and have) great respect for the quality of work that underlies their positions on public policy. But somewhat mischievously, I asked the CEOs present to tell me what spending they themselves proposed to cut, knowing that like many others, they would feel that was a job for someone else, which of course was their immediate reaction.

On another occasion, I met with the heads of the major banks and their chief economists. They started off saying flatly that what the government needed to do was cut public spending by 20 per cent. When we added up their specific suggestions, though, it came to less than 2 per cent. Then they insisted they'd have another crack and came up with a magnificent 4 per cent. The fact was that few of those demanding Draconian cuts in public spending had ever thought through the pain that these cuts would cause to vulnerable people – the poor, the unemployed – and few of them when faced with the need to do so were truly prepared to come to grips with the implications of their own rhetoric.

An important goal for me was to throw open the process of budget consultation. Although there are valid reasons behind the tradition of budget secrecy, particularly when it comes to tax changes, an excessive emphasis on secrecy in the past meant that some ideas were never adequately aired before they became hard government policy and unacceptable mistakes were made. We started our consultations with a televised meeting with economists from think-tanks, business, and labour (where, as I mentioned in the last chapter, the participants ganged up to support Crow). Then, at Elly Alboim's suggestion, we organized a series of four televised public consultations in the various regions of the country. The idea was to have a frank discussion of the issues facing the country and to push people with opposing views to consider the trade-offs necessary to get ourselves back on an even keel fiscally and economically. This was essential to getting the public onside for what eventually had to be done.

This also set a precedent that we built on as we set up the process for the second budget. In this case we decided that the House of Commons finance committee, which was chaired at the time by Jim Peterson, should become the prime consultation vehicle. Under Jim's leadership, the committee abandoned the traditional approach to pre-budget consultations, which consisted of inviting a series of interest groups, each in sequence, to declaim their irreconcilable demands. Instead, the committee arranged to hear testimony from diverse groups seated side by side – an industrial organization and a trade union, for example – which forced them to engage in a conversation about the trade-offs necessary to confront our fiscal problems. This process was crucial in establishing the building blocks of success for the second budget, when there were more complex issues to chew on.

In the short period that we had to come up with our budget, we didn't have time ourselves for delicate craftsmanship. We focused on a relatively small number of big-ticket items at the same time as we tried to squeeze a little out of each department. The Unemployment Insurance system had been sick for a long time, and we knew we had to lay out a plan for that. Defence was an area where we believed we could find savings. We also knew we had to keep a freeze on public sector salaries, because to do anything else would blow the attempt to restrain spending. Strong resistance to our plans came from Ottawa-area MPs, who were afraid of the potential impact of the freeze.

Then I got a phone call from David Dodge and Don Drummond. "We've got real trouble," they told me. "The caucus is getting to the prime minister."

When I went to see the prime minister to lay out my plans, it was obvious that he did not see the need for attacking the deficit as aggressively as I was preparing to do. For obvious reasons neither cabinet nor caucus was happy about starting life as a government with budget cuts and the promise of more to come.

Jean Chrétien was concerned that this budget was going to end the government's honeymoon – a day no prime minister wants to hasten. The truth is that if there is not some tension between the prime minister and the finance minister, one of them is probably not doing his or her job. But among Jean Chrétien's strengths were the lessons he had learned in his many years as a minister. One of those lessons, which became central to our relationship, was derived from Trudeau's decision in 1978 to announce a dramatic package of expenditure cuts in a televised statement to the nation without even informing his finance minister: Jean Chrétien. To his credit, the prime minister was determined not to undermine me the way he had been undermined, and so after arguing with my logic and assumptions – the first of many such confrontations – he swallowed his reservations and backed the thrust of the budget we were preparing.

What remained was "the speech." David Dodge has since reminded me of his bafflement when I first arrived at Finance and asked to see the draft of the budget. What on earth is he talking about? he wondered. To him, the budget was the charts and graphs showing government revenues, the tables outlining spending and projections for economic growth. My, how economists love their charts. He only later realized that what I was asking for was a first draft of the budget speech I would eventually deliver to the House of Commons. I wanted to work from the start on the speech, which from the department's perspective was something of a secondary document. But from where I sat, the speech was of the essence, because it was the document that would unify all the measures we would implement in a compelling and persuasive way.

Anyone who has worked closely with me will tell you that preparing a speech can be a long process, replete with dozens of drafts, as I flesh out my thinking in the course of creating the text. Scott Clark, who eventually succeeded David Dodge as deputy minister, suggested we hire a speechwriter named Larry Hagen, who had formerly worked for Joe Clark. Understanding the importance I placed on the speech, Scott arranged for Larry to attend the CMOs so that he would fully understand the logic behind the decisions we were making. Larry was a very hard worker with a beautiful prose style. He had a tiny office, filled with cigarette smoke. (Yes, a lot has changed!) He beavered away at draft after draft, and he cared passionately about every word. We had wonderful disputes over language and the emotional impact it would have. Larry was also eloquent about the social impacts of the budget cuts on the vulnerable, and brought that sensitivity to the table. He was an important member of the team that prepared most of my budgets through the 1990s, until he died prematurely of a heart attack. That shocked us all, and we missed him greatly as a colleague and as a wonderful human being.

But Larry wasn't there for the first budget, so in the days before I gave the speech in February, I went over it scores of times, alone or with Terrie and others, tinkering with the text and with my delivery. I also tried to go over it with Sheila, who quickly demurred. She pleaded budget secrecy, but later admitted that she knew she'd have to watch me give it in the House of Commons for close to an hour, and felt no human being should have to go through that twice.

And then came the day. Everyone is familiar with the tradition of finance ministers wearing new shoes on budget day, though it is a tradition honoured more in the breach than in the observance, and I did it only once as finance minister. Jean Chrétien, however, remembered a more obscure tradition, which was to replace the glass of water on my House of Commons desk with a glass of gin, which I discovered when I took my first big swig a few minutes into the speech. Some have said my delivery improved marvellously after that.

"The days of the government simply nibbling at the edges are over," I told the House of Commons. "The practice of endless process without product is gone. Our task is to put an end to drift. We need a new architecture for government and for the economy."

I pledged to get the deficit below $40 billion in the coming year and below $33 billion the year after that. I made it very clear that with the short period we had had in office, this budget was only just the beginning. It was important to say that as a government, we were serious about our Red Book commitments to create jobs, with an infrastructure program and support for apprenticeships. But I also said we were going to have a good hard look at all government programs, including the transfers to the provinces that made up such a large portion of our expenditures.

Initially, the public and editorial reaction to the budget was quite positive. I was not surprised by this. Officials in the department were telling me that our budget was tougher than all but one of Michael Wilson's, and I knew one litmus test for us was going to be whether we were more fiscally responsible than the Conservatives had been. But unlike my subsequent budgets, this one was not a success with the markets, whatever the public thought of it. Pete de Vries, who was the master of the numbers at the Department of Finance, and who in the years to come played a crucial role in fashioning every one of my budgets, found himself on a plane to Toronto the next morning filled with Bay Street analysts who were returning home after budget day and was shocked by their surly mood.

Part of the reason for this mood was undoubtedly my decision to set relatively modest deficit-reduction targets. This was deliberate. I thought the only way to restore confidence in the budgetary process was to ensure that the department would never again over-promise. I always understood that we would take a short-term hit for this, but believed it would pay off in the longer term.

I had planned a major national tour to sell the budget, and one of the early stops was at the *Globe and Mail* for a meeting with the editorial board. On the way there in the cab, David Dodge, expecting a bit of a fight, repeatedly reminded Terrie and me of the importance of keeping our cool. One member of the *Globe*'s editorial board, Andrew Coyne, came at us pretty hard, partly because we had included in our budget cuts changes to Unemployment Insurance that the Tories had promised but never implemented. We responded that these were the rules of the game – we had to reflect what we were doing at that moment, no more and no less. At another point he demanded to know what I knew about running a business. This baffled me. If he had asked me what I knew about government I might have understood, but this question was really infuriating. Still, I kept my cool, remembering David's advice. Then there was a sudden eruption from David himself, who at that point did everything but jump up and throttle the folks across the table. I thought Terrie was going to hug him.

What shocked me, though, was not what I confronted in Toronto – whether on Front Street (where the *Globe* is located) or a few blocks away on Bay Street. What shocked me was the international reaction. After I completed my Canadian selling tour, I headed out to the world's financial capitals – New York, London, and Tokyo – where most of the holders of Canadian bonds were. We had cut pretty deep, I thought, especially given that the Canadian economy had not yet recovered from the recession, as the American economy had. We had done a lot in just a few months to prove our fiscal bona fides, and done it at some political risk. I thought we had done enough to win some credibility in their eyes and earn some breathing room. Instead, these foreign investors paid no attention to the budget's details, only the bottom line, and so they viewed me as just another one in a long line of Canadian finance ministers who showed up every year, promising to clean up Canada's act and never delivering. With that kind of attitude in the capital markets it was evident that at the slightest sign of difficulty there would be upward pressure on our interest rates. And that would make the difficult task of moving toward a balanced budget all but impossible. What if another U.S. recession intervened before we had even started to recover from our own? The moment of truth might be even closer than we had thought.

CHAPTER TEN

The Big Budget I

The bond market was hardly new to me. At Power Corporation and later at Canada Steamship Lines, I had enough dealings in the world's financial capitals to know how important credibility was. When you go to the market or to a lender and say, "We want to buy three ships, costing $200 million, and need to borrow $150 million," getting the money at a reasonable cost depends on your credibility. Now, there I was, Canada's minister of finance, back tapping the capital markets, and instead of being believed and trusted – which was the reaction I was accustomed to – I was being greeted with a skeptical shake of the head. Just another Canadian finance minister who was going to pay a premium for being a serial disappointment.

We had another problem as well. Canada had the highest debt-to-GDP ratio among the G8 countries, except for one. That was Italy, which on the face of it had dug an even deeper hole than we had. Yet it was not subjected to the same kind of market pressure that we were. Why? Because Italy's debt was largely held by Italians, while ours was mostly in foreign hands. We didn't just have a fiscal issue; we had a sovereignty issue, because foreign lenders were much more likely than our own to act on a momentary shift in sentiment and move their money elsewhere, forcing us to jack up interest rates.

In the years to come, we were able to address this problem by rolling our debt into longer term bonds. We paid higher interest rates when we did this, but it meant that we did not have a ninety-day clock running on our debt, exposing us to a sudden flight in inter-est rates every time there was an economic shock, either here at home or abroad. But this was 1994, and the ticking of the debt clock was thunderous.

One stop on my post-budget tour in the spring of 1994 was Japan. I was surprised to see on the schedule that my officials had lined me up to meet the minister responsible for the Japanese post office. When I asked why, I was told that the post office was the largest savings institution in Japan and that it held a lot of Canadian debt. When I arrived for the meeting, I heard someone whisper "Canada" into the minister's ear. He had a large tabbed binder that obviously contained information on a variety of countries. I could see that most of them had just a few pages of documentation. I could also see that there was a thicker tab on one particular country, which I assumed was some struggling place in the developing world. When our conversation began, of course, I realized as he flipped to it that the oversized tab was for us.

I had stood up in the House of Commons on budget day in 1994 thinking that I was delivering a pretty sound document. By histori-cal standards, it was. I remember Preston Manning, then leader of the Reform Party, coming to the finance committee one day when I appeared and remarking that I was clearing the bar only because I had set it at three feet high. Jim Peterson slipped me a note com-menting that that was pretty good when you were standing in a hole six feet deep.

The "hole" he was talking about was the fact that the govern-ment's largest single expenditure was servicing the debt: thirty-six cents out of every dollar. Things were so bad we had long since stopped borrowing to build a stronger future; we were borrowing to pay the interest on debt governments had incurred to pay the inter-est on debt that previous governments had incurred, if you get my drift. While my first budget may have succeeded by the standards of my predecessors, it had not passed what I now believed was the critical test for the markets – that of re-establishing Canada's fiscal credibility. This was the marker we simply had to hit in my second budget. I believed I had one more shot at it, but that was it. If I could not restore Canada's credibility in the 1995 budget, there might be no reversing the vicious cycle of rising interest rates and increasing deficits and debt.

I had no trouble convincing my officials at Finance that this was the case. But they had seen previous finance ministers come to similar conclusions and fail to take the drastic steps necessary to set us right. The markets weren't the only ones who had experienced serial disappointment.

As I prepared for the next budget – certainly the most challenging I would ever produce as minister of finance – I knew that success would depend on the team I had working with me. I had been critical of the department, but I also made it clear from the start that my plan was to restore its reputation as the elite of the public service, in terms of intellect and accomplishment. Indeed, the right people were all there; they knew what to do. The problem was that there had not been the political drive to achieve what they knew needed doing. At the top of the department were people such as David Dodge, Scott Clark, Don Drummond, Ian Bennett, Pete de Vries, Paul-Henri Lapointe, and Munir Sheikh who could have been making their mark – and lots more money – elsewhere. They were public servants because they believed in the importance of the department's work. Some of the other officials who struck me as falling into this category were Kevin Dancey, who had left one of the big accounting firms to come to Finance as head of the tax section, and Len Farber, who seemed to have been weaned on tax policy. When I got into an argument with the department over taxes, I often had my way, but I quickly learned that when Len said no it was time to stop pushing; he was invariably right. Susan Peterson was also part of the core team, working on federal-provincial relations, social policy, and the Canada Pension Plan, as was Barbara Anderson, whose knowledge of the North and Aboriginal affairs was invaluable. Later on we also recruited Jackie Orange to head up our efforts to give new life to Canada Savings Bonds.

We also recruited an outsider. David Dodge mentioned to me that there was something called the Clifford Clark visiting economist program, which was designed to bring outside scholars into the ministry. This seemed ideally suited for Peter Nicholson. Crucially, as the Clifford Clark scholar, he would not be lodged in my office as an adviser but would operate from within the guts of the department, where he could examine the issues from the inside but with the perspective of an outsider. He contributed significantly in the year to come with the development of the so-called grey and purple books that laid out the macroeconomic context in which we were working and foreshadowed the program of investments in areas such as education and research that we would initiate once the deficit was under control.

Finally, I was fortunate in the appointment to Finance of two MPs who brought particular skills to the job. Doug Peters, as secretary of state for financial institutions, brought an outside expertise to our debates that balanced the department's institutional memory. David Walker, my parliamentary secretary, added a Western perspective and passion for the social responsibilities of government.

It was a tremendous team, though I have to admit with regret that I did not make much progress in making the department less male, white, and anglophone than it had always been.

Soon after joining us in the department, Peter Nicholson put the challenge of the deficit in particularly startling terms. He asked what the deficit would be in five years if we maintained the status quo. "Would you believe $60 billion?"

There was a stunned silence.

"Look," Peter said, articulating the point I made everywhere I went in the coming years, "this fiscal problem isn't a matter of ideology; it isn't something that should separate left from right. It is the arithmetic of compound interest. And if we don't deal with this, no government is going to be able to achieve the social objectives the public wants it to."

It was a powerful argument. It was also clear to me that if we could break out of this vicious circle, there would be an equally dramatic "virtuous circle" of lower interest rates, declining deficits and debt, and a stronger economy. This was what we were going to need to face the growing Asian competition that was no longer simply a speck on a faraway horizon.

One of the elements in the vicious circle was that governments of all stripes had employed what was called the "hockey stick approach" to the pain required in attacking the deficit – always deferring real cuts to sometime in the future. Repeatedly, finance ministers had laid out plans for expenditure reductions that when illustrated on a graph looked like the blade of a hockey stick resting on the ice for the first couple of years, with the shaft representing the cuts jutting sharply upward only in the third or fourth year. Of course, governments never really got to the shaft of the stick, and therefore very little ever happened. To change this, I insisted on "two-year rolling targets." That is to say, in each budget we would lay out what we needed to do in the coming two years only and not make faraway promises. That meant our progress could be tracked in close to real time. It also meant that for the moment, we could keep everyone's eyes fixed on the Red Book promise of getting the deficit down to 3 per cent of GDP, even though I was already determined to eliminate the deficit altogether.

Another equally important innovation in budget planning had already been adopted in our first budget in the form of a "contingency reserve." One of the little secrets of economic forecasters is that they design their models on the basis of past experience, then plug in what seem to them reasonable assumptions, and hey, presto! You have a forecast. Ask them what happens if the price of oil doubles, or a war unexpectedly erupts halfway across the globe, or the Asian banking sector collapses, and they say, "Well, that's outside our assumptions." The problem is that something unexpected *always* happens. And although you can have good surprises as well as bad, it was the bad surprises I was worried about. In order to have a truly robust plan for conquering the deficit, we needed to have a "contingency reserve" that would act as a shock absorber against bad economic news. In other words, if catastrophe struck – or even something much less than catastrophe but large enough to throw off our planning – we needed to be able to take the shock without rushing in an emergency budget or, worse still, allowing it to deter us from our path. Governments had included "contingency funds" in their budgets before, but these had been designed to deal with unexpected expenditures. Ours was not for spending but for dealing with unforeseen bad economic news. If the news was good, on the other hand, the money would automatically be used to reduce the deficit and eventually to pay down debt, thus lowering our borrowing costs.

Just to give us one additional level of assurance, when we calculated our budgetary plans, we used "prudent" assumptions. In other words, if the economists were predicting growth between 2 and 3 per cent, we might make our calculations on the basis of 1.8 per cent growth. This was the opposite of what previous governments had often done, preferring to work with the sunniest possible scenarios, which made their budgets look good on budget day but quickly diverged from economic reality. Sad to say, as I sit here writing in 2008, it is a bad practice that the current government has resurrected.

These policies really showed their worth after the September 11, 2001, attacks. When the terror struck out of a clear blue sky, not only was there a sudden, unexpected economic shock, affecting both the stock market and the underlying economy, there were also new and entirely unanticipated demands for expenditure. As a result of our belt-and-suspenders budget planning, we were able to absorb $8 billion in new spending over the next few years for border security, intelligence, and the military, including our commitment to Afghanistan. We did all that, and we were able to do it without falling back into deficit.

As we approached the difficult job of cutting spending, Peter Nicholson developed the concept of what he called the "four pillars": spending by federal departments, transfers to the provinces, Unemployment Insurance, and Old Age Security. These categories accounted for nine-tenths of the government's costs (excluding servicing the debt, of course). It was clear to me that we needed to keep two objectives in my mind as we cut. First, we had to make structural changes that would not only yield a reduction in the deficit right away but would ensure that governments did not easily lapse back into their old habits once the short-term crisis had been bridged. And second, we had to make sure that the pain would be evenly spread. I was convinced that individual Canadians would not accept a program of restraint if they believed that they were being hit while others were escaping untouched.

I had already signalled in my first budget that we were going to conduct a comprehensive review of government programs. I had long believed that the structure of government was out of whack. Our spending was in the wrong areas, and governments had tended to adjust it with incremental cuts to particular programs or, more frequently, incremental increases, without ever re-examining their priorities in a fundamental way. That was the reason for the "program review" I announced in the budget. Originally the idea was to conduct this review over five years. Marcel Massé, the former clerk of the Privy Council under Mulroney, who had run for us in 1993 and been appointed president of the Treasury Board, was to chair the review. Marcel knew the ins and outs of the government in a way that I could never hope to, and he was perfectly suited to the job. The idea was that he would lead a panel of ministers, including some of the left-leaning ones, who would conduct the exercise, in the hope that it would win some buy-in from cabinet.

What I did not foresee was that I would return from my alarming tour of the capital markets after the 1994 budget convinced that the five-year exercise I had envisaged was going to have to be completed in time for the 1995 budget – less than a year away. When I came back, I asked David Dodge and Don Drummond up to my office on Parliament Hill. They didn't need persuading from me that the deficit should be a priority; but I was probably the only one there who truly believed we could make it happen politically. I no longer believed that we could simply restrain the growth in government spending and let economic growth – and the increased tax revenues that would bring – look after the rest. "We're going to have to cut our way out of this mess," I said. "We're up against a very tight timeline. When the next U.S. recession comes – and it may come soon – we won't be able to weather it by cutting interest rates. We need to borrow too much and we have too little credibility with the markets to allow us to do that. We cannot afford to have the 1995 budget fail. We need to come in with a budget that will get us to the Red Book target of a deficit no larger than 3 per cent of GDP. But we also need to open a path to something more dramatic than we had ever discussed in the election campaign: the elimination of the deficit."

Talk about preaching to the converted!

I told them that we were going to start the process of cutting right then and there. Everyone has heard of planning on the "back of an envelope." Well, that day, I literally took out a large brown envelope, and as David and Don suggested targets for spending cuts, I began writing numbers on the back of it. I knew that we could not get to where we needed to go without cutting transfers to the provinces – something that was going to be enormously difficult politically because the provinces deliver many of the services, such as health, education, and welfare, that most directly affect people. But I also believed that if we were going to ask the provinces to take a substantial hit, as they would inevitably have to do, we had no choice politically but to cut our own expenditures just as deeply or even deeper.

We started by setting our goal, which was to cut the government's program spending roughly 20 per cent. We knew that we couldn't do it all in a year, but we needed to get on track to doing it within two years. Once we had decided on the total number we needed to hit, we worked back through the government's departments and programs to find the savings we needed. We went through department after department. David and Don might suggest that a 30 per cent cut was feasible in a particular department based on their own in-depth knowledge, and I'd say, "Why not 35 per cent?" Then we wrote it down. The only area we kept sacrosanct from absolute cuts was

Indian Affairs, where the rate of spending growth was restrained to a level below population growth.

At first, some in the Finance Department felt this was just a starting point for discussions with individual departments and that we'd have to go through a lengthy exercise of research, consultation, and negotiation with each one to make sure our percentage targets made sense. But I knew perfectly well we simply couldn't do it that way. I was accused of using arbitrary numbers and I agreed. I was told I was being unreasonable and I agreed. If I wasn't arbitrary and unreasonable, we would be nickeled and dimed and delayed to death. Once we got into bargaining with ministers and departments, we'd be ground away. Eventually, we'd be forced to make an across-the-board cut to meet our targets, which would defeat the exercise by failing to set any priorities at all. We had no alternative. Or actually we did: that we would fail.

When I explained the situation as I saw it to Marcel Massé, he quickly agreed. I gave him and his very able deputy, Wayne Wouters, the list of targets and said, "This is what we have to achieve." One crucial tool for Marcel to succeed was to have access to the Finance Department's numbers. Control of the numbers was a key component in Finance's power within the system. But Marcel needed to be told everything to do the job. It was so contrary to the department's traditions that Terrie and I had to pressure the department repeatedly to ensure the continued flow of information. It worked because Marcel was convinced from the beginning that our analysis of the problem was right, and he was enthusiastic about his role in the process.

That did not mean that the program review process would be an easy one. It began with a series of one-on-one meetings with ministers in which I gave them the number that had started life on the back of that brown envelope (although I chose not to mention that fact!). This would nearly provoke a coronary. The minister would invariably start out by arguing that the target was unreasonable, and usually by questioning my sanity for even suggesting it. But I was not prepared to yield. The next step was for the minister to go before the program review committee led by Marcel to outline how they were going to achieve their designated cuts. The committee quickly acquired the wry nickname the "Star Chamber" – after the 16th-century British court that was legendary for its arbitrary power. The program review committee was told they could alter the specific targets for cuts to each department, but it was a zero sum game: if they wanted to lower the target on one department from 20 per cent to 10 per cent, they could; but then they had to cut deeper elsewhere. The members of the committee, led by left-leaning ministers such as Brian Tobin, were stalwarts about their work and kept the pressure on. Most ministers eventually accepted the deep cuts expected of them, even where they were driven to measures that they found personally difficult.

We knew that for all this to succeed, we needed to make an irrefutable intellectual case to cabinet for what we were doing. We knew we couldn't win over every single minister, but we needed to get a critical mass of support, including the prime minister. The set-piece opportunity to do this was at a cabinet "retreat" that Jean Chrétien had called for June.

We didn't retreat far. The meeting was held in the Pearson Building on Sussex Drive, from which we could see the Ottawa River coursing between the Parliament Buildings on the south bank and many of the large departmental buildings on the north. In my presentation there, I laid out the critical situation that confronted us as a government. I explained that rising interest rates were already throwing off the projections contained in the 1994 budget. We were okay for the moment, I said, because of the large contingency reserve. But the 1995 budget would have to be historic in scale: cutting at the "four pillars" and setting structures in place to make sure we did not slide back. There was plenty of grumbling, as might be imagined. Some questioned the accuracy of the Finance Department's economic projections – understandably, given the woeful history of these projections under the Tories. But no one questioned the 3 per cent deficit target laid out in the Red Book. In other words, my mandate had been reaffirmed – in principle, at least.

Truth be told, one day David Dodge came to me and said, "Here are the cuts we're going to make in Finance, twenty per cent if we are to hit our target."

"Whoa!" I said. "We can't cut Finance that much. We're a special case. We have no programs. We're at the heart of this process."

Then, in his gravelly voice, David reminded me what this exercise was all about: *everyone* had to put something in the collection plate. We made the cuts.

Many of my colleagues hoped that a committee of their peers would sympathize with them; they did not understand the degree to which the process had won unlikely allies such as Brian Tobin. The rule at the program review committee was that if a minister did not identify the cuts necessary to reach the target, the committee would do it for him. John Manley's case turned out to be crucial for the success of the process. His department, Industry, and its extensive subsidies to business, had been slated for a 35 per cent cut. My feeling was that if we were going to cut transfers to the provinces for areas such as health care, we could not possibly continue subsidizing businesses to the degree that the Department of Industry had been doing. Ralph Goodale, meanwhile, who was at Agriculture, was being asked to eliminate the Crow rate subsidizing grain transportation, which was seen almost as a right of citizenship by Western farmers.

Nonetheless, John Manley decided to go around the process and appeal directly to Jean Chrétien. But the prime minister cut him dead, telling him to deal with the committee. When John failed to propose a way to reach his department's target, the committee went through the department expenditures itself and came up with a 60 per cent cut that, as you can imagine, had a powerful effect on other ministers.

There was only one minister canny enough to stymie the process. Herb Gray, Solicitor General at the time, was the most experienced man in government. He had a kind of reverse charisma that had turned him into a press and parliamentary favourite during his time as interim leader after John Turner stepped down. We all held him in high regard for his enormous discretion and accumulated political wisdom. Herb struck on a unique approach with regard to the Canadian Security Intelligence Service (CSIS), which was within his ministry. It was simply too secret to have its budget revealed to the program review committee, he explained. We wanted him to share his plans for cuts notwithstanding the need for secrecy, because we did not want him to put us on the spot later by offering up something outrageous to deflect us. But Herb continued to put us off at every turn, always pleading secrecy. In the end, we never truly found out whether CSIS reached its target – or if it did, how it was done. Because a relatively small amount was involved – his was not a big-spending department – we signed off on it.

I remember walking into a Finance Department meeting and saying, "I guess Herb and CSIS have won. We'd better tell them."

Karl Littler looked up at the ceiling as if to indicate a listening device and wisecracked, "You probably already have!"

As I mentioned, one major hiccup in the process arose from the fact that, believe it or not, there was no single set of government books and, therefore, no single set of numbers. Finance had its numbers; Treasury Board had its numbers; and the departments had their own. As a result, even after ministers did detail how they were going to meet the percentage cuts we had imposed, we realized that in many cases the cuts they were proposing failed to meet the percentage according to our calculations at Finance. There were probably no meetings more painful during this year than the ones in which I told ministers who had turned themselves and their departments inside out to meet their targets that they had to give just a little more.

Throughout the fall, ministers continued to go to the prime minister on individual issues. Often there was a compelling case to be made. This led to a series of very difficult meetings between me and the prime minister. In part, this was because he simply did not subscribe to my view that overcoming the deficit was crucial to Canada's future success. Like his adviser Eddie Goldenberg, his inclination was to think that the deficit was a political problem to be managed, and no more. The prime minister's view was that the Red Book target of getting the deficit down to 3 per cent of GDP – his suggestion – was a worthy goal. But unlike me, he did not regard it as the foundation for whatever else we might want to do as a government. He even got into a long argument with Don Drummond one day in which he insisted that a few simple accounting changes (along the U.S. model) would go a long way to reducing the deficit number. The problem was, from my perspective, that the markets would see that as a shell game and that it would do nothing to restore our credibility: just the opposite.

Our meetings were bruising ones. "I disagree with you," he would tell me the five or six times we met privately to discuss the developing budget plan. He acknowledged that we had made a political commitment to the 3 per cent target, but if we missed it by a year or two, he thought people would understand. Through all of this, I never threatened to resign. But there's no doubt that that possibility lurked behind our difficult negotiations. Still, in every instance, until almost the end (and we'll get to that later), I ultimately won the point with the prime minister. But in every instance it ground away at our relationship. In future years, although the issues were less difficult, we kept our contact through the budget process to a minimum.

Every battle we won – and ultimately the one battle we lost – whether at the level of the prime minister and me, our staffs, or the department and the Privy Council Office (PCO), resulted in emotional scars and a growing distance between us. Meanwhile, the relationship between the PCO and Finance was so bad that the clerk of the Privy Council, Jocelyn Bourgon, worked up her own set of economic and fiscal numbers that were different from Finance's. This caused terrible confusion when the prime minister and I met one on one, since we did not even start with a common factual base. Eventually, I had to arrange for a meeting of Jocelyn, Eddie, Terrie, David Dodge, and me to sort this out. We insisted that while the PCO had the right to brief against us with the prime minister, we all needed to work from the Finance numbers if we were going to have a rational debate. The clerk accepted this result, but as the prime minister's main adviser she continued to oppose our plans ferociously.

We only won the battles we did because the prime minister decided to allow me to charge ahead, despite his many reservations and those of the people around him. It was Jean Chrétien's absolute resolve to back me up as finance minister that enabled us to accomplish what we did. I am proud of our accomplishments together, which were the product of a partnership. But his support did not mean that he shared my feelings of urgency about the fiscal crisis; nor did it mean that the strain didn't tell, and tell deeply on both sides.

By December 1994, we had won a lot of battles at the ministerial level and higher and were getting the coming 1995 budget into reasonable shape. But there was growing resistance from ministers, more and more of them being prepared to go around me to the prime minister. Finally I went to see him and laid out my concerns. We met just before cabinet in what proved to be a stormy session between the two of us. I strongly reiterated what I had said many times before, that we absolutely needed to show the country we were willing to cut close to home if we were going to expect sacrifices of others.

The prime minister said that he did not agree with my targets.

I replied, "Prime Minister – I'm not backing off." He did not reply, but he did indicate his displeasure. At that point we had to break to go to cabinet.

I was determined to push ahead but obviously wondered what would happen when all this eventually hit the proverbial fan, which it did much sooner than I expected. Perhaps fifteen minutes into the meeting, one of my cabinet colleagues made an open appeal to the prime minister, saying that he and other ministers were being asked by me to do impossible things. Around the table it was obvious that other ministers were getting ready to join the parade.

I was about to react when Jean Chrétien jumped in: "Let me say just one thing before this goes any further. There's no need for any of you to come and see me, and there's no need to debate this here. I support the minister of finance." Bang! End of discussion.

CHAPTER ELEVEN

The Big Budget II

G etting the prime minister on board was one thing. Convincing the public of the need to undertake these cuts, and convincing the markets that we were serious about doing so, was something quite different. After the 1994 budget, David Dodge recruited Peter Daniel, a former CBC reporter and senior official at Foreign Affairs, to head up the department's communications team. Peter made one stipulation before accepting the job, which was that he be part of the budget preparation meetings. As it happened, that was precisely the way we wanted to organize our communications effort. In the following years, Peter would be enormously helpful in co-ordinating our approach to communications with the public and with the markets. It was he who brought Elly Alboim and David Herle more deeply into the budget-planning process. They wove together the many elements of an effective communications plan, being careful to translate our policy ideas into language that Canadians could understand and support. One of our objectives was to build on our experience during the 1994 budget process of consulting and communicating extensively before budget day. We were going to have a lot more to communicate in the 1995 budget, but we also had a whole year to prepare.

Part of our preparation involved an expanded role for Members of Parliament. Informally, I met with most of the caucus, one on one or in small groups, to discuss our budget preparations during the course of 1994. Furthermore, we decided that Jim Peterson's parliamentary finance committee should play the major role in public consultations instead of the Department of Finance. This embodied my view that the role of MPs should be expanded – something I elaborated on when I became party leader and eventually prime minister. Playing this consultative role on the budget, the finance committee also offered me the venue for a major statement in the fall of each year, beginning in 1994, outlining where we were, how we saw the economy, and where we were headed. The first of these statements, in 1994, was as crucial as any public appearance I ever made in my years as finance minister. It was where I made the case to Canadians for what I was doing and what I intended to do.

For some time, I had been using a phrase in our internal discussions that we had to convince the public and the markets that we were going to meet our targets "come hell or high water." By the time we began to prepare my remarks for the economic and fiscal update before the committee, the phrase had lost its impact for me. I took some convincing that it would still sound fresh to those hearing it for the first time. But as I began working on my two-day presentation with the help of Peter, Elly, David Herle, and Larry Hagen, the phrase became the core of the message. Indeed, looking back at my time in business and politics, it pretty well sums up the way I came at a lot of things.

I had several challenges in making my presentation. I had to prepare the public for what was going to be a very tough budget. I also needed to reassure the markets that not only were we on the right course, but we were picking up speed. The communications team developed a graphic presentation using PowerPoint, which at the time was a relative novelty, that grabbed remarkable attention, especially with the television media.

On the first day, I laid out the history of our economic and fiscal difficulties, showing the depth of the problems we faced and their long-term structural nature. On the second day, I laid out the rudiments of our plan. I explained how cutting the deficit would help lower interest rates, creating a self-reinforcing positive cycle. And I made the commitment to meet the 3 per cent deficit target "come hell or high water."

I absolutely believed that we would meet that target when I said it. But in the months to come it sometimes seemed like it would be a near-run thing.

While the review of government programs was being played out at least partially in public, because of leaks by the various bureaucratic and political players, we were working more quietly on the issue of transfers to the provinces. One obstacle we had was the mixture of transfers, all operating under different rules.

Our idea was to lump all of these transfers into a single consolidated fund that would be smaller than the sum of all the transfers that preceded it. At first, we called this the Consolidated Federal Transfer, a fairly bureaucratic name. Then, because it dealt in theory mostly with social spending, it was called the Canada Social Transfer. At the last minute, after the budget had already been printed in fact, Sheila Copps, who was deputy prime minister, and Diane Marleau, who was the health minister, insisted that it be renamed the Canada Health and Social Transfer (CHST). We designed the CHST in part as a cost-cutting exercise; however, the cuts were not immediate but phased in over time to give the provinces an opportunity to adjust. To make the cuts easier to absorb, the CHST gave the provinces considerably more flexibility in how they spent the federal transfers, with the important condition that they live up to the Canada Health Act. As it turned out, the provinces tended to hit hardest at welfare and post-secondary education when they made their own cuts. Eventually, we would address each of these areas, through the national child benefit and the Education Budget of 1998. I know that these changes produced real hardship for individuals, as well as for some of our most important institutions. But without these changes the hardships would have been much greater later on.

By November, the budget was in pretty good shape when we were sideswiped – just as I had feared we might be – by an event outside of our control. Without warning, an international financial crisis struck, beginning in one country but leaving others such as Canada with weak balance sheets as collateral damage. This was the peso crisis of December 1994, which was provoked by a lack of transparency by the Mexican authorities. The Mexican government had increased spending ahead of its presidential election earlier in the year. Political violence, including the assassination of the leading presidential candidate, led foreign investors to start pulling money out of the country. The outgoing president was reluctant to devalue the peso, and in the early going, the degree to which this was draining Mexico's foreign currency reserves was not obvious to the outside world. When the realization hit, there was a massive run on the peso, followed by a dramatic devaluation. That created a further exodus of foreign capital.

The collapse of the Mexican economy was only averted by an international rescue package developed in significant part by Robert Rubin, the U.S. treasury secretary. Bob and I were in frequent contact through this crisis. He needed allies. The Europeans were reluctant to see international institutions such as the International Monetary Fund (IMF) get involved because they felt that the United States had blocked assistance to Europe in previous crises. In the end, the United States gave loan guarantees and conducted currency swaps worth $20 billion (all figures here in U.S. dollars). The IMF offered a credit arrangement of almost $18 billion. The Bank for International Settlements contributed a line of credit worth $10 billion. And the Bank of Canada pitched in with currency swaps worth approximately a billion dollars.

Naturally, the peso crisis spooked international investors, who began looking around for other vulnerable countries with unresolved fiscal problems, and we were near the top of the list. It didn't help that in January 1995, the *Wall Street Journal* published an editorial that said Canada had become an "honorary member of the Third World" because of our debt. The resulting pressures on the dollar meant that the Bank of Canada had no choice but to increase interest rates in response, and this threw all of our budget projections out of whack. As it happened, news of the 100-basis point (or 1 per cent) rise in interest rates reached me just as I was about to begin a presentation to cabinet. I explained to my appalled colleagues that the rise meant that if we were going to hit our targets, we needed even more dramatic cuts than we had already imposed. I also informed them that a team of IMF officials had recently visited the department (as they periodically did) and had argued that our commitment to cutting the deficit was still not adequate – something that further bolstered my case. Most ministers had already "given at the office," and more than they felt they could, but they were going to have to give again. Now the human resources department and the Unemployment Insurance system – which had been partially spared by Lloyd Axworthy's social security review, which wasn't due to report for another year – were also going to have to swallow huge cuts.

This was very tough medicine. But it proved the logic behind jettisoning the "hockey stick approach" in favour of strict short-term targets. This meant we could not use an unexpected event to defer tough decisions. This is precisely what "come hell or high water" meant.

If there was any benefit to the peso crisis, it was that my colleagues could now plainly see what I had been saying all along. Our deficit problem made us vulnerable, terribly vulnerable. Something happening half a continent away could kick the feet out from under us. It had happened once and it would surely happen again if we didn't do something about it. I believe this is the moment when the cabinet really came together with determination to meet the commitment we had made in the campaign to get the deficit down to 3 per cent of GDP. In my own mind, it confirmed an even more ambitious goal: eliminating the deficit altogether.

One last area of government spending where I was still struggling, however, was the fourth and final pillar: assistance to seniors. There were huge issues related to the Canada Pension Plan (CPP), of course. Since the CPP was a joint federal-provincial program operating with a set of liabilities that were entirely separate from the federal balance

THE BIG BUDGET II   149

sheet, however, I dealt with it on a separate track, and I will get to that in the next chapter. In this budget, what I had set my sights on was a reform of Old Age Security (OAS), a program paid for directly from federal government revenues.

Inevitably, as Canada's baby boomers aged, there were going to be more and more eligible recipients, and relatively fewer working-age people to support them through their taxes. This was a problem that was still unfamiliar to most Canadians, though it was certainly understood by the markets. Moreover, there was a serious issue of equity, with the most prosperous generation of seniors ever tapping huge amounts of money from the Treasury regardless of their personal wealth, at the expense of their children and grandchildren. We considered a number of options for the 1995 budget but eventually settled on a proposal for a sharper clawback of benefits through the income tax system: in other words, taxing back more of the benefits from better-off seniors.

That having been said, we knew that reforming seniors' programs had been a "no-go area" ever since Michael Wilson had tried partly to de-index benefits in 1985. At the time, Brian Mulroney had been confronted outside the Parliament Buildings, with TV cameras rolling, by a senior named Solange Denis. "You lied to us," she said. "You got us to vote for you, and then goodbye Charlie Brown." Within a few days, the government backed off its proposals.

As we developed our own ideas, nearly a decade later, I decided to take an hour and visit Madame Denis, who still lived in the Ottawa suburb of Vanier. I knew that the media would run to her for the thumbs-up or thumbs-down the moment the budget was out, and that her verdict could be critical to public acceptance. The department was very jittery about my excursion because of the potential that she could blow the wraps off a politically sensitive element of the budget. I explained my plan in detail to Madame Denis and once she understood it, she endorsed it.

As it turned out, though, our problem was not Solange Denis. I had told the prime minister I believed we needed to make definite progress on seniors' programs in the 1995 budget. We had an aging population, and the baby boomers would start to retire in 2011, imposing huge new burdens on a potentially debt-ridden federal government. Besides, if we did not do it in the context of attacking other forms of expenditure, we would never again have a political context in which it was possible. I also felt that if farmers were sacrificing the Crow rate and provinces were losing on social transfers, we could not ignore this major area of government spending: it was an issue of fairness.

Although the prime minister understood all these issues and shared many of my concerns, he was extremely reluctant to take on the seniors, especially with a Quebec referendum in the offing. In fairness to him it must be said that his worries were especially intense because, historically, those cheques from Ottawa had been an important part of securing federalist support in the province. He and I clashed on this again and again. And the seesaw battle continued right up to the threshold of budget day. In fact, the department had taken to operating with two drafts of the budget, one printed on blue paper and the other on pink paper, each with different text with regard to seniors. The top Finance officials were deathly afraid that somehow the wrong button would be pushed and the wrong version of the budget would find its way into the media's hands.

With eight or nine days to go, many of my departmental officials had come to the conclusion that the battle was lost, but I was still unwilling to concede defeat. Over the previous year there had been many battles that had seemed lost for a time but I had not given up on, and we had eventually won them. As a result of those battles, I was by this time pretty much *persona non grata* with the prime minister, though. In a meeting with David Dodge, Peter Nicholson, Elly, and Terrie, I decided that it might be worthwhile to have Peter make one final approach. Peter had a closer relationship with Jean Chrétien than any of us; his father, a Liberal member of the Nova Scotia legislature, had been a friend of Jean Chrétien.

So Peter dutifully went off to 24 Sussex to make this last pitch. The prime minister, I was later told, listened as Peter explained the "four pillars" and how important it was to address each one of them. It was early evening, and as the sun went down, no lights were switched on and the room grew very dark. After about ten minutes of Peter's presentation, Jean Chrétien stopped him dead. He told Peter that Finance should defer to his political judgment on this and that he was convinced the budget would be a success without taking on the seniors' issue. Peter came back to the department and reported mournfully that he had fouled off a couple of pitches from the prime minister, then flied out weakly in centre field. He said that the prime minister had complained bitterly that I did not seem to understand how to take no for an answer. It was something he had said to me personally a few days before; and I had replied that if I had been prepared to take no for an answer, we never would have got anywhere attacking the deficit over the last year.

This turned out to be the most difficult moment in my already strained relationship with the prime minister – until the few days before I left cabinet in 2002 – and it turned on an issue of pure policy. The prime minister, as was his right, was pushing back hard on what he regarded as a core political issue. I felt that it was a matter of principle that the government be seen to be taking all its fiscal challenges seriously in the 1995 budget, fearing that anything less would be seen as a failure of resolve by the bond markets that would drive us farther into a hole. I was also very concerned about fairness between the generations – something that underlay my whole approach to the deficit and the debt.

As budget day approached, I had to face the fact that on this one issue, Jean Chrétien would not be budged. Having won so many battles, I found it hard to lose this one – a question of personality and character, perhaps, as much as principle. But I also believed this was our last shot at fixing Canada's fiscal mess and restoring our credibility – and that if we blew it, that was it. I had a meeting with Terrie, Elly, and David Herle to consider my options. One was to resign, which some of my advisers advocated. But for me, the issue was whether this budget was good enough without the seniors' package to restore the government's fiscal credibility. One adviser argued that we had got 95 per cent of what we had set out to do, and that it was enough to satisfy the markets, which was our principal goal.

I was later told that there were contingency plans in the Prime Minister's Office (PMO) and the Privy Council Office (PCO) to replace me and rush in a substitute budget, and that some didn't believe that would be altogether a bad thing. The clerk, I learned, was urging that I be replaced, and was canvassing potential replacements with the prime minister. In the end, though, I decided that the budget would demonstrate our absolute commitment to getting the deficit down to 3 per cent of GDP, which we had promised in the Red Book and which would constitute, by far, the most substantial attack on the deficit ever.

I told the prime minister that I would pass on the seniors' issue for now, on condition that I could commit in the budget to reform in 1996. He agreed. The moment of crisis passed. And subsequently I came to the conclusion that on this issue he was more right than I was.

By the time I stood up in the House of Commons to deliver the budget speech, certainly the most significant I ever delivered, and arguably one of the most significant in Canadian history, I knew it was going to be a success. Every year on budget day, the media go into a "lock-up" many hours before the budget is delivered. They are given the budget documents and access to Finance and other department officials but are not allowed to publish or broadcast any of the information they have until the finance minister begins his speech. Many media outlets bring Bay Street analysts into the lock-up with them to help assess the budget so that they can get their stories out the minute the finance minister starts to speak and the lock-up ends. Of course there are always many Finance officials, including ministerial staff inside the lock-up, to brief reporters and to respond to their questions. I knew from reports coming out of the lock-up that day that the financial analysts were giving the budget a very positive review. I also knew that the international media – and the international markets – would take their cue from those analysts. We had done it!

When I rose in the House of Commons to deliver the 1995 budget, an acute observer would have noticed that a number of seats normally occupied by senior cabinet ministers were filled by others. This was not because they had decided to forgo the opportunity to hear my dulcet tones, although that may have been a side benefit. It was because we had taken the unprecedented step of sending cabinet ministers out far and wide across Canada and to key foreign financial capitals so that markets at home and abroad would have evidence of our government's resolve.

The success of the 1995 budget was not due to one person or even one government department. It took a prime minister's support and the backing of cabinet members whose ministries had to make the expenditure cuts called for, and a caucus who knew they would have to work on what might be a hard sell in every big city and small hamlet in the country. I made the speech, but if ever there was a collective effort, this was it.

As important as the immediate success was, something larger had also been accomplished: we had established a new social contract with Canadians in which the principle of zero deficits played a central part. There was no other country that went as far and as quickly as we did. And there were other countries, notably the United States, which followed a similar path, and then abandoned it, squandering the benefits of the balanced budgets and burdening future generations with the responsibility of paying for low taxes and high spending in the here and now. In this country, ordinary citizens have embraced a belief in fiscal discipline, and they are now the ones who need to keep governments on the straight and narrow.

CHAPTER TWELVE

Time . . . and Generations

O ne of the great challenges of democratic government arises from the temptation of political parties to make election promises that they know, or should know, would be unwise to implement. It also leads any government that is thinking about deep structural reforms to hesitate, because the costs of those reforms may come before the next election, while the benefits surface only later. It encourages short-term planning – short-sighted planning, in fact. When we came to office in 1993, we faced a number of such dilemmas. The deficit fight, as was famously said, meant short-term pain for long-term gain. We were fortunate that the public was mature enough to recognize this was necessary. But as I mentioned in the last chapter, we also had a broader issue of fairness between generations, involving not only the deficit – which was, in effect, one generation taking out loans that its children would have to pay – but also the Canada Pension Plan, which would soon tip into insolvency without dramatic change.

And then there was the GST.

The Goods and Services Tax, since its inception, has been good policy and bad politics. A succession of governments has faced this contradiction. Brian Mulroney's government, which introduced it, delayed revealing the details until after it had secured re-election in 1988. Arguably, the political fallout contributed more to Brian's political demise, and that of his party after he had left the scene, than anything else he ever did. Replacing the old but invisible

Manufacturers' Sales Tax (MST) with the omnipresent GST, paid at the cashier by every Canadian every day of the week, inflamed public opinion. And yet, the tax made eminent economic sense. The MST really was a "tax on jobs," as the Mulroney government argued, and it really did curb investment that could create employment. At the time, they also insisted that the switch to the GST was "revenue neutral," meaning that the new tax would not generate any more income for the government than the old one did. In a bit of sleight of hand, Brian later claimed that the GST was such a prodigious revenue-earner that he deserves credit for our government eliminating the deficit! I think I am content to let history adjudicate that claim. But the fundamental importance of the GST as a building block in the federal government's balance sheet is undeniable.

Unfortunately, many years later, the continuing unpopularity of the tax led Stephen Harper to promise a reduction in the rate of the GST, something that no doubt won him some crucial extra votes in January 2006 – but at what cost! To keep that promise he forced the government to take a $12 billion to $13 billion reduction in revenues. As a result, he removed the government's cushion against falling back into deficit, and left himself with no room to cut personal income taxes or to accelerate the tax relief manufacturers needed to modernize machinery and plants to partially compensate for the rising dollar. The Conservative government did all this without even leveraging the GST reduction to induce the provinces to harmonize their sales taxes fully – which would have been some compensation.

But in between Brian Mulroney's and Stephen Harper's GST woes was the little matter of how we, the Liberals, were going to handle the same hot potato. In Opposition, some of our MPs wanted to take advantage of the stunning public reaction against the tax by promising to "scrap" it. Jean Chrétien was not among them, however. His experience as a finance minister, as well as his naturally cautious nature, meant that he was reluctant to box himself into a promise that would be difficult to keep. He appointed a caucus committee led by John Manley and Diane Marleau, which took the responsible position that the revenue generated by the GST would have to be found elsewhere. This became party policy.

Of course, one of the fundamental principles that the Red Book embodied was that all our promises would be costed. Here is what the Red Book said: "A Liberal government will replace the GST with a system that *generates equivalent revenues* [my emphasis], is fairer to consumers and to small business, minimizes disruption to small business, and promotes federal-provincial fiscal co-operation and harmonization." No one who read this passage in our platform document could be in any doubt as to what the official policy of the party was. But what party platform documents say – even the Red Book, the most closely examined platform document ever in Canadian politics – and what candidates say on the campaign trail can sometimes be quite different. Furthermore, what candidates say can sometimes be different from what voters hear. In the 1993 election campaign, some Liberals weren't especially careful with their language, promising to "scrap" or "kill" the GST, wording that would lead some voters to think that the party's policy was much more adventurous than it actually was. Sheila Copps went so far as to say that if the tax were not abolished, she would resign. Once we were elected, my challenge was, like it or not, to deal with the expectations created by some Liberals on the hustings while trying to achieve the more precise goal we had laid out in the Red Book.

Indeed, as finance minister, my challenge was more than just addressing an election promise. I had made restoring our fiscal credibility a fundamental element of our policy, and the way in which we addressed the GST would be a significant marker of our credibility both to Canadians and to our lenders. I set the department to work coming up with options. But the fact was that replacing the GST with another tax would inevitably have shifted the burden elsewhere. Simply redesigning the GST as a retail value-added tax would have invited the justified criticism that the GST was being disguised instead of replaced. We did work hard on harmonizing the GST with provincial sales taxes – and made headway in the Atlantic provinces – but ran into a brick wall in Ontario, where Mike Harris turned against it, despite having espoused the idea on the campaign trail.

As we were wrestling with these issues, I remember having an argument with Terrie, Elly, and David Herle. "Look it, I never said I would scrap the GST and to the best of my knowledge Jean Chrétien never said he would scrap it, and I don't see why we have to do anything beyond what we said in the Red Book." But they pointed out that there was videotape of Jean Chrétien going further than that – a political fact we had to reckon with. The problem was that not everyone saw this situation the same way. The prime minister's attitude was simply to ignore it and get on with life – certainly not to apologize. Sheila Copps's position was that we should simply eliminate the GST. But I was the finance minister and I needed to deal with the situation, and clearly, neither of these two options were the answer. I needed to lance the boil, and in the end I saw that the only way to do that was to admit that we were not going to succeed in "scrapping the GST," to apologize, and to move on.

To pretend that harmonization of the GST with provincial sales taxes (which was a good idea) or some more gimmicky solution (which would not have been) met the standard established by some of the language used in the election campaign would only invite derision and undermine our credibility, which in my case, as finance minister, was deeply connected with the faith of the markets and the public in our management of the deficit. The prime minister – always reluctant to admit a mistake – was clearly unhappy with my decision; nonetheless, I was determined to go ahead and do it. Terrie worked closely with Eddie, who was trying to make the best of a bad situation. There may have been a difference in opinion about the approach I was taking, but there were no surprises. I made a statement in the House of Commons in which I made it clear that we would not change the GST. Then I went to a press conference in the national press theatre, where I said, "We made a mistake. It was an honest mistake. It was a mistake in thinking we could bring in a completely different tax without undue economic distortion and within a reasonable time period."

Sheila Copps decided she had no choice but to keep her election promise by stepping down and fighting a by-election (which she subsequently easily won). Jean Chrétien disagreed with her decision, as he had done with mine, and tried to dissuade her, but to her credit she was determined and stuck to her guns. I do not remember him ever talking directly to me about the GST apology, but he communicated his displeasure publicly in many ways. In the House, he never associated himself with the apology. He was quoted in the media as saying that I had "created a problem" for the government, and he was said to believe that I had gone "too far" in making the apology. Terrie was stunned because she believed that despite a tactical difference of opinion between the prime minister and me, the decision to apologize had been worked out with the PMO in minute detail. Jean Chrétien continued to refuse to make any apology himself for many months, even when an angry voter in a CBC Town Hall confronted him just before Christmas. His response inflamed the issue once again, and he was forced into a series of increasingly more straightforward expressions of regret. He thought I made a mistake apologizing. I thought he missed an opportunity to staunch the bleeding once and for all.

As we began to prepare for the 1996 budget, it became clear that the issue of the government's ability to fund its Old Age Security requirements when the baby boomers begin to retire in 2011 was no longer the concern it had been for me a year earlier. Actually I realized this when reflecting much later on something Scott Clark had said just before putting the 1995 budget to bed: "You haven't just hit your targets here, you've eliminated the deficit." He did not mean, of course, that we would do it in one budget, but that it would be accomplished within a few years. That brought home to me the reality of what we had done. This meant that by 2011 the OAS would no longer be in jeopardy, and the drastic reforms I had envisaged were no longer required, proving once again the healing powers of a virtuous circle.

This did not mean, however, that Canada's pension problems were behind us. Far from it. We were facing the complex task of reforming the Canada Pension Plan (CPP).

When we took office in 1993, we actually had two financial time bombs dropped in our laps: the deficit and the CPP. The big difference between them was not their scale – the unfunded liability of the pension plan was comparable to the national debt. The difference lay in the fact there was virtually no public pressure to face up to the problems of the CPP. Remarkably, many young people had begun to assume that they never would get a government pension, but there were no headlines about a "pension crisis," and even the markets seemed to take little notice. This always amazed me. In a sense, it worked to our advantage. The CPP is jointly run by Ottawa and the provinces. Because I was able to work on the problem with the provincial ministers outside of the full glare of public attention, we were able to focus, to a remarkable degree, on fixing the plan for future generations instead of worrying about how it would all look at the next election.

In 1995, the actuary's report revealed that to maintain the soundness of the CPP, contributions would have to rise from the rate at the time of 5.8 per cent to reach more than 14 per cent of employee income. Even though that amount would have been split between the employee and employer, it was nonetheless staggering. What had happened is that the flaw in the architecture of the CPP, which had been there from the beginning, was finally being fully revealed. When the plan began in the 1960s, there were eight workers for every one of pensionable age. But then, as Canada's baby boomers grew older and the demographic bulge moved upward, that ratio began to change – to five to one when we took office and barrelling toward three to one in the early decades of the twenty-first century. The CPP was never a savings plan; there was never some big pool of money out there to pay the pensions, as you would have with most company pension plans. The CPP was based on the idea that today's pensioners would have their stipends paid out of the contributions of today's workers. The problem was, as the ratio of pensioners to workers shifted, the ability of the workers to sustain the burden was increasingly compromised. This also raised an issue of fairness between generations. Workers paying big CPP premiums in the late twentieth and early twenty-first centuries might find that by the time they were ready to retire, the system was collapsing and there was little or no pension for them.

That was looking at it from the point of view of the ordinary citizen. But from the point of view of the federal government, the looming crisis in the CPP posed an additional challenge. At some point, the markets would clue into the fact that this was a fiscal disaster in the making. Canada's baby boomers were going to begin retiring in 2011, which was not that far off. If we reached 2011 with large numbers of Canadians potentially falling into financial distress because the CPP had failed them, I knew that the federal government would be on the hook through Old Age Security and the Guaranteed Income Supplement, which are funded by Ottawa alone. Where would the money come from? The possibility that the demand for pensions would go straight to the general revenues of the federal government was real. Even the perception that they might was going to make Canada seem even more suspect financially than it already was, with all that entailed. In that sense, getting the CPP back on track was not just about pensions, it was about maintaining the solvency of the country.

The reform of the CPP was unusually complex because the CPP is jointly administered with the provinces, as I mentioned earlier. Changes to the way it is managed need the approval not only of the federal government but also of two-thirds of the provinces containing two-thirds of the Canadian population. That includes Quebec, even though Quebec has its own pension plan, in part because it generally follows the same principles in running its plan. Of course, all the provinces saw the problem with sustaining the pension system in the long term, but they also came at it from very different ideological viewpoints. Resolving the problem would need either an increase in payments or a decrease in benefits, or a combination of the two. While Mike Harris's Ontario Tories could be counted on to resist increases in premiums – which look from some perspectives, but are not, like taxes – the NDP governments out West could be expected to argue just as strongly for maintaining benefits.

Despite their ideological differences, the provincial finance ministers showed their determination to solve the system's problems. The constructive spirit shown by Ontario's Ernie Eves, Alberta's Jim Dinning, Manitoba's Eric Stefanson, New Brunswick's Edmond Blanchard, Newfoundland's Paul Dicks and Saskatchewan's Janice MacKinnon was typical. Dinning's leadership was crucial, because Alberta had been concerned about the CPP for years and even toyed with the idea of creating its own separate pension fund along the lines of Quebec's. Even Quebec's finance minister, Bernard Landry, was prepared to play along. He was the most determined separatist in the Bouchard government and it would not have astonished us had he been pushing another agenda. However, Landry saw that the Quebec Pension Plan (QPP) itself needed reform to be saved, and our process gave his government cover for making some difficult decisions.

By this time, Barry Campbell, a highly respected international lawyer and businessman, had become my parliamentary secretary. Thus I asked David Walker to lead a process of consultation that took him across the country, into small communities as well as large cities. He spoke to pensioners, and actuaries and investment advisers. An important element in the process was that wherever he went, a representative of the province he was in would accompany him. He included the local MPs as well. And of course, senior officials from the Department of Finance were also there every step of the way.

In the end, we reached a consensus that the increase in premiums should be held to 9.9 per cent, and we were able to protect most of the CPP's benefits. At Finance, our approach to pension reform, which required in-depth coordination with provincial officals, was skilfully developed and led by Susan Peterson, the assistant deputy minister responsible for relations with the provinces, and Bob Hamilton.

Munir Sheikh devised the mechanism to ramp up CPP premiums relatively quickly to create a surplus in the fund. The thesis was that the surplus would be invested over time and would generate a second stream of revenue for paying pensions and thus eliminate the need for ever-rising premiums. We believed that working people would accept an increase in premiums if it was coupled with a fundamental reform that would guarantee their future pensions and not just patch up a cranky, leaky old system for a few years. Of course, sound as this idea is in principle, the creation of a cash fund also raised a whole other set of questions, such as how large it should become, how its assets should be invested, and who would manage them. It would defeat the whole enterprise if we just ended up with a large pool of cash that politicians invested according to their inclinations and ambitions (something that was alleged to have happened with Jacques Parizeau and the QPP).

We needed the fund to be managed exclusively in the interests of the pensioners. To that end, part of our plan was to set up the Canada Pension Plan Investment Board, responsible for managing the money in the CPP fund, completely independently from government influence. We gave the board a clear mandate – to maximize the fund's return on investment without taking an undue risk of loss. There were to be no other goals or objectives, no political interference of any kind. The mandate could not have been simpler: do the best job for CPP members.

Years later, the wisdom of this approach has become even more apparent as many other countries have set up "sovereign wealth funds" with their national assets, which all too often are accused of making investments with political motivations that will cost them financially in the long term.

A word about sovereign wealth funds. They have become a huge issue in the last decade, which has seen many new state-owned or state-controlled funds roaming the world searching out investment opportunities. Already we are seeing strong reactions to these entities and talk of legislation to control their activities.

I believe that governments around the world – when they act – should establish a very clear line of demarcation between funds that are primarily agents of government policy and funds that are pure return seekers. I expect that governments will begin to put restrictions on those that fall into the first category, but I hope they will largely exempt funds in the second group. It will be essential for the Canada Pension Plan to be seen as independent of government control. And the best way to be seen as independent is to be genuinely independent.

There is, however, one area linked to CPP reform where I feel we should have been able to do more. Disability costs had increased sharply in the late 1980s and early 1990s, though we had begun to bring them under control by the time CPP reform was on the table. Some of the provinces felt that disability benefits should be withdrawn completely from the CPP, as one way of reducing the costs of the pension plan. My position was that we were coming at this from the wrong angle. It is wrong, I argued, for a country as rich as Canada not to have a comprehensive system of support for the disabled.

I grew up in the era when polio's ravages were a part of everyday life. For my generation of children there were reminders of the toll the disease had taken: boys and girls in class in leg braces or with withered arms. Later, I had some experience of the difficulties the families of the disabled face; Sheila's nephew Douglas is confined to a wheelchair. Then, when I was finance minister, Terrie would often bring her brother Stephen, who is handicapped, with her to work when he was visiting town, and he became an important part of everybody's life.

We needed back then – and need now – a joint federal-provincial program that ensures as much as possible a level playing field across the country for the disabled, providing enhanced benefits and improved services to everyone who needs them. Only if that were implemented could I have supported re-examining the relationship between disability benefits and the CPP, and I felt that the national disability program had to be in place first. Unfortunately time did not allow for this to happen, and it is one of the greatest regrets of my life that we were not able to make more progress toward a truly national disability program built by both orders of government. It's time to revive that idea and do the job properly.

In retrospect, it may seem strange that at a time when the federal government was cutting transfers to the provinces and federal-provincial relations, as a result, were severely strained, we were able to work together so constructively on the CPP. We were able to do so for two reasons. First, because the CPP is a joint federal-provincial program, and neither the provinces nor Ottawa were in a position to blame the other if the system were to fail. It was, perhaps, to para-phrase Benjamin Franklin, a case of finance ministers hanging together or hanging separately.

That being said, I believe there was an even deeper reason, one that the cynics may find difficult to accept. Quite simply, the finance ministers of that era, all wrestling with inherited deficits of one kind or another, were not prepared to transmit the consequences of the broken retirement system on to subsequent generations. In short, we were determined to do the right thing, and we did.

As I write, the last actuarial report on the CPP says it is now on a sound footing looking forward seventy-five years – the furthest out that actuaries are able to project. We had succeeded in saving the pension system, and we are one of just two G7 countries to have done so.

CHAPTER THIRTEEN

Tipping the Balance

Mitchell Sharp, a man with generations of political experience, once remarked to me that I had become the most powerful finance minister ever. Too powerful in his view. Perhaps, but if so, this was a result of the desperate fiscal situation in which we found ourselves. In any event, this picture of my influence overlooked the fact that in one crucial area of government policy in which I was deeply interested, my role in the government's decision making was relatively limited. That was the province of Quebec.

First of all, there was the matter of party politics. In the rest of the country, the era where a single individual can dominate the organization had long since passed. As a result, with a few notable exceptions, the party outside Quebec settled into a more normal phase after the 1990 leadership race, and my supporters continued to play significant roles as riding or provincial executives, candidates, and organizers. In Quebec, it was different. There, all power flows from the Quebec lieutenant, who is named by the prime minister; and in Quebec, the bitterness over the leadership race never ended. Thus I had no involvement with the party organization in Quebec whatsoever, nor did those who had supported me. While I got along well with André Ouellet and Marcel Massé, many of the party's leading organizers in Quebec didn't much like me and I didn't much like them. My friends in the party were on the outs and frankly had no interest in working their way in.

When I first became minister of finance, I was also assigned responsibility for Quebec's regional development agency. My task there was fairly specific, however. With the help of my Quebec assistant, Benoit Labonté, who later went on to become mayor of Montreal's Ville-Marie, I set about cleaning up the mishmash of programs that previously existed, refocusing them on small and medium-sized businesses. I also added a component of "social economy," supporting the Regroupement économique et social du Sud-Ouest (RESO). This is a wonderful organization founded by Nancy Neamtan in Montreal, which helps lift people out of poverty through sound entrepreneurship and the development of business skills. I was very enthusiastic about this element of my job as regional development minister. However, being in charge of a spending department was clearly a conflict of interest as I set about attacking the deficit, and the prime minister eventually decided to relieve me of those responsibilities.

Party politics aside, it was not altogether surprising that I was kept at a distance from the Quebec file. Jean Chrétien was the senior minister from Quebec in every respect and had devoted a considerable portion of his career to the management of Canada's relationship with his home province. Moreover, he and I had differed deeply in our approach to Meech Lake and to Quebec more generally.

In my view, as someone who has lived in Quebec for forty years, a commitment to Quebec and a commitment to Canada are not contradictory; indeed, they reinforce each other. Most of the French-speaking Quebecers I know are both Quebec nationalists and Canadian nationalists, and no one should be offended by that. I have always believed that the more confident the rest of Canada feels about itself and the more confident Quebec feels about itself, the more confident each will feel about their relationship.

On the one hand, I believe that if Canadians are going to compete in the world, they will need world-class post-secondary education and national social programs in health care and child care. The federal spending power that is essential to building these programs, which are under provincial jurisdiction, was confirmed in 1999 when our government signed an agreement on the social union with the provinces. On the other hand, I believe our federation is "asymmetrical" in the sense that the provinces have their distinct needs and aspirations that should be recognized. This is especially true of Quebec, with its unique challenge as a province with a majority French-speaking population in the midst of English-speaking North America.

The idea of recognizing the particular needs of individual provinces is nothing new. Pierre Trudeau himself acknowledged this when he agreed to the so-called "Cullen-Couture agreement" giving Quebec a role in selecting immigrants to the province. But asymmetry has also been recognized in other ways for other parts of the country. The Auto Pact, for example, which my father and Lester B. Pearson signed, was very much an agreement aimed at sustaining automobile manufacturing, which existed primarily in Ontario. Similarly, when I was minister of finance, at the suggestion of then National Resources Minister Anne McLellan, we enacted specific tax changes to kick-start development of the oil sands, which existed only in Alberta and now in Saskatchewan.

For me, this was a very personal issue. My father, half-Irish and half-French Canadian, was raised in French. I grew up in the mid-dling space between the "two nations," speaking English at home but being educated in French as a boy because of the depth of my father's feelings about his francophone roots. When Sheila and I moved to Montreal as young people, it gave me a tremendous opportunity to reconnect with this francophone heritage in the midst of the flowering of the Quiet Revolution. As much as I shared the excitement of that period, for me, it was not only about Quebecers but about French Canadians across Canada taking control of their collective destiny. Naturally, given my upbringing, I was a fervent supporter of bilingualism. I remember the sadness I felt shortly after I was elected as an MP for Montreal when I was invited to speak at "Le Club Richelieu" in Windsor. These were the sons of the French Canadians with whom my father and I had picnicked with when I

was a boy in Belle River, St. Joachim, and Pointes-aux-Roches. I
began my speech in French only to be interrupted by the chairman
after about five minutes. "Mr. Martin, would you mind switching
to English?" he asked. "Many of us here don't understand that
much French."

I do not have many regrets about my political career, but one of
them is that I was not able to contribute more to addressing the mutual
incomprehension between many among our anglophone and francophone populations. It pains me that the relationship between
multiculturalism, which I fervently believe in, and its roots in the confederation of the two founding nations, is so widely misunderstood.
Confederation was born out of the union of two peoples and two
religions, English and French, Protestant and Catholic, historically
perpetually at war with each other. It was the necessity of accom-
modating each other that created the space for multiculturalism, which
is more than the tolerance of others; it embodies mutual respect and a
recognition of the richness each wave of newcomers brings. Our
society is always changing as a result. Thank heavens we have not been
afflicted with some of the agonies that have troubled so many
European countries in integrating new populations in the last few
decades. In this country, true multiculturalism is a source of pride, and
that fact is rooted firmly in our heritage – a heritage that includes the
Aboriginal peoples of the continent.

My deliberate exclusion from the Quebec file by Jean Chrétien
was not entirely a bad thing. It allowed me to focus on Finance, on
issues where my weight could be fully felt, and where the prime minister and I could find a *modus vivendi*. Having the two of us working
on the Quebec file was, to be frank, a formula for perpetual conflict,
which would not have helped me in the principal task I had before
me. I had few Quebec responsibilities and had neither the time nor
the desire to take on any more. Still, with the election of a Péquiste
government under the sovereigntist hard-liner Jacques Parizeau in
1994, everyone knew that it would not be long before there would
be another referendum on Quebec sovereignty. As a Quebecer and a

Canadian, I was naturally going to be involved in the referendum campaign. And as minister of finance, I had clear responsibilities.

One of the strongest arguments against separation had always been economic. Canada's feeble economic performance in the late 1980s and early 1990s, however, combined with Ottawa's fiscal crisis, had greatly undermined the force of that argument. The 1995 budget had been a significant element in reviving the economic argument as an effective weapon for federalists. And of course, the weaker the separatist cause became, the better off Canada, and indeed Quebec itself, would be fiscally and economically. Shortly after the 1995 budget, I gave a speech in New York aimed at reassuring investors that a sovereigntist victory was unlikely. I hoped to avoid having to pay a premium on our borrowing because of market fears of a "yes" victory.

The "no" side in the fall 1995 referendum was by law led by provincial politicians, which put those of us in Ottawa in a secondary role, at least officially. Nonetheless, like many federal politicians from Quebec, I was in demand in the province from the moment the campaign got underway. I gave several dozen speeches, and my message was well received. I talked, as others did, of the value of the Canadian passport and of Canada's social safety network of pensions and old age benefits. More specifically, as minister of finance, I emphasized that separation, if it ever came, would come at a very severe financial and economic cost.

I also gave one major campaign address that did not go over so well. In a speech to a business audience in Quebec City, I attacked the separatist claim that trade had become internationalized and that the North American Free Trade Agreement (NAFTA) would guarantee Quebec continued access to its traditional markets in the United States as well as in the rest of Canada. I said three things. First, that separation was separation, and there was absolutely no guarantee that Quebec would be allowed to join NAFTA as a separate country. Second, that entry into NAFTA would be subject to a new negotiation with the United States and ultimately a Canadian veto. And third, that anyone who thought that NAFTA was sufficient to assure Quebec of the existing level of access to the Canadian market was deluded. You only had to look at the softwood lumber dispute between Canada and the United States to understand that being in NAFTA was one thing, and that being part of a unified country was quite another when it came to trade. Included in the speech were a few lines to the effect that separation would threaten 90 per cent of Quebec's exports as well as close to a million jobs.

There is a difference, of course, between having your job threatened and actually losing it. But it was, in retrospect, a mistake to assume that such a nuance would stand up in the whirlwind of a referendum campaign. Parizeau had a heyday, immediately picking up on what I said, translating it into "Martin says a million jobs will be lost." By the time I was able to react publicly, Parizeau had succeeded in spinning the Quebec as well as the national media and turning my intervention into a gaffe that dominated the news through a cycle of a day or two.

What really turned the campaign upside down, and gave the sovereigntists their best shot ever at winning a referendum, was Jacques Parizeau's decision to step back and allow Lucien Bouchard to become the de facto leader of the "yes" campaign. Bouchard was a much more appealing figure than Parizeau, and he had achieved a kind of secular sainthood among some Quebecers after his near-death encounter with what was known as a "flesh-eating disease." I personally believe as well that he embodied Quebec's disappointment at the rejection of the Meech Lake Accord. Whereas Parizeau represented a leap in the dark, which was the federalists' greatest weapon, Bouchard represented the pain of rejection, which was the sovereigntists' greatest strength.

It has become part of the mythology of the referendum that the government did not order the development of a complete set of contingency plans in case the referendum was lost out of fear that they might leak and affect the result. Whatever was happening at the PMO and the PCO – and I was not privy to that – at Finance we definitely were preparing for the worst. From early on in the referendum campaign, the department was working with the Bank of Canada on what had to be done to steady the markets the day after the referendum. About ten days before the vote, I got a call from David Dodge. He told me that it was more important for the minister of finance to be back at work in Ottawa, while at the same time preparing to react to anything that might hit us, than to remain out on the campaign trail. In particular, he was very concerned about a potential run on Canadian financial institutions, a number of which had very significant exposure in Quebec. If something like that started to happen, and it could happen any day, the government might have to react in a matter of hours – something that it would be difficult for me to effect if I was beating the bushes somewhere up the Saguenay. A run on a commercial bank, for example, would require the Bank of Canada to inject liquidity into the system. But the government might also have to organize a consortium of banks to backstop any institution in trouble. David felt strongly that a calm reassurance from the minister of finance that the system was sound could be critical in preventing panic from spreading across the system.

We also had significant concerns about the government's own balance sheet. The potential scenario was much worse than Canadians, and even most outside experts, ever realized. Indeed, had the markets understood how dicey the situation was, in all likelihood we would have experienced major problems in the latter part of the referendum campaign before the result was even known. Remember that we were still in the first year of the fiscal plan laid out in the 1995 budget and it was less than a year since the Mexican peso crisis. The reason for our vulnerability was associated with our huge debt but was quite technical, which may explain how it escaped notice at the time and since. Most of Canada's debt in this period was in short-term instruments, which meant that we were exposed to a very rapid run-up in interest rates. To make matters worse, by coincidence, there was a "bunching up" of these loans coming due, and needing to be renewed, within the weeks immediately after the referendum. That meant we could be forced to refinance a large portion of our debt at the worst possible moment. In the view of David Dodge and Don Drummond, a "yes" vote in the referendum could very quickly result in a liquidity crisis with huge downward pressure on the dollar and upward pressure on interest rates. Don estimated that if there were an "investors' strike" – that is, a situation in which the markets would not lend to us at anything but preposterously high rates – the government could actually run out of cash by mid-December and be unable to pay public servants or issue cheques to seniors. It was a disaster scenario and it was not at all difficult to imagine.

As bitterly as we had complained about the *Wall Street Journal* describing us as a Third World country in terms of our fiscal situation, the truth is that there was a very real danger that we might have to throw ourselves at the feet of the International Monetary Fund (IMF), if that became our only resort, in the case of a referendum loss. The department was actively considering what kind of approach it would make to the IMF if that became our only resort. Of course, even we did not understand how quickly and deeply we would have been plunged into a post-referendum crisis in the case of a "yes" vote. Finance officials had heard rumours that the Quebec's Caisse de dépôt – the fund that manages the Quebec equivalent of the Canada Pension Plan – was buying up Canadian dollars, presumably on the instruction of the Quebec government, to give itself as much flexibility as possible in anticipation of an early declaration of independence. It was only later that we learned that Jacques Parizeau had prerecorded a televised statement that would have launched the province on a fast track to independence.

On referendum night, I could barely stand to watch the results come in on the television we had specially set up in the Department of Finance for the occasion. Terrie and David Dodge would poke their heads in my office from time to time to let me know how it was going. Mid-evening, as the results trickled in and the outcome teeter-tottered back and forth, David went to a meeting at the PCO to discuss plans for the next day. Whether there was a contingency plan at the centre or not, for our part, we had a thick binder, gaming out every possible outcome and eventuality.

Thank heavens, I did not have to go out that night and try to stem an economic and fiscal crisis. The "no" side won by a margin of 50.58 per cent to 49.42 per cent – saved by a margin of fifty-four thousand votes. But the close call left a deep mark on all of us. After the referendum, we accelerated the program of rolling much more of our debt into longer term instruments. We paid a premium for doing so, but it also allowed us to sleep more peacefully following the scare we had experienced in October 1995.

After the referendum, given the agonizingly close results, the government had to respond in some way. Ironically – and this has largely been forgotten with the passage of time – Jean Chrétien's initial response was to enact many of the elements of the Meech Lake Accord. He ensured that Parliament belatedly recognized Quebec as a "distinct society" and adopted a statute that gave the regions, including Quebec, a veto over major constitutional change. He also offered to hand over skills training to exclusive jurisdictions (something I was concerned about as finance minister because I felt it limited the federal government's ability to ensure job mobility). The entire package was no more than an echo of the Meech Lake Accord because it was done by federal statute and not embedded directly in the Constitution, which is part of the reason it has subsequently been forgotten. It has also been forgotten, I believe, because much of what seemed so controversial in the late 1980s had become obvious common sense in the aftermath of the referendum.

Following the referendum, the prime minister decided that the rules needed to be set for what many feared could become a never-ending series of such events – the "neverendum," as it was called. I fully agreed with him that it was intolerable for the sovereigntists to be permitted to set the rules of the game as if no one else had a legitimate stake. The question in the 1995 referendum was, if possible, even fuzzier than the question fifteen years earlier. It was outrageous to think that a PQ government might try to effect separation with a

razor-thin mandate on a question whose precise meaning even constitutional lawyers had trouble figuring out.

As a Quebecer myself, I felt strongly that the government of
Quebec had no right to tear my province out of my country on an
unclear question with an uncertain mandate. For all those reasons, I
completely agreed with Jean Chrétien's decision to refer the issue to
the Supreme Court of Canada in 1996. Some of those most closely
associated with me in Quebec, notably Dennis Dawson, felt very differently about the federal government's attempt to impose clarity for
future referendums. He spoke out against it in public, as was his right,
which the Chrétien people regarded as an act of defiance related to
our rivalry over the leadership. It was not, but so be it.

Where Jean Chrétien and I parted ways was not on the question
of the Supreme Court reference but on whether it was wise to have
Parliament legislate on the matter *after* the court's very strong judgment in 1998 laying out the requirements necessary for separation in
response to the government reference. My feeling was that the
Supreme Court judgment, with its reliance on international as well
as Canadian law, supplied federalists with a more compelling case
than any piece of federal legislation, which might appear to be just
another volley in the continuing exchange between sovereigntists in
Quebec City and federalists in Ottawa. The argument the court made
that sovereignty was not something that could simply be grasped or
proclaimed by the government of Quebec but would have to be
granted by the international community, of which Canada was an
important part, was incredibly powerful in Quebec. It constituted
the high ground from which we as federalists were best positioned to
fight. My concern was that the Clarity Act advocated by the prime
minister would rob the Supreme Court judgment of some of its
authoritative power. That being said, I agreed that clarity was an
absolute requirement for the future. And so, once the cabinet decision was made to proceed with legislation, I supported it fully.

CHAPTER FOURTEEN

Into the Virtuous Circle

During my post-budget tour of the financial capitals after the 1994 budget, I gave a speech in New York, as is the custom for Canadian finance ministers. Afterwards, Jim Wolfensohn invited me up to his office high in a tower near Wall Street. Jim and I had been good friend for decades. Even before I joined Power Corporation in the 1960s, he had been recruited by Maurice Strong to be chairman of Power's Australian subsidiary, and that's how we got to knew each other. His career as an investment banker took him first to Britain and eventually to the United States. He would later become the president of the World Bank – one of the ablest to ever hold that position. But at the time, he was running an investment firm along with his partner, Paul Volcker.

Volcker had been chairman of the Federal Reserve Bank in the 1980s and had wrestled inflation to the mat by jacking up interest rates to unprecedented levels. In fact, it was thanks to Volcker that interest rates hit 22 per cent back in 1981, the day Ladi Pathy and I bought Canada Steamship Lines. Needless to say, the memory of this fact crossed my mind as we shook hands. Volcker is a towering man who looked all the more imposing looming over Terrie, who just clears five feet in heels. At the time, Bill Clinton was early in his presidency and deeply engaged in his own struggle to combat the deficit, which turned out to be one of his great accomplishments as president. Volcker seized the opportunity to impress on me some of his thoughts about what had been going wrong in the industrialized world.

His central point was that fiscal and monetary policy had been at odds with each other. Fiscal policy refers to the way governments try to manage the economy by changing taxes, spending, or borrowing. Monetary policy refers to the actions of central banks – such as the Bank of Canada – to manage the economy by changing the money supply. When they go hand in hand, fiscal and monetary policy can be powerful tools. When they work at cross-purposes, they can cancel each other out – or worse, they can have unintended negative effects. This had been my precise concern when I decided not to renew John Crow's term as governor of the Bank of Canada. Crow was inflexible in pursuing his own monetary policy, and appeared to feel he did not need to take account of the government's fiscal policy. Volcker argued that the way out of our economic doldrums was to bring fiscal and monetary policy back into concert. If governments could get control of their deficits, there would be less inflationary pressure in the economy and that would allow central banks to ease interest rates. Although he didn't use the phrase, he did speak to the concept of a *virtuous circle*, as officials at Finance called it, which could emerge if we got ourselves out of the *vicious circle* of bigger deficits and higher interest rates. In other words, just as the negative features of our existing economic practices built on one another, if we could turn the momentum around, it would be the positive elements that would multiply.

I really believed in the virtuous circle: completely. My experience in business was that what made an economy go or not go was interest rates more than taxation. If you are going to make an investment, what you have to know is whether you are going to make a profit. If you have to pay taxes on that profit, of course you would rather have them lower than higher. But if you can't make a profit, or you can't expand due to high interest rates, then the level of taxation isn't going to be your main concern. That's why I believed deficit elimination should come before tax cuts. My fundamental aim was to get our balance sheet in shape in order to keep our interest rates low.

I have always been an optimist about Canada, and in private conversations, I began to argue that if we stuck to our policies, Canada was on the threshold of an economic "Golden Age." I really believed that to be true but followed Terrie's advice never to say that in public, out of concern that it might strike some people as a less-than-sober attitude at a time when we were still struggling to eliminate the deficit. Then, one day, in an interview the forbidden phrase slipped out. Of course, it made headlines and evoked a furious response from columnists and editorials, accusing me of overreaching. It also evoked a furious response from Terrie. Still, in retrospect we were at the beginning of a Golden Age, the second-longest period of growth in Canadian history and the longest sequence of budget surpluses ever.

Even I was astounded, however, at how quickly it all happened. After the 1995 budget, interest rates fell faster than anyone expected, which made it less costly to service the debt and easier to meet our fiscal targets. As investors saw that we were serious about meeting – and soon exceeding – those targets, it took a further premium off interest rates, which in turn made it easier for us to restructure our debt. Lower interest rates also made it easier for Canadian businesses and consumers to borrow money. Moreover, the Canadian economy was showing signs of having completed its sometimes-painful adaptation to the era of North American free trade. If any one of these factors had been missing, the virtuous circle might never have asserted itself – or at least it wouldn't have spun us so quickly out of the mess we had been in.

Somewhat mysteriously, the Canadian dollar remained unacceptably low. That made it easier for Canadian industries to sell their products abroad but understated our national wealth and weakened the incentive for Canadian business to invest in new capital equipment. I learned very early on as finance minister never, ever to comment on the dollar, even if I was concerned about it. The wrong note from me could easily upset the markets. On the other hand, David Dodge and I were convinced that the international investor community did not understand how effectively we had turned around our fiscal situation. On one occasion, David and I went down to Wall Street to talk up the dollar. As we emerged from the last meeting of the day, there were camera crews on the street outside and I steeled myself for what would come next. As was David's habit, as soon as we cleared the building, he pulled out his pipe and lit up. I don't remember precisely what I said when we were questioned by the reporters there, but I do remember being concerned that I might have overstepped the bounds in commenting on the dollar. I needn't have worried. The controversy the next day was all about whether it was appropriate for the minister of finance to be seen in public in the company of a smoker!

I knew economic growth alone would carry us a long way toward reducing the size of our debt in relation to the size of our economy: what is called the debt-to-GDP ratio. After all, by definition, it can be improved either by reducing debt or by increasing growth. I also wanted to reduce our interest payments on the debt, however, which at this time made up the biggest single category of spending for the federal government – more than health care, education, defence, or anything else. In fact, interest payments were eating up more than one-third of the federal budget every year! I also wanted to reduce the amount of Canadian debt held by foreigners. There was only one way to do both: chop away at the debt in absolute terms – paying it down, in other words. Once again, it was no surprise to me that this happened, only that it happened as quickly as it did.

As I write these words, compared to the early 1990s when I became finance minister, our debt-to-GDP ratio is below 30 per cent compared to 71 per cent at its peak, government interest costs are 15 cents compared to 36 cents on the dollar, and Canadian debt held by foreigners is 7 per cent compared to 44 per cent of GDP.

Still, I don't want to make it sound as if this positive momentum was entirely self-sustaining. Absolutely not. One of the most fundamental decisions we made in these years was what came to be called the "no deficit rule," which sometimes became a source of tension between me and other ministers, and between me and Jean Chrétien –

who had other priorities, as a prime minister must. As I've said before, economic and fiscal forecasts are often unreliable because they never foresee the unforeseen, and the unforeseen is a feature of economic life as it is of life in general. Whoever first announced that it is tough to make a prediction, especially about the future, had it right. Forecasts are not very robust in the face of surprising events, whether positive or negative. Furthermore, under the previous Tory government, the forecasts were usually overly optimistic. The fact is that private sector economists can and do change their forecasts every quarter, or even more frequently as new information comes in, while the government reveals its projections in the budget and then has them hanging out for the world to see for more than a year before the final numbers are known. For private sector economists, there are almost no consequences for getting a forecast wrong, or for changing it every quarter. For governments the consequences can be huge.

I was determined that once we reached a balanced budget we would never again in my time fall into deficit. I believed this was the only way to maintain our credibility. What that meant was that if we ever got a forecast wrong, it was going to be wrong on the upside – meaning we would come in with a larger surplus – not on the downside, where we would risk falling back into deficit. If the economy performed worse than expected, then we had the built-in contingency reserve to protect our forecast; if it performed better, then we would run a surplus, which could be used in part to pay down more debt and reduce the interest costs for next year. More virtuous circle.

It is important to understand that the no-deficit rule was a sharp break with tradition. In the postwar years, many economists argued that you did not need to be in the black every year, as long as budgets were balanced over the course of the economic cycle, so that deficits during slumps would be paid off with surpluses in good years. Whatever the economic rationale for that approach, it didn't work in the real world of politicians. Once you break the spell – once governments find they can get away with borrowing instead of taxing to pay the bills – it is almost impossibly tempting for politicians to do it again and again until the debt is out of control. How many times have politicians talked about the three-year cycle as the time period to climb out of deficit, only to extend the cycle when the moment of truth arrives. The fact is, in most instances, going into deficit is simply a sign of bad fiscal management, the proverbial canary in the coalmine.

We needed to do things differently for two very important reasons. First, the debt we had built up over so many years left us vulnerable to a financial crisis that could plunge us into a catastrophic downward spiral that might take decades from which to recover. Our debt was equivalent to 70 per cent of our annual gross domestic product! The no-deficit rule enabled me as finance minister to set a goal of getting the ratio of debt-to-GDP down to 30 per cent. Ralph Goodale, who succeeded me in that role when I was prime minister, went even further, setting the target at 25 per cent.

The second reason for the no-deficit rule was a question of fairness among generations. If the government was borrowing to build infrastructure that would benefit the generations to come, that would not be a problem. As individuals, we borrow to buy a house knowing that we will be able to live in it for many years. But in the decades before I became finance minister, the federal government had been borrowing each and every year just to pay its current bills. That's like having $40,000 in take-home pay but spending $50,000 and making up the difference by adding $10,000 a year to the Visa bill. You'd better win the lottery, because otherwise you are on your way to bankruptcy. When governments do this – running up debt to pay for current consumption – it is like asking their children and grandchildren to pay their grocery bills. That just isn't fair.

This made sense to me, but I did not realize how much it would resonate with others until I found myself talking with a group of seniors after the 1995 budget. One lady really took me to task over spending cuts, and the audience was completely with her until I answered her off the cuff by saying, "Ma'am, all you're telling me is that your grandchildren should pay for your lifestyle. Don't you think you owe them more than that?" The mood in the room instantly changed. I had won them over, and I used that argument a lot from then on.

Was I saying then, or am I saying now, that a deficit should never be permissible? No, I am not. If Canada ever finds itself in a deep recession, balancing the budget by hiking taxes could make a bad situation worse. But what is unacceptable is to overspend or to cut taxes too much out of political expediency when times are good. That destroys the government's room for manoeuvre when the inevitable economic slowdown occurs and threatens to throw the country back into the bad old cycle of unremitting deficits and growing debt. As I write, I fear that that may well be precisely what the Harper government is close to doing.

Am I saying that governments should never cut taxes? Of course not. Once we had eliminated the deficit and set the debt on an inexorable downward track, I brought in the largest tax cuts in Canadian history. But cutting taxes must be weighed against our needs for health care, education, research, child care, and so many other services we depend on. Furthermore, nothing could be more unfair than making our children, already saddled with debt service costs that are properly ours, suffer tax increases in the future to pay for the tax cuts we enjoy today. Again, I fear that is precisely what the Harper government has done.

The business community, here and abroad, has long contended that centre-right governments are better fiscal managers than centre-left governments. Historically, in Canada, it has actually been the reverse, as it has in the United States. This comparison is even worse, I fear, when instead of a centre-right government we have a government that is very far to the right.

The Conservatives argue, in effect, that a federal government without fiscal elbow room is a federal government that cannot spend foolishly – especially in areas of provincial jurisdiction. What nonsense! A federal government that threatens to tip back into deficit weakens the whole country, at every level of jurisdiction. It is the strength of the federal government's balance sheet that affects

Canada's interest rates – rates that in turn affect every province, every business, and every individual. And it is only the federal government that has the geographical reach to make sure that we have the money to ensure we are healthy, educated, and well cared for across the land, whether our particular region is in a boom or a bust or somewhere in between.

From my perspective, one of the most important aspects of the no-deficit rule was that it implanted in the public's mind the need for a sound fiscal policy so that politicians would pay a price at the polls if they started to stray. In fact, the growing public support for the no-deficit rule was crucial to our success. You only need to look south of the border to see what happens if the public does not impose this discipline on the politicians: in the United States, the mighty efforts of the 1990s to overcome the deficit hangover from the 1980s were quickly squandered in the first years of this century.

When we made the no-deficit rule, it was beyond our wildest imagination that we would later be criticized for our cautious approach. But by the late 1990s, there were frequent complaints about the regularity with which we outperformed our budget predictions. Jean Chrétien was one of those critics, truth be known. This led to one of the few light-hearted elements in our relationship. Every year, he would make a bet with me that we would end up doing better than I predicted in the budget, and year after year he was right. Eventually he claimed that I owed him $700. I guess I do.

As I was preparing the 1998 budget, I recall telling the prime minister that I expected that the fiscal year 1997–98 would be the one in which we eliminated the deficit, and I hoped to be able to announce as much when the final numbers came out, which would not happen until the fall. He persuaded me against my better judgment to make the announcement in the February 1998 budget instead, months earlier than I planned. That left me and my officials at Finance with the task of how to reveal our achievement to the public. We worked on all sorts of formulations. Finally, Larry Hagen, who was writing the budget speech, suggested: "We will balance the budget next year.

We will balance the budget the year after that. And we will balance the budget this year." It had a declaratory ring, and yet by leaving the current year to the last, it hinted at my own sense of caution. Nonetheless, I sweated bullets over whether it would turn out as we hoped till the revised numbers started rolling in that fall, making good on my promise.

The no-deficit rule, plus some of the structural changes we put in place in the 1995 budget, created a cultural change in Ottawa. It became almost universally accepted that no new spending could be launched outside the rigid fiscal framework we had laid down in our budgets. Although the problem never entirely went away, I worried less and less about ministers trying to go round my back to the prime minister to plead for new spending. One potential problem that did arise was the prime minister's commitment in the 1997 election to the "fifty-fifty formula." The formula was that for every dollar in surplus that arose in the future, fifty cents would go to new spending and the other fifty cents would be devoted to a combination of tax relief and deficit reduction. I had no desire to have a straitjacket put on me as finance minister in this way. However, Jean Chrétien was probably the shrewder politician here. The promise conveyed the gist of his priorities to the public. Eventually I came to like the communications value of the commitment, but I didn't like the balance it struck. In my government, Ralph Goodale altered the rule to allocate equal shares to new spending, tax cuts, and debt reduction.

As we emerged from the era of deficits in the late 1990s and found ourselves entering a world of surpluses, we confronted a new problem, which was the pent-up demand from a governmental system that had been restrained for so long. Almost every department of government could naturally make a case – and often a good one – for restoring some of the programs that had been cut back or cancelled. The provinces had their own set of demands emerging from a combination of their own problems and the cuts we had made to the CHST. At the same time, many businesspeople and economists, not to mention the Reform Party, were arguing that our tax structure was out of whack compared with that of our competitors. For my part, as discussed earlier, I felt it was vital to make headway in paying down our debt because the costs of servicing it were so colossal.

In this environment, it would have been easy on the spending side to spread a little pixie dust in every direction (a budgetary approach favoured by my successors in the Conservative Party) without creating the critical mass in any single area to make a noticeable difference in the lives of Canadians. I wanted to make sure that what funds we were able to free up for new spending were sufficiently concentrated to make a difference, and that each budget had a clear theme that the public could understand, even if it did try to address other needs as well. While there were many things that could be done with our new-found surpluses, nothing was more important in my view than helping Canadians to build up their knowledge and skills. Education is both a social and economic program. In fact it is the foundation for a country's success in both areas. Although we specifically framed the 1998 budget around education, we began to nurture this theme as early as 1995. Over several years, our aim was to address the issue of education at every point in the continuum, from early childhood learning through student debt to parents' savings for their kids' university education, scholarships once they get there, and assistance for the nation's research institutions.

I was lucky that I was able to rally a fair degree of consensus around the idea of a knowledge agenda at the time. David Dodge, Scott Clark, who succeeded Dodge as deputy minister, and the Department of Finance were on board, as were Terrie, Elly, David Herle, and Kevin Lynch, then the deputy minister at Industry. All of us recognized a growing public thirst to rebuild our educational system from top to bottom. At the PMO, Chaviva Hošek and Eddie Goldenberg were also enthusiastic. We had great support from the universities and teaching hospitals, as would be expected. Further, this was an area where we were able to forge a consensus with the provinces. It is only in retrospect that it seems strange to me that an initiative of this kind should have been led by the federal Department of Finance. The truth is that within a couple of years of the 1993 election, we had pretty much got accustomed to dominating most policy debates (with the exception of Quebec). It may have seemed peculiar to Mitchell Sharp, but it didn't to me.

We took the first step on this agenda in early 1996. Although we had not yet eliminated the deficit, we had done better than we had hoped. There was some money left over even after putting our contingency reserve toward paying down debt. The department, led by Scott Clark, came up with the idea of the Canadian Foundation for Innovation (CFI). It was clear to us that Canada was slipping badly on the international intellectual table because of the stresses on our great research institutions, which included, of course, our own cutbacks in both direct spending and transfers to the provinces. Although we did have some niches of excellence, they were dwindling. We didn't have adequate facilities for cutting-edge work in biology, genetics, physics, chemistry, and geology; and increasingly we were having trouble retaining the top brains in these fields, much less attracting new ones.

This issue really hit home for me, quite literally, at the insistence of my close friend Brian Aune. Shortly after the 1995 budget, he organized a meeting at my home of some of Canada's leading medical researchers, including Dr. David Mulder of McGill University, where they explained to me the degree to which Canada's best and brightest were leaving the country.

Paul Davenport of the University of Western Ontario and his fellow presidents from the major research universities also made this urgent point with me at a meeting in Ottawa. Something had to be done.

My view was there was simply no reason why the universities of Toronto or Montreal or any one of our major universities should not take their place alongside Harvard or Cambridge, to be counted among the great universities of the world, or that smaller institutions such as the University of Waterloo, for example, should not be recognized alongside M.I.T for their international-class excellence in research and technology.

One of our concerns was to make sure that however we spent the money, it would not create continuing pressures on the budget year after year. The idea behind the CFI was to make a one-off contribution (which could be topped up from time to time, as circumstances permitted) to an arms'-length foundation that would fund state-of-the-art laboratories, equipment, and research. Furthermore, because it would be a foundation whose existence went beyond a single budget cycle, important research would be insulated from the vagaries of year-to-year budget pressures. You can't cut research spending in one year, increase it the next year, and cut it back again the third year, and hope to build an effective research and development (R&D) program. This approach, which we used again in later budgets to establish other foundations, came under attack by the Auditor General, who argued that the money they received put them beyond parliamentary scrutiny – a criticism I entirely rejected. Parliament voted the money. The foundations are totally transparent in their spending and are always ready to meet with parliamentary committees to discuss what they are doing.

As we began to think about creating the Foundation for Innovation, there were some concerns about provincial reaction. Ottawa had long played the dominant role in funding research and development, but because our plan was to work directly with universities, which are in provincial jurisdiction, I understood we might have an issue. For that reason, I called up Jim Dinning, who was then Alberta's treasurer, and said that I would like to see Ottawa come into the field with some big money. I told him that it would be helpful to me at the federal level if he raised a little ruckus in public and demanded to know why the federal government didn't get off its backside and do something. He said, "I think that's a great idea. We have a similar program in the works, and if you were to move on this, it would make a perfect match." I also spoke to Ernie Eves, the finance minister in Ontario at the time, in a similar vein, and he had much the same attitude. Crucially, when I approached the Quebec universities, I was able to win their support as well, ensuring that the foundation would not be greeted as an intrusion into Quebec's jurisdiction. The CFI was announced just before the 1997 budget; it received $800 million initially and has continued to grow since then. It was the beginning of what proved to be a highly successful series of initiatives over the next decade that reversed Canada's brain-drain and began to restore our potential as an R&D leader in the world.

One of the truly exciting aspects of being minister of finance at this time was that I was able to fund the ideas of those with brilliant insights.

This happened when world-renowned medical researcher Dr. Henry Friesen came to see me for twenty minutes and stayed most of the afternoon. Dr. Friesen was the head of the Medical Research Council of Canada. His idea was to transform the council into the Canadian Institutes of Health Research, a network of thirteen member institutes that specialize in issues ranging from cancer research, aging, and infectious diseases all the way to genetics, nutrition, and Aboriginal people's health. What made it really innovative – and caused us to back it – was that it was a true network, yet was built on the individual strengths of each institution.

Working together they were able to shape a national health research agenda for Canada, turning knowledge into action, commercializing new technologies, and improving the health of Canadians and our country's economy at the same time. Since its beginning, the CIHR has more than doubled the number of researchers it supports, to more than eleven thousand, and it continues to make great progress.

That being said, the politics of reinvesting in education turned out to be more complicated the more ambitious we became. There was a perpetual tug of war between the universities and colleges on the one hand and students on the other about where any new money for higher education should go. Naturally, the educational institutions wanted bricks-and-mortar and operational funding and research grants, while the students wanted direct financial aid.

These were years in which students faced increasingly high tuition fees in many provinces, as well as more and more demanding educational requirements for the best jobs. Student debt was sky-rocketing. The federal government had long been in the business of providing student loans, which complemented the student bursary programs that existed in many provinces. There was big take-up on federal student loans but also a high rate of default, and many complaints from former students in the early years of their careers who felt hobbled by their debts. I had a lot of sympathy for the students. David Brodie, in my office, not long out of university himself, became their biggest champion in the Department of Finance. The most logical way to address their problems would have been to relate the repayment of loans to income after graduation. To put it simply: a newly graduated doctor who went to Africa to work with the poor would not be expected to pay back her loan as quickly as a classmate who quickly established a lucrative practice in downtown Toronto. Unfortunately, many student groups fiercely opposed this kind of reform, and while Lloyd Axworthy floated the idea as part of his social security review, their opposition killed it. In the end, we did negotiate at length with the provinces and enhanced our student loan program with greater funding, but we never made the more fundamental changes that would have made the most sense.

In my view, we also had to do something to help parents and families save for the increasing costs of post-secondary education. One proposal that became highly contentious inside the department was a major enhancement to the Registered Education Savings Plan (RESP). Unlike the Registered Retirement Savings Plan (RRSP) on which it had been loosely modelled, the existing RESP was not generous enough to encourage much take-up by the public. In fact, for that reason alone there was some sentiment in the department for winding it down. Terrie had different ideas. She believed strongly that if we were going to make education a priority, we needed to give ordinary Canadians a stake in our plan. As important as it might be to build labs for researchers and give loans to students to go to university, many middle-class Canadians felt terrible anxieties about their ability to save for their kids' university education. For them, education had often been the key to making their way in the world, and they wanted the same for their children. But the idea of an enhanced RESP was strongly resisted by "tax purists" in the department who generally did not like the tax system to be used as an instrument of social policy. I gave the lead on the file to Don Drummond, one of the most principled and imaginative public servants with whom I have ever worked, and someone who shared the department's negative view of the RESP. It is a tribute to his professionalism and that of the department that despite the fact they resisted the RESP idea on tax policy grounds, once I had made the decision they committed themselves to developing the best mechanism they could. Don had extensive conversations with financial advisers to understand what kind of incentives would be most attractive to encourage parents and grandparents to save for education.

In the end, we announced a greatly enriched RESP, in which the amount that could be put away for each child would be raised, the rules would be made more flexible, and Ottawa would contribute a grant to a child's RESP equalling 20 per cent of the contributions made by parents and grandparents. The program has been a tremendous success – and I've just made the first year's contribution for my grandson, Ethan, and am about to make the first contribution to his new baby brother, Liam.

At 6:00 a.m. on January 23, 1998, the phone at my bedside rang. It was Jim Peterson, by this time the minister responsible for financial institutions. I admit I had trouble processing what he had to say, and not just because I had been roused from my sleep. He told me that he had just got word that the Bank of Montreal and Royal Bank were going to announce plans to merge later in the day. This couldn't be right, I thought. The banks all knew that we had a review of financial institutions underway, led by Saskatchewan lawyer Harold Mackay, which was going to report within a matter of months. I quickly showered and shaved and headed into work.

Within half an hour of arriving at the Finance offices at Laurier Esplanade, I took the call from John Cleghorn, CEO of the Royal Bank.

Cleghorn was and is a friend of mine. He has made a great contribution to Canadian life, as a business leader and in areas of public concern such as education, conservation, and the military. But this was not a chat among friends. It was true, he told me: the banks were about to announce their merger plans.

I was furious.

These two banks were trying to make an end-run around an orderly process of considering changes to the banking system that was well underway. By refusing to wait for the Mackay report, and the government's decision about its recommendations, they were catching their competitors who had respected the process flat-footed. It was clear to me that they had decided they were going to have trouble convincing Ottawa of the need for mergers, and hoped that if they presented their plans as a *fait accompli*, they could win the public debate.

Well, that was not how it was going to be.

I had a fiduciary responsibility, as I saw it, not to allow those banks that had respected the process to be taken advantage of by those who didn't. Moreover, if the government flinched now, there was going to be a wild scramble as the other banks tried to find partners. (Indeed, it wasn't long before the TD Bank and Canadian Imperial Bank of Commerce [CIBC] announced their merger plans.) Even Scott Clark, who was generally a supporter of bank mergers as a matter of policy, shared my belief that we had to state publicly without delay that we would make the decision about the future shape of the banking system according to the process we had established and not be stampeded by the banks. Before the morning was out, I gave a press conference making it clear that I was not happy, and that whatever was going to happen, it was not going to happen on anyone's timetable but the government's.

The policy decision was by no means a simple one. The banks were facing intense international competition at a time when U.S. and foreign banks were growing enormously in size. Arguably, the Canadian banks needed to bulk up to defend themselves at home as well as to take advantage of opportunities abroad. They also needed to have huge resources to service the gigantic transnational companies that were increasingly dominating global industry and commerce. Politically, there was considerable support for this view among some elements in the Liberal caucus, particularly from the Toronto area. They rightly regarded the banking sector as one of the engines of prosperity in their region, and saw the mergers as a necessity to move Toronto into the big leagues internationally. Their fear was that without mergers Toronto would become no more than a regional banking backwater, servicing some of Canada's needs but not much more.

But the statements of the banks caused some head scratching among officials at Finance, as well as many in the business community. To them it seemed unrealistic of the banks to talk, as they did in their merger announcements, about "going global." If they had spoken about first becoming major North American institutions, that would have been more realistic – at least in the medium term. Their public statements left many observers with the uncomfortable feeling that the banks had an abstract notion of adapting to globalization but had not really thought through what their role might be. Moreover, there was a real danger that the mergers would *reduce* the banks' interest in going global as they created a less competitive environment here at home. These were business decisions, however, arguably outside of my remit.

But what was clearly my responsibility was the important question of competition here at home. This was not a problem in Toronto, Montreal, or Vancouver. There would always be competition there. But in smaller centres and in specific industries, it was an issue. If you were a small or medium-sized business in Toronto, you could get financing locally. But try being an entrepreneur in Moose Jaw or Renfrew. What was the chance that these mergers would occur without a substantial reduction in the number of bank branches, and of bank interest in Canada's smaller centres?

Furthermore, I also had to consider the implications for the banking sector as a whole. If four of the six biggest banks merged, there would be enormous pressure on the two remaining banks to find a partner. The probable outcome would be that one of the merged big banks would gobble them up and we would be left with two large banks. What would happen then if one of them got into trouble, as has happened with even larger banks abroad? Fortunately, the Canadian banks have been much better managed than many of their large international competitors. Nonetheless, the consequences of a major banking crisis in such a reduced field would obviously be much worse, and the potential that the government would end up holding the bag as a result much more serious.

It was well-established practice every year that Gordon Thiessen and I would meet with the bank CEOs for a freewheeling discussion. In the aftermath of the bank merger announcements – and my quick reaction – however, there was a very different tone to our annual meeting. Peter Godsoe of the Bank of Nova Scotia had already spoken publicly against the trend to mergers, and he wasn't shy about saying the same thing to all of us behind closed doors. Soon the meeting became a shouting match between the bank heads, with Terrie, Scott Clark, Gordon, and me looking on, fascinated. At one point, Matthew Barrett, head of the Bank of Montreal, pleaded in vain with his colleagues that the industry shouldn't be parading its differences in front of the minister of finance. I remarked dryly that they shouldn't desist on my account.

The debate about the mergers continued for nearly a year behind closed doors and in public as we waited for various pieces to fall into place: the Mackay task force report as well as those from the Competition Bureau and the Office of the Superintendent of Financial Institutions. In December 1998, I announced my decision: the mergers would not be allowed. My position was that mergers might be contemplated, but not if it endangered the stability of the financial system or if it occurred at the expense of competition. I made it clear that it is not enough to have a few bank branches scattered around the country. Somebody in Moose Jaw who wants a loan has to be able to get one, and on a level playing field with someone in Toronto. It is worth mentioning that in the aftermath of the decision not to allow the mergers, instead of closing branches, the large banks began selling them to smaller competitors. This trend – along with the potential entry of new players in the banking sector permitted by changes in the Bank Act and more expansionist credit unions – may allow for the development of a more competitive banking system better able to meet the needs of consumers and allows the big banks some of the flexibility they wanted.

Among the many MPs I was close to in my Finance years, one of the most extraordinary was Shaughnessy Cohen. It wasn't just her name that was remarkable. She was a smart, hilarious, indefatigable parliamentarian and always the life of the party. She first sought the Liberal Party nomination in Windsor-St. Clair in 1988. This was the successor riding to my father's Essex East. Dad made it a practice not to get involved in nomination fights but on this occasion showed enough body language for folks to understand that he actually supported Shaughnessy's opponent. And then something out of the ordinary happened. My mother, who had never taken a public position on a political matter contrary to Dad's, became an open supporter of Shaughnessy. Shaughnessy won the nomination that year but lost the election.

After that, Shaughnessy developed a close friendship with my mother. She would drop by the house, and the two of them would sit in the kitchen and chat. My father would be in the library, pretending to read but straining to hear whatever chat – political or just social – was passing between them. At Shaughnessy's instigation, I am sure, they would raise their voices just enough to tantalize my father at the start of a story, then deliberately drop them low at a crucial juncture, with the well-aimed intention of driving him nuts.

After she won her seat in 1993, Shaughnessy made as big an impression around the Parliament Buildings as she had in our kitchen. I often had to pass by Shaughnessy and her circle of caucus friends in the government lobby on my way to taking my seat in the

House of Commons, and if there was something she wanted from me as minister, she had no compunction about stopping me in my tracks in a loud voice and then cross-examining me about the total inadequacy of the Department of Finance on whatever issue she happened to be concerned about that day.

In December 1998, Shaughnessy collapsed in the House of Commons with what proved to be a ruptured aneurysm. That evening, a group of us sat vigil at the hospital, but it was only a matter of time. A few days later, I delivered the eulogy at Shaughnessy's funeral in Windsor, which was attended by almost as many Opposition MPs as Liberals – a tribute to her infectious warmth. I said that she was now up in heaven, arguing politics with my father.

Sheila, who was very involved with the "Politics and the Pen" event held in Ottawa each year, was instrumental in the establishment of the Shaughnessy Cohen Prize for political writing, whose recipients have included Jane Jacobs and General Roméo Dallaire.

Politicians sometimes need to be reminded that no one is irreplaceable. Well, almost no one. We will truly never see anyone quite like Shaughnessy again.[1]

---

[1] The journalist Susan Delacourt, who was a close friend of Shaughnessy, wrote a fine and touching biography after her death, which I would recommend to anyone interested in learning more about her remarkable life and personality.

CHAPTER FIFTEEN

Taking on the World

I believe that a finance minister's work internationally can be every bit as important as the work at home, because in a world of interdependent markets, no one can succeed in a world in chaos. The many meetings that take place among finance ministers and central bankers attract relatively little attention outside the business media. To make matters even more remote from the average Canadian, the world of international financial management is populated with an alphabet soup of organizations – the IMF, the WTO, and the G7 – whose discussions may seem arcane to all but the specialists.

And yet, the issues are big ones. In my time, they involved several international crises, each of which threatened our prosperity here in Canada, caused untold suffering in the countries directly involved, and foreshadowed issues we are dealing with to this day.

We also grappled with the stranglehold of Third World debt and aid that affected the very survival of some of the poorest people on earth.

Despite their importance, I find these issues hard to convey to the reader, to lift off the page effectively. This may be an instance where a picture is worth a thousand words, especially if we can explain that the child in the picture does not lack a school because of a typhoon or some other natural disaster but because of a failure in his country's banking system. Or if we can show a destitute family ground into poverty and explain that their hopeless situation is not caused by war, or disease, but by the fact that the world's financial architecture was built for another era.

And I still feel passionately that if we get the right structures in place, we can help make sure that the globalization process the world is going through today works to the benefit of Canadians – who are a trading people – and of humankind.

At my first G7 finance ministers meeting, which was held near Frankfurt, Germany, a meeting was arranged between Lloyd Bentsen and me. Bentsen was Bill Clinton's treasury secretary at the time, but he was best known for his eviscerating riposte to Dan Quayle during the 1988 vice-presidential debate after Quayle compared himself to JFK. "Jack Kennedy was a friend of mine," Bentsen replied. "Senator, you're no Jack Kennedy." I had my own brush with Bentsen's historical memory at this first meeting, held in a castle in Kronberg, built for a daughter of Queen Victoria whose son became Kaiser Wilhelm II. In an attempt to make small talk I remarked to Bentsen that I had heard the castle had also once served as General Eisenhower's headquarters near the end of the Second World War. He didn't seem as surprised at this insight as I thought he might have been. "That's right," Bentsen replied in his Texas drawl. "I came here, and it was in this room that I tried to persuade him to run for president as a Democrat."

"Isn't that interesting," I said lamely.

For me, the attraction of the world stage did not come from the chandeliers and the fancy locations. It came from the impact of its issues – their sheer scale, and the daunting mechanics of addressing them. Globalization, the environment, poverty, disease: these were places where Canada had to make a difference. I began, of course, as a rookie among the G7 finance ministers but, as my years in Finance mounted, ended up being the dean. In my first years at Finance, my focus, naturally, was mainly domestic. On the other hand, it had always been obvious to me that the success of our economy was based on our ability to compete internationally, which meant we had a vital interest in the way the international trading and financial systems operated. If I had any doubts, the Mexican peso crisis had driven this truth home: we could do everything possible within our borders to get our house in order and still get sideswiped by problems abroad.

Along the way, over the course of many meetings in many far-flung places, I made some good friends and some important allies. Just after the 1997 election here in Canada, the G8 summit was held in Denver, Colorado. Tony Blair had recently taken power in Britain as leader of the first Labour government in nearly two decades. My office had arranged for me to have a bilateral meeting at the Denver summit with my British counterpart, the new chancellor of the exchequer, Gordon Brown, whom I had never met. When I arrived in Denver, I went to the official reception hosted by Bill Clinton. Every Democratic Party operative in the Denver area was there, and the president spent his time introducing this mayor and that congressman, and, oh, say hello to my friend in that corner there.

After about ten minutes of this, I wandered back to the summit shuttle bus to go through some documents. Already sitting in one of the seats reading was a man with unruly black hair. "Are you Gordon Brown?" I asked.

And he replied, "You must be Paul Martin."

"So," I said. "Why don't we have our bilateral meeting right here and now."

He agreed immediately – something that we both found all the more agreeable because of the consternation this would create with our departmental handlers. Forty-five minutes later we were well on our way to becoming fast friends. He was open. He was smart. And, to my surprise, he shared more of my fiscal philosophy than I expected from a Labour politician. As our friendship grew over the many encounters we had at finance ministers' meetings in the coming years, it was not lost on either of us that our relationships to our respective prime ministers were very similar – although that was something we rarely discussed. Our bond was really forged from a common set of values and a similar approach to public life.

At the Denver summit, the G8 leaders indulged in a form of summit ad-hockery that I have long believed to be counterproductive. The meeting was held only six months or so before the famous Kyoto conference at which the protocol was signed, so the issue of climate change was very much on the agenda. Under pressure from the Europeans at the summit, President Clinton declared that the United States would commit to a 7 per cent decrease in greenhouse gas emissions by 2012. He made the commitment, as I learned at the time, without consulting Bob Rubin, his treasury secretary, who felt the number had been pulled out of a hat. Jean Chrétien then increased Canada's objective to a 6 per cent reduction.

I think that these impressive promises – which were made by other governments as well in this period – were at the root of the international community's long-term policy failure on global warming because they were unattached to implementation plans. High-flown rhetoric was never harnessed to practical action. Our electorates and the world thought we were doing something when we were not. A more realistic approach, one that tied our commitments to specific plans, would have let everyone see precisely what we were doing or not doing, and monitor our performance. There is no doubt that the climate crisis confronting us is more urgent and threatening than we realized a decade ago. But much more would have been accomplished if governments around the world had taken their own rhetoric seriously – something Stéphane Dion did when he became minister of the environment in 2004. There was no intention to deceive at Denver, or at Kyoto for that matter, but there was a colossal failure both to plan ahead and to follow up.

In my role as finance minister internationally, my preoccupation quickly became how to encourage the evolution of the world's markets and financial institutions in order to ensure the global financial stability Canada required to grow. Several things were apparent to me. The first was how vital multilateral institutions such as the G7 were to Canada, because without them we would simply be excluded from the tripartite U.S.-Europe-Japan management of the world economy. Second, as a small-market nation heavily dependent on exports, we had more at stake in a well-functioning global financial system than almost any other country. Third, we were very much a junior member of the G7 club, and could only have influence by a commitment to sound finance at home and a reputation for generating sound ideas that could command the attention of the larger economies.[1] Finally, it was obvious that while the G7 countries were still the bedrock of the international financial system, they were losing relative weight with the emergence of new giants in Asia and elsewhere in the developing world. For this reason, I felt it was important to start drawing these emerging economies into world decision making, which would, incidentally, also help Canada because of our dependence on a multilateral system that works. I believed that the G7 countries could not lecture the newly emerging countries on their economic management from a lofty height; we needed to engage them in a process in which we would work together for our mutual benefit. This strongly held belief drove my actions throughout my time as finance minister and prime minister, and still does in my post-public career.

The fact is the international financial architecture that had developed following the Second World War was no longer adequate, and was likely to become less so over time. The reforming vision that created the IMF and the World Bank at the end of the war was needed again. We badly needed a new set of reforms that took into account the massive economic changes in the world since the demise of the Soviet Union in the late 1980s and early 1990s.

[1] My father once recounted a remark made to him by the venerable Belgian statesman Paul Henri Spaak to the effect that some of Dad's influence representing a relatively small country in international forums derived from his longevity as a foreign representative for Canada and the experience he was able to draw upon. Admittedly, Spaak, who had been his country's foreign minister seven times as well as prime minister three times over a period of thirty years, may have had himself in mind as well when he made the remark. But this insight did reinforce my view that continuity on the international stage was important and that it had been a mistake, for example, for Canada to treat the CIDA agency as a revolving door or a stepping stone to higher office, meaning that the assets due to experience and longevity were never allowed to accumulate.

For a precedent for what had to be done, I'd ask you to go back to the start of the twentieth century for the most instructive example. In 1907 and 1908, there was a financial crisis in the United States that led to panic and a run on the banks. Banker and financier J.P. Morgan stepped in and organized a coordinated effort, arranging loans to shore up his country's ailing banks and plummeting stocks. He virtually single-handedly averted a collapse of the U.S. financial system. But after it was over, it became clear that because of the growth of the U.S. financial sector, a single person would never be able to accomplish such a feat again. This realization eventually led to the development of the whole domestic regulatory regime for financial institutions in the United States, an evolution that continues to be thickened and strengthened to this day.

My first experience with international turbulence as finance minister occurred early on with the Mexican peso crisis, which was resolved primarily by the action of Bob Rubin and the U.S. Treasury. After it was over, I felt that this might be the last time, given the growth and increasing seamlessness of the global financial system, that one country even working through the IMF would be able to come to the world's rescue.[2] In short, I felt the J.P. Morgan example in the United States at the turn of the last century had just been replayed on a global scale for the last time, and I was certain that the world's regulatory system was going to have to reinvent itself.

The alarm bell was rung by the Asian financial crisis of 1997. The details may seem complex, but the underlying problem was fairly straightforward, and like the Mexican devaluation crisis in 1994, an important element was a lack of transparency camouflaging inappropriate or inconsistent policy.

---

[2] As an aside, the American initiative in itself was controversial. The Europeans felt that the United States had not always been helpful when problems had arisen in countries important to Europe, but were able to bend the IMF to their will when the problem was in their backyard.

It went something like this. Countries such as Thailand had been under huge pressure from the International Monetary Fund (IMF) to open up their markets to foreign capital investment. This was really a reflection of an attitude at the IMF that every economy should function pretty much like those in the United States or Europe, but the IMF had not thought through the issues of transition. Unfortunately, while there was enormous pressure to liberalize the way investment flowed into these markets, there was no parallel pressure to regulate their capital markets or to ensure financial transparency. As these developing countries opened up their capital markets in the 1990s, they enjoyed huge flows of international investment from banks, mutual funds, hedge funds, and so on. Much of that money went into institutions such as local banks as short-term U.S. dollar loans. These banks would then turn around and lend the money out to businesses and individuals for much longer periods, say ten years, and those loans would be in the local currency, such as the Thai baht.

The ticking bomb in this situation was that anything that spooked the international investors could lead them to pull their short-term money out. Of course, that's exactly what happened, and the Thai banks had no easy way to respond, since they had already lent the money out in long-term loans denominated in baht. To make matters worse, Thailand had pegged its currency to the U.S. dollar – a policy it sustained with reserves of U.S. dollars. When investors started pulling out, the Thai central bank quickly used up those reserves trying to keep the baht at its pegged rate. Nobody knew this was happening until the bottom fell out. The Thais then had to unpeg the baht; it came under attack from international markets and dropped like a stone. That left Thai banks with the impossible task of paying back their U.S. dollar loans with the devalued baht. It made for a dizzying spiral.

Thailand was only one of a number of countries in a similar pickle. As the panic spread, the "Asian Tigers" had their feet knocked from under them one after another. Thailand's problems surfaced in the summer of 1997; by August, Indonesia had hit the skids; and by December, the world learned that South Korea was in deep trouble too.

Korea was a particular concern because it was the eleventh-largest economy in the world. Bob Rubin jawboned the big American banks to discourage them from pulling the plug on their Korean loans, which would have had disastrous consequences. He phoned me over Christmas to ask that I intervene with Canada's "big banks" to do the same. I told him that our big banks were more like the mid-sized American banks that he had chosen to leave off the hook. Still, I knew our banks would co-operate, and when I asked, they did.

Not long after this Russia defaulted on its debt, and a month later, a major U.S. hedge fund – Long Term Capital Management – got into such trouble that it took a major effort by the U.S. central bank to bail it out. Each of these incidents posed a huge threat to the global system. Things got even worse in October 1997, when word began circulating that Brazil, too, would need a financial aid package. Needless to say, this cast a pall over most of Latin America.

In a global financial crisis, there are those countries who are hit and whose people suffer, sometimes terribly, and those who try to help. In the Mexican crisis, Canada was hit but Canadians came through it well because the crisis did not last too long. We would not have been so lucky had we become entangled in the Asian crisis. Every night when I went to bed, I said a small prayer of thanks that the 1995 budget had succeeded, and that its healing power was being recognized by the markets. We were not being hit, and that meant we could help.

Every year, the IMF and World Bank meet in Washington for their annual meetings. One of them was held in 1998, in the midst of the Asian financial crisis. Bob Rubin called me up and said that Bill Clinton would like to meet to discuss the crisis with a group of about two dozen of the finance ministers and central bankers attending the meetings. Bob asked Gordon Thiessen and me to come over to the Willard Hotel, which is a stone's throw from the White House, at three-thirty that afternoon. Now, not all those present were that keen about wedging this into their already overloaded schedules, but when the president of the United States asks for a meeting, you obviously show up. The problem was that he didn't. Not at three-thirty, anyway. It turned out that we had been asked to come an hour early so that the Secret Service dogs could do their work, which included German shepherds sniffing down the finance ministers. More grumbling. It was at the height of the Monica Lewinsky scandal to boot, so more than one of us thought that this all might be a photo op to demonstrate the president's determination to keep working on substantive issues. By the time they piped "Hail to the Chief" over the loudspeakers, we were getting pretty fed up.

As a group we were deeply knowledgeable about the Asian crisis, since we were grappling with it every day. When Bob Rubin threw the meeting open, he asked me to begin and I lobbed an easy question at Clinton, as did several others, to which he replied with fairly general answers. So, just to be mischievous, I decided to raise something much more technical, something really tough. Clinton handled himself beautifully. Suddenly the meeting came alive. We talked for two hours and it was pretty clear that he knew and understood the situation as much as anyone in the room. When he had to leave, there was a standing ovation.

It was in this period that Bill Clinton described the Asian financial crisis as the world's worst in fifty years, which was an overstatement. But it was helpful in making the case for the reforms I believed now had to be put in place. There was talk for a time of an international bankruptcy court, which would allow countries in financial trouble to reorganize their affairs systematically, just as corporations can. Ultimately the idea didn't fly, in part because of the opposition of many developed countries and the large international banks. I then championed, with Gordon Thiessen's strong support, the idea of "collective action clauses" in lending agreements, which would allow a country in trouble to change the terms of its debt with the agreement of a majority of its creditors (instead of the 100 per cent otherwise required, which was almost impossible to obtain). This was strongly supported by the developed countries, but many developing countries said this would stigmatize their debt, making it harder for them to get loans; so I decided that Canada, which by this time had become the darling of credit markets, would start inserting such clauses into its own loan agreements as a way of demonstrating that there was no stigma attached. Collective action clauses are now no longer the exception but more and more the rule.

There were many other ideas in the air. Canada's contributions to these debates were enhanced by the superb public servants I had working with me, including Tom Bernes, Ian Bennett, Louise Frechette, Jim Judd, and Jonathan Fried, all of whom went on to yet more distinguished careers in public service domestically and abroad. Paul Jenkins, who was senior deputy governor at the Bank of Canada, was also an extremely valuable voice in these discussions. One of the most important changes to which we contributed was the establishment of an organization that would systematically share best financial practices.

This proposal was originally opposed by Hans Tietmeyer, from Germany, one of the most influential central bankers of his era. Someone – not me, though I wish it had been – suggested that the way to overcome his resistance was to ask him to convene a committee to examine the concept and report back. He agreed and a few months later, it had become his idea, and the Financial Stability Forum was born. The forum played an important role in containing the international contagion of the recent sub-prime mortgage crisis.

Hans wanted to limit the permanent membership of this group to the G7 and a few other countries, however, which I strongly opposed. While an early supporter of the forum I argued that excluding the world's emerging giants, such as China, India, and Brazil, was a failure to recognize the real world. I didn't win this argument, but I continue to believe this is a flaw in the makeup of the forum that will inevitably have to be remedied.

There is a never-ending struggle between regulators and the private sector in its ceaseless search for profits – a struggle in which national borders are invisible and the regulators are always playing catch-up. For this very reason, those managing the major economies need to act together. I was on the cutting edge of financial innovation when I left the business world twenty years ago, and as finance minister I had a watching brief on the emergence of new financial instruments. Still, after I left government and became acquainted with the intricacies of many modern financial techniques, I was amazed to learn how much things had changed, and not always for the better.

This phenomenon of business leaping ahead of the regulators was clearly what happened during the "sub-prime crisis." Many of the United States' most important financial institutions were deep in the business of securing shaky loans to homeowners who could not handle it when the housing market went sour. And the ripples weren't just local or national. They were international. For instance a bank went under in the United Kingdom, and several small municipalities in northern Norway were bankrupted by the sub-prime crisis. In the end the Federal Reserve had to step in to save Bear Stearns – a venerable Wall Street financial institution.

Now, imagine, if you will, in the not too distant future, as the Chinese and Indian economies grow in sophistication, what will happen if there is an equivalent sub-prime crisis, only this time rooted in China. Or if a major hedge fund headquartered in India topples. Will Chinese and Indian investors be the only ones to suffer? I doubt it. Who will step in to deal with the international consequences? And how far away from its source will the financial tsunami strike? That is why the Financial Stability Forum and the other exclusive clubs based on past Western hegemony that are supposed to have an important role to play steering the global economy will eventually have to open their doors much wider.

The same was true of the G7, but here I was more successful in making the argument. While the Asian crisis was the result of problems in only a few countries, the rest of the world had to bear the consequences as contagion spread from economy to economy, from continent to continent. Afraid of a global meltdown, the G7 finance ministers sought to convince the governments of emerging economies to adopt the framework of financial rules and regulations that existed within the G7. We did not succeed. They simply ignored us.

They did so for two reasons: First they felt we talked a better game than we played, and second and more importantly, they ignored us because they were not at the table at the time we came up with our solutions. Their criticisms were dead on! Quite simply, too many of them felt they had been harmed in the past by the strictures imposed on them by the IMF, which is essentially the G7 in different guise. They had been asked to open their financial markets, for instance, before they had the capacity to absorb or regulate the new inflows of capital. As a consequence when the inflows quickly turned to outflows, their middle classes were reduced to poverty and their poor to starvation.

For these reasons I came to the conclusion that the emerging economies had to be at the table with us – and not just temporarily – if we were to deal with today's financial crises and to prevent tomorrow's. I spoke to Larry Summers, who had by this time succeeded Bob Rubin as the U.S. treasury secretary. He agreed with me and together we made a list of those that should participate. I went out and sought their agreement, country by country. Initially the concept encountered some resistance from Germany, but we overcame that. Everywhere else there was enthusiastic acceptance.

When I spoke to Gordon Brown, it quickly became apparent that he and I had very similar agendas. Both of us wanted to build on the G7 system to include the newly emerging economies, and both of us wanted reforms to the IMF that would make it more responsive to the needs of the developing world. The difficulty was that as we played the same corners, we kept bumping into each other. Eventually, we had a chat and agreed that he would focus his energies on reforms to the IMF and I would concentrate on building a parallel group to the G7 with much broader membership of finance ministers and central bankers. This worked well, and we were able to make progress on both fronts.

Thus the G20 was born. I became its first chairman. The first meeting was held in Germany, the second and third in Canada, and it has become a permanent and valuable fixture on the international financial scene.[3] As time passes, I hope its members will always remember why it came into being. History shows that as the moment of crisis passes, so does the push for reform. Crisis prevention will only occur if governments constantly challenge the conventional wisdom of the day. The G20 must continue to do this, because human nature being what it is, it is a lot harder to get governments to focus on crisis prevention than it is on crisis resolution.

The G20, like the G7, brings finance ministers and central bank governors and their respective deputies together at the same table. I was extremely fortunate that Gordon Thiessen and David Dodge were Canada's central bankers in my time. We are never the biggest country in the room and our representatives stand out only if they are of a quality that enables them to do so. The weight of Gordon's and David's interventions at the table and the respect in which they were held made being Canada's finance minister easy. Not that we always agreed!

At a G7 meeting during the Asian crisis in Washington I said to the central bankers present: "You are going to have to loosen up considerably on money supply if we are going to get through this." This was at Blair House, a stately early-nineteenth century manor house across the street from the White House. My message was not unlike that of the other finance ministers: "We have to get consumers buying."

The Japanese, who were still in their own, longer term economic doldrums, said that they could not loosen up. I had quite an argument with some of the European representatives too, who also said no.

---

[3] The members of the G20 are Argentina, Australia, Brazil, Canada, China, France, Germany, India, Indonesia, Italy, Japan, Mexico, Russia, Saudi Arabia, South Africa, South Korea, Turkey, the United Kingdom, the United States of America, and the European Union.

"You're making a mistake," I said. "There's not much we can do in Canada on our own. We could open up the floodgates and it wouldn't have much impact. I'm telling you that if the Japanese, Europeans, and Americans don't do something, we are in real trouble here."

After the meeting, as the big cars rolled up to take the ministers and central bankers away, I was waiting by the door for Gordon Thiessen, with whom I had the habit of walking back to the hotel after these meetings (and getting lost), when Alan Greenspan came over and we struck up a conversation.

"You're right," he said. "Your analysis is correct."

"Well, you were remarkably quiet while I made the case," I said. "Are you going to move?" I can't remember his exact words, but effectively he closed ranks with his fellow central bankers. He did say, however, whatever he did would be in the United States' interest.

When I told Gordon about this later, he remarked that the resistance to what I was suggesting came because central bankers believe their responsibility is only to their country's self-interest, and indeed that is as it should be if the international system is to work. My rejoinder was that for the big countries, at least, action on these global dangers was in their national self-interest.

Alan Greenspan certainly wasn't influenced by anything I said. But, as a result of problems in the U.S. financial sector, the U.S. Federal Reserve soon started loosening the purse strings. I think that the action he took there, along with his intervention to prevent the collapse of the hedge-fund Long Term Capital in 1998, averted what could have been a much deeper crisis. Today he is being criticized for unduly increasing the U.S. money supply, but the fact is that in this particular instance, Greenspan's actions lifted the world economy at a time when it badly needed it. The problem is that if a comparable crisis were to emerge tomorrow it is hard to imagine that the U.S. Federal Reserve could have as dramatic an impact if the major central banks in the world sat on their hands, as they did in the late 1990s. Shades of J.P. Morgan. It is here that the rubber hits the road.

European thinking continues to be dominated by the fear of hyper-inflation born of Germany's experience during the 1920s and 1930s. Similarly, U.S. thinking continues to be dominated by the desire for growth, as a result of its experience during the Depression. When you realize that these are eighty-year-old traumas, whose memory still dictates very different approaches to managing the economy, you can imagine how difficult it will be to have a cohesive approach among the central banks when they are joined at the table by the huge economies of China and India, each locked into their own historical experiences. Making globalization work will increasingly require a level of international dialogue and co-operation that was not needed before the rise of these economies, and the others who will follow. Like it or not, the line between national interest and global interest is becoming much fainter.

If I were to draw a few lessons from the Asian crisis or indeed from the more recent sub-prime credit crunch, they would be:

1. Given the complexity and interdependence of today's global financial system, the need to resolve periodic financial crises, let alone prevent them, means that we can no longer rely on the United States alone, nor can we rely even on the United States, Europe, and Japan working in concert. China, India, and the other regional economic powers have to be at the table.

2. The agenda for that table has to be forward-looking. One of the reasons the international financial system seems to lurch from crisis to crisis is that the major powers make changes to patch up the wounds of the last scrape but rarely adopt reforms that would prevent the next crisis.

3. The Financial Stability Forum was created to mitigate, if not prevent, future crises. Its membership, which is currently much too restricted, should expanded to include the emerging economies.

4. The developed world is not in a position to lecture the developing world on how to regulate its financial affairs. The same

lack of transparency that triggered the Mexican and Asian crises underlay the sub-prime crisis that began on American soil. We are all in this together.

5. Long Term Capital Management and Bear Stearns were bailed out because the potential consequences of their failure were unthinkable. We need to prepare for the day when something similar occurs in China or India, at a point when their international significance is as great as that of the United States. This is important for Canada's financial stability. It is one of the principal reasons I pushed to create the G20.

It was during the Asian financial crisis that I first met Anwar Ibrahim, who was Malaysia's finance minister as well as its deputy prime minister. Although Anwar had been appointed by Mahathir bin Mohamad, the country's long-time autocratic prime minister, he was independent-minded, and completely at ease within the international community. I found him interesting and knowledgeable, and I quickly got to like him. I also saw him as a positive force for change on the Asian side of the Pacific and was pleased to be able to host him on an official visit to Canada.

In contrast to Mahathir, who was inclined to meet the demands of the international community with a stiff forearm, Anwar was an economic liberal and a crucial link between the G7 and the countries in Asia. At one point during the Asian financial crisis, Indonesia looked like the next domino to topple. Almost incredibly, Indonesian president Suharto was not taking phone calls from President Clinton. At a meeting of G7 finance and foreign ministers, we realized that it was important to penetrate Suharto's entourage and impress on him directly the scale of the peril Indonesia's economy was facing. Surprisingly, none of us knew Suharto or his foreign minister well enough to intervene. Jim Wolfensohn, who was then president of the World Bank, suggested connecting through Anwar, who was indeed able to get to Suharto and convince him to pick up the phone when the president called.

Anwar shared many of the international community's concerns during the Asian financial crisis. Mahathir, in contrast, was inclined to blame international investors for the region's problems. Anwar also became identified with opposition to the prime minister's heavy-handed political style and the cronyism that prevailed in government contracting. Mahathir reacted to all this as a threat to his regime, which it was, and fired Anwar in September 1998 amid rumours of a police investigation. A few days later, Anwar participated in a rally of nearly one hundred thousand people demanding reform. A few days after that, he was dragged into court and accused, rather bizarrely, of corruption and sodomy. He was badly roughed up. The trial was presided over by a judge who received a judicial promotion soon after rendering a guilty verdict. I denounced this travesty as it unfolded, as did everyone from Amnesty International to then U.S. vice-president Al Gore.

I did everything I could, both publicly and privately, to help Anwar through these tribulations and make sure the international community did not lose sight of his plight. I wrote to his wife, Wan Azizah Wan Ismail, a physician and a formidable political leader in her own right, on a number of occasions. More importantly, I also phoned her from time to time, knowing full well that her phone would be bugged and that the Mahathir regime would therefore know that international concern was not going away. I asked Canada's High Commissioner to Malaysia, John Bell, to keep a close eye on the proceedings, and he was able to pass a message of support from me to Anwar during his trial. In the near term, these efforts did not get Anwar out of jail, but they may have kept him from getting roughed up more than he already had. I also wrote to Anwar directly in prison, and although those letters never got through to him, he subsequently told me that a friendly jailer had told him about them, which helped sustain his spirits. On one occasion during this period, I happened to sit down at the same table as Mahathir at the annual economic forum at Davos, Switzerland, and pointedly raised the topic of Anwar's imprisonment, much to Mahathir's displeasure.

I am not sure what good that did, but it did remind him once again that the world had not forgotten Anwar Ibrahim.

When Anwar was finally released in 2004, Jim Wolfensohn phoned me to help organize his departure for Germany for treatment on his back, which had been injured during prison beatings. Since then, Anwar has taken up an international academic career, and has now returned to Malaysian politics, where he is effectively the leader of the opposition. We continue to be good friends.

(As I write this in the early summer of 2008, I have just learned that Anwar has been threatened with arrest once again, in a repeat of the earlier scenario. It cannot be a coincidence that a series of by-elections are scheduled in the near future. I have already spoken to his closest adviser to see what I can do, along with – I'm sure – many others in the international community. I hope that everything will have been resolved for the better by the time you read this.)

While the reforms we undertook in the wake of the Asian financial crisis were going to benefit the emerging economies as well as ourselves, they were entirely inadequate to address the difficulties faced by the poorest countries on earth, many of them in Africa, who could only dream of the troubles faced by the Asian Tigers.

During the late 1990s, a movement called Jubilee 2000 began to urge the elimination of the debt of the world's poorest countries. The Jubilee movement was strongly rooted in the Christian Church, though it also attracted many secular figures, including various rock stars and movie actors. The name *Jubilee* came from a passage in the Old Testament Book of Leviticus referring to the freeing of those enslaved by debt from their obligations every fifty years.

At one of the G7 finance ministers meetings, I mentioned the movement to Gordon Brown.

"I was at church the other day," I said, "and I started really catching it from the parish priest on this issue of debt relief."

Gordon, whose father was a Church of Scotland minister, laughed and said, "Well, I was just at church and the same thing happened to me."

I turned to Bob Rubin and Larry Summers, both of whom are Jewish, and jokingly remarked that they would have to come to church one Sunday just to get connected with what was going on. In fact, both were very much involved, as we all were in developing the policy that led to a reduction in the indebtedness of poor countries, particularly in Africa and Asia over the next few years.

In 1996, the G7 launched an initiative to reduce the foreign debt of the world's poorest countries, dubbed the Heavily Indebted Poor Countries Initiative (HIPC). Although it began to make a dent, it clearly was not having the dramatic effect we had hoped, and at a Commonwealth finance ministers meeting in 1998, I spoke on behalf of my colleagues in calling for a comprehensive review of the system. Following from this, Canada became the first country in the world to go beyond the G7 commitment when Prime Minister Chrétien announced the Canadian Debt Initiative, which set us on a faster track to relieving the debt we were owed by the world's poorest countries. But at the international level, things were stalled. As a result, the IMF/World Bank meetings in 2000 at Prague took on a new significance.

These were the years of massive street protests every time a major international organization convened a meeting, whether it was the IMF, the G7, or the World Trade Organization. Prague was a central meeting place in which it was possible for all sorts of protestors, ranging from the most deeply committed Christian activists, to anti-globalization leftists, to anarchists spoiling for a fight to gather and express their views. Prague was bristling with temporary street fences and riot police ready for the onslaught. The anti-globalization move-ment was inspired in part by a sense, similar to that behind the Jubilee idea, that the process of globalization was occurring on terms that were lopsided in favour of the rich and often disastrous for the poor. Within my own Finance ministry, there was an increasing recognition that the issue of debt in developing countries needed to be addressed. It was an issue on which I was determined to lead. The crushing debts taken on by many developing countries were compounded by rigid policies at the IMF that forced many of them to cut their already-meagre public services to meet debt payments. This had pushed some of the poorest lands on earth into a further downward spiral.

In Prague, the G7 finance ministers met at the same time as the IMF/World Bank meetings, as they normally do. The G7 generally works on the basis of "consensus," which often means that it moves when the United States is good and ready. And I knew they were not yet there on the debt issue. Larry Summers, who had succeeded Bob Rubin as U.S. Treasury secretary in 1999, was eager to move but had not yet persuaded the Clinton administration to do so. I decided that Canada should step out on the debt issue publicly in order to create some momentum. It should not have been a surprise to the other finance ministers, because I had spoken plainly and repeatedly against delay inside the room. Nonetheless, it did seem to come as a shock when we issued a press release calling on the rich nations to immediately grant a moratorium on debt service payments by eligible countries. I then announced that Canada would even further accelerate its program of debt forgiveness and begin its own moratorium on debt service payments immediately. In short, we were no longer prepared to wait for the consensus to develop. We were going to lead and asked others to join us.

Larry Summers and I had become friends when he was Bob Rubin's deputy at Treasury. He is brilliant and many of us believe if he put his mind to it, a Nobel prize in economics could still be his. But he is no one's idea of a diplomat. When he bumped into me in the hall, with staff and media all around, he loudly said, "What in God's name have you done?" I replied directly to his challenge with cameras whirling and microphones open as our aides tried to pry us apart.

The next day, after tempers had cooled, there was as usual a closing press conference. Because of his reputation for bluntness, Larry expected questions from the American press about his relationship with his colleagues. Not surprisingly, given our corridor confrontation the day before, the first of these questions was put to me. Of course, I replied that Larry was a person of great diplomacy and tact.

Next, someone asked Larry what he thought about my initiative on debt relief. "I can't believe Martin did that. It was the stupidest thing I ever heard of," he replied, or words to that effect.

And then, when the cameras turned away, he looked over at me with a huge grin on his face. I've been dining out on that story ever since.

I am proud to say that over time, one by one, the other industrialized countries followed our lead to accelerate debt forgiveness to the poorest countries of the world. This has made a significant contribution to the welfare of millions of people, particularly in sub-Saharan Africa.

It was also during the Prague meetings that I got a call from Ruth Thorkelson saying that Bono was in the city.

"Bono wants to see you," Ruth told me.

My reply was: "Who?"

"The leader of U2," Ruth said.

"What?"

Despite the fact that I started off with what I'd call "an incomplete knowledge" of U2's repertoire, by the end of the most complete briefing any minister has ever received from his staff on any topic, I was an expert.

I had a small meeting room at the end of a corridor, to which there was a steady stream of finance ministers and central bankers, whose comings and goings excited absolutely no interest from either my staff or the other national delegations in the vicinity. When Bono arrived, however, secretaries and pinstriped Finance types lined the corridors flashing their cameras. It was as if the Pope had dropped by for a chat. The question of who would attend the meeting with me, I later learned, was a matter of intense negotiation among my staff.

Bono and I quickly hit it off. We discussed my decision to take a forward position on debt relief, which was obviously the root of his enthusiasm. But, surprising as it may sound, we connected because he is also a policy wonk, deeply interested in the minutiae and mechanics of international aid. In fact, he is as knowledgeable as anyone out there.

When our meeting was over, Ruth "volunteered" to accompany Bono down to an interview he was doing with CNN elsewhere in the building. Along the way, he asked her what she thought of some lyrics he was working on and serenaded her with what she later recognized as "Beautiful Day," when it was released sometime afterwards. I'm told Ruth bought ten thousand copies of the CD.

It was at the CNN interview that Bono paid me one of the more memorable compliments I have received in my career: that I was a "f——ing great guy." To my regret, my publishers rejected this as a potential title for this book.

On the final day of the meetings in Prague, unbeknownst to those inside, the demonstrations outside were turning into full-scale riots. I was able to return to my hotel but did so without Terrie, who was attending other meetings in her role as executive director of the World Bank. As a result, she got locked in the conference centre for better than eight hours. Her phone call to me made Larry Summers's language earlier that day seem positively decorous in comparison. I suspect that when the Prague summit was all over, I was more popular with Ruth than I was with Terrie.

On the morning of September 11, 2001, I was at the farm in the Eastern Townships, working out on a stationary bike. Just before nine o'clock, Sheila came into the room and told me that a plane had crashed into the World Trade Center. I didn't think much of it. We had all heard of Piper Cubs or other small planes flying into buildings before. Twenty minutes later, she came in again and said I really needed to come upstairs.

"Why?" I said.

"Well, I told you, a plane hit the World Trade Center, and now a second one has hit the other tower."

And so, like a lot of people that day, I came to my television with a sense of utter disbelief. This was an attack on a colossal scale, unimaginable before that day. It was first and foremost a human tragedy: children left without mothers or fathers; parents without sons and daughters.

After the initial shock had worn off, I realized that this was also a strike at the heart of the world's financial markets. As finance minister, there were questions I needed to think about and address. How were the markets even going to function? Would there be a liquidity crisis?

I phoned Jonathan Fried, my G7 deputy, and asked him to get in touch with David Dodge, by now governor of the Bank of Canada, right away. "You've got to phone David and suggest he connect with the other central bankers to make sure that we don't have a liquidity crisis." By the time Jonathan and I next spoke, that had been done, and I said we needed to have a parallel connection among the G7 finance ministers. I started working the phones. Normally, when I would try to contact my fellow finance ministers, my office would have to arrange a time for the call to go through. But on this occasion, it was no problem tracking them down because most of them were glued to their televisions.

At one point, Sheila interrupted me and asked me to get off the line.

I said, "What do you mean? I've got urgent work to do. I'm talking with the other finance ministers."

She replied, "I want to speak to our children, and I want you to as well."

Paul Jr. was living in Singapore at the time. Jamie was in Toronto. David and Laurence were in Montreal. "Singapore's a long way from New York City," I said, "and besides, it's the middle of the night there."

All she said was: "Get off the phone. I want to speak to my sons. If I can't reach out and touch them, I want to hear their voices." I got off the phone.

Almost every time I tell that story, it seems, someone tells me of something very similar happening in their own family.

At the time of September 11, before the creation of the American Department of Homeland Security, the U.S. Customs Service was still part of the Treasury. One concern that occurred to us almost immediately after the attacks was that Canada would be side-swiped as the United States tried to secure its borders against further infiltration. It didn't help that reports soon circulated in the United States that some of the terrorists had entered the country from Canada – a claim that was proven completely false, but was nonetheless repeated by some American politicians and media personalities with an isolationist agenda. Luckily, I was quickly able to persuade Paul O'Neill, the new U.S. treasury secretary, that if the Americans sealed off their borders, it would count as a victory for the terrorists. This resulted in what eventually came to be known as the "Smart Borders" initiative, which aimed to secure a free flow of goods and people across our border while making sure that we felt safe and secure whichever side we were on.

Interestingly, as time went on I discovered in my discussions with O'Neill that I sometimes had more intelligence information from the United States than he did. Our officials were getting it directly from their American counterparts who wouldn't share it with other U.S. agencies. As the 9/11 Commission later confirmed, the coordination within the agencies of the American government was deeply flawed, sometimes leaving even cabinet secretaries in the dark on intelligence being shared with allies.

In the weeks and months that followed September 11, one of the ironies was that the terrorist attacks in the United States struck such fear among the security services around the world that it was not easy to organize a coordinated response from finance ministers. The G20 was scheduled to meet in India not long after the attacks, but everyone was receiving the same advice: it was too dangerous to travel. This is crazy! I thought. I suggested meeting in London or Washington, and those suggestions were shut down too. I kept saying, "You are letting these people paralyze us. This is exactly what they want."

Eventually, I invited my G20 colleagues to Ottawa, thinking that it might be easier for them to escape the travel restrictions imposed by their governments if Canada was the destination. This turned out to be the case. Karen Martin in my office did an amazing job in organizing the meetings in a matter of a few weeks. It was gratifying that Canada was regarded as a safe haven in a world in turmoil. More importantly, by convening meetings of the G20, which included the G7 ministers, it sent a signal to the world that the system could not be paralyzed. At the G20, we were able to establish a new mechanism for tracking international terrorist financing – an important counter-strike against them in the wake of September 11 – and an initiative the G7 never could have realized on its own.

We also ended the paralysis that was affecting the other international institutions and soon the IMF, the World Bank, and others started rescheduling postponed meetings. But as we know, the world did not return to normal.

CHAPTER SIXTEEN

Getting Quit

In August 1998, I announced that Terrie O'Leary was being appointed as Canada's executive director at the World Bank. For eight years, Terrie had been tirelessly at my side. She had helped shape my policies in Opposition, staffed my office with wonderful effect in government, supported me fiercely when I was right, and let me have it between the eyes when she thought I was wrong. She knitted policy decisions, which she always understood deeply, with political considerations involving the public, the caucus, and the party that she usually understood better than I did. I would dearly have liked her to stay, but I understood that the intensity of those eight years was taking a toll. Terrie is someone who never does anything halfway. For some reason, after eight years she had wearied of waking up to my phone calls in the morning and staying late into the night at the office – mostly long after I had left. She has continued to be a close friend to this day, but she wanted a change.

I had no doubt that Terrie would make an exceptional executive director at the World Bank, an institution I knew well. In my experience Terrie is someone who has never found her level. She has always surpassed it. She ended up staying at the World Bank for two two-year terms, and I was often told by her colleagues in the international community, as well as by then World Bank president Jim Wolfensohn, that her energy and intelligence stood out in that world as it had here in Canada.

I knew that Terrie was going to be hard to replace, but we did eventually fill the position. I assembled an excellent new team. Ruth Thorkelson, who had a strong social policy background and brought the sensibilities of a Westerner to the job, moved up to become my chief of staff. Scott Reid, who had an excellent understanding of the workings of the media, and a good rapport with the press gallery, came on board as my communications adviser. He was soon joined by Melanie Gruer, who was a real find. All three excelled at their new jobs, were great people to work with, and would later become important members of my staff in the Prime Minister's Office.

Before she left in the summer of 1998, Terrie, along with David Herle, had arranged to have lunch with me on St-Denis Street in Montreal. Their message was straightforward: I should start considering seriously what I would do if the leadership of the Liberal Party opened up. If I was serious about succeeding Jean Chrétien, I should begin to think about the organization I would need to run once he announced his decision. If I had learned anything from watching Jean Chrétien's own campaign in 1990, it was how valuable it was to have run before. I had a network of people across the country who had been committed to me, and many of them had remained unusually close. It was no secret that I was the likeliest front-runner if the job opened up, and many of my supporters from 1990 were already positioning themselves for the next race.

But this was a long-term enterprise. It was preparation for a day we did not expect for some time. No sign of this could be clearer than Terrie's departure. I would hardly have willingly dispatched my closest and most valuable adviser to Washington in 1998 if I were girding myself to battle for the leadership of the Liberal Party in the near term. Just the opposite. The very fact that David and Terrie had to sit me down and focus me on the matter is a token of how completely absorbed I was at the time in my job at Finance, which increasingly drew me into the international issues that most fascinated me. Their message that day was pretty simple: I needed to tend my domestic political garden too if I still hoped to run for the job of leader some day. In short, I should do what I could to maintain my profile in the party and the country.

This wasn't hard for me to do. My role in the government had been crucial to our fiscal success, and the public understood that. As a result, I was inundated with requests for speeches from the party and general public across the country. Meanwhile, my supporters played their part in the Liberal Party organization, even if they occasionally chafed at the secondary roles to which they were often relegated.

So much in this period is now viewed through the lens of retrospect that it is worth recalling the degree of co-operation that still existed at the time. David Herle, who was later unfairly demonized by the Chrétien camp, was invited to make an important presentation on public opinion to the annual caucus retreat in 1998, which was held in the prime minister's home riding of Shawinigan. At election time, party organizers were always keen to have me figure prominently in television ads, and I duly co-operated.

Still, it would be ridiculous to deny the element of rivalry in my relationship with the prime minister. Part of the reason that Terrie's departure proved to be something of a turning point was that she had played the pivotal role in maintaining cordial relations with the PMO staff. That included Eddie Goldenberg, of course, but also Peter Donolo, who was often a moderating influence. Terrie's relationship with Donolo was quite close, and they had both been among the group of Young Liberals who had approached me in 1982 to speak at their convention. Terrie and Peter Donolo had been very effective in managing the public dimension of my relationship with the prime minister and keeping any simmering tensions between our respective supporters from coming to a boil in front of the media. A few months after Terrie left for Washington, Jean Chrétien appointed Donolo to be Canada's consul general in Milan. He was replaced as Jean Chrétien's director of communications by Françoise Ducros, who regarded me and my staff with suspicion, and wasn't shy about sharing her doubts with friendly reporters.

Nonetheless, at this same time Jean Chrétien had allowed the race to succeed him to begin informally. Jean Pelletier pulled me aside one day and told me that the prime minister would run for re-election one more time and that would be it. Although Jean Chrétien never spoke directly to me about this, it became clear that he had given some of my potential opponents the go-ahead to begin organizing. We heard this directly from people around Sheila Copps and were able to infer it indirectly through the actions of Allan Rock. As the tempo picked up in 1999, we established a trust fund to begin fundraising for my leadership bid.

All this coincided with growing restlessness in caucus. To some degree, this was the inevitable product of our years in power. In our parliamentary system, there are often MPs of quality who become frustrated over time with their lack of influence when their own party is in office. It was also clear that having been a supporter of mine in 1990, while not necessarily a fatal obstacle to advancement, was not helpful. As MPs became identified with me, or expressed their dis-satisfactions in other ways, their chances of advancement declined correspondingly. Unlike Brian Mulroney, who had held his fractious party together for so long in part by a meticulous attention to the individual needs and personalities of his caucus, Jean Chrétien did little to cultivate the ordinary MP.

As the biennial meeting of the Liberal Party approached in March 2000, some of my supporters in caucus were clearly getting wound up. The more rambunctious among them saw the meeting as an opportunity to push Jean Chrétien out before another election, even though there was no leadership review at the biennial that would have made this even technically possible. I was absolutely opposed to making trouble for the prime minister at this meeting. So were those working most closely with me. What sense would it make? I also have a visceral dislike of party in-fighting. My goal had never been to knock Jean Chrétien off but to replace him. Believe me, though, there were plenty of MPs at the time who didn't share my aversion to fight-ing it out right then and there.

In order to calm the troops and avert a party crisis at the biennial meeting, my senior organizers gathered together some of my caucus supporters a few days before the convention. They met at the Regal Constellation Hotel near the Toronto airport. David Herle, I later learned, gave a PowerPoint presentation in which he made it clear that Jean Chrétien's position was secure and should not be challenged. The message to my supporters in caucus was to use the meeting to position ourselves for the time when the leadership opened up and not allow it to become a festival of open defiance, which would not advance our cause. As Michael Heseltine discovered when he played a central role in removing Margaret Thatcher as prime minister and leader of the Conservative Party in Britain, the one who wields the hatchet can end up being seen as too divisive a figure when it comes time to choose the new leader.

I was aware of the Regal Constellation meeting beforehand and knew the general approach David was taking, though I did not consider it a big deal. He debriefed me on the phone afterwards, but, given what happened later, I was remiss in not thinking through the implications. That set the scene for one of the most embarrassing moments I ever experienced in politics.

Despite David's advice, a number of MPs couldn't contain themselves and spoke up in the next few days, calling on Jean Chrétien to step down. On the Tuesday evening of convention week, CBC News led with a story revealing the fact that the Regal Constellation meeting had taken place. The report made it clear that David's advice was to lay low during convention week. In the context of the outspoken remarks of some of my supporters, however, it looked to some people as if there was a plot to oust the prime minister. Normally, the role of the prime minister's advisers would be to play down a story like this, but from the moment it broke they did the opposite: torquing the story with reporters as hard as they could and building it up as an act of open rebellion orchestrated by me. The next morning, I made a pre-arranged appearance at an early morning meeting of Liberal women at the convention. I was completely unprepared for the media frenzy that confronted me when I came out. I still didn't think it was much of a story – or, perhaps I should say, didn't realize that it was. When reporters asked me about the Regal Constellation meeting, I said that my staff met with members of caucus all the time – which hardly satisfied the scrum.

Ideally, in any interaction with the media, you have an exit plan: a door nearby through which you can disappear. In this case, though, there was no door nearby, no place to go. As it became apparent that my replies weren't satisfying the reporters, I decided to end the scrum. But I had to leave the conference floor in the Westin Hotel by a series of three escalators. There were cameras in front of me and cameras behind. There were reporters shouting questions to me from every direction. My endless, silent escalator ride was an instant television hit: it ran and ran all day. That afternoon, in an attempt to recoup, I held a second scrum in which I explained more about what had happened at the Regal Constellation, having been "re-briefed" by David and Scott Reid. But it was much, much too late to change the impression that we had planned an ambush on Jean Chrétien – an impression that his coterie was keen to sustain.

A few days after the convention, I was in the House of Commons on what is called a "duty day," which simply means taking your turn sitting at your seat so that there is some cabinet representation in the chamber. I received a note saying that the prime minister wished to see me. When I arrived at his office, he was sitting with Jean Pelletier and Eddie Goldenberg, and he was clearly in a furious temper. He confronted me with a memo purporting to be the minutes of a conference call in which a group of my organizers were planning to swoop in for the kill in the aftermath of the convention. The transcript was marked with initials such as DH, SR, and RT – David Herle, Scott Reid, and Ruth Thorkelson, in other words. I took a quick look and saw right away that it was a complete fraud and I said so.

The prime minister said, "No, it is not." He was mad as hell.

And then I blew my cork: "Wait a minute here. I am telling you this is a fake. Are you calling me a liar? This is despicable."

And he said, "I don't believe you." I may then have used language that I would not repeat here.

"Go ahead and investigate," I said. "I want you to investigate."

About this same time, mysterious brown envelopes began to circulate to the media, containing the same phony transcript. Most reporters immediately recognized it for the garbage it was. Inevitably, however, there were a few who reported on it without first establishing its authenticity. The whole dirty tricks campaign was plainly got up by someone close to the Chrétien camp, whether authorized or not.

It had all degenerated into a disgraceful mess. To take some of the steam out of growing media enthusiasm for the "civil war in the Liberal Party" story, Scott phoned some reporters and said that we would "down tools" in the interest of party unity. And we did do what we had already done – this time with better effect – which was to urge our supporters not to make a public show of disunity. But we were not about to dismantle the organization we had built for the leadership campaign the prime minister had repeatedly signalled would come sooner or later.

A week or two later, Pelletier phoned me and said that he had established the memo was fake. I replied that my people and I were owed an apology by the prime minister. We are still waiting.

The rivalry between Jean Chrétien's supporters and my own had become a problem. It was damaging me; it was damaging the prime minister; and it was damaging the party. As it happened, Michel Camdessus, who was then managing director of the International Monetary Fund, was due to step down in 2000. There is a long-standing tradition, which continues to this day, of a European leading the IMF and an American heading the World Bank. There was some talk among finance ministers at the time about the possibility of breaking this pattern and opening up the processes in both institutions. As a successful finance minister, having by this time overcome the deficit in Canada and become active in wrestling with international financial crises, my name came up. But it was never much more than cocktail party talk. My interest had always been in the World Bank, where my close friend Jim Wolfensohn was in charge. If that job had been open, which it wasn't about to be, I might have been interested. But in any event, it quickly became clear that the Americans would not loosen their grip on the World Bank, in which case the Europeans were not inclined to do so at the IMF. So there was no issue.

Nevertheless, some of those around me were urging me to quit. Most importantly, Sheila felt that I should get out of politics. She believed that I could do as much in private life as I could staying in politics, and that I would be perfectly happy beginning the "third career" I had always talked about right then and there. At the time, Terrie also felt I should get out. She believed that since the deficit had been conquered, the government had drifted from its moorings. She argued that my credibility was being undermined by my continued association with the government – a source of disagreement between us, to be frank. David Herle, for his part, thought that I might be better positioned to run for the leadership from outside the government, as John Turner and Jean Chrétien had both done. But that simply wasn't in my character. If I got out of politics, I was going to get out and get on with my life. Quitting government or politics as a "play" for the leadership wasn't something that even remotely tempted me. Furthermore, as the dean of the G7 finance ministers at a time when the global sands were shifting dramatically, I was in a position to influence economic policy in a direction I felt was best for both Canada and the world, and I was not about to walk away from that.

That fall, the prime minister decided to call an early election. As a result, when we brought in our fall economic and fiscal statement a few weeks before, it amounted to an annual budget. Not just any budget. We brought in the biggest personal tax cuts in Canadian history. It was an important milestone in our long fiscal journey. We had conquered the deficit, started paying down the debt, reinvested in crucial social programs, and now we had sufficient funds to provide tax relief on an unprecedented scale.

Any personal relationship with the prime minister was by this time utterly non-existent, but politically we continued to work together. I spoke extensively across the country during the campaign. In Quebec, the party's television ads put me in the shop window. On one occasion, John Rae asked me on short notice to take the red-eye flight to Vancouver to introduce Jean Chrétien at a rally, which I dutifully did. On the stump, the prime minister sometimes promoted a Liberal vote as a "two-fer": that is, a Liberal government gave you two for one, Jean Chrétien and me.

During the election, the prime minister sent strong signals in public that this would be his last campaign, partly in response to opinion polls indicating that while the public continued to support the party, they were tiring of his leadership. After the vote, which produced a larger majority for us, Jean Chrétien had his usual con-sultations before announcing his new cabinet.

"Well," he said to me, "you have been minister of finance for a long time. Don't you think it would be time for a switch?" He offered me Foreign Affairs. In a way it wasn't surprising. After all, it was the post in which my father had served with great distinction. But it was not for me.

"I've got to tell you," I said, "I am probably doing more in terms of foreign policy right now at Finance than I could do as minister of foreign affairs." It was in no sense a negotiation. He made the offer. I declined. He said he would keep me in Finance as I wished.

When the cabinet was sworn in at Rideau Hall, there was as usual a reception afterwards. Jean Pelletier approached me and confirmed our earlier conversation to the effect that Jean Chrétien would not run again. "Bide your time," he told me, "and there will be a leadership convention." We also heard again from supporters of Sheila Copps that the prime minister had indicated directly to her that he would not run again, but there was never any discussion of the matter between me and the prime minister, nor did I expect that there would be, given our strained relationship. Most of the signals pointed in the same direc-tion: it was time to move the leadership preparations into high gear.

The economic package I had delivered before the election made the usual February budget redundant. The next budget came in December 2001 as part of the government's response to the shock of September 11. The terrorist attacks had imposed many unexpected new costs, including our deployment to Afghanistan, as well as measures to beef up domestic security. It was the result of our long-term fiscal discipline that we were able to absorb very substantial new spending on security. With the use of the "prudence" reserve I had always built into my budgets, we were able to do so without slipping back into deficit. The budget allocated $6.5 billion to intelligence, policing, border screening, and the military. It also included more than a billion dollars for the high-tech "smart borders" program we wanted to put in place, to keep trade moving freely without allowing terrorists to do the same. It was an important budget. The demands on Kevin Lynch, now my deputy minister at Finance, to find a way to meet these sudden demands for spending without breaking our fiscal framework were huge. But because of Kevin's earlier experience at the Department of Industry, he had the ideal background for the task, and we were able to pull it off.

It was in this context that Brian Tobin, who had returned to federal politics in the 2000 election and become industry minister, decided to push for a billion-dollar cross-Canada broadband infrastructure program. I very much respect Brian, and to be truthful, if I had been at Industry at the time, I can imagine myself pushing for something equally bold. He was obviously counting on the prime minister to help give him what he wanted. But his proposal would have cracked the fiscal framework that we had worked so hard to establish. Moreover, I thought it was unwise to invest heavily in a hard-wire technology that would soon be rendered obsolete by the emergence of wireless broadband.

When the story of our disagreement hit the press, I was obviously concerned, because for most of my tenure at Finance we had been successful in keeping internal disagreements over budgets out of the public eye. At that point, from my perspective, it became an issue not just of policy but also of budget discipline; in other words, if we yielded after Brian had gone public it would have encouraged others to end-run the process in the same way. But it never came to that. I said no and heard nothing more about it from the PMO. At the time, I believed this was because some people in the PMO, including Eddie Goldenberg, had doubts about the wisdom of his project on policy grounds, and they took my side, notwithstanding the deep divisions between us politically since the biennial.

I am told that Jean Chrétien has subsequently said that he gave Eddie instructions to allocate a preliminary $100 million to Tobin's scheme (rather than the $35 million the budget actually contained). I was unaware of this at the time. My relations with the prime minister at this point were so poor that we no longer had direct contact. Indeed, I would say it was the first budget in which I was not certain that I could rely on his support for my final decisions. However, with regard to Tobin's broadband proposal, I simply assumed that the prime minister had decided not to let the tensions with me get in the way of maintaining fiscal discipline and was not fighting me on the point for that reason.

There were, however, other instances where these tensions were more obviously at play, with real-world consequences – and not for the good. One involved a miscalculation of federal tax payments affecting several provinces, but Manitoba in particular, which had received more than they should have. It was the fault of the Revenue Department, a separate ministry. By default, however, I became the lead minister trying to clean up the mess. At Finance, we came up with a formula that relieved the affected provinces from having to pay back the money they had mistakenly received. But this created an issue with other provinces, who would complain that they were being short-changed. I held a meeting involving the affected ministers, including Stéphane Dion, who was at Intergovernmental Affairs, to explain my approach. Stéphane raised some very reasonable objections, which I went back to Finance to work through. Once I had done that, Stéphane came fully on board.

At that point, someone at the Privy Council Office raised concerns, to the effect that I was trying to run the government behind the prime minister's back. The objection was that I was calling meetings of ministers to discuss major policy matters outside the formal PCO structure. This was nonsense. I was merely trying to work out a solution to a problem with the relevant ministers as I had always done. As a result of the PCO's intervention, however, the prime minister decided to assign John Manley, by this time deputy prime minister to take the cabinet lead on the file. I explained to John when we met that Stéphane and I had worked out the solution that was acceptable to the concerned ministers, but John, asserting his authority, said he was not sure he agreed and wanted to study the matter. At that point, I was fed up. I told him the solution was in front of him and it was now his file to handle. For whatever reason, John then recommended our proposal be rejected. None of the ministers who had been consulted understood this, and neither did the government of Manitoba. Unfortunately, I did – only too well!

It was in this atmosphere that Johanna Leffler, one of my advisers at Finance, who had also become a good friend, remarked to me that if I were serious about the party leadership, I would have to leave the government: "You cannot challenge Jean Chrétien when you are sitting in his cabinet." My reply was that I had no intention to challenge the prime minister, only to organize to succeed him. The events of the coming months would take care of this little difference of opinion.

It was soon after my discussion with Johanna, on May 30, that Jean Chrétien arrived in an obviously agitated state at an unusual Thursday-morning meeting of cabinet. He said that the race to succeed him was getting out of hand: it was destabilizing the government. "I want this all to stop," he said. "No more organizing. No more fundraising." It was a stunning suggestion, absurd really. He had given the go-ahead for the race to begin, and now that Allan Rock, John Manley, Sheila Copps, and I were out organizing, he was trying to call a sudden halt. I had no intention of doing that. The loss of momentum and the blow to morale would have been huge and possibly irreparable. I had a clear lead on my rivals, and a precipitous halt would have hurt me more than anyone else.

Those who worked for me at Finance would all tell you that I was never very good at briefing them after cabinet meetings. I went back to my office that day and returned to my work. A few hours later, Tim Murphy came in and said, "What the hell happened at cabinet today?" I realized that I had goofed, leaving my staff unprepared for the fallout.

"How do you know about it?" I asked. Tim told me that the Chrétien people were spinning all over town that he had walked into cabinet and stared me down.

"The hell he did," I said. It was only at that moment that I realized that Jean Chrétien had launched a full-scale attack.

Whether it was a well-planned attack is another matter. Some of those around me were certain that it was. I am not so sure. The night before the fateful cabinet meeting, a couple of MPs who supported me had met with some union leaders to discuss the leadership. During that discussion, I was later told, there was some talk about how my supporters would cope with Denis Coderre and Martin Cauchon, cabinet ministers who were strong Chrétien supporters in Quebec. As I understand it, word got back to the prime minister a few minutes before cabinet that I was "trying to take them out." This was all idle talk – of which there was an abundance at the time – but it obviously sparked a reaction from Jean Chrétien, who heard it before I did.

Planned or not, we had clearly entered a new world. I had a speech the next morning in Hamilton and was flying there that night. As I was sitting in my hotel room preparing for the speech to the Federation of Canadian Municipalities, Tim Murphy came by and told me that the PMO wanted changes to my text.

The political drama between the prime minister and me was unfolding against the backdrop of a policy dispute that had intensified as our relations deteriorated. I had grown increasingly concerned that as a nation we had neglected the importance of our cities. To a

At home on the farm. (Deborah Samuel, *Vista* Magazine)

Drawn to the flame: Campaigning in LaSalle-Émard to get into parliament. (Martin family)

Elected, to my father's great delight. (Martin family)

Running for the leadership of the Liberal Party in 1990. The hard-fought campaign created a lasting gulf with the eventual winner, Jean Chrétien. (Martin family)

Participants in my leadership campaign.
Back row left to right: Benoit Labonté, Earl Provost, Jean-François Thibault, Lloyd Posno, Jean Lapierre, Jean Marc Fournier, Georges Farrah, Terrie O'Leary, Joe McGuire, Zoe Rideout, David Herle, me, Chris Peirce, Linda Hays, Anne Marie Tingley, Lou McGuire, Carsten Jensen, James Cowan, Georges Rideout, Richard Mahoney, Michael Marzolini, Ralph Goodale
Middle row: Kim Doran, Jim de Wilde, Alan Alexandroff, Dennis Dawson, Mike Robinson, Dove Hendren, Sheila Martin, Iona Campagnolo, Mark Resnick, Marian Maloney, Kaz Flinn
Front row: Jamie Deacey, Robert W. Peterson, Ron Caza, Jeff Cowan, Jacques Hudon, Anne Champoux, Jonathan Herman, Ken Tilley, Norbert Thériault, Todd Burke, Jonathan Schneiderman, Doug Richardson (Photo by Jean Marc Carisse)

All smiles in the Prime Minister's Office between Prime Minister Jean Chrétien and his Finance Minister. (Dave Chan)

Fewer smiles. (Dave Chan)

Handshakes with two of the people who helped me most during our toughest deficit-fighting days at Finance: David Dodge (above) and Gordon Thiessen (below). (Dave Chan)

An informal cottage meeting of my friends and advisers known as "The Board." Left to right: Ruth Thorkelson, Richard Mahoney, Mike Robinson, David Herle, John Webster, Elly Alboim, Terrie O'Leary, Véronique de Passillé, Michele Cadario, Scott Reid, Brian Guest, Pietro Perrino, Karl Littler, Dennis Dawson, John Duffy, me, Tim Murphy. (Karen O'Leary)

Chairing a meeting of my advisers.
From left: Pietro Perrino, Johanna Leffler, Richard Mahoney, Tim Murphy, David Herle, Dennis Dawson, Karl Littler, Jim Pimblett, me, Michele Cadario. (Dave Chan)

With my first Cabinet at Rideau Hall.
Back Row left to right: Helen Scherrer, John Efford, Liza Frulla, Ethel Blondin Andrew,
Andy Scott, Gar Knutson, Denis Paradis, Jean Augustine, Joe Commuzzi, Albina Guarnieri,
Joe McGuire, Mauril Bélanger, Carolyn Bennet, Aileen Carroll
Middle Row: John MacCallum, Stephen Owen, Bill Graham, Stan Keyes, Bob Speller, Joe Volpe,
Reg Alcock, Geoff Regan, Tony Valeri, David Pratt, Jacques Saada, Irwin Cotler, Judy Sgro
Front Row: Jack Austin, David Anderson, Ralph Goodale, David Anderson, Anne McLellan,
Lucienne Robillard, me, Governor General Adrienne Clarkson, Pierre Pettigrew, Jim Peterson,
Andy Mitchell, Claudette Bradshaw, Denis Coderre, Rey Pagtakhan. (Dave Chan)

Sheila and me with the 2006 campaign staff, RCMP, and the staff from 24 Sussex.
Back Row left to right: Hilary Nicholson, Mirka Orankiewicz, Lucja Grabowiec, Sayla Nordin,
Scott Reid, David Herle, Gord Langlois, Heather Watson, me, Robert Asselin, Michele Cadario,
Scott Feschuk, Gary Stuart, Sylvain Cote, Jim Pimblett, Mario Dionne, Josh Drache,
Roger Charbonneau
Middle Row: Jay Strauss, Anita Vandenbeld, Jamie Cote, Véronique de Passillé, Terrie O'Leary,
Sheila Martin, Melanie Gruer, André Fortin, Jonathan Moser, Dave Chan, Guy Legros
Front Row crouching: Taras Zalusky (and daughter Alena), Kevin Bosch (and son Ronan),
Rhiannon Andrews, Orli Namian, Alphee Moreau, Marlene Floyd. (Brigitte Bouvier)

The moment when I was sworn in at Rideau Hall by Alex Himelfarb as Canada's 21st Prime Minister, on December 12, 2003. (Dave Chan)

degree, this was a constitutional issue. Because the cities are entities created by the provinces, the federal government does not have a direct constitutional relationship with them; and although their work can often have the most immediate effect on the most basic elements of our lives, they have a limited tax base. A city may invest in an industrial park to create jobs, for example. It will need to provide sewers and roads to the new businesses. Some of the people travelling to their new jobs will need enhanced bus service, and their co-workers who drive will put additional stress on existing municipal roads. Out of all this, the federal and provincial governments reap additional personal and corporate income taxes. But the city gets only a modest bump in property tax revenues. It bears the largest costs, in other words, yet the municipality receives the smallest tax harvest of any of the orders of government.

These arrangements were fine in 1867. However, I believed we now had to come up with creative ways around the constitutional barriers. After all, Canada is an increasingly urban nation. The cities are the setting for some of our biggest issues, whether it is immigration, mass transit, schools, or violent crime. The cities are also the throbbing commercial centres at the heart of globalized trade. As I have said many times, Canada may compete with China or Japan, but the tougher competition is between Toronto and Vancouver on our side of the Pacific and Shanghai and Tokyo on the other.

At the time, the *Toronto Star* had started to campaign for a federal focus on Canada's biggest cities – mirroring my own thoughts, though my goal was broader – to include all municipal governments and not just those of our biggest cities. Urbanization was producing gridlock in downtown Toronto, but at the same time it was making it difficult for smaller centres to keep their hospitals open as population declined. We thought hard about what a New Deal might entail, and we developed some ideas about giving municipalities a broader and more stable tax base, appropriate to their responsibilities.

We also began to kick around ways of bringing municipal leaders more directly into national debates. After all, did the mayors of

Toronto, Vancouver, and Montreal not have at least an equal need to discuss immigration and mass transit as the premiers of smaller provinces where those issues did not loom so large? Did the mayors of Saskatoon, Winnipeg, and Edmonton not have just as much reason to speak to Aboriginal issues as their premiers? It should be said as well that it is not just the large metropolitan centres that need to be considered in this context. Canada's smaller centres and rural communities face their own challenges as the large urban centres grow in wealth and population.

Not everyone in Ottawa was enamoured with this line of thinking, and not just because it was liable to cost money. At a political level, there was the memory of the Department of Urban Affairs, created under Pierre Trudeau, which had been an irritant for the provincial governments, who saw it as an intrusion into their jurisdiction. When I used the phrase "New Deal" in a speech to the Federation of Canadian Municipalities in Ottawa, the *Toronto Star* pumped it into a headline, which was fine by me, but which created tension with the PMO, where the inclination was to leave well enough alone. But for me the need for a national municipal policy was indisputable. The question was not whether, but when. So I decided that I would outline more specifics when I addressed the next meeting of the Canadian Federation of Municipalities, coming up in Hamilton.

Francie Ducros, the prime minister's director of communications, had shown increasing interest in my Hamilton speech even before the cabinet showdown with the prime minister. Now out of the blue, word came to me through Tim Murphy that the PMO wanted to take the unprecedented step of censoring parts of my speech. Jean Chrétien and I had had differences on many subjects over the years, but the PMO had never arrogated this role. "I am not changing a word," I told Tim. "This has never happened before and to hell with them." I delivered my speech on Friday morning precisely as I had planned.

Meanwhile, trouble was looming over another speech that I was scheduled to deliver that night. Tony Dionisio, Toronto leader of the

Labourers International Union who supported Brian Tobin's leadership bid until he withdrew from the race earlier in the year, had invited me to speak to a gathering in Toronto. We started getting word that the prime minister wanted me to cancel that appearance and attend a speech he had decided to give, also in Toronto, to the Ontario wing of the federal Liberal Party. I have long had a practice of never cancelling a speaking engagement at the last minute except in the most extreme cases. I told my staff to tell the PMO that I would not cancel my plans, which had been in the works for weeks.

You can't be in competition with the prime minister, was the message I received indirectly from David Smith – one of the few Chrétien strategists who was still trying to keep channels open. The word, as it reached me, was that I needed to introduce the prime minister and pledge my loyalty.

I said, "Wait a minute. Are all the candidates being asked for an oath of fealty? If not, why should I?"

I did agree to come and make an introduction, however, but only if they could change the timing, since it conflicted directly with my earlier commitment. That was not on, either.

Chrétien's people made sure that the media knew all about this dispute. Naturally, there was a large posse of reporters who showed up for my speech "loaded for bear." When the time came for the scrum, I said that I was going to "consider my options." It may seem naive, but this whole thing had exploded from nowhere in just two days. I genuinely did want to consider my options, and was going to do it on my own time.

That weekend, Eddie Goldenberg phoned me at the farm and asked me point-blank to make a declaration to the media that I intended to stay in the government. I said that I could not do that because I was still mulling over the options. Eddie told me that I had to phone the prime minister then. I said that if the prime minister wanted to discuss this, he should call me. He did not. Eddie and I had several conversations, but no one was budging. Finally, on Sunday morning, Sheila and I drove into Montreal, and it was there, that afternoon, that I took a call from the prime minister. We spoke only briefly before he handed the phone to Eddie. Eddie said he had drafted a letter of resignation for my signature explaining my reasons for quitting and stating that it was by mutual agreement. But I wasn't interested. There *was* no mutual agreement. I knew that I was almost certainly going but did not say so on the phone. I wanted to resign on my own terms the next morning. Terrie phoned David Dodge at the Bank of Canada to reassure him that I would make an announcement of my decision before the markets opened on Monday.

Toward the end of the afternoon, Sheila and I got in the car to drive back to Ottawa. As I drove, I leaned over and switched on CBC Radio to listen to *Cross Country Checkup*. That's where we heard that John Manley was being sworn in as finance minister.

And that's how I "got quit."

CHAPTER SEVENTEEN

The Next Level

"Getting quit" turned out to be more liberating than I had anticipated. It enabled me to talk about my own policies more freely – though not, as I explain below, as freely as I would have liked. I could, however, now organize for the leadership without restriction. That in turn meant that Jean Chrétien had to lift the ban on campaigning for all the potential candidates. He could hardly have me outside the cabinet campaigning at full tilt while preventing his preferred successors inside the cabinet, such as Allan Rock, John Manley, and Sheila Copps – anyone but me, in other words – from doing the same.

It was by this time indisputable that the party and the caucus did not want to face another election under the same leadership. The same was true of the public: the prime minister had even signalled his intention to step down before the next election during the 2000 election campaign. What was infuriating about Jean Chrétien's posture in this period was that notwithstanding those strong signals, he began to talk tough in public – "I'm the little guy from Shawinigan. No one's going to push me around."

I will admit that this got me going. I don't look for a fight, but if somebody wants one, they are going to get one. I think this goes back to a very basic decision when you get into politics. You need to understand that politics can be a rough game at times. If you aren't prepared for that, best to take up another line of work.

Meanwhile, there was a parallel track behind the scenes. Shortly after the 2000 election, Dennis Dawson phoned me to say that he had been summoned for a chat with Jean Pelletier. Pelletier had suggested that the party's biennial meeting, at which there would be an automatic leadership review, and which would normally occur in March 2002, should be delayed by a year. In this scenario, the biennial meeting, when it eventually did occur, could easily be converted into a leadership convention to replace Jean Chrétien. According to Pelletier, this would avoid forcing the party through a divisive leadership review process, when the prime minister was planning to step down eventually anyway. Pelletier apparently recognized that the prime minister was unlikely to achieve the level of support he needed to survive a review.

Taking this into account, after some negotiation as to precise dates, my supporters on the national executive, who formed a majority, agreed to delay the meeting until February 2003.

In the weeks after my departure from cabinet, there was a warm gust of support for me from the party and the public. I went on a national speaking tour, attracted significant crowds, and had an enthusiastic reception everywhere I went. Anne McLellan, at this time a senior minister in the Chrétien government, introduced me when I attended the Calgary Stampede. A number of ministers discreetly contacted me to reconfirm their desire that I be the next leader. I received many calls from long-time party members whom I knew, and some of the people associated with me, such as David Herle, Karl Littler, and Michele Cadario, were flooded with offers of support. Yet none of this in itself meant much so long as the prime minister was dug in.

What set the cat among the pigeons, however, was a feature in the *Hill Times*, an Ottawa publication popular with the media and political insiders. The *Hill Times* published a list of MPs who supported me alongside a list of those supporting Jean Chrétien. Since my list was considerably longer, the PMO applied pressure on MPs to switch their names into his column, which a number of them did. Some of my closest associates still in cabinet, such as Ralph Goodale and

Anne McLellan, were told to make sure their names were on the Chrétien list as well. Eventually the lists pulled into a virtual draw.

As sometimes happens in politics, however, a modest success can lead to an overreaching mistake. The caucus was scheduled to have its annual summer retreat in Chicoutimi in August. A few days before the meeting, Don Boudria and Martin Cauchon announced with some fanfare a list of ninety-four MPs who, they said, had pledged their support for the prime minister in a future leadership review – just more than half the caucus. This time, however, some MPs began stating publicly that their names should not be on that list. Pretty soon the total was tumbling well below 50 per cent. It was a tactical blunder on the part of the Chrétien camp, and was read by the media as a sign that the party had reached a "tipping point."

From the time I "got quit," we had all expected the Chicoutimi caucus meeting to mark a crucial turn in the road for Jean Chrétien's leadership. Still, perhaps I was more relaxed about the event than I should have been. After arriving at Chicoutimi, I headed out for a caucus golf game. I ignored Jim Pimblett's caution that I should not do my pre-game stretches in sight of the press photographers. The result was that the next morning every paper in the country featured a truly awful picture of yours truly. To this day, the photo is still occasionally resurrected from the archives. I've often wondered if I could sue the photographer for libel; probably not, since I'm told truth is a valid defence in such circumstances.

Shortly after arriving in Chicoutimi himself, the prime minister gave an aggressive speech attacking some of the ideas I had been publicly proposing to reform Parliament and give MPs more clout – seemingly a signal that he planned to take no prisoners during the caucus. The next day, as I entered the caucus room, Richard Wackid from the party whip's office handed me an envelope, which I stuck in my back pocket without opening. So when the prime minister gave his address to caucus, his declaration came as a surprise. He sought to buy himself some more time as prime minister by offering to resign in February 2004 – a full year later than the biennial, which had been scheduled at his request for February 2003, just six months away. Later, when I checked the envelope, I discovered that it contained a note signed by the prime minister saying that he was planning to make an announcement about his future.

As I sat in the back of the room, I was besieged by caucus supporters offering me conflicting advice. Some felt that this was another manoeuvre that would inevitably be followed by yet another after that, with Jean Chrétien determined not to go until he had destroyed my chances of succeeding him. They urged me to insist that the party should go ahead with its established timetable, with a biennial early the next year in which there would be a leadership review. Others took the view that as unsatisfactory as it might seem, Jean Chrétien's pledge offered a path to our goal without further strain to the party. I shared this latter view.

In order to make my intentions known, I needed to figure out an appropriate place. Some of the other potential leadership contenders held "scrums" with the media outside the caucus room, but I have never liked the chaos of scrums and did not think that it would be sensible that day for me, as potentially the next prime minister, to react in that kind of forum. Brian Guest approached the prime minister's staff to see whether I could use the microphone that had been set up for the prime minister to hold his press conference, but they refused. So there was a scramble to find a hotel room with the proper audio hookup for the media. All of this took far too long and so when I came out, paid a brief tribute to the prime minister, made my statement, and then left without taking any questions, it was a bit of an anti-climax – or so the assembled reporters obviously felt. My brief remarks conveyed what I wanted, however: that I would accept the prime minister's timetable to avert further damage to the party.

Fifteen months passed from the Chicoutimi caucus meeting till the leadership convention, which was scheduled, after a bruising fight by the party executive, for November 2003. For me, it was very different from the leadership race of 1990. This time, instead of being the underdog, I was the favourite. This time, instead of having to put together an organization from duct tape and binding twine, the challenge was to make room for newcomers in an organization already bursting with talent.

It was well known that I had a large group of intensely committed supporters that had been nicknamed "The Board" by my longtime personal assistant, Thérèse Horvath. Thérèse had been in Pierre Trudeau's PMO, where she worked very closely with Jim Coutts. Later on she became Raymond Garneau's assistant. When he was defeated in 1988, my first act was to commiserate with him. My second was to ask if I could hire Thérèse. It was one of the best decisions I ever made. She has been with me ever since, and I could not function without her. Her ability to deal with people is extraordinary. In opposition, in the minister's office, in the Prime Minister's Office, or out of office dealing with Africa and the wide range of Aboriginal issues that involve me now, she has the knack of making everyone feel special, a knack that has turned night into day for me on too many occasions to count.

Thérèse's nickname for the group of my closest advisers stuck. The Board was a name that none of them relished, but it became their media moniker. I used the term myself, mostly because I knew it bugged them. The group did not issue membership cards, and it changed composition with the passage of time. But a snapshot of the group taken at Terrie and David's cottage in the Gatineau Hills a few days after the Chicoutimi caucus captured the group fairly well as it then was. It included Terrie and David, of course. Elly Alboim, whom I came to know as finance minister, brought his exceptional policy mind and communications skills. Michele Cadario, who had long been a road warrior in my cause, painstakingly building my organization across the country, became campaign director in the leadership campaign. Véronique de Passillé, who was president of the Young Liberals at the time, and Pietro Perrino, an important strategist for the provincial Liberals, were my main organizers in Quebec; Dennis Dawson was one of my principal advisers on the province. John Duffy had been involved in drafting my policy platform in 1990 and would do similar service now. Brian Guest, a passionate advocate for cities and the environment, now also became communications director. Karl Littler was an exceptional organizer who would lead our effort in Ontario along with Charles Bird. Scott Reid, who had left my staff by this time, was working closely with Brian on providing media and communications advice. Tim Murphy, an experienced organizer, formidable policy adviser, and a former member of the Ontario Provincial Parliament, continued to work as my chief of staff. Richard Mahoney lent his unsurpassed knowledge of the party and network of personal contacts. Ruth Thorkelson, who had also gone to the private sector, was in charge of debate preparations.

John Webster was *éminence grise* of the campaign. He had a commanding presence and was always the calm in the middle of a storm. A steadfast and loyal friend, he was at the centre of both of my leadership and election campaigns. Mike Robinson, meanwhile, provided a key link to the party elites, and Francis Fox did the same, concentrating on Quebec.

It was more than just a political organization. It was a network of close friends whose relationships had been forged through many political campaigns over many years. Interestingly, most of them had significant histories in the party as activists and organizers that pre-dated my own entry into politics. They provided me with a cadre of advisers who knew me exceptionally well, who were my most loyal supporters as well as my sternest critics. The intensity of their personal relationships sometimes made it hard for newcomers to penetrate – or at least gave them the impression that it would. At times, it also gave my opponents, inside and outside the party, a ready target to shoot at. Often this was presented in the form of an attack on Earnscliffe, the Ottawa firm where many of them worked from time to time. I think a fair examination of the record would show, however, that these attacks, which often insinuated conflicts of interest, were never backed up with even the flimsiest of evidence. I know these people very well, and they are as honest as they were loyal.[1]

In addition to The Board, who provided the core of the campaign organization, I also needed to raise the funds to fuel it. Gerry Schwartz and Heather Reisman had been close friends as well as supporters since I had first got to know them in my 1990 bid for the leadership in which Gerry, a celebrated Bay Street entrepreneur, led the fundraising effort and Heather co-chaired my Ontario campaign. I was very grateful that Gerry agreed to head up my national effort once again. Guy Savard, one of Canada's most able merchant bankers, raised contributions in Quebec. Together they not only raised sufficient money for the leadership, there was enough left over to pay off the Liberal Party's $3.5 million debt from the Chrétien years.

From the outset of the leadership campaign, we knew that the likelihood was that we would win. In retrospect, I regret that in our zeal to turn that likelihood into a certainty we alienated some of those in the party who supported other candidates. I do think, however, that we were successful in broadening my already-large base in the party. One of the priorities of the "insiders" on The Board had to be to make room for those who were only just making up their minds to support me. In British Columbia, Mark Marrisen, for example, had been a Chrétien organizer in 1990. Admittedly, in Quebec, the scenario was more challenging. The depth of antagonism between our organization and Jean Chrétien's was so great that few had any interest in crossing the divide. Jean Chrétien's former supporters mostly looked to other candidates such as Allan Rock and Brian Tobin and when they left the race either gravitated to Sheila Copps or simply dropped out altogether.

---

[1] Stephen Harper set up an inquiry into federal polling contracts under the former separatist minister Daniel Paillé, which was clearly aimed at Earnscliffe. No doubt to the Harper government's disappointment, Paillé found nothing irregular but did chide the Harper government for its own polling practices.

For me, party renewal implied much more than a change of leader. It meant reaching out to a whole new generation of voters, and doing so in areas where few had recently if ever voted Liberal. By the end of the leadership campaign, the Liberal Party had its largest membership in decades. The Quebec organization had been infused with life and the party in British Columbia was stronger than ever. Besides former Chrétien supporters, we had also reached out to the Trudeau wing of the party, and some party legends such as Marc Lalonde, Otto Lang, and Tom Axworthy came to play important roles.

It was important that the leadership campaign also send messages of inclusion to Canadians outside the party who had not recently supported the Liberals. Many of the themes of my campaign were about reaching out. For a long time, I had believed that the Liberal Party could do more to attract voters in Quebec and Western Canada who had felt excluded by some of our policies, and often simply by our tone of voice. One of the first trips I undertook after Chicoutimi was a swing through the Western provinces, where I was greeted by an enthusiasm that suggested they did not have to be a perpetual graveyard for Liberals. I also believed my "cities agenda" would connect with people in places such as Quebec City, East End Montreal, and Calgary, where the party had been especially weak.

I continued to make democratic reform an important part of my message to Liberals and to the public. At the broadest level I was concerned, as many people are, about the declining interest in politics among Canadians. I thought the place to start was with parliamentary reform. Unfortunately, over the course of forty years or so, Canadians had seen the influence of individual Members of Parliament eroded as the power of the prime minister and the executive branch of government grew. It was, sad to say, a Liberal prime minister who once described MPs as "nobodies." What has happened is that MPs, who form the most personal link between individual citizens and the government in Ottawa, have been gradually disempowered. They vote according to the dictates of their party, and too often, when their party is in power, no one in the government cares particularly what they have to say. No wonder fewer and fewer Canadians are bothering to vote.

To address this, I developed a series of proposals aimed at reducing party discipline on MPs, giving them a greater role in initiating and shaping legislation, strengthening parliamentary committees, giving MPs a role in overseeing government appointments, and creating an independent ethics commissioner. Although the devil, as always, is in the details, the underlying impulse behind these proposals was more important: to reconnect Canadians with their democracy.

From the start, the leadership campaign went well. Extremely well. So well, in fact, that I sometimes felt frustrated by the front-runner's role, which invariably is to be cautious, when my own inclinations were to engage the party in real debate. Yet to stake out new territory far from the place the Liberal Party had occupied under Jean Chrétien was to invite yet another round of party in-fighting with the sitting prime minister. For instance, he fiercely attacked the proposal I had made to allow parliamentary committees to choose their chair-persons by secret ballot (rather than, as tradition had it, by the prime minister himself). Eventually, the Canadian Alliance introduced a motion to flush out the Liberals on the topic; the issue was only defused when the prime minister agreed to a free vote in the House on the matter. Not surprisingly, MPs voted to empower their committees rather than preserve the prerogatives of the Prime Minister's Office. Jean Chrétien also sought to ratify the Kyoto agreement, but still with no plan in place to implement it – a concern that Anne McLellan, still a senior minister, was bold enough to raise publicly. In the House, I was forced to choose between the treaty I supported and the government's promises without preparation, which I regarded as a shell game. In the end, I decided that the principle was too important not to support, even if a plan would have to wait until I had the reins.

One of the most perplexing decisions Jean Chrétien made in the last months of his leadership was to introduce a "reform" of the party financing system that seemed designed to hobble the Liberal Party. No one would argue that party financing in this country was perfect.

Yet the effect of the legislation was to force the Liberal Party, without any period of transition, to develop a system along the lines of the one already perfected by the Reform/Canadian Alliance/Conservative Party over more than a decade. There was simply no time for us to develop a large base of small donors, as the legislation required us to do. The president of the Liberal Party at the time, Stephen LeDrew, described the law as "dumb as a bag of hammers." Ironically, while it was a substantial irritation to me as Liberal leader, the debilitating effects of the legislation on the party were gradual and not truly felt until after I stepped down and was replaced by Stéphane Dion. It was Stéphane, I am sad to say, who suffered most from legislation that might reasonably be interpreted as having been aimed to get at me.

The paradox of the leadership campaign was that it was a great success from the narrow perspective of securing a victory in the Liberal leadership, but in many ways it did not set up the party for the coming election as well as it might have done. When Allan Rock and, some time later, John Manley withdrew from the race long before the convention, it was an acknowledgement that the party had made up its mind. Only Sheila Copps remained in, and she never gathered the support to be in serious contention. Because the media had no contest to report on inside the leadership race, they focused on the ancient rivalry between Jean Chrétien and me, which now had a new dimension: effectively, there were two leaders of the Liberal Party at the same time.

Early in 2003, I laid out the elements of the dilemma this situation created for my leadership campaign as explicitly as I could in a statement to reporters in Sherwood Park, Alberta. I told them that loyalty to the current prime minister could not be allowed to preclude the public discussion of controversial ideas. I said plainly that there could only be one prime minister at a time, and that the positions I put forward were not demands on the current government but policies I was proposing for my own.

There was, however, another element to this strange situation that was unknown to the public and the media at the time. I could declare publicly that there was only one prime minister at a time, to free myself up to discuss new ideas in public. But the reality that change was coming at the top was naturally affecting the expectations of those in office. Tim Murphy was more and more often approached by ministers in the Chrétien cabinet seeking approval for their departmental plans for the future.

In order to circumvent some of the stifling constraints of the situation and to kick-start the renewal of the party, our campaign opened up a mammoth exercise in policy consultation, led by Mark Resnick and aided by Ruth Thorkelson, Peter Nicholson, and John Duffy, in which we drew hundreds of academics, party members, and policy analysts into lively debates on everything from parliamentary reform to health care to Aboriginal policy. I also mounted a series of town hall meetings with voters of every stripe across the country, organized with the help of think-tanks such as the Canada West Foundation and Canada25. These provided the kind of forum I have always enjoyed, letting loose with plenty of free-flowing debate and lots of time for questions and answers. The policy wonk in me relished the chance to delve into a wider range of issues, much beyond what I had dealt with in Finance.

Once summer turned to fall, our challenge became how to sustain public interest in the campaign. I had long ago intended to go to the polls within months of becoming leader and prime minister, in order to secure my own mandate from the electorate. That meant that the leadership convention in November was an important stage from which to speak to Canadians. Unfortunately, by this point, the media's interest was really flagging. In many ways, it was more like many American party conventions, where the outcome is already known ahead of time, than what we are used to in Canada. Brian Guest had suggested inviting Bono to the convention; we had by this point developed a good relationship born from our mutual interest in Africa. I was taken with the idea because his star quality would go a long way to elevating public interest in the developing world among Canadians. Many of my staffers hoped that Bono would perform as well as speak at the convention, but that was not to be. Still, it was great for the family to have him hang out with them for much of the day.

We arranged for Sheila Copps to give her pre-vote speech in a hall that we made sure was packed to cheer her on. As the certain victor, I did not speak at the convention until after the vote was over. I spent a lot of time preparing for my keynote address, as I invariably do for big speeches. I talked about my belief in Canadian ambition: to be a more substantial presence on the international stage; to create a more prosperous, competitive, and advanced economy; and to do much more to educate our children, look after our seniors, create opportunity for our Aboriginal peoples, end the marginalization of our disabled, and improve our health care for all. In particular, I made the case for attacking wait times in our medical system as a visible sign that we were serious about reforming medicare.

I think it went well, setting the tone I wanted as I approached my return to government and to the electorate in a different role. But later in the convention, my staff told me, to my surprise, that I also needed to make some off-the-cuff remarks to a general meeting of the delegates when they met with the new party executive. My message was that the Liberal Party often ends up becoming too dependent on the government when the party is in power, which is not a good thing. When, as inevitably happens, Liberals find themselves back in Opposition, the party structure has often atrophied and is not up to the job. The government will make the decisions it must, I said, but the party should remain independent, even challenging the government at times. As often happens, in my experience, the universal opinion seemed to be that this off-the-cuff address was the better speech.

During the convention, I did everything I could to ensure that Prime Minister Chrétien got the praise he deserved for his decade in office. There was a tribute evening at the convention, and we made sure our supporters were there. In my speech, I said I was proud of what we had accomplished under his leadership, which was true. There was no need to dwell on our cool personal relationship. Behind the scenes, however, things were not going smoothly. To that point, the PCO and the PMO had refused to provide me with any briefings whatever in preparation for the transition. Once briefings began, they were not always as complete as my transition team would have preferred: for example, we did not have access to some departmental officials who would have been helpful as we planned the reorganization of government departments. It would also become clear in the coming weeks that the PMO was not happy about me playing the semi-official role that I inevitably assumed in the weeks before I took office, and which was imposed on me by the prime minister's decision to delay the handover: meeting with the premiers at the Grey Cup and touring parts of Halifax that had been devastated by Hurricane Juan are two examples of this role.

The prime minister had said publicly and repeatedly that he had no intention of stepping down before February 2004, the date he had announced at the Chicoutimi caucus so long before. Naturally, I planned for the transition on that basis, anticipating that I would call an election for the early spring, very soon after taking office. This was not something I would be able to do any earlier because the Conservatives had not yet held their leadership convention, and there was a pending redistribution of parliamentary seats that would benefit the West. I had long believed that the West needed a larger voice in Ottawa and the Liberal Party, and I was not about to call an election at a time when it would do the opposite.

Soon after I was chosen leader, however, word reached us that the prime minister was actually planning to step down much sooner. At one time, this would have been welcome, but at this late date it complicated our transition plans. We then got the indication that he would stay until his original date only if we asked him to, something that would have seemed laughable after we had had so long to prepare for office. So I left him to choose his own date of departure.

In retrospect, many have assumed that this dance over timing was about the release of the Auditor General's report on the sponsorship program. Perhaps, but the fact is, the prime minister had already guaranteed that the report, which dealt with problems on his watch, would only be released on mine. Let me explain that. The Auditor General can only report when Parliament is meeting. By proroguing Parliament as he did, Jean Chrétien ensured that this would not happen until I was prime minister, whatever the ultimate date of the handover. Once Parliament is prorogued, there are technical requirements to bring it back into session, including that it start off with a throne speech and the subsequent debate. The idea that having relinquished the leadership of the Liberal Party, but not yet the office of prime minister, Jean Chrétien would summon Parliament into a new session in early 2004, have a throne speech, table the Auditor General's report, take the heat that was rightfully his, and then – at that point and that point only – hand over the Prime Minister's Office is too absurd to take seriously. The fact is Jean Chrétien could easily have chosen to have the Auditor General's report tabled and made public while he was prime minister – but he opted not to do so.

Whatever my predecessor's calculations, the Auditor General's report was not a preoccupation for me at the time. I had not seen the report, and did not anticipate how incendiary it would be. After all, the Auditor General had issued a previous report on the same program, and although it had been a problem for the government, it was hardly devastating. Terrie had warned me, when she tried to persuade me to leave before the 2000 election, that Jean Chrétien would try to "wait me out." I think the jury is still out on whether that was his original intention. Where she was absolutely right was that he would leave a "time bomb" when he went – something I had believed he cared too much about the party and the country to do.

Surprisingly, Jean Chrétien and I had virtually no direct contact during the transition. For some reason, however, he insisted on a face-to-face meeting to tell me his revised date of departure, which turned out to be December 12. We met briefly in his office, along with some aides, but our encounter was extremely awkward. He remained behind his desk and certainly had no intention of saying anything of substance. When we met the media afterwards, I said a few words, and he said quite a bit more. When a reporter asked me

THE NEXT LEVEL 251

a question, Jean Chrétien announced the scrum was at an end. For a split second I was poised between continuing to speak or letting him have his day. I decided on the latter. My time would soon come.

Over the next few days, my main preoccupation was putting together the cabinet – for me, as for most prime ministers, one of the most difficult tasks the job entails. As Frank McKenna once remarked to me, the problem in choosing a cabinet is not so much finding the people to do the jobs as it is having to say no to the many good people for whom there is no room. There were several principles with which I approached the task. The first was that this would very much be a transition cabinet. I was hoping to have many new Members of Parliament in caucus after the coming election, and to recruit quality candidates the newcomers needed to know that there would be opportunities for them. So everyone would be told that an appointment now would not guarantee a claim on a cabinet post after the election. Second, it was important that some of the prominent ministers from the previous government step aside, both to create openings for newcomers and to make it clear to the public that this government was as much about change as it was about continuity. Third, I wanted, through my cabinet selection, to demonstrate a commitment to greater representation by women, as well as a stronger voice for the West.

Allan Rock indicated to me that he was prepared to remain in cabinet, but he also suggested an exit ramp, which was the post of ambassador to the United Nations. I was happy to offer him the latter, knowing that he would be superb at the job, which indeed he proved to be. John Manley presented a greater challenge. He wanted to be foreign affairs minister, but like most prime ministers, I was determined to play much of that role myself, and felt there was too much potential for conflict if he returned to a job he had occupied for a time under Jean Chrétien. As an alternative, he would have considered staying at Finance, but I had already decided on Ralph Goodale, who was a natural for the post. Of course, John's very close association with Jean Chrétien in the latter years of his government meant that almost any differences between us on policy matters would play themselves out in the media as an extension of old battles now better forgotten. When I met with John, I raised the possibility of his taking on the job of ambassador to the United States, for which he would be well suited. He asked whether I would consider making the ambassadorship a cabinet-level job – a constitutional peculiarity in my view – and whether he could report directly to me; in both cases I said no. John said he would consider my proposal, but I did not hear back from him for several days. Then, word reached me that he was planning a press conference to announce that he had been offered the ambassadorial post but had turned it down. I didn't believe this was possible. I called him to see whether he had made up his mind, but he said he wanted more time. In the end, I heard the news like everyone else, through the media.

Sheila Copps was a special case, as so often in her career. There had been extraordinary bitterness in the Hamilton area between Sheila and my supporters, including two MPs, Stan Keyes – who had supported her leadership bid in 1990 – and Tony Valeri. Late in the 2003 leadership race, there was a signal through one of her organizers, Joe Thornley, that she would like to be appointed ambassador to the United Nations Educational, Scientific and Cultural Organization (UNESCO), which I was prepared to do. When I met with her during the transition, however, I was stunned to hear her declare that she intended to run again. Whether there was a miscommunication through Thornley or she had changed her mind, I do not know. However, her determination to run again created an inevitable clash. Due to redistribution, if she stayed where she was, she would be vying for the Liberal nomination with Tony Valeri, a man of great talent whom I was determined to put into cabinet. We suggested two alternative seats, one of them a safe Liberal seat, in fact. In this latter case, I asked John Turner if he might be able to help. He approached Beth Phinney, an incumbent MP from Hamilton who had intended to run again. Beth agreed to step down, which would have left the nomination open for Sheila.

When John picked up the phone to relay the offer to Sheila, she declined.

In retrospect, one regret I have about my first cabinet was not including Stéphane Dion. My advisers were split. David Herle and many of the other anglophones around me were enthusiastic about his inclusion. The advice I got from others, however, particularly in Quebec, was the opposite. In any event, I did not put Stéphane in my first cabinet, though I always intended to bring him back in at some point, as indeed I did as environment minister after the spring election.

At the same time, I did something unusual on Stéphane's behalf. I had made it policy that constituency nominations in the coming election would be open to all comers, allowing the party's stock of candidates to refresh itself thoroughly for the first time in a decade. When it became clear that Stéphane was in danger of losing his nomination to a strong supporter of mine, however, I departed from my policy and stepped in to make sure he would be renominated.

Putting together the Prime Minister's Office confronted me with a different problem. As I soon discovered, while some MPs may be sitting by their phones waiting for the call, many people of quality not in elected office have personal or professional reasons to prefer staying out of the daily pressure cooker of the PMO. This challenge was all the greater when it came to Quebec. The Quebec media had long complained about the fact that my entourage was mainly anglophone, and that I was getting advice only from outside Quebec. This was just wrong. Montreal is less than two hours away from Ottawa, and throughout my years as minister Sheila and I never moved our home, continuing to return to Montreal every chance we had. I was in continuous contact with people such as Dennis Dawson, Francis Fox, Pietro Perrino, and Jean Lapierre, as well as Lucie Santoro, who was on my Montreal staff, and of course with my two former legislative assistants Benoit Labonté and Claude Dauphin, both of whom are now councillors for the city of Montreal. Such people didn't need to be in my Ottawa office to contribute to my thinking on Quebec issues or national issues. The media just didn't get it, because it all happened more than two hundred metres from Parliament Hill.

The situation changed when I became prime minister. As some of my advisers who did not join the PMO quickly found out, if you are not on the staff, you cannot possibly remain in the loop on every significant issue. Too much happens too fast. There cannot be a "kitchen cabinet" second-guessing the staff at every turn, because at the PMO the thinking is in the doing. But it was terribly difficult to recruit people to pack up and head out on route #40 to live in Ottawa. Not only is there a feeling in Quebec that, politically, the National Assembly is where it's at, the truth is that in Ottawa, for all the attempts over the years to make it bilingual, the working language is predominantly English, even including some meetings where most of the people in the room happen to be francophone. Even Francis Fox agreed only to a six-month stay in the PMO as principal secretary. After the election, he was succeeded by Hélène Scherrer. Brian Guest was named deputy principal secretay.

Among my advisers who were already in Ottawa, most were keen. Only Terrie and Elly declined to come on board. Tim Murphy became chief of staff, with Ruth Thorkelson as deputy. Scott Reid was director of communications, and Melanie Gruer became press secretary. Mario Cuconato was tour director of operations. Peter Nicholson came in as a senior policy adviser. After the election, Karl Littler joined as head of cabinet operations, Michele Cadario directed the regional political desks and Steve McKinnon was responsible for the party office. Véronique de Passillé was my new legislative assistant, preparing for question period and in charge of overall briefing, while Karen Martin became my director of appointments.

A few days before my government was sworn in, we made a remarkable catch for the Liberal Party. Scott Brison, who was one of the brightest stars in the Progressive Conservative Party, a one-time candidate for the leadership of that party, and an opposition finance critic who had jousted with me daily from the Opposition benches, announced he was crossing the floor to join our party. Scott was very much a "progressive" conservative who did not feel at home after the merger of the PCs with the old Reform Party/Canadian Alliance under Stephen Harper. It was a clear signal that there was a large segment of the public that had lost their traditional home with the PCs and would be looking to us as an alternative.

The day before the swearing-in of the new government I made my calls to the new cabinet, and a few to those who did not make it and perhaps hoped that they would. Some who had aspirations, such as Joe Fontana, took their exclusion with good grace. In Joe's case, I always planned to bring him in after the election, as I did. Others did not react so well. I offered Maurizio Bevilacqua the cities portfolio, but at a below-cabinet rank. I wanted to make this a major focus of my government, but I had no intention of infuriating the provinces, in whose jurisdiction the municipalities were, right before an election by establishing a new ministry of urban affairs. But Maurizio declined. Instead, I appointed John Godfrey, who was to have had another portfolio, and he came into cabinet after the election a few months later.

Finally, on December 12, 2003, Sheila and I went to Rideau Hall for the swearing-in. I had retained many of the strongest ministers from the previous Liberal government, but about half of the cabinet were newcomers to that role. It was a great moment.

CHAPTER EIGHTEEN

Taking the Reins

The cabinet swearing-in at Rideau Hall was very special. In addition to the vice-regal ceremony with the Governor General, we had a "smudging" ceremony conducted by Elmer Courchene, the senior elder of the Sagkeeng First Nation, to which the grand chief of the Assembly of First Nations, Phil Fontaine, belonged. Elder Courchene burned sage, then enveloped us in the smoke by fanning it with an eagle feather in an ancient ritual of purification and healing. It was symbolic, of course, but I was determined that it was not going to be just symbolism. Our native peoples have had far too much experience of being brought in for decorative effect, then being ignored. I wanted Aboriginal Canadians to see that they were an integral and important part of our society. I wanted to establish a partnership with them based on mutual respect rather than dependence.

For me, establishing a respectful relationship with Aboriginal Canadians and providing the means necessary for them to take control of their own destinies was a fundamental goal I set for myself as prime minister. It marked my last weeks in office just as it marked the first day. Though the achievements of the Kelowna Accord in 2005 have been squandered – the word is not too strong – by my successor, I believe that there will be a day not far off when the principles of that agreement are resuscitated as a matter of historical justice. The reaction of native schoolchildren to the smudging ceremony was especially gratifying to me; we received hundreds of appreciative letters. There is a limit to what we can do about what past generations have suffered; but there are no limits to what children may accomplish with their lives, except those we impose on them. Our Aboriginal population is the youngest of any demographic group in our country, which presents us with our greatest opportunity and our greatest challenge.

There was also another symbolic change with larger significance that I made to the swearing-in. I had a special ceremony for parliamentary secretaries. One of the factors behind my push for parliamentary reform was the need to enhance the role of Members of Parliament. Under previous administrations, parliamentary secretaries were rotated to the back-benches every two years, regardless of how well they performed. They were also totally dependent on the goodwill of their ministers for any tidbit of responsibility that might fall their way. I decided to change the system, giving them a status akin to that of junior ministers in the British system. This meant they had special responsibilities assigned to them in a mandate letter from the prime minister. Many of them went on to do exceptional work.

My experience with my own parliamentary secretaries gave me the insight to do this. A number have been mentioned in this book. All were accomplished individuals, some of whom went on to be successful ministers. Roy Cullen was a senior public servant before entering politics. Bryon Wilfert, once a successful municipal leader, has become one of the country's leading experts on Asia. Despite being a rookie MP when I was prime minister, Navdeep Bains played a crucial coordinating role with caucus during the difficult times of minority government. John McCallum, one of Canada's brightest economists, brought his expertise to bear as one of my parliamentary secretaries and as secretary of state for financial institutions.

Andrew Telegdi was not only an expert on immigration, he was hugely helpful on dealing with the challenges of Canada's Aboriginal people, and was from the beginning a driving force behind the government's science and technology agenda.

As I began this new mandate I had some overarching principles in mind. I have always believed that our generation has a duty to the next, and the one after that. Some people talk about "intergenerational equity," which in plain language means leaving our country and the world in as good shape or better shape than what we inherited. At first, this can seem like not much more than a platitude, but it has been a constant aim through my career. Fairness to our children and grandchildren was a crucial reason for getting a hold of the deficit problem in the 1990s. The same was true with reform of the Canada Pension Plan. It had always been my intention that once we got Canada back on a sound fiscal footing, we would have the resources to invest in our children's lives. That started when I was still finance minister and we launched the learning agenda and the National Child Benefit.

Now as prime minister, I set out to do much more. When I took office in late 2003, health care was the dominant priority for Canadians, as it had been for many years. I made fixing the system my most important commitment in my first election campaign. I promised to cut the long wait times that frustrate and, in some cases, literally sicken Canadians. And within a few months, I achieved a historic ten-year health-care agreement with the provinces, with wait time targets and substantial additional funding to achieve them.

What was equally ambitious was that I wanted to establish a national system of child care. Everything we have discovered during my lifetime about early childhood development has reinforced my view that cultivating young children's minds would help improve their life chances. Some of my Liberal colleagues felt that since we had promised a national system of daycare in the Red Book, a new commitment would be met with derision. But we made the commitment, added the dimension of early childhood learning, and built a national system by the time I left office.

There cannot be a Canadian alive today who does not realize that the environment, also, is a generational issue. When I was a young man growing up in Canada's industrial heartland but working most summers in the bush or at sea, I was moved by the need for conservation of our wilder spaces. Since then, like many people, I have seen the dangerous effects of the depleted ozone layer, a decline in biodiversity, and now climate change. Neil Armstrong made history when he stood on the moon's dusty surface back in 1969. But for me and for many of my generation, the most dramatic image to emerge from the space program was that picture of the Earth, a green and blue round ball covered in clouds framed by the emptiness of the universe. I have never understood how anyone could look at that picture then look at their children and not ask themselves, What in God's name are we doing?

My economic policies, including the cities agenda and my efforts to enhance trade with the emerging economic powerhouses in Asia, were also about developing a long-term strategy that would hand future generations the tools to prosper in a changing world. This is why I thought it was so vital that Canada be part of reforming the international financial and trading systems along multilateral lines, to make sure that there would be a role for us. Even my belief in a more robust Canadian foreign policy – in Africa, Haiti, and the developing world more generally – had to do with the fact that the prospects of the young populations in these distant parts of the globe were intimately linked with those of our own children.

By the time I walked into my new office after the swearing-in, I had had a lot of time to think about what I wanted to do as prime minister, and how I would do it. Later, I would be criticized for having too many priorities. I accept that I had a great many. I might even accept that my agenda was too large for the political circumstances in which I found myself. I do not, however, accept that my agenda was too large for the country. I had, of course, envisaged at least four years as prime minister. It quickly became clear that I might not have that privilege, and that the sponsorship issue might blot out any other matters of policy. And so, I decided, I would get my agenda out anyway. I thought it was a compelling vision for the country and would help us win the election. But I also believed that if we stumbled at the polls, it would be a guide to future governments and policy makers.

The Conservatives have tried to undo much of what we accomplished. But the day will come when we find our way back as a nation to the principles and policies I laid down. The delay will cost us, I am sure. The children who miss out on the chance to enrich their minds in their earliest years will never get that lost time back. The Aboriginal people who do not get the education or economic opportunities they deserve will be affected all their lives by our collective failure. We will eventually make a serious start on containing greenhouse gases, but we will have lost more precious time. It will take time to rebuild our role as an independent force in the world. And the trading opportunities we are squandering in China and India, for example, will take years to recover. But all of this will come over time.

I have no regrets about my desire to shake things up as prime minister. That's why I wanted the job. Still, it took a while for me to adapt my management style to the peculiarities of the office. Whether in the business world or at Finance, I had never been one to respect rigid hierarchies. I preferred talking directly to the expert on an issue, whether he or she was the head of marketing or a director-level official in the Ministry of Finance. As finance minister, I didn't have much taste for the pablum that makes it up through two or three levels of bureaucratic editing to the desks of many ministers. If something was on my mind, I went to the expert, not his or her boss.

The problem was that while I could do that at Finance, it was much more difficult as prime minister. Instead of sitting down with the front-line policy makers, you meet with the officials in the Privy Council Office and five or six ministers, then set a general direction. When they come back to you with their recommendation, you say yes or no or send them back to the drawing board. That took some getting used to. Another thing that took getting used to was the hand-holding that some of my cabinet ministers seemed to need. As minister of finance, I liked to have as much scope as I could carve out, and my contact with the prime minister was as limited as I could manage it. I remember Jean Chrétien telling me that this was pretty much the way he had handled his relationship with Pierre Trudeau when he was a minister. What I discovered as prime minister is that not everyone likes to operate that way.

That having been said, and despite the burden of the sponsorship issue (which I will deal with in the next chapter), I was able to lay out my ideas and aspirations for the country in the leadership campaign, my first months in office, and in the platform for the 2004 election. I also wanted to reshape the political balance within Canada and within the Liberal Party. Western Canada is our most economically dynamic and fastest-growing region. Yet our central institutions have not reflected that. Westerners expressing the region's entrepreneurial spirit have sometimes been treated like visitors from outer space in Ottawa. As finance minister, I had done what I could to redress that; as prime minister, I hoped to do much, much more.

In my home province of Quebec, meanwhile, the Liberal Party had allowed itself to shrink into a smaller and smaller redoubt. The bitterness over the failure of Meech Lake, and the reluctance of the federal government to convey its understanding that Quebec as the home of the largest francophone population in North America has a special responsibility, had taken us outside the political mainstream there. The issues between the governments in Quebec and Ottawa are substantive, as they are with any province. In many ways, however, sending the right message to Quebec is also a question of tone.

In the little more than two years I had as prime minister, we made enormous headway on many of our most ambitious goals. What the public saw in Parliament and in the media, day in and day out, however, was the sponsorship issue. As a consequence, the 2004 election campaign turned out to be very different than the one I would have chosen to run. After that election, I confronted the almost daily crises and challenges thrown up by minority government. And then there were difficulties of my own making: I wanted to do too much, too quickly, for the bureaucracy to absorb and I did not always communicate my objectives to the public as clearly as I saw them myself.

Like any prime minister, I was heavily dependent on the public service to achieve my goals. At the top of the bureaucracy is the clerk of the Privy Council, who is at the same time the prime minister's deputy and the master of the bureaucracy. Alex Himelfarb was the clerk when I took office, and at first I regarded him with some trepidation, since he had been closely associated with my predecessor. As the first weeks turned to months, however, my confidence in him grew. Tim Murphy, who was Alex's counterpart in the Prime Minister's Office, felt the same way. Not too long after I took office, Alex, who was obviously uncertain about his place on my team, took a trip to Australia to think things out. I later learned that when he came back, Tim sat down with him and talked things out. After that, there were no issues between us. He shared my enthusiasm for ideas, and my desire to get things done (perhaps too quickly sometimes), which helped establish our bond. In time, I saw that he was prepared to serve me just as loyally as he had served Jean Chrétien. Alex has a first-class mind. He is also innovative and, when we had determined on a course, was able to surmount many obstacles, bureaucratic or otherwise, on our behalf.

In addition, Alex brought some of the public servants I had most admired over the years into the PCO, including Jonathan Fried, who had worked with me on international issues at Finance as my foreign affairs adviser, and Dale Eisler – a distinguished former journalist from Saskatchewan and later chief of communications at Finance – as head of PCO communications.

When I was sworn in, I also made a number of changes to the structure of government, some of which worked out quite well, while others did not. In retrospect, it was probably more structural change than was necessary so soon. The alterations we made to the Treasury Board under Reg Alcock were important for modernizing government. Splitting the Human Resources Department in two enabled

Ken Dryden, as minister of social development, to concentrate his energies on getting us a national child-care system. Anne McLellan took over the new Ministry of Public Safety and Emergency Preparedness, which was an important adaptation to the post–September 11 world. Later, in the wake of the SARS crisis, I would establish the Public Health Agency, and appointed Dr. Carolyn Bennett, who was a great success as the first minister of state for public health.

But the split between Foreign Affairs and International Trade was not a success. That proposal, which had long been contemplated at the PCO, was strongly opposed by some members of my transition team on the grounds that if anything, trade and foreign policy were becoming more closely interlinked. Personally, I did not feel strongly about the matter. In the end, I decided to let the PCO go ahead with the change, but the resistance of many senior public servants produced spectacular bureaucratic turf wars over the issue. To my surprise, the PCO's plan came to be seen as a hobby-horse of mine. It wasn't; but I did let it play out, which probably was a mistake.

In the first few weeks of office, I oversaw the preparation of a speech from the throne while Ralph Goodale, as finance minister, developed the first budget of the new government. We knew that these were in a sense the formal prelude to an election that I intended to hold shortly, in order to seek my own mandate with the public.

One important part of preparing for an election was to recruit new candidates. We were very successful in bringing on board a group of leading Canadians with a natural background in areas such as business, labour, municipal government, and social justice, too many to name.

As well, along with Scott Brison we attracted two former PC Members of Parliament, John Herron and Keith Martin, to the Liberal banner.

In addition, we were successful in recruiting many able individuals who, although they might not have national reputations, were important figures in their local communities. Collectively, these recruits sent a strong signal in English Canada that we were a party whose reach was wider than ever.

Of course, for every candidate of this calibre I managed to lure, there were many others who declined. Often, it was because of family or business concerns. The harsh truth is also that many people who have been successful in their lives – whether it is in business, public service, sports, or in the community – are reluctant to sacrifice the reputations they have succeeded in building up over decades to the bitter attacks that characterize so much of our public life. The challenges facing women are particularly tough since they are often expected to balance family and career in a way that many men are insulated from.

But nowhere was the challenge more formidable than in Quebec. As I've noted, many Quebecers have tended to regard Ottawa as increasingly remote from their concerns. The most crushing blow for us, however, was the Auditor General's report on the sponsorship program, which hit Liberals particularly hard in Quebec, where the tawdry affair had unfolded in an especially intimate relationship with the national unity project – almost literally wrapped in the flag. We could see the impact of this on our fortunes in quite specific ways. We had up to that point enjoyed many contested nominations in the province. Suddenly we were having a hard time attracting quality candidates. Some of those who were going door to door said they felt the public blowback hot in their faces. Some were taunted on front porches where they would have once been welcomed. In this context, it was particularly gratifying to me that Jean Lapierre, who had left politics after my defeat in 1990 and pursued a very successful media career, chose to declare his candidacy even after the release of the Auditor General's report. It was quite simply an act of political courage.

I had always wanted to change the dynamic of the party in Quebec, which meant appointing a Quebec lieutenant who could make that happen. Jean Lapierre was born in the Magdalene Islands, had been the MP for Shefford, and is a passionate Quebecer. Despite his passage through Bloc Québécois in the wake of the failure of Meech Lake, he is a strong Canadian. He often played a bridging role, helping Quebec to understand the rest of Canada, and the rest of Canada to understand Quebec. He was a strong and innovative minister, and he continues to be a good friend to this day.

By early April, the redistribution of seats was in place and we had recovered slightly in the polls from the initial blow created by the Auditor General's report. There was some debate over whether I should abandon my original plan to go for an early election, and govern for a while, giving me a chance to plant my agenda more firmly in government and in the public's mind. To do so, however, would have branded the new government as a lame duck – an impression that would only have been reinforced as the sponsorship issue continued to simmer. I also wanted a public mandate for the agenda I had set out. I consulted with both ministers and political advisers before dropping the writ, although I was never really in much doubt personally that I would go in the spring. On May 23, I went to the Governor General to ask for an election to be held on June 28. I understood how difficult the election would prove to be; and it was evident that the sponsorship issue would force me to run a very different election campaign than the one I had planned.

On the simplest and most personal level, the experience of leading my party through an election was not as novel or bewildering to me as it must be to some first-time leaders. You are jammed into an airplane for week after week, with forty of your best friends – the press corps – riding just five or six rows behind you. You may wake up at an ungodly hour in Halifax, have a "media availability" on the wharf, give a luncheon speech to a service club in Thunder Bay, and end the day with a rally in an arena in Winnipeg. Although I have long ago seen the toned body of my youth metamorphose into something, shall we say, less toned, I have always been blessed with a strong constitution and lots of energy. I can go long hours without exhausting myself, which is what you have to do on an election campaign. I can also sleep on planes. Furthermore, throughout the Chrétien years, the party had routinely asked me to conduct a national speaking tour parallel to the prime minister's during elections. These tours were almost as extensive as his, but with none of the support a party leader enjoys. I was used to schlepping around the country on scheduled aircraft, suffering long waits in airport lounges and at hotel counters. The "leader's tour," with its retinue of logisticians, made the campaign a relative breeze. Nothing, however, made as much difference as having Sheila by my side. Her presence meant that on the flights between events, I could retreat with her and take my mind away from the campaign.

The main challenge was having the mental composure to step back and play the role you can most usefully perform in the campaign: that of salesman-in-chief. I loved it. I had got into politics to sell my vision of what the country could become. But this meant that I did not have much direct contact with the campaign managers, David Herle, John Webster, and Lucienne Robillard. Lucienne was new to the campaign team, but I had watched her over the years as a cabinet colleague. No matter what portfolio she assumed she mastered it quickly, knew what she wanted, and got it done. She also was a person of very strong integrity and conviction, exactly what we needed at this particular juncture. I dealt with them and the others on the ground mostly through Terrie and Tim, who came with me everywhere on the tour. When I would ask to see the overnight polling numbers, Terrie would tell me that wasn't necessary; it wasn't in my job specs and wasn't going to help me concentrate on what I had to do. If I really wanted to see them, I generally had to go behind her back.

Though the kaleidoscope of towns, villages, factories, landscapes, hotel rooms, crowds, cameras, and candidates can get a little confusing on a leader's tour, there are a few simple rules. For example, one of the great things about political rallies is that they are invariably festooned with signs that have the name of the party candidate and the riding in which the candidate is running. If you are a party leader: read these signs. That way, as the days and places and people all become a blur, you will never forget the name of your good friend "X," or what riding, let alone what province, you are in, when you go on to commend him or her to the local voters.

One thing I did not like about the leader's tour was that I was often booked into halls too small to accommodate the Liberal supporters crammed into them. This is an old political trick, to make the rally look good on TV. Better to have five hundred people sardined into a room registered by the fire inspector for two hundred than to have them looking lost and lonely in a hockey arena. The problem is that as the candidate, it is very difficult in a loud, crowded room full of cheering supporters to take the mike and appear prime ministerial. No doubt this is what happened to Howard Dean in the 2004 presidential race when, carried away with enthusiasm during a rally, he let out his famous yowl. This does not connect well to the TV viewer, in his or her pyjamas, placidly sipping a cup of Ovaltine before bed. I was never quite that bad, but I do remember Terrie taking me down after one especially throaty and agitated performance standing on a table in a Burlington pub. "For crying out loud," I said in my defence. "If you don't want me looking and sounding like that, don't book me into that kind of event." But of course the local candidates always loved those sweaty, overpacked rallies, whatever the TV viewers made of me, so they never really went away.

In December, 2003, when I took office as prime minister, there was every reason to believe that the coming election would be fought on health care. It had, for many years, been the number-one issue for the public. Because of the federal government's sound financial stewardship, we now had the resources to reinvest in the system. And as a new prime minister, I would be able to open negotiations with the provinces with a clean slate. The Liberals were the founders of the national medicare system. The Conservatives, under Stephen Harper, were – to say the least – suspect in their commitment to it. There was every reason to believe that we could win on that issue, and it did prove to be a bulwark of our platform.

There was one hiccup in the run-up to the campaign, however, when Pierre Pettigrew, whom I had appointed minister of health, mused publicly about "experimenting" with the private delivery of publicly funded health-care services. Of course, it should go without saying that many of the services we receive through medicare are already privately delivered. But the matter of private delivery of care is often confused with what I regard as the fundamental issue: whether we have a publicly funded system that covers everyone and guarantees universal access. What Pettigrew said was unremarkable in Quebec, but it touched a sensitive nerve in the rest of the country, where some people mistakenly saw it as a less-than-complete commitment to medicare. It took a day or two to get that one back in the box – another lesson, as if one were needed, about how passionate feelings are on this issue, and how difficult it can be to navigate.

During the campaign, I met with a group of cancer patients at a YMCA near Toronto. I heard a presentation from Michael Decter, the health-care expert, and Dr. Terry Sullivan, the head of Cancer Care Ontario, on how to reduce waiting times for cancer treatment. I was very moved by this encounter: on the one hand, I could see and hear people who desperately needed life-giving care and, on the other, experts who knew there was a way to make sure they got it, if only governments would do their part. I told them I was going to put the message I heard that day on the national agenda. I hoped that this event would be instructive to the media, helping them – and through them, the public – to understand why I felt so strongly about waiting times. Ironically, this event did not get much coverage. It happened to come the same day that Ralph Klein raised the prospect of radical changes to medicare in Alberta that would challenge the principles of medicare going back to my father's day. Paradoxically the Alberta premier's intervention helped us to make our case to the voters for enhancing the existing system.

But health care was just one part of our platform. I have always believed that a party should enter an election with a carefully considered policy document. That is what the Red Book was all about. Still,

I was not naive enough to think that parties win on their platforms alone – or even primarily because of their platforms. Often relatively trivial or completely unexpected incidents, surprising media coverage, or gaffes by the leaders or their candidates can play a substantial and even determining role in the outcome. It quickly became apparent in the 2004 campaign that our challenge as a party was not to reach out to new groups with our agenda but to retain the loyalty of voters who had long put their faith in us. Our core vote, in the cities, in Ontario, and especially in Quebec, was bleeding away. The sponsorship program had become the locomotive for the Opposition campaigns.

We might have weathered that if it were not for another issue – this one a ricochet from the government of Ontario. Dalton McGuinty's Liberal government had taken office in Ontario just a month and a half before I took over as prime minister. One of his centrepiece promises in the election campaign was that he would not raise taxes. Soon after the election, Premier McGuinty came to see me at 24 Sussex, where we discussed a number of issues. Almost off-handedly as he left, he mentioned that his government "might have to do something on health premiums." Nothing in what he said prepared me for his government's first budget, brought down on May 18, just days before I called the federal election. It introduced a "health premium," which was in effect a tax, ranging from $60 to as much as $900 depending on income. Coming when it did, where it did, in the province where the federal Liberals had historically had their stronghold, and creating not just a tax issue but also an issue of political trust, it was a heavy blow to our fortunes. I remember that most of our Ontario MPs thought the health premium was a bigger problem than the sponsorship issue, particularly in the first weeks of the campaign.

The Conservatives, under their new leader, Stephen Harper, understandably wanted the election to be about the sponsorship program. I wanted it to be about our future and the kind of Canada we wanted. I knew that despite their disgust over sponsorship, most Canadians did not share Harper's view of what we were or what we should become. He had a long career behind him in which he had shown himself to be firmly in favour of dismantling many social programs, including important elements of medicare. He had been such an over-the-top decentralizer that he had at one point talked about Alberta erecting a "firewall" from Confederation and creating a kind of provincial autarky within a limply federated Canada. He had also made it very clear that he was not a supporter of the Charter of Rights and Freedoms as it was evolving through the courts. I had trouble believing that anyone would be attracted by this pinched vision of Canada.

Fortunately for us, Harper's candidates scored many own-goals on our issues. It was the usual thing to which we had become accustomed from the Reform and Alliance parties. The Conservative organization outdid even its predecessors in mid-June with an official party press release headlined "Paul Martin Supports Child Pornography." Really. Almost unbelievably, Stephen Harper's response was to refuse to apologize, though he said that he thought the headline "was a bit strong" and directed that it be changed. Somehow they failed to understand that this kind of preposterous slander reflected on them among voters and not on me.

I never lost my confidence that we were going to win the election, although I would not have bet heavily on a majority. My organizers were not so sure. Roughly halfway through the campaign, David Herle and John Webster met me at the Ottawa airport when the tour plane arrived there for one of our few down days, and rode with me back to 24 Sussex. They wanted no one else in the room when we talked. David laid out some of the polling data on which he based his sober assessment: we were slipping behind. In government, I have always found polls less useful than focus groups, which can help you figure out how to communicate with the public about the policies you have developed. A poll can't tell you much about whether to balance the budget, how quickly, or when. In elections, however, I get much more interested in the polls, because they are the quickest and most effective way of knowing whether your message (and that of your opponents) is getting through.

As the three of us sat in the little sunroom at 24 Sussex, they laid out a two-pronged shift in strategy. It has always been John's strongest ability to look at a situation, however bad, and see a road out of it. First, in English Canada, he recommended that I move away from a concentrated attack on Stephen Harper and his values, which had already penetrated quite effectively to voters of the centre and left. The problem was that many of those turned off by Harper and his agenda were fleeing to the NDP, in part, no doubt, in disgust over sponsorship. We needed to make very clear to progressive voters of all stripes that the only effective way to prevent a Harper government was to re-elect us. "You let me worry about Harper," David said. "You have one job in the remaining days of this campaign: convince Canadians that you'll cut wait times in the health-care system if you are re-elected."

In Quebec, if anything, the problems were more acute. The Bloc Québécois had managed to turn the sponsorship issue, with its links to national unity, into a comprehensive condemnation of the federalist system in the minds of many Quebec voters. David made it clear to me that the Quebec campaign I had imagined, in which we reached out to nationalist voters, had instead become a fight to save the furniture as federalists stampeded into the Bloc Québécois camp, or resolved simply to sit this election out. We were in deep trouble, he told me, in danger of being reduced to a small rump of seats in heavily anglophone and allophone ridings. In that context, he recommended that we remind Quebecers of what was at stake. A massive Bloc Québécois victory would potentially lead us back into the swamp of referendum, uncertainty, conflict, and doubt.

The strategic turn in English Canada was the easier of the two to accomplish (though, interestingly, many reporters had so much trouble understanding why we would turn our sights on the NDP that they almost failed to report it). Personally, I had no problem reaching out to voters who were considering the NDP and reminding them of the stakes in this election. Changing tack in Quebec was much more difficult. The party there was deeply attached to our original strategy of wooing voters back from the Bloc Québécois. A strategic change now required a more muscular approach from my national organizers toward the management of the Quebec campaign.

Given the issues and those stakes, there was no one better to make the case for federalism and the Liberal Party than Stéphane Dion, with his unique combination of intellect and passion, alongside Pierre Pettigrew, who like Dion had joined the federal cabinet in the wake of the 1995 referendum. It would have been easy for Stéphane, given his exclusion from cabinet just a few months before, to play the dog in the manger. But that isn't Stéphane. To that point, he had devoted his energies almost exclusively to his own riding, but he leapt at the opportunity to play a bigger role on a wider stage. In the final weeks of the campaign, he barnstormed the province, going on every radio talk show and speaking at every public meeting he could.

In the last days of the campaign, many commentators in the media wrote us off. I was certain, however, that a victory was still there for us. I felt the turn at a speech I delivered in Toronto to a meeting of the Women's Executive Network, organized by my friend Pam Jeffrey. I could feel the rising anxiety among this group of accomplished and progressive women about what a Harper government would do to the Canada they believed in. The anxiety was all the more acute because Harper had begun speaking in public as if victory was already his – and many in the media had started believing it.

I hatched the idea of going on a cross-country tour in the last hours of the campaign. I started by dipping my foot in the Atlantic in Nova Scotia, and with the time-zone advantage was able to fly to Gatineau, Quebec, on to Toronto, then Winnipeg, Regina, and Vancouver – ending the day by putting my feet in the Pacific. Perhaps because he believed the election was in the bag, Stephen Harper spent much of his time in the final days in Alberta, where the results were never in doubt. It was a gift to me because it painted such a contrast.

Of all the major polling firms, only one predicted a Liberal victory. On election night, CTV's pollsters revealed their biases by all but declaring us defeated before the votes had even been counted. But

David Herle knew better. Whether it was our mid-campaign course correction that made the difference – and I am inclined to think it was – our support rallied tremendously in the last forty-eight hours before voting commenced. David could see from his research as we rounded the last corner into the stretch that we were pulling back into contention and then opening up a gap.

But such was the overwhelming opinion of commentators and pollsters that we would lose, that even Sheila was shaken. I learned much later – indeed only when I started on this chapter of the book – that on election day she went into David's hotel room where he was trying to get some badly needed sleep, stood over his bed, woke him up, and said, "David, tell me you're not lying to my husband!"

On election day, as usual, I went to vote in my constituency in Montreal and then retired to the Queen Elizabeth Hotel to rest and prepare to watch the evening's results roll in. David dropped by and gave me his final reading: we would win more than a hundred and thirty seats and a minority government. When the results came in, they were just as David had predicted. We had won. We had been reduced to a minority, but we had fought back from what many had considered certain defeat, and won.

CHAPTER NINETEEN

Sponsorship

All of us strive to be masters of our own destiny in an uncertain world, many elements of which are beyond our individual control. This is as true of politicians as it is of anyone else. There are, however, differences. Politics is played out in the public glare. Furthermore, in politics, there is always someone actively trying to prevent you from reaching your goals. A win for you is almost always a loss for someone else; and of course the reverse also applies. To a degree, you can calculate the odds of various possibilities and make your decisions accordingly. For example, it was obvious to me that if I stayed on in politics after 2000, I might inherit a Liberal Party whose stock of goodwill with the public was somewhat depleted. I considered that possibility and believed that through a combination of ideas, organization, and force of personality I could revivify the party and the government, and convince Canadians that I represented change. I always knew there was a risk that I would be proved wrong; it was a calculated risk I was prepared to take.

In politics, as in life, however, there is also another form of uncertainty – what Donald Rumsfeld memorably dubbed the "unknown unknowns." A freak storm may knock down your house or a cancelled flight may lead you to miss the meeting at which you could have sold your million-dollar idea or landed a part in a Broadway show. It is difficult to calculate what you can't anticipate. And in politics this is a particular problem. Modern governments are enormous and complex. No one knows, or can know, everything that is going on. Yet our system rightly says that there needs to be responsibility and accountability at the top.

For me, the sponsorship issue fell into this category of "unknown unknowns." When I made my decision in 2000 to stay in politics, with the intention to run for the job of Liberal leader when Jean Chrétien stepped down, the sponsorship program was a ghostly presence on my radar. As I have said before, because of our differing views on Quebec, because of our competing political organizations in Quebec, and because of our personal rivalry, the prime minister excluded me from any close participation in the Quebec file. This was his baby. In my Finance years, I accepted this, albeit a little resentfully. To Jean Chrétien's credit, I had been fully empowered in Finance at a crucial moment in history. The portfolio had given me great latitude to pursue my interest in international affairs. And, to be frank, my English-Canadian supporters had been divided among themselves – and often from me – over Meech Lake; there was not much enthusiasm among them for poking that particular beehive with a stick.

Given the sway I had over the direction of the government in the 1990s, it is perhaps understandable that people assume I must have known more than I did about the inner workings of the sponsorship scandal. "Paul Martin was practically running the government; how could he not have known?" The answer is threefold. First, as important as the finance minister's job is in setting fiscal policy and directing resources to priority areas, the role is not one of oversight. Finance is a small policy department, despite its outsized reputation and clout. It does not oversee the disbursement of funds, as the Treasury Board does, nor does it audit them. Second, no one in a renegade program has an interest in phoning up either the minister of finance or the people in the department and saying, "Guess what? We're siphoning off public money." Conspiracies – which is what this was – are by their nature secretive. Third, Jean Chrétien's organization and my own were virtually at daggers drawn in Quebec. The last person to whom anyone in this conspiracy was likely to talk was me, or anyone close to me.

Whether I liked it or not – and I definitely did not like it – my time as prime minister would be marked by a scandal that was the fruit of mismanagement and malfeasance by others. I understand the anger of Canadians; indeed, I share it. In retrospect, it is easy to see why many of them took their anger out on me and the party I led: where else could they direct their rage? I dealt with the scandal as openly and honestly as I could, and though some have criticized this openness as a political mistake, I have no regrets for doing what I believe was the right thing. But you will understand my anger that in my time as prime minister, the scandal prevented me from devoting my whole energies to my dreams for Canada.

The consequences of the sponsorship scandal were actually much broader than any missed opportunities for me and my government. Consider where we were politically in this country before the Auditor General's report was ultimately tabled in February 2004. Separatism, and its Ottawa proxy, the Bloc Québécois, were in full retreat. The polls suggested the Liberal Party was poised to move back into francophone Quebec in a way that it had not done since 1980. The NDP continued to wither on the vine, as it had been doing for a decade. The Conservative parties were finally getting their act together, but many "progressive" conservatives were uncomfortable with the new creature coming into being and were looking for another home. It is no exaggeration to say that the sponsorship issue revived separatism and the separatist parties in Quebec, lifted the NDP back on its feet, and lubricated the unity of the right. The ultimate product is a government now led by the most right-wing prime minister in Canadian history, representing barely more than one-third of voters, confronted by a centre-left electorate divided among four parties. That is what the authors of the sponsorship program and those who suborned it by looking the other way have to answer for.

The first inklings I had of what would become the sponsorship scandal came, as they did for most people, through the pages of the

Globe and Mail. Like everyone else, I knew the government of Canada had long been in the business of supporting local festivals and suchlike. That had been happening since I was a child. In this context this specific program – what came to be known as the "sponsorship program" – had been initiated by Jean Chrétien after the referendum to raise the profile of the federal government, particularly in Quebec. What was new, unusual, and unknown to me, as it was to most people, was the degree to which the sponsorship program was mismanaged and that unscrupulous people were illegally profiting from it. When the first stories broke, it seemed like small beer, worth investigating and sorting out but not much more than that. Jean Chrétien asked the Auditor General, Sheila Fraser, to look into it. And the news stories kept coming. Naturally, the Opposition jumped on each incremental revelation. It was an escalating political problem, but still far short of a defining national issue. The Auditor General's first public report on the issue generated some discussion and concern, but it remained a second-order issue for the public. Polls at the time showed that health care remained at the top of Canadians' political concerns, with government integrity and accountability far, far down the list.

In 2002, not long after I had "got quit" from cabinet, the prime minister wisely appointed Ralph Goodale as minister of public works – a job that no sane man would have wanted at the time but one that Ralph was perfectly suited for by virtue of his probity and unimpeachable integrity. From what Ralph has told me, starting the day he was appointed, he managed the portfolio with almost no direction, or even interaction, with the prime minister, beyond the initial instruction to find out what was wrong in the department and fix it. Less than a day into the portfolio, Ralph announced that he was suspending the sponsorship program. Shortly afterwards, he threw out the advertising agencies to whom the job of managing the program had essentially been contracted out. And then he referred a number of specific elements of the program to the RCMP for further investigation. Finally, he sent an electric jolt through the government system, telling other ministers that he had ended any contact with the ad firms involved and suggested they do the same. All that in a matter of weeks.

In addition to the RCMP investigation, Sheila Fraser continued her audit of the sponsorship program. It was pretty clear from the stories now leaking in the media, as well as from the growing scope of the RCMP's investigation, that there were going to be some serious revelations. Her report was ready for release in November 2003. For Jean Chrétien, it certainly would have been a bitter pill to swallow on the eve of his departure from politics. It would also have been an act of political responsibility and a gift to the future of his party to have accepted the report when it was due. But whether it was out of a preoccupation about his legacy or bitterness toward me – and only he can answer that – he decided to take the steps that would delay its publication until after I had replaced him at 24 Sussex. It is one of the many ironies in this sad affair that Jean Chrétien and those around him were later so critical of my handling of the Auditor General's report, when he and they had chosen, with great deliberation, to throw the responsibility for dealing with their mess into my lap.

When I came to office in December, in part on Ralph's advice, I cancelled the sponsorship program as virtually my first act. Ralph became finance minister when the cabinet was sworn in, of course, but because he had been minister of public works, he had been briefed by the Auditor General in the fall. When I finally had the report in my hands, I skimmed it, realized it would be a looming issue for the new government, and handed it over to a cabinet committee led by Anne McLellan that included the new minister of public works, Stephen Owen. I knew we had a big train coming, but I still did not recognize the scale of the political disaster the Auditor General's report would create. This was due in part to Sheila Fraser's vivid characterization of the report in the press conference she gave on the day it was released to the public – something no one could have anticipated.

There was an argument for reacting to the Auditor General's report in an understated way. That approach (for which many of my critics, including Jean Chrétien, have argued) would have simply been to say that the Auditor General had spoken and that the criminal matters arising from what she had found would be investigated in due course by the RCMP. End of story. The problem with that was that this whole affair was more than just a criminal matter, deeply serious though that obviously was. Everyone, including the public, understood that this was a deeply political program as well. It was important that those who had committed criminal offences be held responsible in a court of law. But the public was also right to demand political accountability, and that was something that I was determined to give them. Of course those responsible would feel aggrieved about being held accountable. Why wouldn't they, and why should that be a consideration?

Both Anne and Stephen felt very strongly about the necessity for an inquiry. I had appointed Stephen as minister of public works in part because of his impeccable credentials as a man of integrity and judgment. He was a former ombudsman in British Columbia and a one-time member of the Law Reform Commission there. I think that he would have seriously contemplated resigning from cabinet had we not initiated a judicial inquiry. In fact, my cabinet was deeply divided on the issue, very much along geographical lines. Few among the Quebec ministers favoured a judicial inquiry. Ministers from the rest of Canada were mostly in favour.

I personally believe that a government whose ethics are doubted – rightly or wrongly – is a government paralyzed. You cannot summon the political will or public support for change unless the people are prepared to give you their trust. That is why I decided to call the judicial inquiry that was led by Mr. Justice John Gomery. I wanted to make it clear that we had nothing to hide and would not sweep anything under the rug. I also announced "whistleblower" legislation to encourage public servants who see something going wrong to speak up. I appointed a special counsel to track down and recover missing funds. And I ordered reviews of government spending and contracting procedures through the Treasury Board.

To those who say the inquiry was a political mistake, I can only reply that the facts do not back them up. The public reaction to the Auditor General's report was spontaneous, immediate, and dramatic. One poll showed us dropping 17 per cent virtually overnight. Elly Alboim told me that in all his years looking at polls, he had never seen anything like it. In the days that followed, I was very open about my own fury at the Auditor General's findings in media interviews, including one on the CBC program *Cross Country Checkup*. As I made my way across the country on a pre-planned swing through eastern Ontario and then on to Quebec City, Winnipeg, and Vancouver, some clever journalist dubbed this my "mad as hell tour." Some of my critics within the Liberal Party later argued that by so openly expressing my disgust at what the report revealed, I raised the profile of the issue and therefore inadvertently condemned the party to eventual electoral defeat. Let's be clear: it was the misdeeds revealed by the Auditor General and later by the Gomery inquiry that damaged the party. My condemnation of them was right in principle and also, as it happened, right politically. That catastrophic drop in the polls the day after the Auditor General's report was released was quickly stemmed and then at least partly reversed as I showed the public that I shared their outrage.

That having been said, we did not win the communications battle over sponsorship in the end. I don't know whether it was winnable. What I would have liked the public to have absorbed was this: the scandal was the work of a relatively small group within the Liberal Party and the government; neither I nor the cabinet had any knowledge of the depth of what was happening in the sponsorship program, nor did most of those in government; I shared the anger and disgust at what had been uncovered; and I would undertake my responsibility on the public's behalf to make sure the facts were revealed, the miscreants were punished, and the structures put in place to make sure this could not happen again.

I don't think I handled the issue particularly well in public. As a politician, I had no problem talking about difficult things. I had made the spending cuts when I needed to, for example, and convinced the public that they were necessary. But I had trouble with an ethical issue like this one, in part because I was so bothered by it. It fed into an easy and cynical caricature of politicians as being devious or corrupt. I was mad about it. I was mad that people I knew had been involved. I was mad at Jean Chrétien for having left me this time bomb. It drove me crazy that I had to deal with this leftover mess when there were so many more important issues I had come into government to confront. In hindsight, it is clear that as a government that had been in power for a decade, we were not going to get the benefit of the doubt. When I stood up in the House and said that I knew nothing about what had happened, it did not occur to me that some would construe it as a claim that I had never heard of the sponsorship program; of course I had. I was saying that I knew nothing of the misdeeds.

The public had a right to be skeptical, of course. The Opposition had a legitimate opportunity to strike. But many commentators failed the elementary test of fairness by repeating the absurd insinuation that as finance minister I must have known. Did anyone really think that people like David Dodge and Don Drummond at Finance were in the know? It was absurd! And if the Department of Finance did not know, how did they think I would be apprised of the sorry facts?

I mentioned this later to a reporter who had been covering politics at the time. "Why didn't you just say that?" she asked. I replied that I must have said it a hundred times.

I simply could not believe, emotionally and intellectually, that anyone thought I had anything to do with this mess. Why would I have jeopardized my reputation for this? And why on earth would anyone have told me about it? My organization in Quebec was barely tolerated by the party there. The Little Sisters of the Poor would have known about the scheme before I did. Those who were involved were my political foes. As the Opposition assaulted me in waves, trying to link me personally to the scandal, I kept thinking someone would stand up and say, "Hey, wait a minute; he's the last person who would have known." But it never happened.

Even at the moment when the Auditor General's report was released, and I called the inquiry, I still had no idea how bad the sponsorship mess would turn out to be. I thought Mr. Justice Gomery would discover that the sponsorship program was handled very poorly by the government and that some money found its way into the wrong hands. I did not expect the level of criminality that was uncovered, nor the links back to the Liberal Party. I could not have imagined the B-movie scenarios of envelopes of cash being wordlessly pushed across tables in dimly lit restaurants. I had no conception that Radio-Canada's news network, RDI, would run the hearings live and that they would turn into a popular daily soap opera in Quebec. Perhaps I should have; but I did not.

The question then becomes: if I *had* known all that, would I have called the inquiry? The answer is yes.

In this same period, shortly after taking office, I also confronted a series of problems involving people who had been appointed by the previous government. Only one of them was linked to the sponsorship scandal, though all of them raised questions of accountability to a greater or lesser degree. There was a mistaken belief among many people, especially in the media, that I had adopted a general policy of "sweeping clean" the government of people closely associated with my predecessor. From my perspective, each of these cases confronting us was a discrete problem, though of course I tried to apply consistent principles when they arose.

The first was Alfonso Gagliano, who had been public works minister during the launch of the sponsorship program. When the issue heated up in Parliament, Jean Chrétien had appointed him as ambassador to Denmark. I was told privately that the Danes were complaining, and said publicly that he was no longer serving Canadian interests in the post. In the circumstances, I agreed with Bill Graham, that as minister of foreign affairs, he should recall him as ambassador. Anyone who says that he was our best possible representative in that post at that time is being disingenuous.

The other cases did not relate to the sponsorship scandal. For instance, I had no intention of removing Jean Pelletier, who had been Jean Chrétien's chief of staff, as head of Via Rail. However, when the former Olympic athlete Myriam Bédard raised allegations of impropriety at the corporation prior to Pelletier's tenure, he was quoted in the media as saying: "I don't want to be mean, but this is a poor girl who deserves pity, who doesn't have a spouse, as far as I know." He should not have commented on the personal life of an employee. Furthermore, I had made it plain that no pressure was to be put on whistleblowers by their superiors. It was entirely inappropriate and a direct challenge to my whistleblower policy. To leave Pelletier in place in the circumstances would have undermined our commitment to public servants that they could come forward without fear if they had allegations or concerns.

At my very first meeting as prime minister with Jacques Chirac a few weeks later, the French president told me he was a friend of Pelletier and that he didn't much like the way I had treated him. Chirac had been mayor of Paris when Pelletier was mayor of Quebec City and they had become friends back then. I told Chirac that I appreciated their relationship but that I was prime minister of Canada and would make my own decisions.

A few days before Jean Chrétien's testimony, I appeared before the Gomery inquiry myself, in more matter-of-fact testimony. Preparing was not difficult. I had nothing to hide, and having my say over the course of many hours might even force the media to grapple with the facts in a way they had been amazingly reluctant to do so far. On the other hand, no one testifying under oath at a televised proceeding is in any doubt about the potential of lawyers to make you look bad. I was the first prime minister ever to run such a gauntlet, and I wanted to make sure that I did not do the truth a disservice. I hired two outstanding counsel, Andrew Davis and Leonard Shore. Two members of my staff, Katherine Levitt and Véronique de Passillé, also helped tremendously with my preparation. They walked me through the kinds of questions I might expect. As was the standard practice, I also met prior to my testimony with one of the commission's lawyers so that they would be prepared for what they were going to hear. In the end, it went exactly as I would have liked it to. For one day, at least, the media had to convey the story that I had tried in vain for so long to communicate in the House of Commons.

One ruling Mr. Justice Gomery made during the inquiry that had huge political implications for us was the initial publication ban on Jean Brault's testimony at the beginning of April 2005. I do not fault Gomery for it; he was doing his job. Brault was also facing criminal charges and was concerned about contamination of his trial by publication of his inquiry testimony. However, the fact that it was legally under wraps magnified public expectations about his admittedly sensational testimony. Within a few hours of his appearance, Brault's claim that large sums of sponsorship money had been funnelled back to the Liberal Party was posted on American websites. It was a big story, available to journalists, political staffers, and news junkies. But the publication ban kept it from most Canadians, who still get their news from televisions, newspapers, radio, and Canadian websites – all of which were prohibited from disseminating a word. By the time the news ban was lifted a few days later, the media had whipped up a frenzy of public expectations and unloaded several days of testimony in a single multi-megaton bombshell. The story broke during my trip to Rome for the funeral of Pope John Paul II, and naturally the travelling media clamoured for my comments right there in the precincts of the Vatican. But for all their ardour to hear from me, my call for the RCMP to investigate could hardly be heard in the din back home.

Before the Brault testimony, the Conservatives and the Bloc Québécois were already hungry for an election. The testimony, and its impact on the polls, had them salivating for one, despite the fact that the polls all indicated that Canadians were not interested in having an election just one year after the last one, on the sponsorship issue or anything else. It was in that context that Ken Dryden suggested I give a televised address to Canadians with a very specific pledge. I thought it was a good idea. In the speech, which ran just more than six minutes, I laid out as clearly as I could, as completely removed from the media filter as was within my power, all that the government had done, including shutting down the sponsorship program, calling the Gomery inquiry, suing the malefactors who had taken government money, and ordering a forensic audit of the Liberal Party's books so that any ill-gotten funds could be returned to the government of Canada. I talked about having established an independent ethics commissioner and a comptroller to oversee government spending. Finally, I pledged that I would call an election within thirty days of Mr. Justice Gomery's final report.

Of course I did not imagine that my address or the election pledge it contained would staunch the Tory and Bloc enthusiasm for an early election. I did hope, however, that it would clarify the issue for the public, telling voters they would have their say once all the facts were known, and that it was the Tories and the Bloc who were set on forcing an election on sponsorship before the facts were known. In the end, we survived a non-confidence motion and avoided an election that spring not because of my pledge but because of a complicated sequence of political events, most of them having nothing to do with the inquiry – a rarity in this Parliament. But that's another story, one that I will defer to a later chapter.

When Mr. Justice Gomery released his preliminary report at the beginning of November 2005, it was a huge media event. Although I had committed to calling an election after the final report, due in just a few more months, the release of the preliminary report triggered another round of partisan manoeuvring for an election, this time successfully. There were no stunning revelations in the Gomery report; those had already come out, day after day in the testimony before the inquiry over the previous year. There were, however, some interesting findings. Forgive me for quoting verbatim:

The Minister of Finance establishes the fiscal framework within which overall government spending takes place. Once that framework is set, departments are responsible for the management of the expenditures allocated to them, with general oversight by Treasury Board. The Department of Finance and its Minister have no oversight role for other departments' expenditures, other than setting the financial context via the fiscal framework.

And later:

Mr. Martin, whose role as Finance Minister did not involve him in the supervision of spending by the PMO *or* PWGSC *[Public Works and Government Services Canada], is entitled, like other Ministers in the Quebec caucus, to be exonerated from any blame for carelessness or misconduct.*

Exactly.

CHAPTER TWENTY

Taking the Lead

The same November weekend I was elected leader in 2003, the Grey Cup was played in Regina. The cleanup in the convention hall in Toronto had barely begun when I got on a plane and headed West for the game in which my hometown Montreal Alouettes would play the Edmonton Eskimos. There was a rumour that I might be asked to make a ceremonial kickoff, which nearly gave David Herle a heart attack. I could fall flat on my back-side anywhere, except in his home town. As it was, I was invited to toss the coin, which even he accepted I could probably manage without embarrassment.

A few weeks earlier, knowing that I was certain to become leader and eventually prime minister, I sent out an invitation for all the pre-miers to meet with me in a room below Taylor Field Stadium before the game for a get-to-know-you session. I'm afraid that our meeting came as a bit of a surprise to the prime minister and, from what I hear, was not received in very good humour. But it was very impor-tant to me that I kick off my leadership (sorry about that!) with a signal that I wanted to work closely with the premiers. Many of the issues that were most important to me – those of Aboriginal Canadians, health care, child care, and cities – would not be solved unless we were able to work together. Of course, this was a casual meeting. I was not yet prime minister, and it was not the time yet for making any decisions; but it did set a tone. I committed to holding annual first ministers conferences – something the premiers had been requesting – with the first to be devoted to health care. Afterwards, we all shivered in the stands through a pretty good game. Montreal was up at the half, but it was all Eskimos after that. It wasn't the result I wanted on the field, and I lost twenty bucks to Doug Richardson, a good friend from Saskatoon, but our meeting that day did contribute to a series of successes over the next two years.

The first discussion of public policy I can remember hearing as a young boy in our household was about health insurance: a program that was the product of tough negotiations between the provinces and the federal government. As federal minister of health and welfare for more than a decade, beginning in 1946, my father was determined to create a national public health-care system in Canada. It is not surprising that, as his son, I have always been an unequivocal supporter of a system that would cover all Canadians and would be publicly financed. Government financing means we pool the risk we all have of falling sick, instead of putting the financial burden on the most vulnerable, the sickest and the poorest among us. This is a deep philosophical commitment for me: it runs in my veins, you might say.

There is, however, a danger with a single-payer system such as ours, as there is with any monopoly: bureaucracies develop inertia and particular interests entrench themselves, to the detriment of those who are sick. That is why it is so important that our public system guarantees timely care. This is what lay behind the Chaoulli decision of the Supreme Court in 2005, which said that when governments put a universal system of health care in place, they must deliver those services in an equitable and timely way. The decision was essentially about wait times and what is reasonable. It will open the door to private health care in Canada if governments can't get their act together and ensure the timely delivery of medical services.

The issue of whether some of our publicly funded health services could be delivered by private suppliers is a different one, on which I am more agnostic, providing quality care is not imperilled. The fact is most doctors work in private practice, and they represent the single largest expenditure in Canadian health care.

Aside from these large philosophical questions, health care faced other challenges by the time I became prime minister. The provinces had begun cutting hospital funding in the early 1990s and I compounded the problem considerably with the cuts in transfers made in the 1995 budget. As we emerged into the era of balanced budgets and surpluses, it was obviously important to reinvest in the system. It also gave us a chance to make sure results, including medical outcomes, would be evaluated and those responsible would be made accountable.

The health-care system is enormously complex and yet very personal in the way it touches our lives. Few of us go through a year without visiting a friend or a loved one in hospital, or perhaps spending time in one ourselves. Most of us go to the doctor from time to time and, if we are lucky, have a relationship with a physician, which can be an important element in our good health. Because of that intimate contact, each of us evaluates the success of the health-care system much more directly than we do other government programs.

During the 2004 election, I had made a campaign stop in St. John's, where I spoke to the Canadian Nurses Association national convention, and I did something out of character for me. I spoke in public about the days I spent in the hospital with polio as a child. I told them about my memory of lying in a bed in a ward with other boys who had polio, and how one day the orderlies had brought a huge machine into the room. I asked the fellow in the bed beside me, who was a lot older, what it was. And he said, "That's an iron lung. You're going to go out of here in one of those. All of us are going to go out of here in an iron lung."

I told the nurses how I remember feeling terribly alone, since my parents could only stand at the window at the end of the ward and wave to me. So there I was, eight years old, faced with the possibility of living the rest of my life in this huge machine and nobody to talk to. At one point, a nurse who was working on the ward came by, and realized that I was upset. So she sat down and started to talk. The next night she came by again, and again she sat and talked with me.

She did this night after night, usually after she finished her rounds.

Then, one day she wasn't there for her rounds and I really felt very badly. It was her day off. But a while later, she turned up at my bedside at the usual time. She had come in to the hospital *on her day off* just to talk to me. I can't remember much about my experience with polio any more, except that one thing: that a nurse came and talked to a little boy, and I'll never forget that.

It was a more personal story than I am usually comfortable sharing in public. But I was glad I did. It felt as if I was saying thank you after all those years and I'm glad to recount it here for the same reason.

Of course, everyone knows that it is harder and harder for those in the health professions to give that kind of care because they are stretched to the breaking point. And of course, there is no way of measuring the tenderness I was lucky enough to receive. What you can measure, however, is how long it takes to get care of any kind: wait times, in other words. You can argue that there is much more to the functioning of the health-care system than wait times. But the time it takes to see a general practitioner or a specialist, or to get into the hospital for an operation, or how long you spend waiting in the emergency room are very good indicators of whether you are getting reasonable access. And that's how most people think about medicare. In a private system, such as in the United States, access to health care is rationed by the ability of a patient to pay; in a public system such as ours, health care ends up getting rationed through waiting lists, and those of us who believe in the future of public health care know they'd better be short.

Shorter wait times should be part of a broader set of reforms that directly relate to people getting better care and more quickly resuming their normal lives, which is why I was determined as prime minister to drive the process: to see the establishment of "benchmarks." If the public could see that it was taking longer for a hip operation or an MRI than the benchmarks said it should, it would help rally public pressure for increased health-care reform. The deficit had been conquered when I was finance minister because public opinion was mobilized behind what had to be done – an important element of which was laying out specific, achievable targets and then meeting them. I was convinced the same approach would work for health care.

In the 2004 campaign, I promised to give the provinces stable, long-term funding for health care at a higher level, with a special emphasis on reducing wait times. The federal government had been in the habit of settling five-year deals with the provinces on health transfers, but they were constantly being renegotiated before being implemented because they were imposed by Ottawa from on high. The result was that Canada's "health-care debate" wasn't really much more than a perpetual federal-provincial squabble about money. Right after the election, I called the promised first ministers conference on health for September in Ottawa.

Before meeting with the premiers, I obviously leaned heavily on Ian Green, the deputy minister of health and Janice Charette, the associate deputy minister. Needless to say, the appointment of the former premier of B.C., Ujjal Dosanjh, as health minister gave us a provincial insight that was invaluable. He was also passionately committed to medicare and had stated that it was an essential component of Canadian citizenship. He was the right person in the right place at the right time. I also sought advice from some of the most knowledgeable people in the country outside the department, including Senator Michael Kirby and Michael Decter, a former public servant with a special expertise in health-care management, whom I consulted many times. I also spoke to Roy Romanow, whose Royal Commission on the Future of Health Care in Canada would play an important role in shaping our policy and influencing the fiscal debate at the premiers meeting. Finally I sought out Monique Begin, who had been the federal minister of health when the Canada Health Act was introduced and who along with Michael Dector had been there whenever I needed their advice.

At the federal level, we had to resolve some issues before negotiations with the provinces began. The first was how much money we were prepared to pony up, and over how long a term. We figured that amount was $42 billion over ten years, including the annual escalators. We were determined to get agreement on the annual increases to the transfers, so that we would not find ourselves back at the bargaining table every two years, confronted with new demands. But this was going to be a bargaining session, and we did not want to reveal our hand before I met with the premiers. In public we announced that we were prepared to put $15 billion on the table, and an "escalator clause" that would regulate annual increases, but we were deliberately vague about what that was and what it would cover. Although the premiers had announced they wanted us to contribute a flat 25 per cent of the health-care system, we did not agree.

The morning before the day of the conference, I met with the three territorial leaders over breakfast to discuss the unique health-care challenges facing the Northern territories. I committed $150 million targeted at long-term health-care reforms in the North because I knew that national solutions to problems don't necessarily work North of 60. From much higher costs due to the vast distances between remote communities, to the severe health challenges in our Aboriginal population, delivering health care presents more problems than most of us in the South would realize.

That evening, I had dinner with the premiers at 24 Sussex to get the discussions started in as informal a way as possible. In his inimitable fashion, Ralph Klein left early in order to visit the casino across the Ottawa River in Gatineau. I told him if he won, the federal government would expect royalty payments. He then returned to Alberta to prepare for his coming election campaign, leaving behind his minister of health, Gary Marr, to represent his province.

The next day I convened the meeting at the Government Conference Centre, which was the old downtown Ottawa train station, across the street from the Château Laurier Hotel. During the election I had promised to televise our discussions, which in retrospect was a mistake. In general, I am a great believer in transparency in government, which is why I made the promise. Unfortunately, the presence of the television cameras tempted the premiers to berate the federal government over their grievances, many of them real and a few imagined. I should have known better. At one point, an open microphone picked up a voice saying "Jesus Christ!" in reaction to something a premier had said. The hunt was on for the guilty party. Later, I had to 'fess up, and told the conference about a call I had received from my Aunt Anita and my Aunt Claire, who had recognized my voice and scolded me for my bad language.

While the premiers went after us in public, we knew we had the resources to address most of their real concerns and did not want to back anyone into a corner. We did not want to respond to their jabs, though it probably would have been good politics. I wanted a win for health care, and politics wasn't going to get that. I understood the premiers needed to vent. I did not want to score points; my goal was to reach an agreement.

Despite the public posturing, the serious negotiations went on behind closed doors. We had a marathon closed-door bargaining session at 24 Sussex, where I was able to take advantage once again of my ability to power-nap while Lucienne Robillard as minister of intergovernmental affairs held the fort downstairs. Unlike the CSL negotiations years before, where I had been forced to resort to sleeping on the library floor, this time I had my own comfortable bed just upstairs, and I was able to retreat unnoticed for twenty minutes to refresh myself and go back at it.

Around eleven o'clock that night, we ordered pizza for the premiers and their staffs inside 24 Sussex – and for the media who were huddled out on the sidewalk. It was only when the TV cameras started to roll on the house manager, Hilary Nicolson, as she arrived with the take-out boxes that it occurred to us that the footage of a health accord catered by a pizza chain might not be the enduring image we wanted for the negotiation. Dalton McGuinty, who, you may have noticed, cuts a slimmer figure than some of us, turned down the pepperoni and bacon special in favour of an apple that Jim Pimblett managed to rustle up from the kitchen.

Eventually, after much back and forth, the provinces, ably led by Premier McGuinty, came up with a counter-offer. McGuinty's chief of staff, Don Guy, went on a walk around the block with Tim Murphy and they thrashed it out. Then Tim briefed Ujjal Dosanjh, Alex Himelfarb, Lucienne, and me. The provincial counter-offer was $41 billion and was within the limit we had previously set for ourselves. Even before McGuinty, who was acting as spokesman for the premiers, presented what he called their "final offer," we knew we were closing on a deal.

All that remained was to put in place the agreement concerning evidence-based wait time benchmarks and provincial targets. I believed that if the Canadian Institutes for Health Information were to report publicly on what was happening on wait times province by province, sector by sector, from heart surgery to joint replacement initially, expanding the list over time, public opinion would drive reform. Eventually, thanks to Premier Campbell and a smaller committee of premiers, the provinces came onside. As a result we named Dr. Brian Postl of Manitoba wait times adviser. This was an important appointment, as he played a crucial role in keeping everyone's feet to the fire.

In the end, we got the deal we wanted for the country, a win for everyone. An extremely important element from the federal perspective was that it allowed for a 6 per cent escalation in costs each year, and had a term of ten years. This made it politically difficult for the provinces to keep trying to reopen the agreement.

From my perspective, something crucial for the future of the federation was that for the first time, unlike previous health-care negotiations, the provinces actually signed the deal, including Quebec. We also signed a side agreement with Quebec, allowing for a separate process of establishing benchmarks. This pleased me because it demonstrated a flexibility that in my view should be considered a normal part of the federal system in this very diverse country. As intergovernmental affairs minister, Lucienne Robillard was instrumental in securing this success, and Jean Charest was so excited with what we were signing that he asked to keep the pen!

Reaching an agreement had taken nearly five gruelling days, but it was worth it. Much of the commentary at the time dwelt on its implications for the survival of our minority government rather than the effect it would have on Canadians' health care. From my perspective, however, by resolving our differences with the provinces on health funding we had achieved my first objective for the new government before the new Parliament had even met. The issue of funding had been disposed of for a decade. So far this has allowed both levels of government to turn their minds away from squabbles over money to the need for further changes to improve patient care, to address issues such as how to improve health-care management and how to stay abreast of new technology.

The health-care agreement was a major success, but it will require further work to close the loop. As the process of establishing benchmarks widens in scope, and targets are set by the provinces in more areas of health care, the federal government needs to make sure that the public has a clear way of monitoring progress, in order to maintain pressure for further reform. The agreement signed with the provinces was quite clear on this point. That being said, all governments have the responsibility of ensuring this transparency and all governments have the responsibility of ensuring the continued reform of the public health-care system. That in essence is what the 2005 health-care agreement was all about.

In Canada, as in many parts of the world, we have tended to think about our health-care system primarily in terms of treating the sick, thereby neglecting the other elements of health, which include the prevention of disease. We received a sudden and dramatic lesson about what this means in 2003, when Canada lost forty-four people in a very short period to Severe Acute Respiratory Syndrome, more commonly known as SARS. The epidemic had begun in south China but very quickly spread to other countries, including Canada, probably because of the close business and personal relations between people in Canada and Hong Kong. The Canadian epidemic was concentrated in Toronto and Vancouver, but the economic and social effects were much broader geographically than the disease. The Conference Board of Canada estimated that the outbreak cost Toronto $1 billion in lost economic activity. Even in Montreal – a city without one reported case of SARS – newspapers reported that the Chinese restaurants were empty.

The crisis exposed our lack of infrastructure for dealing with such a public health emergency. I did what I could at a symbolic level to quell people's fears, which, despite the seriousness of the outbreak, were somewhat exaggerated. I was upset by the images of Canadians walking their own streets wearing protective breathing masks, so I made a public visit to Toronto's Chinatown during the leadership campaign, popping into shops along Spadina Avenue and meeting with leaders of the Chinese community in a restaurant along with Tony Ianno, the local MP.

When I became prime minister, I was determined that Canada would never again be caught unprepared in a crisis like this. I appointed Dr. Carolyn Bennett, a Canadian physician of wide experience and the MP from St. Paul's in Toronto, as the first-ever minister of state for public health. In the next two years thanks to her drive we created the Public Health Agency of Canada, headquartered in Winnipeg, where there already was a laboratory for studying the world's most infectious diseases. To head the agency we appointed Dr. David Butler-Jones as the first chief public health officer of Canada. He proved to be an articulate and outspoken advocate for public health, and with Dr. Bennett's support helped turn the Public Health Agency into an organization with the capacity and the mandate to prepare for future crises. The truth is that we still have a long way to go in developing techniques of preventing the spread of disease. But I believe the creation of the Public Health Agency will be seen as a major step in Canadian health care, and that it will continue to grow in importance. There are many reasons for this, including the continued failure of the world to understand the need to deal with the health issues that flow from globalization.

At an Asia-Pacific leaders meeting I attended in Korea when the threat of bird flu was on everyone's mind, I was asked by the prime minister of Malaysia why British Columbia had engaged in a mass chicken cull, killing some thirty thousand chickens. I explained that this was the best way of preventing the spread of the disease. One of the other Western leaders then asked the Asian countries why they did not engage in the same kinds of mass culls that the West did when they were faced with the threat of bird flu. We were told that if a farmer discovered bird flu among one of his ten chickens and slaughtered all ten – as he should – it would wipe him out. What he was more likely to do was to go to market with his chickens and sell them all fast, thereby ensuring the disease would spread. Asked why the government didn't step in, the answer was that most Asian countries did not have the money to engage in the kind of prevention that we did, and even if they did the Asian market system simply did not lend itself to the kinds of action we could take in the West.

The discussion that ensued was quite an eye-opener for both sides. The Western leaders appeared to come to grips for the first time with just how different the market system was in much of Asia with its myriad of small farmers compared to big agriculture companies of the West. On the other hand, many of the Asian leaders appeared to understand for the first time that the threat of a pandemic was not an issue that could be put on the back burner. The problem was that this discussion – an important bridge across the cultural divide – occurred just before the mandatory photo op, which, as in so many international meetings, meant that all serious discussion came to an end.

Subsequently at my request Canada convened a meeting of ministers and officials from the relevant countries to follow up on the opening created by this discussion, and to ensure that the concerns of the world's leaders were conveyed to the World Health Organization, which welcomed this alarm bell. Not long after that, the threat of the pandemic subsided, however, and as with so many international crises, once it was over the leaders went on to other things, and once again the WHO found itself a voice crying in the wilderness.

The fact is, however, there will be further pandemic threats, and we cannot continue to wait for them to descend upon us before we come to grips with what they represent. I raise this because I know that the Public Health Agency of Canada will play the key role in dealing with prevention in Canada, but I would also hope it will play a leadership role globally in ensuring that prevention not reaction becomes the order of the day whatever the health threat, fulfilling Carolyn Bennett's dream.

CHAPTER TWENTY-ONE

Sharing the Wealth

The beauty and the challenge of Canada is its diversity. Some of us live in Newfoundland outports or small prairie towns. Others inhabit the high-rise towers of Montreal, Toronto, and Vancouver, or the sprawling suburbs that spill far beyond their boundaries. But we are all Canadians, and part of being Canadian is having similar expectations of what our governments can and will do for our health, education, well-being, and economic development. That principle is broad, simple, and easy for most of us to understand. But the mechanisms for transforming that principle into a practical reality are often complex and arcane. Discussions about them are often played out in the public sphere as federal-provincial squabbles. The public hears the heated rhetoric – which grows more and more tiresome – but for the most part it is only a few policy specialists who understand the details.

When we agreed on the health accord in Ottawa in the summer of 2004, we ended up putting $41 billion on the table for the provinces, and you may think that was the end of the story. But it wasn't. The support Ottawa gives the provinces for health care is distributed among the provinces according to a relatively simple formula based on their population. So Alberta receives roughly the same amount of support per person as New Brunswick does, for example. The problem, of course, is that the provinces fund much of the health-care system from their own provincial tax bases, which may be very different depending on the wealth of the province. That's where equalization comes in.

The idea behind equalization is fairly simple: that Ottawa should transfer money to the poorer provinces to make sure their citizens enjoy similar levels of services to other Canadians. That principle is enshrined in the Constitution in just a few words, but it takes many more to explain how the system works. Under the equalization system, provinces receive money based on a formula that compares their relative wealth – or more specifically, their relative ability to raise taxes inside their borders. The less wealthy provinces are then given "equalization payments" from federal funds to help them close the gap. Those calculations were made every six months, and they shifted according to the changes in the economies of the different provinces. So equalization payments to some provinces could go up and down like a yo-yo. The way the formula worked meant that a serious economic downswing in one of the richer provinces could plunge a poorer province suddenly into an unanticipated deficit through no fault of its own. Because the payments were unpredictable. and because they represented an important part of many provincial budgets, some provinces could never be sure whether they could fulfill their health-care obligations.

That's why, at the health-care conference, we planned another meeting with the provinces and there we agreed to make changes to the program. First we agreed to provide an additional $33 million to assist the less prosperous provinces in meeting their commitments during the ten years of the health-care agreement. Next we made changes to ensure greater stability and predictability, essentially smoothing out the variations in equalization payments by changing the period of time on which the calculations were based to a three-year moving average, to reduce sharp fluctuations and make payments more predictable.

We then committed to a mandatory review of the system every five years to determine whether the overall amount Ottawa was transferring to the provinces should be raised or lowered, and finally we created a panel to report back on the fairness of individual provincial shares of the equalization pie.

If all of this sounds terribly complicated that's because it is – not the principle, it's in the Constitution – but the formula, ay, there's the rub! When I was at the Department of Finance, I was told there was only one person who understood equalization, a fellow named Doug Clark. You can imagine my mixed feelings when I went to his retirement party.

And then there were the Atlantic accords. Not long after I became finance minister, Premier Clyde Wells had appealed to me to help find a solution to Newfoundland and Labrador's fiscal problems that would allow the province to lift itself up rather than be perpetually dependent on federal assistance. I spoke to Ralph Klein about this and he was very sympathetic to Wells's concerns. Unfortunately other provinces were not, but I always kept in mind the need we would eventually have to deal with – the intractable financial problems facing Newfoundland and Labrador, as well as Nova Scotia, their sizable deficits and incredibly high debt loads. Both provinces were caught in a no-win situation. Each of them was in such severe financial straights that we had to find a way to repair their balance sheets and I felt it would be better if the solution was based on their own resources.

This is why I sought to strengthen the Atlantic accords. Nova Scotia and Newfoundland and Labrador were on the brink of new oil and gas developments that promised to transform their provincial economies and lift them out of their relative dependence on the rest of Canada. If the accords had been left as they were, much of what they gained in oil and gas revenues would have resulted in reduced transfer payments. In other words, the governments of the producing provinces would not be the prime beneficiaries of the Atlantic oil and gas boom. That would have deprived them of a unique opportunity to shuck off their debts and set off on a new economic and social path. These provinces (and particularly Newfoundland and Labrador) had an opportunity to pull themselves out of an historic hole, not with federal bailouts, but with money they generated within their borders. It would have been a national as well as a regional misfortune not to let them to do so, an unforgivable missed opportunity.

The accords went back to the time of John Crosbie and the Mulroney government. The problem was their real benefits would have ended just when both provinces were about to realize them. I wanted to allow the two provinces the immediate lift they would get from their new oil and gas revenues and extend the arrangements long enough for them to launch themselves on a new economic course. I was not prepared, however, to perpetuate the arrangements indefinitely. They needed to have a termination date.

Unfortunately, our ability to reach a deal was complicated by the fact that we had a negotiating partner in Danny Williams, the premier of Newfoundland and Labrador, whose negotiating style was not exactly built around "getting to yes." During the 2004 election campaign, I had pledged to ensure that Newfoundland and Labrador and Nova Scotia would be the primary beneficiary of the offshore developments. When Williams raised the issue during the first ministers meeting on health in September 2004, I reiterated my intention to keep my promises to Newfoundland and Nova Scotia. I gathered all the premiers in the room and asked them whether they were prepared to accept that I was going to take action to strengthen the accords. "Speak now or forever hold your peace," I told them. No one spoke except for New Brunswick's Bernard Lord, who did not object but indicated he was not very happy.

I do understand, given their history, why Newfoundlanders like to have a provincial leader who is a visible champion ready to take on the powers that be, and I had no problem with that. But when Williams ordered that Canadian flags be lowered at the provinces' government buildings, I drew a line in the sand and said I would not negotiate with him until they went back up. In any event, we kept at it with John Hamm, the premier of Nova Scotia, and came close to a deal early with him. The problem was that Hamm would not sign until Williams did, which meant that after the flags went back up we had to go through a couple more months of talk before we ratified the deal. My basic purpose was to put both provinces in a position where their debt and deficit positions would improve to the point where they were on a closer footing to the other recipient provinces. This meant they had to use the monies primarily to retire debt. Both premiers agreed to do so. Both kept their word. I hope their successors will honour that understanding.

I stand by the measures I took to strengthen the Atlantic accords. My goal was to provide both provinces with a new start so that in the future they could win through their own efforts. I regret, however, that the negotiations have been perceived as a unique one-off. First of all, the Atlantic accords had been in existence for fifteen years. Second, our intention to proceed was set out at the health-care meeting and everyone knew it. Third, every province enjoys one-off arrangements, though they take various forms. The Auto Pact had enormously benefited Ontario over the years, and subsidies to aerospace have benefited Quebec, just as the accords will benefit the two Atlantic provinces. But these other arrangements were much less controversial, because they were not wrapped up in the public's mind with the equalization system in which every province has a stake.

The other thing I regret in all of this is that Energy Minister John Efford, who fought vigorously for the accords, and his native province, was attacked at home when the federal government insisted that the deal reflect a fair balance and that it have a termination date. Just as I believed that Williams and Hamm fought for their provinces, so did Efford as the federal minister for Newfoundland and Labrador fight for his province. He also fought for the national interest, as was his responsibility, and this should be recognized.

The federal government has a well-established constitutional right to develop programs and spend money in areas of primary provincial jurisdiction. This spending power is what allows Ottawa to launch or maintain national programs where the issues themselves are national in scope or have national implications. The spending power is what enabled my father and Monique Begin to bring in health insurance and medicare, and what enabled me to introduce a national system of child care and put in place a new deal for the municipalities.

As I have said before, one of my preoccupations as finance minister, and later as prime minister, was to make sure that my generation would live up to its responsibilities to the generations to come. This is why as minister of finance (despite many late-night debates with my departmental officials, who disapproved of the measure), I was so supportive of the government's decision to extend maternity and paternity leave to a full year. I remember describing those debates to my daughter-in-law years later, after she gave birth to her second child. Watching the two parents cope with two children under the age of two, and talking to their friends in similar situations, I was certainly glad my view prevailed.

This is also why I reacted the way I did, one day in 1996, when a paper arrived at my office, authored by the social policy expert Ken Battle at the Caledon Institute, an important social policy think-tank. The covering letter was almost apologetic, saying that I probably didn't have time to read the whole document, but perhaps I could take a look at the executive summary. The paper outlined an imaginative scheme for using the tax system to get money to the families with children most in need. It was well known that poor families often found themselves in a "welfare trap." If mom or dad went out and got a job, usually at the bottom of the pay scale, they not only lost their welfare payments (as well as having to pay taxes and other premiums on their paycheques), but they also lost the many other benefits they and their children received, including, for example, dental and supplemental health care, eligibility for nutritional and early education programs, and so on.

Ken's idea was groundbreaking: he proposed that the federal government would provide monthly payments to low-income families with children through the tax system. That would allow us to use a sliding scale of need, so that when someone took a job, they didn't suddenly get cut off from financial support. In exchange for Ottawa taking over the burden of income support for these poor families with children, the provinces would guarantee that the money they saved would be redirected to other programs for helping poor children through early childhood learning, for example, or better nutrition, public health, and dental programs. And these programs would be available to the families of the working poor, who often have been frozen out in the past.

I thought the scheme was ingenious, and I phoned Ken up one Sunday morning to talk about it. We didn't know each other at the time, and he was plainly a little startled at being peppered with questions from the minister of finance as I played devil's advocate, trying to suss out any vulnerabilities. At the end, the conversation left me convinced this was the right thing to do, and that we had the resources to do it.

I was very lucky at the time to have Pierre Pettigrew as my colleague at Human Resources. Obviously, Ken's idea could not succeed without provincial buy-in. Pierre quickly forged strong relationships with his provincial counterparts across the political spectrum. The agreement Pierre worked out with them over the coming months for the National Child Benefit embodied my view of federalism.

True, the federal government was getting directly involved in an area of provincial jurisdiction. But not every national program involves the national standards required of the Canada Health Act. In this instance the federal government was able to build on the provinces' individual accomplishments, allowing each great latitude in determining their specific needs and in developing the programs to address them. Truth be told, there are considerable benefits in competitive federalism where provinces attack similar problems in different ways and learn from one another's successes and failures. Thus when I revived the idea of a national child-care strategy after I became prime minister, I was building on what we had already accomplished for the neediest of our children.

My interest in early learning and child care went back to the 1980s, when I first met Dr. Fraser Mustard, the brilliant Canadian scientist and physician who had conducted pioneering work on the relationship between early nurturing and future health and development. He walked me through his thinking about the way in which the minds of infants and young children are wired neurologically, and how that is affected by the care they receive from their very earliest moments, long before they reach school. It was the exposure to Dr. Mustard's ideas that led me, along with Chaviva and Terrie, to lace the Red Book in 1993 with so many proposals for daycare, nutrition, and literacy. Later on, Margaret McCain, who worked on similar issues, and co-chaired a task force on early learning in Ontario with Dr. Mustard, had a similar influence on me. The ideas of Fraser Mustard and Margaret McCain make it abundantly clear that a child who is well-fed, secure, loved, and well-educated is likely to be a stronger, smarter, more well-balanced, and better contributing member of society.

The debate that ensued was sometimes framed by my opponents as a question of whether children were better off in the home with a parent or in an institutionalized setting. I'm afraid the cattle had long ago left the barn on that one. Whatever some social conservatives might prefer, most Canadian families find the need to put their children in child care at some point, and often for several years until they reach school age. I am also at a bit of a loss to understand how the opponents of child care think that single mothers, not to mention Aboriginal Canadians and immigrants, can acquire the skills and education they need to thrive without adequate child care.

In the Red Book, we had put the emphasis on a national daycare strategy that unfortunately fell foul of our absolute priority to get control of our finances in the mid-1990s. But now the time had come. We started working on our strategy as soon as we were elected, and it was developed under the guidance of Ruth Thorkelson in my office and Yaprak Baltacioglu at the PCO. Ken Dryden was the minister who went out and made it all happen. The idea was not to impose a one-size-fits-all child-care plan on the provinces. The provinces already had different approaches to for-profit and not-for-profit child care, for example. Furthermore in the latter case, some charged parents a fixed daily rate, while others had a scale related to income. I didn't think it was our job in Ottawa to impose our strictures on each of these issues.

The idea was to build a national child-care program based on provincial structures in place and working together to fill in needed gaps. Ken is quite simply a star, and not only because of his hockey career. His low-key seriousness and obvious goodwill meant that he was extremely effective in building relationships with his provincial counterparts, and because of this he achieved a profound level of commitment from the provincial social development ministers. Unfortunately, because the provincial systems were so different, and the level of attachment to child care so varied, discussions involving all the provinces tended to drift toward general "principles" that would have led us to committing very large sums of money under the vaguest of rules.

Therefore our approach quickly became to focus on a bottom line: to make sure that each province made substantial progress toward more regulated child-care spaces and toward enriched early learning. While the starting points and the paths to that objective might vary, the important thing was that the goals be defined for each province in a readily measurable way. None of us wanted to reach a national agreement that amounted to us transferring a large amount of cash based on general principles and nothing but provincial goodwill.

Eventually, Ken started negotiating individual agreements with the provinces, beginning with Manitoba because they already had a well-developed system that emphasized early childhood learning. Our idea was to establish as much as possible a model for the rest of the country. Because the provinces were so different the negotiations were tricky at a technical level. Some provinces, such as Alberta, had highly measurable minimum standards with regards to space and staff-to-child ratios, for example. Other provinces, including Manitoba, had more sophisticated goals, related to the quality of curriculum, that were also more challenging to measure. Nonetheless, the province-by-province approach proved to be much more effective than trying to cobble together a single national agreement. It was also a recognition of the asymmetrical reality of Canada. In the months that followed, we signed first with Manitoba, as we had planned, and then with the other provinces one by one, until at the end we had a truly national agreement.

These signing ceremonies were joyous occasions, in part because they were invariably attended by child-care workers who were proud to have their work recognized in such a visible and substantial way. There was only one problem from my point of view. We usually set up the signing ceremonies so that Ken would sit beside the provincial minister and ink the documents, while I stood behind them smiling proudly at what we had accomplished along with the premier. But the cameras didn't start flashing until they stood up for the ritual handshake – with me now having disappeared from view behind Ken's six-foot-four frame.

It is a tragedy that when they came to power, instead of building on what was a major breakthrough, the Conservatives decided to cancel the early learning and child-care program. They replaced it with a gimmicky political contraption rather than a serious effort to address the issues involved, and then after the election they reneged on their own promise to create more daycare spaces. Sadly, it is not just the children as individuals who will have lost precious years of opportunity, but Canada as a nation. What gives me some solace is that the agreements we achieved in my time as prime minister represent a template that a future government will inevitably draw upon. I mean "inevitably." This is not about whether, but when.

I realize that the provinces face immense financial pressures, and one of the reasons it is important that the federal government remain fiscally healthy is to do its part in relieving those pressures. I have never believed, however, in the so-called "fiscal imbalance" between Ottawa and the provinces. A fiscal imbalance implies that Ottawa has greater taxing powers or debt raising authority than the provinces, and that is quite simply not the case. There is one order of government,

however, that does suffer from a fiscal imbalance and that is municipal government.

While health care and child care were by no means easy issues to
navigate with the provinces, my desire to see our municipal governments become the economic and social catalysts they should be raised
even more complicated issues of federalism and how it should work.
Our municipalities are constitutionally creatures of the provinces.
They are where people live, but they do not have the revenues or the
decision-making powers adequate to their responsibilities. I think
Canada's municipalities and especially our great cities are too
important to be languishing in the background as national policy is
made and national issues are confronted. I was all too aware,
however, that if the federal government appeared to be crowding in
on the provinces' turf, the effort to strengthen our municipalities
could end up in a jurisdictional mess.

In my time at Finance, the cities agenda had become more and
more important to me. As prime minister, I finally had the chance to
do something, ably assisted by Brian Guest, the prime advocate for
the cause among those closest to me.

What we came to call the New Deal for Cities and Communities
marked the first involvement of the federal government in urban affairs
in twenty-five years. Pierre Trudeau's decision to create an urban
affairs ministry in the 1970s had ended badly. The Trudeau-era ministry had tried to use the Canada Mortgage and Housing Corporation
as its point of entry into urban issues, only to be rebuffed by the
provinces. A lot had changed in twenty-five years. Canada had become
even more urbanized, cities were under greater financial pressure, and
our understanding of what made great cities had evolved. But how to
get back in the game without offending the provinces?

Part of the answer were the infrastructure programs our government had first established in 1994 as a way of creating employment.
Over the years we had developed good working relationships with
the provinces and municipalities as we sorted out common priorities

for infrastructure. Frequently we shared the costs three ways, though increasingly the municipalities were having trouble financing their share. Once I became prime minister, I was convinced we could leverage the goodwill accumulated over the years to get back into the discussion of urban policy. At the same time, we could direct our investments in infrastructure increasingly toward greener and more sustainable projects. This time, there was no push back.

As prime minister, I had two goals in the near term. The first was to help the municipalities get the revenues they needed to undertake their responsibilities. Of course, that was tricky because the municipalities are provincially created entities, most of which rely heavily on property taxes and provincial grants. We did feel, however, that we had a couple of levers. One was to refund the GST that municipalities paid. This would provide a significant new revenue flow. Even more importantly, we also decided to divert five cents of the federal tax on gasoline to them, something that seemed sensible, since municipalities maintain roads and run our mass transit systems.

The second goal was to get municipal leaders more deeply involved in those national issues in which they had special experience and responsibilities. As it happened, on the same day as my second throne speech, October 5, 2004, there was a meeting of Canada's twenty-two big-city mayors in Ottawa. I decided that I should invite them to 24 Sussex for an informal get-together over drinks. As the conversation buzzed, I was off in one corner talking with a couple of the mayors and the ideas were flying around. It occurred to me that we should get everyone involved. So I got their attention and said we should have a collective bull session right there. Some of the mayors were standing, some were sitting on the spiral staircase leading up to the second floor – and we got all into it. Then I offered them a place at the national table – literally. We moved into the dining room, crowded around the big table, ordered more food and drink, and away we went for two hours while I questioned them on what kind of targeted investments we should be making in Canada's large cities. This was the first time that a group of this kind had been able to have a direct discussion with a prime minister – something that went a long way toward building goodwill for what I wanted to do.

In my first government, I had appointed John Godfrey to be parliamentary secretary with responsibility for the cities. The fact that I did not put him in cabinet was not a reflection either on him or on the cities agenda as a priority, quite the opposite. I did not want to provoke a constitutional spat with the provinces over our relationship with the municipalities right before an election. Immediately after the election, I appointed him minister of state for infrastructure and communities. This was an inspired appointment. One of the challenges John confronted from the start was the inherent tension among municipalities. He asked me, "So you want me to do cities: down to what size?" I replied, half facetiously, "No village too small!" I received a lot of criticism subsequently for "diluting" the cities agenda, but my objective was that all communities, whatever their size, deserved our attention, not only because all citizens, wherever they lived, deserved our attention, but because all communities had their issues. For instance, it is ludicrous to discuss regional economic development without rural governments at the table.

This isn't to say there weren't problems. The big cities made a claim for the most resources because of their size and rates of growth, while the smaller communities made special claims based on the problems of isolation and depopulation. Nonetheless, we acted quickly. In the 2004 budget, even prior to the election, we announced the 100 per cent GST rebate to all municipalities.

David Miller, the mayor of Canada's largest city, Toronto, and a former NDP candidate, became strongly supportive in public, as did Bob Chiarelli from Ottawa, Dave Bronconnier from Calgary, Pat Fiacco from Regina, Larry Campbell in Vancouver, Peter Kelly in Halifax, Gérald Tremblay in Montreal, and many others. During the 2004 election, I had also received an enthusiastic response to a speech I made in Edmonton at a big-cities conference, in which I elaborated on my plan to give municipalities a share of the federal tax on gas to develop their infrastructure. Some of my political advisers would probably complain that the cities agenda, which was always more driven by policy than politics, was less successful at the level of ordinary voters. After all, the architecture of the plan offered the municipalities greater fiscal resources and more autonomy in planning their projects, making it harder to stamp the federal government's "brand" on new subway stations or water plants. So be it.

After becoming minister, John Godfrey devised what proved to be an exceptionally successful strategy – in which he was assisted by a task force led by former Vancouver mayor and former B.C. premier Mike Harcourt. John quickly recognized that the most effective way forward was to embrace the variety and complexity of our urban life. Instead of developing a single, rigid national mould and then trying to cram each particular municipality into it somehow, he decided to go after the provinces one by one, with the aim of signing three-way deals involving the city, the province, and our government. Although he worked on the major cities in parallel, his first target was Vancouver, where we were assisted enormously by the B.C. premier and former mayor of Vancouver Gordon Campbell and his constructive view of the way federalism should work.

Campbell's help came at a very difficult moment for us in the House. In April 2005, we were being threatened constantly with defeat by the combined forces of the opposition parties. Although he was only a week away from launching his own re-election campaign, at the signing ceremony in Vancouver on April 15 Campbell appeared with a large number of B.C. mayors from all parts of the province, and the deal was universally heralded as a great success and a sign of good things to come for other provinces, cities, and communities if only our government could survive long enough to achieve them. It was a real morale booster at a tough time. I flew back to Ottawa that night, and as soon as I got off the plane, well into the small hours of the morning, I phoned John Godfrey back in Vancouver, who was in a bar celebrating with his staff. He was a little surprised to hear me ask, "Who's next?"

The B.C. agreement was not only the first; it created a gold standard that we followed elsewhere. It was important because it involved the Union of British Columbia Municipalities in a direct way, and as we found out, in British Columbia and elsewhere, one of the best ways around the urban-rural and big city–small city divisions was to involve these associations, and allow them to do much of the log-rolling and compromise among themselves. So, for example, the B.C. agreement stated that while municipalities of more than twenty-five thousand people could not use the infrastructure money for roads but had to devote it to public transport or other sustainable development, smaller communities had more freedom.

After the B.C. agreement, we were able to get the ball really rolling and signed deals with most provinces, even as the media and consequently the public were focused on the dysfunctionality of the minority Parliament and the almost daily intimations of the government falling. We actually got a little rivalry going, at one point, between those working on the cities file and those working on child care, over who was ahead in the race to sign up provinces.

Interestingly, in the negotiations to get the NDP's agreement on our budget in the spring of 2005, Jack Layton and his advisers had only the vaguest idea of what to ask for. We offered to speed up some of our plans for the cities, notably increased funding for public transit, that we were intending to go ahead with anyway. This worked splendidly for us and allowed Layton to claim a policy victory.

Despite all this progress, we actually needed one more budget to complete our agenda. Had we been re-elected in 2006, we would have been able to give the commitment on gas tax revenues more permanence by enshrining it in law. Our idea was to make a fifteen-year legal commitment. I said this during the election campaign and I was glad to see the new Conservative government pick up on at least this part of the new deal. This will allow the municipalities to borrow against that expected stream of revenue, and create truly sustainable municipal development.

The New Deal for Cities and Communities accomplished three things. The simple act of creating a ministry dedicated to the interests of cities and communities denoted a new respect for them. It meant that there was a place in Ottawa for mayors and councillors to discuss their problems and their hopes. By taking them seriously (by involving them, for example, in formal budget consultations), we were treating them as a mature order of government.

Second, by treating the municipalities as full partners in decision-making, not only on infrastructure matters but on issues as various as immigration settlement, housing, community safety, economic development, and urban Aboriginals to name a few, we were edging our way toward a new way of doing business in Canada. There had been tripartite agreements for urban development before, in Winnipeg and Vancouver, for example, but during our time in government, we increased the number of such agreements, focusing on their specific needs. Most of these were in the West, but we were within days of signing a major agreement with Toronto and Ontario when the government fell.

We also created "sector tables" under the auspices of the Canadian Federation of Municipalities, which, had they been fully developed, would have allowed the cities, provinces, and federal government to sit down and talk about specific challenges such as immigration, or ports, or housing where a group of cities and towns shared a common problem. These meetings would have been called by the cities, not the federal government, limiting provincial push-back.

All of this was done while working with the provinces. Indeed, when we signed the gas tax deal with Quebec on June 22, 2005, Jean Charest declared, "This is the most important agreement between Ottawa and Quebec City in recent years. This is proof that the federal system can benefit Quebec and show good results."

Finally, we managed to make the existing infrastructure programs increasingly "green," by dedicating ever-larger percentages of the funds to municipal water and transit projects. We insisted that the funds the municipalities reaped from the gas tax be invested in what we called

"environmentally sustainable municipal infrastructure." Every municipality, large or small, had to sign an agreement promising to show
how each new investment had led to a measurable improvement in
air quality, water quality, or reductions of green house gases after
five years. And each municipality had to produce a thirty-year "integrated community sustainability plan" relating these investments to
four aspects of long-term sustainability: environmental, economic,
social, and cultural. Over time, this requirement has encouraged and
rewarded longer term thinking about issues like sustainability and
global warming in Canadian communities of all sizes.

The reason that we were able to embark on these large new initiatives
with the provinces, whether it was health care or child care or the
cities agenda, was that we had managed our fiscal situation so well
in the 1990s. I have always taken the view that the strength of the
federal government's balance sheet must not be compromised. That's
the balance sheet the international markets look to first, and the one
that has the predominant effect on our interest rates, and the investment we are able to attract. In fact, the soundness of the federal government's balance sheet has as great an effect on the borrowing terms
the provinces confront as do their own books. That's why, except in
an extraordinary case such as Alberta when the price of oil is high,
Ottawa's fiscal position should be the best in the country. When I
was minister of finance, that took priority over everything. By the
time I became prime minister, things had opened up, it is fair to say,
precisely because of the attitude I had taken in the previous decade.
We now had a strong balance sheet. We now had surpluses instead
of deficits, and it was right that some of that money should find its
way into the hands of the provinces and municipalities. Together
there was a lot we could do.

CHAPTER TWENTY-TWO

Green and White

Like most Canadians, I have worked and lived most of my life in cities. And like most Canadians, part of my attachment to our country comes from the sheer scale and beauty of the land. When I was a young man, I found summer jobs that took me out on Lake Erie and then to northern Alberta, the Beaufort Sea, the Saguenay, and Hudson Bay. I hiked, canoed, and fished in some of the wildest places in Canada. All this was long before the words *ecology* and *environment* entered daily discourse. As I have said before, when I was young my love of the outdoors began to translate itself into strong feelings about conservation. In those days, very few people had begun to understand the interdependency of the natural world and the future of the human race. Like many people, it was only as the science progressed and the problems facing us increased that I became concerned with the larger issues of biodiversity, the ozone layer, and greenhouse gas emissions, to pick a few examples. In fact, I think it is fair to say that although this understanding had deepened considerably by the time I went into politics in 1988, it is only in the last decade that the science – and the public's understanding of it – has led us to face the fact that our very future as a species is now in play.

After the 1990 leadership convention, I asked to be environment critic. That job introduced me to a circle of Canadian environmentalists, including Elizabeth May, Stephanie Cairns, Louise Comeau, and David Runnalls among others, with whom I started consulting regularly. As opposition critic, I attended the Rio conference, chaired by my friend Maurice Strong, and grappled with some of these issues as they played out on a global scale. I had a chance to deepen my understanding of the ideas circulating internationally, and meet some of the important people behind them. Rio also marked me because of the appalling contrast between the commitments made by government leaders in that international forum and their actions after they headed home.

This experience coloured my view of how countries acted during the Kyoto process, where the undertakings we and the other countries made contained no substantive measures that would ensure their implementation. After we signed Kyoto, I argued for a fully articulated plan. To their credit, as environment ministers, Christine Stewart and later David Anderson made an effort to develop one. But they were fighting an uphill battle. Of course the conflicts were not only out in the community, with industry, but also internal; the departments of Environment and Natural Resources had deep philosophical differences, as well as disputes over bureaucratic turf. When the vote on ratification took place, after I was out of cabinet, I supported it. But I continued to express my deep reservations about this kind of policy making by photo op.

By the time I came back to government as prime minister, some people had concluded that meeting our Kyoto targets was impossible. This was not my view, but it was clear that they were extremely ambitious and were getting more ambitious every day that passed. By this time, Canada was about 20 per cent above its 1990 emissions level and its target was to get to 6 per cent below the 1990 level. Still, we had signed an international treaty and Canadians expected us to do our best to meet those commitments. I was determined to have a go, but this time we were going to have a plan to get there.

Under the direction of Brian Guest and Johanna Leffler (who collaborated with Desirée McGraw and Louise Comeau, two leading environmentalists, and a small group of environmental policy experts), the preparation for my environmental agenda as prime minister was well underway even before I became party leader. After the 2004 election, Stéphane Dion took over as environment minister. His arrival at the department proved crucial beyond even my expectations. He threw himself into the job with his characteristic energy, enthusiasm, and intellectual rigour. You have to remember that any program was inevitably going to be dauntingly complex. There was a complex scientific dimension. There were individual industrial sectors with which we had to negotiate and which did not hesitate to try outfoxing the system by offering up changes that were already underway for other reasons in the hope that the new regime would not have any impact on them. We were also hamstrung by controversial commitments made by the previous administration to cap the costs that industry would face to comply with emissions reduction targets. The provinces, of course, were significant players, for both constitutional and political reasons, and the provisions of the Kyoto treaty itself were complex. Finally, to be credible to the public, the whole package needed to be acceptable to important elements of the environmental community, who would be sought out by the media to give their imprimatur (or withhold it). In a way, it was the towering complexity of these issues that made Stéphane ideal to take them on.

Of course, the Environment department was not the only one concerned with this issue within government. When I became prime minister, the Department of Natural Resources had primary custody of the Kyoto file, and it took some effort to shift the balance. Brian Guest, collaborating closely with Stéphane among others, co-ordinated the development of what was called "Project Green," an umbrella under which we could place several elements of our environmental platform, including climate change. Before Christmas 2004, Brian gave me a detailed proposal, which included an ambitious attempt to reach our Kyoto targets. The plan included restrictions on greenhouse gas emissions that could be ratcheted up over time, as well as incentives for Canadians to make energy-saving changes in the daily lives. He also argued that we could earn international credits under the treaty by making environmental investments outside our borders that would also benefit our Canadian industries. I personally hoped that in the long term, we might be able to use Canadian technology to help developing countries in Africa, for example, to grow through the kind of green initiatives that would benefit them as well as us.

By developing a thorough costing and economic modelling we allayed some of the concerns of the Department of Finance. If there was a bureaucratic obstacle remaining, it was the Department of Natural Resources. Although the plan was transformed considerably as it fought its way through the bureaucratic process, we managed to get significant elements into the 2005 budget. We were beginning to break the logjam that had helped paralyze the government since Kyoto first emerged on the horizon. Canada at last had a very detailed plan for coming to grips with carbon emissions, even if we did not communicate this as clearly as we might have done.

The 2005 budget contained both spending and tax measures to reduce greenhouse gas emissions, including incentives to use wind power and other sustainable sources of energy. There were also conservation programs, including one encouraging homeowners to retrofit their houses to conserve energy. There were tax incentives to industry to develop less wasteful energy usage and money for environmentally sustainable infrastructure in our cities. There were also more traditional measures to enhance our natural environment, including our parks and waterways. It was quickly dubbed the "greenest budget ever," and rightly helped establish Stéphane's reputation as one of the world's most effective environment ministers and Ralph as Canada's greenest finance minister.

The plan that underlay Project Green was a judicious mix of regulation, tax incentives and disincentives, and emissions offsets. We recognized that when the United States finally turned on this issue, it would turn on a dime. In fact, its municipal and state governments were already showing Washington the way.

We wanted to prepare Canadians to participate in the international emissions trading system that would inevitably follow. We also wanted

Canadians to be able to take full advantage of the huge market for environmental technologies that will be in increasing demand as the world comes to grips with what may prove to be its greatest challenge.

As finance minister, I had set up an agency to develop environmental technologies, and it has been very successful, but it could be doing so much more. Almost every major problem the world has faced in the last two centuries has been resolved in part through technological advances. In 2000, Canada set up a pilot project for carbon dioxide sequestration, for example, in Weyburn, Saskatchewan, and I am happy to see the Harper government is now pursuing our lead on this. We have the right geology for carbon storage in this country, and we need to make sure this, and the development of a wide range of advanced environmental technologies, is an industrial and governmental priority.

In the same vein, we have not worked hard enough at finding technological fixes for coal-generating power plants. It is clear that the rapidly developing countries of Asia will continue to burn coal, increasing their production of carbon dioxide. The incentives and disincentives should ensure that no new plants will be built without the capacity to fully utilize newly developing technologies for carbon sequestration.

One of the other environmental issues that preoccupied me as prime minister was the preservation of fishing stocks. John Efford, who was my original natural resources minister before he had to step down due to ill health, and Fisheries Minister Geoff Regan had long argued that Canada needed to get a hold of the problem of overfishing off the nose and tail of the Grand Banks – outside our territorial waters. One on occasion, Mark Watton, who staffed the Atlantic desk in the PMO (and who was very deeply concerned about the issue), arranged for me to join a Fisheries Department surveillance flight out of St. John's. Below us they showed me a big fishing boat that two months earlier had cut its illegally sized nets to avoid capture by our people trying to police the fishery.

The problems off our shores were really just local symptoms of an international disease, and while our prime concern is the Nose and the Tail of the Grand Banks, ultimately a global solution is required. Some of the poorest countries on earth, including many in Africa, for example – countries that have always depended on local fishing for the very sustenance of their people – were the victims of huge industrial fishing fleets from much richer places such as Spain or Taiwan. These fleets sailed just outside territorial waters, vacuumed up the fruits of the sea, scraped the bottom of the ocean bare, destroyed the fish-stocks and the environment that produced them, then moved on to the next place, indifferent to the devastation they left behind. The global commons were being ruined – with every major fishing stock under threat – and I felt strongly that we needed to address this as a global issue. Canada – with the death of the Atlantic cod fishery as a terrible example of failure – was in a position to exert influence, speaking from bitter experience.

Geoff Regan, as fisheries minister, took the lead, and the push to increase global concern became a consistent element of our foreign diplomacy. I met with Britain's Tony Blair, Ricardo Lagos of Chile, France's Jacques Chirac, and George Bush, and argued for a "global commons" approach. I also met with Russia's Vladimir Putin, Japan's Junichiro Koizumi, Portugal's Santana Lopes, and Spain's José Luis Rodríguez, whose countries were among the worst offenders. Everyone agreed on the principle (albeit a bit defensively in some cases) that fish stocks were the property of humankind and should be managed as such. What I was looking for was an international agreement that would start with the North Atlantic but then go beyond it to manage fishing in international waters according to scientific and environmental standards, with the agreements monitored by an international organization as well as the coastal states. We had made reasonable progress at the leaders' level but by the time I left office had not yet achieved an agreement that would permit us to get officials doing the detailed work required. Who can doubt that fish stocks will collapse, just as our cod fisheries have done, if we do not adopt a global approach?

It was in the North that my feelings about the country, the land, our people, and the environment came together most closely. I had fallen for the North as a young man, working in the Arctic in the summertime, and the place has never lost its allure for me. It is remarkable that this vast expanse – which few Canadians know truly well, and which many will never see with their own eyes – can nonetheless have such a powerful hold on us. Of course, being a Northern country is very much part of how we see ourselves. Quebec singer Gilles Vigneault wrote the lyrics "Mon pays ce n'est pas un pays, c'est l'hiver" – *My country isn't a country, it is winter*. It became a very popular song that applies to all Canadians, whether they are digging themselves out of a snowbank in the Saguenay or walking into the January wind on Portage Avenue. While other peoples may define themselves by moments in their history that are memories rather than experiences – whether it is the adventures of cowboys or the lost glories of empires – we define ourselves in part by our geography, and especially the vast Arctic North.

When I was at Canada Steamship Lines in the late 1970s, and before we had become partners, Ladi Pathy approached me to see whether we were interested in forming a joint venture with Fednav, the government and Upper Lakes Shipping to build and operate an Arctic-class bulk carrier. I jumped at the chance. It was always part of my conception of the North that commerce would play a role in maintaining our sovereignty, along with our Aboriginal peoples, Arctic science, and the military. We built the MV *Arctic*, which at the time of its first operation was 51 per cent owned by the government of Canada and 49 per cent by the three shipping companies. The ship is a combination of bulk carrier and ice-breaker. One of my regrets about leaving CSL was that after I entered politics, the company lost its interest in the North somewhat, and when the government decided to sell its share in the ship, CSL did not take the opportunity to snap it up. Today, it has become part of Ladi's fleet at his company, Fednav.

When I became prime minister, I had two goals in mind for Canada's North: enhance the living conditions of the people that live there and assert our sovereignty over its land and waters. The two are intimately connected. Making life better for Northerners – in particular the Inuit, who live in some of the most remote areas of the territories – will allow many of them to stay on their ancestral lands, which will in turn reinforce Canada's sovereignty. Internationally, our work to improve the lives of those who inhabit our North underscores our sovereignty. (Both Russia and Norway have made similar arguments in defence of their own claims.) And the history of the Canadian Inuit on the land and ice constitute part of our claim too; it has been a source of frustration to some Inuit leaders that we have not made this case more strongly. Of course, the military must play a role in maintaining our sovereignty, but the territories are so immense that no purely military land- or sea-based solution will ever be enough.

As I've said, making the North a place where people want to continue to live is not just a matter of justice and citizenship; it is also part of making sure we control one of our most precious and certainly our most delicate geographical resources. We know that as the ice-cap melts, the emerging shipping lanes will be more and more attractive, and the potential environmental disasters more and more of a concern. At the same time, the natural resources that have been imprisoned and inaccessible underneath the ice will be more and more tempting to exploit. It is estimated that a quarter of the world's remaining oil and gas reserves lie in the Arctic Basin. At the same time, the changing conditions in the North will likely open up opportunities for a commercial fishery that will have to be carefully managed.

We need to make sure that we are sovereign over the economic development of the North, so that the environment can be fully protected, and the economic benefits accrue primarily to the people whose land it has been for millennia. Our existing case, under the UN Convention on the Law of the Sea (which controls development in the North), is irrefutable, even if there are some small boundary issues. But we need to assert our rights wherever we can, as strongly as we are able. We can no longer take them for granted or assume that nobody else covets this bitterly cold land and the freezing waters that course through it. For this reason, our government provided more funding for the International Polar Year – $150 million – than any other country and used this to coordinate our efforts.

Science is a big part of Canada's approach to the North and we are the leader in many areas of study across the Arctic: ocean currents and ice dynamics, understanding of the treeline, caribou and reindeer habitat and migration, and the Arctic coastal fisheries, to choose a few examples. These activities cement our territorial claims as well, giving us an important base of knowledge about the North. In particular, our effort to map the land and sea, including the seabed, is fundamentally important. Canada has had a program for mapping the continental shelf, which has been used to help determine boundaries in the North since 1958, but we injected new funds to scale up our efforts. As I write, it is reported that Canada is preparing to claim an area of the continental shelf the size of our three prairie provinces, stretching to the North Pole, as well we should.

Replacing Canada's aging ice-breakers is an element in ensuring our presence in the North, but the area is so vast that no number of ships could ever patrol it adequately. That's why we invested $110 million to triple our satellite surveillance capacity for the North. We also increased support for the Canadian Rangers program, which enlists Northerners, mostly Inuit, to patrol thousands of square kilometres of territory in the most remote parts of the North on snowmobiles in some of the most inhospitable weather conditions on earth. Why no one has ever made a TV show about these guys, I will never know!

We also created a new joint task force for the Canadian Forces, which undertook the largest ever military exercise in the North involving land, sea, and air units, along with the Coast Guard, RCMP, and environment and emergency preparedness teams. I was very interested in this particular exercise of our sovereignty. Indeed Sheila and I went to Pangnirtung along with Nancy Karetak Lindell to watch part of the exercise. Most Canadians have never had the pleasure of visiting Pangnirtung, an Inuit community perched beside a spectacular fjord on the edge of the Arctic Circle on Baffin Island. If it weren't so inaccessible, its stunning beauty would be as familiar to Canadians as Lake Louise.

Of course, we don't ever want our North to become as familiar as our Rocky Mountain parks. The Northern wilderness is too delicate to sustain that. For too long we have nurtured the North as part of our national mythology, but seldom have we given a thought to it as a place where people live and where exotic creatures and plants have long clung to life in an inhospitable environment. But the evidence grows more and more overwhelming that climatic and environmental changes mean that we cannot any longer indulge in this kind of benign neglect.

My minister of Indian and northern affairs, Andy Scott, and I were fortunate to have the direct input of three remarkable Northerners in shaping our northern policy. Ethel Blondin was minister of state for northern development and the MP for the Western Arctic. A Dene, she spent part of her childhood on a trapline and grew up in residential schools. Nancy Karetak Lindell represented Nunavut and is Canada's first female Inuit MP. She was born in what is now Arviat – formerly called Eskimo Point. Both of these women overcame enormous challenges to establish distinguished careers at the highest levels of government. Larry Bagnall, the MP for the Yukon and parliamentary secretary for Natural Resources, led the fight against drilling in the Arctic National Wildlife Refuge in Alaska. Along with Andy, they helped develop an approach to Northern development that involved the co-operation of the peoples and the governments of the territories, rather than being imposed from the top down, as had been the case in the past. In this way, it foreshadowed our approach to the Kelowna Accord, which embraced all the First Nations, including those living in the North.

On December 14, 2004, in Ottawa, Andy, Ethel, and I announced our Northern strategy with Premiers Paul Okalik of Nunavut, Joe Handley of the Northwest Territories, and Dennis Fentie of the Yukon, almost exactly a year after I became prime minister. It aimed to bring the quality of life in the North up to the standard that Southerners enjoy. It addressed issues as various as housing, education, the environment, economic diversity, Aboriginal languages, sovereignty, and devolution of powers to the territories, acknowledging that each territory would need to seek its own path and address its own most pressing concerns. With $210 million on the table to get started, and the promise of more to come as the territories fleshed out their individual plans, we were on track to bring about lasting change for the better for our Northern citizens and a stronger foundation for Canada's sovereign rights in the North.

CHAPTER TWENTY-THREE

Into Africa

You won't be surprised to hear that I think my father was one of Canada's great foreign ministers. His experience in the international arena began at the time of the League of Nations and was further shaped by the Second World War and its aftermath. Immediately after the war, Canada had the third largest navy in the world. It was in a position to develop nuclear weapons, though we chose to renounce that possibility. We played an important role in the formation of international institutions, such as the United Nations, and in some of its more muscular interventions in world events, including the "police action" in Korea and the peacekeeping mission after Suez. It was from this experience that the notion of a "middle power" emerged, and the related idea that Canada could find a role as an "honest broker" among the great powers of the world.

The problem is that world no longer exists. The Cold War ended with even more stunning speed than it began. New powers emerged, particularly in Asia, that have created a very different world than the one represented in today's institutions such as the G8 or the United Nations Security Council. Even before all of this had begun to play itself out, the concept of Canada as a "middle power" had increasingly cast us in the role of handmaiden to the great power to our south, the little friend that could convince the behemoth to be reasonable.

By 1993, this idea had degenerated into Canada hosting a meeting between President Clinton and Russian leader Boris Yeltsin in Vancouver. There we provided the hotel rooms and the scenic mountain backdrop but played no part in the discussions. Even if at one time there had been some truth in the idea of a middle power playing a brokerage role, it was looking increasingly dubious in an era where the Bush administration had adopted a "with us or against us" unilateralism. This attitude may have reached its apotheosis in the Bush administration, but it had precursors in the Clinton administration, notwithstanding its greater openness to multilateralism. Remember it was Clinton's secretary of state, Madeleine Albright, who coined the term *indispensable nation* in the context of the all-but-forgotten Desert Fox operation against Iraq in 1998. The full quotation is: "If we have to use force, it is because we are America. We are the indispensable nation. We stand tall. We see further into the future."

It goes without saying that our relationship with the United States is fundamental to our well-being as a nation. The United States is our nearest neighbour, our largest trading partner, and our closest ally. However, the relationship has matured over 140 years. It is determined in part by our governments, of course, and waxes and wanes as any relationship does, but always within a fairly narrow band. This is because it is shaped to an even greater degree by the millions of business, educational, and cultural contacts that occur every day between people without any direction from governments. This is why the relationship is so strong. It is also why our role in the world need not be constrained by that relationship. To be sure, we will be far more effective if we have the support of the world's superpower, but I believe that we will have the greatest impact on the direction of world events if we select an objective carefully and choose those opportunities where we can play a leadership role.

Our foreign policy should reflect our own interests and values. (I do not, by the way, subscribe to the view that there is much inherent conflict between them.) And in many cases, that will put us in concert with the United States. But where our foreign policy clout will be greatest will often be in places where the Americans are less, rather than more, active. We frequently have opportunities to show leadership in regions such as Africa and the Caribbean, for example, that are less central to American foreign policy. In order to show leadership, however, we have to back up our rhetoric with resources. The real problem with our foreign policy has not been, as some have had it, that we have cast ourselves in the role of the world's stern grandmother but rather that we talk a good game but don't deliver.

This view led me to the conviction that Canada had to re-energize its military. Canadians have long treasured our distinguished service as peacekeepers, dating from the era of my father and Lester Pearson – and rightly so. During the recent decades, however, it became clear that the "classic" peacekeeping role we played for so many years in Cyprus, for example, patrolling a clearly demarcated ceasefire line between former military foes, was no longer what world events were demanding. We had moved into an era in the Balkans, for instance, in which peacekeepers were called upon to play a much more robust role, helping to create the peace rather than just preserving it, and even helping to rebuild failed or failing states. At the same time, through the course of many governments, including during my stint as finance minister, Canada's defence capacity had been whittled away.

On the advice of the minister of defence, Bill Graham, in February 2005, I appointed General Rick Hillier as chief of the defence staff. I was impressed with the man, his leadership abilities, and his vision for our military. He advocated a concept called the "three-block war" to describe its mission. The notion was that in many of the turbulent regions in which it was expected to operate, Canada's military might be called upon to manage humanitarian relief on one block, stabilize a ceasefire on a second, and fight a combat mission on the third. This was not a rejection of our peacekeeping tradition but a revision to suit tougher times, and I supported it. General Hillier had a vision for the Armed Forces and a plan – including a capability to deploy forces quickly when needed. I had given a lot of thought to the role and capabilities of our armed forces when I was out of office, and I found that General Hillier's views – admittedly based on a deeper understanding – were very similar to my own.

Soon after his appointment, I had an important meeting with General Hillier and some of his senior staff in a small meeting room near my office on Parliament Hill. Bill Graham and Pierre Pettigrew were there along with their deputies, as well as Alex Himelfarb and my foreign policy adviser, Jonathan Fried. I laid out my priorities. I knew that General Hillier was a strong proponent of Canada's role in the NATO mission to Afghanistan, which had been triggered, of course, by the 9/11 attacks. They had been masterminded from al-Qaeda's bases in Afghanistan, which were under the protection of the Taliban government of the day. I, too, supported the mission, but I also wanted to make sure that it was set in the context of other priorities.

"Canada's role in the world is not simply to support a great power," I said at the outset. "Canada has its own perspective that it needs to articulate through its military and foreign policies." First, I believed that the world community could not stand passively by in the face of the slaughter in the Darfur region of Sudan. I was certain there would have to be a substantial increase in the number of international peacekeepers in the region, and although the African Union might not think it right for our troops to be on the front line, we would want to put in more military advisers and supply funding for the equipment and training of troops from Africa. In addition, as the hemisphere's largest francophone nation, I said we should shoulder special responsibilities in Haiti. Finally, I advised him that I believed we might one day be called upon to play a military role as peacekeepers if there was ever an Israeli-Palestinian peace pact, and that I wanted us to be in a position to do so.

The burden of my message to General Hillier was that our commitment in Afghanistan had to be shaped in the context not only of other current commitments but potential new ones. He assured me that he understood, and that whatever the next stage might be in our Afghanistan mission, it would not preclude our capacity to deploy elsewhere.

Why, you may ask, was Darfur – part of a faraway country of which Canadians knew little – so high on my list of concerns? My particular interest in Africa goes back to my youth, when I first spoke to Maurice Strong about a career in Third World development. While life took me in a different direction, it was never far from my mind. As finance minister I did whatever I could to lead on the issue of Third World debt and I was proud of Jean Chrétien's leadership in rallying the developed world around a coordinated approach to Africa at the G7 summit in Kananaskis, Alberta. As prime minister, I was lucky to have an energetic international development minister in Aileen Carroll, who shared my views and passions. She refocused the Canadian International Development Agency (CIDA) to put more emphasis on Africa, and helped rescue the flagging international effort to get retroviral drugs to Africans living with HIV/AIDS. When our government was eventually defeated in 2006, we were in the process of doubling our aid to Africa even faster than the G8 had committed itself to doing.

To me, it made sense for Africa to be a Canadian priority. Nowhere on earth are there so many failed and fragile states whose populations need the support of the international community. As I will discuss later, Canada was a leader at the United Nations in developing the notion that the international community has a "responsibility to protect" people when their political structures fail to do so. And since we are a developed country that was never a colonial power, and no one suspects us of neo-colonial ambitions, we are able to come to this work with "clean hands." We are ideally situated to play a role in Africa.

When I came to office, the crisis in Darfur was about a year old. It was clear that there was an ethnic cleansing, which some have even characterized as genocide, of the black African tribes taking place at the hands of Arab militiamen, who were doing the killing with the connivance of the Sudanese government. Humanitarian groups working in the region were concerned that the flow of refugees was overwhelming their capacity to cope, as thousands of people arrived at the makeshift camps, starving and without possessions, every day. Still, the "CNN effect" – the attention drawn to any conflict once television takes an interest – had not yet kicked in, and would not do so for some months. This was shaping up like the Rwanda massacres, of which the international community was forewarned, but somehow never galvanized into action, with ghastly results.

For all its agonies, Africa has never been a place to which the Americans have devoted much diplomatic capital. To me, Darfur presented a perfect opportunity for Canada to play a leadership role in keeping with my broader philosophy of our foreign policy. The world was sitting on its duff while a massacre was taking place. We set up a task force with representatives from Foreign Affairs, CIDA, and Defence to coordinate our response. General Roméo Dallaire, by this time a Senator, brought his experience in Rwanda to help us to understand the military issues and also helped us to raise the domestic profile of the crisis. General Dallaire has a profound, personal understanding of what it means to see people laid waste by massacre – and no one had a greater appreciation for the moral cost of standing by and doing nothing. Mobina Jaffer, who was Canada's first African-born Senator, had already been Canada's special envoy to Sudan for several years, and knew the ground down to the tribal and village level. Bob Fowler, a distinguished Canadian public servant and former UN ambassador, continued in his role as the prime minister's African envoy – a position he had first held under Jean Chrétien. By the spring, Allan Rock, whom I had appointed as ambassador to the United Nations, organized what he termed a "posse" of countries at the United Nations that pressed the case for urgent action on Darfur to members of the Security Council.

Once it became clear during the summer of 2004 that the African Union was willing to take the lead, I decided that Canada would jump in with money and technical support. When Allan phoned me to say that $25 million was needed for helicopters, we made the announcement within four days. We also sent armoured personnel carriers to the region to equip the African Union troops for Darfur. Although the force mounted by the African Union was smaller and less capable than it might have been, Canada's efforts helped launch it into the field, with others, including the European Union, following behind us. I spoke to George Bush about this during my visit to his

Texas ranch, saying that Canada was going to take the early lead in Darfur, in terms of money, equipment, and training, and that I hoped the United States would quickly follow. He agreed. When we acted, the United States did swing in behind us massively, as President Bush had told me it would.

In November 2004, I travelled to Khartoum and met with Sudan's president, Omar al-Bashir. It was a frustrating conversation. Bashir's army had clearly been in cahoots with the Arab Janjaweed militia that was slaughtering people in Darfur. He feigned ignorance when it suited him and airily pledged compliance when that suited him better. At the time, his government was obstructing Canada's efforts to get equipment such as the armed personnel carriers we had given the African Union into the area, and was even preventing our diplomats from getting visas. He said he would sort it out, which of course he did not.

In Sudan, I went to a displaced persons camp near Khartoum. The conditions were bad, but not as bad as some of the more distant refugee camps, I was told, in part because out there the Sudanese government was putting up obstacles to humanitarian aid. As we drove along the dusty road on our way out of the camp, one of the Sudanese security vehicles in our convoy hit a young girl from the crowd that had assembled to greet us. When Sheila and I heard what had happened, we went to the hospital where they had taken the injured girl – Widad Isa was her name – to bring her a teddy bear and a few toys. She was staying in a room that seemed to us quite comfortable, though we later learned she had been moved there after the Sudanese authorities learned we were coming to her bedside. At the time, it did not seem that her injuries were serious. When Canadian officials checked on her after I had left the country, however, her condition had become more serious. Eventually we saw to it that she and her father were flown to London so that she could get better care, and they returned to Sudan after her complete recovery.

Canada's leadership role in Darfur was recognized by the world community. In fact, by the spring of 2006, after I left office, the international negotiating team working for a solution to the Darfur crisis consisted of the United States, the European Union, the United Kingdom, and Canada. As ambassador to the United Nations, Allan Rock continued to play an important role. Yet ultimately international efforts have fallen short of what was needed. The truth is that the African Union force was never robust enough to do the job in the face of the Sudanese government's stubborn opposition. Instead of an AU force of seven thousand troops, we needed a joint AU/UN mission of something more like twenty-five thousand. This has now been agreed to, but the deployment is proceeding at a snail's pace.

There was ultimately an agreement among the G8 to assist in creating the capacity for the African Union to put together an action force of seventy-five thousand for use in such conflicts.

As I write this, however, nothing is happening. I had suggested that the G8 should provide the funding for equipment, training, and salaries in order to get the force into a state of readiness. If we were serious, we would have pursued this, but we ran out of time. The simple fact is, in Africa, we avert many murders, but our feeble efforts allow many more to occur. The African Union has its problems, but it is Africa's best hope, and we have to make it work.

The suffering of people in places such as Darfur – where as many as three hundred thousand people may have died and more than 2.5 million (most of them children) have been displaced, according to the United Nations – should give us all pause to reflect on the bounty of wealth and peace we enjoy in this country. It should give us some perspective on our own lives, and perhaps also on our politics. One great disappointment I felt as prime minister was how our efforts in Darfur, as imperfect as they were, were reduced to crass politics in the context of the minority Parliament here in Canada.

In the spring of 2005, the government was facing the prospect of a vote of non-confidence. Even if we were able to secure the support of the NDP, which we eventually did, we also needed to corral the votes of several of the independent MPs to survive. Among the independents was David Kilgour.

Kilgour had been a junior minister under Prime Minister Chrétien and a supporter of mine in the 2003 leadership. However, I decided not to include him in cabinet. In April 2005, he announced that he would sit as an independent, citing the sponsorship scandal, same-sex marriage, and Darfur as his points of contention. When the question of the non-confidence motion arose, he was neutral in public but privately made known his intention of voting against the government. Fair enough. But the public posture he adopted in laying out a price for his vote struck me as cynical and self-serving. He said he wanted Canada to commit five hundred soldiers to peacekeeping in Darfur. No one was more interested in finding a solution to Darfur than I was, of course. But it was also perfectly clear that the solution to the crisis had to have an African face. We were already the second or third largest supporter of the African Union in Darfur; NATO was not getting involved. The idea that five hundred Canadian troops out there on their own in that huge territory would make a decisive difference was ridiculous. None of the Canadians who were on the ground in Darfur supported the idea of a unilateral Canadian force, nor did General Dallaire, whose experience in Rwanda gave him the most authoritative voice on the subject here in Canada.

General Dallaire and I met with Kilgour to explain our position. I made it very clear that we rejected his proposal, and that he could vote as he pleased. As it happened, we were working behind the scenes on Darfur at that very moment. We had made a decision to commit $170 million, mainly for trucks and other equipment, as well as eighty logistical troops, likely to be based in Addis Ababa. Kilgour seized the moment of our announcement for further public grandstanding, and to make official his decision to vote against the government. He dressed his decision up in the clothing of principle, but I believe it was an expression of little else but his desire to avenge his exclusion from cabinet.

You can imagine my frustration when the media reported the announcement of our new commitment to Darfur as an attempt to snag Kilgour's vote, which was already lost precisely because we had rebuffed his demands! If anyone had followed the story in detail and with precision, they would have understood how farcical the whole episode was. In the end, Kilgour's press conference certainly blunted the effort to rally public support to the cause of Darfur, but happily it had no ripple effect in Africa or internationally, where our commitment was understood and welcomed.

A few weeks after I was in Khartoum, I travelled to Libya, which was a key element in the Darfur crisis because of its border with Sudan and its prominence in the African Union. It was to be a fascinating diplomatic adventure, as any encounter with Libyan leader Muammar al-Gaddafi inevitably is. Gaddafi has been the ruler of Libya since 1969, espousing a highly individual ideology of Islamic socialism. He lives in a huge tent outside of the capital, Tripoli, and keeps hours that are uniquely his own.

Like other Western leaders, I felt able to meet with Gaddafi in this period because he had moderated his international policies considerably in the previous few years. Over time, Gaddafi had shifted his foreign policy interests away from the Arab world, where he had been a folk-hero of sorts, to seeking a leadership role in Africa. His co-operation was crucial to maintaining a route for humanitarian relief from the Mediterranean to Darfur, whose northwestern corner touches on the southeasternmost part of Libya. This overland route limited the potential for interference by the government in Khartoum.

Although I was well acquainted with sub-Sarahan Africa, I was relatively new to the Maghreb. So the trip was also an education for me, and, it offered a chance to raise some commercial issues as well. Because Canada's relations with Libya had warmed more quickly than those of the United States, Canadian companies had stolen the march on their continental rivals in helping the Libyans to revitalize the aging infrastructure of their oil industry. Petro-Canada and Nexen were bidding on various contracts in Libya and were keen for me to show the flag. SNC-Lavalin had been present in the country for some time in a major way. I had extensive discussions with many of Gaddafi's ministers and officials, some of them surprisingly satisfactory, in which we discussed the pace of economic, political, and social reform in the country. Dan McTeague was with me, and he argued strenuously on behalf of a number of Canadian consular cases but without much immediate progress.

Over a long lunch in Tripoli, Gaddafi and I spoke mainly about the African Union and Darfur. He treated me to a lengthy lecture on his philosophy of the world, embodied in his "Green Book." When he was finished, I was content that my job in Libya was pretty much done. But some time during the afternoon, I was informed that Gaddafi had invited me to his tent palace in the desert outside the city. Our Canadian diplomats were very excited because this was an unusual honour that was not always extended, even to the leaders of European nations who, on the face of it, were more central to Libyan foreign policy. Jacques Chirac, for example, had recently visited and had not been invited.

The tent was larger and more elaborate in structure than any other I have ever seen. Inside, however, it was austere, if comfortable, with the austerity broken only by the presence of a large TV screen. The meeting, which began around ten-thirty at night, turned out to be another elongated affair. Though our talks did not range beyond what we had discussed earlier in the day, I expected that when it was done, the Canadian reporters gathered outside were going to be very keen to talk with me, and I was trying to think what I could possibly say. When I eventually emerged, however, I discovered that the pressure was off. While Gaddafi and I were inside the tent, the reporters who were outside had been stationed not far from a group of Gaddafi's camels, two of which chose the occasion to have sexual congress. This proved to be far more interesting to the Canadian press corps than anything I could ever say.

While the media's attention was elsewhere – I mean the minority parliament, of course – we were also working on some fundamental reforms to the principles and mechanics of the international system, with the hope of preventing future Darfurs. One of the most successful diplomatic appointments I made as prime minister was Allan Rock as ambassador to the United Nations. Allan was not only crucial in coordinating action on Darfur, as I have already said, he was also a leader in reforming the United Nations. On these issues, the main burden of diplomacy fell to him, and he proved a worthy successor to the many illustrious Canadian diplomats to hold the job of Canada's envoy to the United Nations. Allan demonstrated how, with a strong-willed person in this post, Canada can punch substantially above its weight.

In September 2004, when I made the annual prime ministerial trip to the United Nations, Allan arranged for me to have dinner with the "High Level Panel" that was charged with assessing the challenges facing the United Nations and proposing approaches to deal with them. The panel was led by the former prime minister of Thailand, Anand Panyarachun, and included Gareth Evans, the former Australian foreign minister and head of the International Crisis Group, a non-governmental association that aims to avert bloody conflict. I raised what I believed to be some of the crucial issues facing the United Nations, emphasizing that its success was crucial to Canada. The Human Rights Commission, which – incredibly – included some of the world's worst abusers of human rights and had been egregiously politicized with a deep hostility to Israel, needed to be replaced. Structures to address the non-proliferation of nuclear weapons and other weapons of mass destruction needed to be revived and strengthened. The Security Council, still dominated by the victors of the Second World War, needed to be enlarged and reformed to reflect the world of the twenty-first century. I also made the pitch for the creation of a leaders' version of the G20, which I saw as an adjunct to the United Nations, though not a creature of it. Finally, I discussed the idea of the "responsibility to protect," or R2P.

The R2P was a Canadian initiative – developed under the leadership of Lloyd Axworthy when he was foreign minister – in reaction to the failure of the United Nations to intervene effectively in the Balkans, Rwanda, and Somalia during the 1990s in the face of terrible and systematic massacres there. The problem was that the United Nations, as a body that represents the governments of states, had always been extremely circumspect when it came to the sovereignty of its members. Kofi Annan, who was secretary-general of the United Nations at the time, challenged the world to find a way to reconcile the notion of sovereignty with the moral imperative to act in the face of these evils. It was an area in which no superpower could take the lead, and so it was the perfect role for Canada. For this reason, Allan Rock took the lead, along with Gareth Evans. R2P had three elements. The first was the responsibility of the international community to prevent outrages against human rights before they happen – to act, for example, as the United Nations and others had failed to do, when the Hutu-led Rwandan government first began exhorting violence against the Tutsi people. The second was a responsibility to act in the first instance by political, economic, and diplomatic means, perhaps, but ultimately militarily if necessary. And the third was a responsibility to rebuild after the crisis was over.

The moral imperative to these responsibilities may seem obvious. But they were deeply controversial. To begin with, while they flowed from the failures of the international system in the 1990s, they were being considered in a quite different context in the early twenty-first century. The United States had invaded Iraq, which created the fear among some countries that the responsibility to protect could be used as a diplomatic instrument for neo-imperialist conquest. Moreover, in the wake of September 11, the focus of the United Nations had been broadened from the "Millennium Development Goals" – an ambitious set of targets to lift the developing world up economically and socially – to include the West's growing concerns about security. Many developing nations at the United Nations resented this shift away from their priorities to ours, and came to see the responsibility to protect through that prism.

The UN summit in September 2005 would address UN reform, the Millennium Development Goals, and the responsibility to protect. It is not too much to say that the responsibility to protect might have been doomed by the resistance it was facing in the developing world had South Africa not stepped out on the issue, making it clear that this was in large part about Africa and saving its citizens from harm at the hands of irresponsible governments. In the end, the process was an almost perfect illustration of how difficult it is to get anything done in a body with hundreds of countries at the table. For this reason, Kofi Annan eventually set up a working group of about fifty countries, but that too was unwieldy, and eventually, it came down to about twenty countries that were deeply involved – not a bad illustration, incidentally, of the principle behind the G20 I had been pushing for.

Still, as the summit approached, some countries such as Jamaica, Pakistan, Algeria, and Cuba continued to oppose it. Allan phoned me to see what I could do to help.

In the case of Jamaica, the problem was that the prime minister, P.J. Patterson, saw the responsibility to protect in the context of the recent ouster of Jean-Bertrand Aristide in Haiti. Though the details of Aristide's flight from Haiti remain in dispute, many, including Patterson, believed that it was the result of direct action by the U.S. government. I spoke with Patterson and was able to persuade him to change his view, partly because of Canada's bona fides in the region and in particular with respect to Haiti, as well as by arguing that no intervention would occur without regional approval. This was important in Africa as well, where Allan worked to refine the proposal to meet some of the concerns, decentralizing the process so that it would operate under the aegis of the African Union.

In the case of Pakistan, I already knew the prime minister, Shaukat Aziz, quite well, from our time as finance ministers. In some ways this was an easier task because when I phoned Aziz, it soon became clear that he had not been aware of the positions taken and the tactics adopted by Pakistan's delegation at the United Nations. He said he would look into the matter, and the fact that I had got through became evident when the Pakistan delegation suddenly dropped its fight at the United Nations.

In a way, the most difficult case was Algeria, which of course had its own colonial legacy with France. The president of Algeria when I was prime minister (and as I write) was Abdelaziz Bouteflika, whom

I knew and greatly respected. I had met him many years before when he approached me at an international gathering and introduced himself. He had been Algeria's foreign minister in the 1960s, coinciding with my father's tenure in that role for Canada, and had known my father quite well. When I phoned Bouteflika to discuss the responsibility to protect, he was very cool to the idea. I used every argument that came to mind, but he was reluctant to budge. Finally, he told me: "This is a very big thing you are asking of me, a very big thing." He gave me no commitment during the call, but the Algerian delegation at the United Nations stopped any active intervention against us, which, as Allan reported to me, was sufficient to make the difference. Another case of personal diplomacy being effective.

Although I did not get as personally involved with Cuba, my officials, including Jonathan Fried, did. They very effectively made the argument that the responsibility to protect was not a pretext for American military intrusion in Latin America. Our long-standing independent foreign policy with regard to Cuba was crucial to our credibility in making this argument. The Cuban delegation did not object to the final text, and this may have contributed to Venezuela's decision in the end to acquiesce as well. I used the same argument with Ricardo Lagos, the president of Chile, who shared Latin America's skepticism. In the end, he also supported the concessions.

When it came my turn to speak to the United Nations in September, I devoted much of my time to the responsibility to protect. In the end, the resolution adopted by the United Nations was weaker than we had hoped. Specifically, it retained a role for the Security Council, where a single one of the permanent members could hold up action with a veto. This is precisely what we had seen during the Balkan wars, when Russia had rendered the Security Council impotent with its veto, ultimately forcing NATO to step in. Still, the adoption of the principle that the international community has a responsibility to the citizens of a country whose government has turned against them was a profound turn in the thinking of the world community. The huge challenge ahead is to give that principle life.

CHAPTER TWENTY-FOUR

Acts of God and Humankind

When I became prime minister, Haiti was in deep turmoil. The populist ex-priest Jean-Bertrand Aristide was losing control of the country, and we were preparing ourselves for the possibility that we might have to evacuate our nationals if the situation got worse. I authorized a small military advance team to go to Port-au-Prince to prepare an exit route for Canadians stranded there.

In February 2004, Aristide fled the country during a rebellion. The American role in Aristide's departure quickly became controversial. Aristide left after his security detail, which was provided by an American-based private firm, told him they could no longer protect him. He was evacuated on an American plane. He later claimed, once he had been whisked off to Jamaica, and then on to South Africa, that the Americans had engineered a coup. It was a charge that the Americans denied, and I did not have any particular cause to doubt them.

Still, in the aftermath of Aristide's ouster, I was struck by the reaction of the leaders of the nearby Caribbean countries, such as Jamaica's prime minister, P.J. Patterson. Many of them raised very strong objections to the American role in Haiti. They felt that as the democratically elected president of Haiti, Aristide should have been supported, or at least left in place, for all his manifest flaws as a leader. I did not share their view. Aristide had conducted himself in a thoroughly undemocratic manner as president, ignoring the constitution and subjecting his political opponents to brutal attacks. That having been said, I thought it was good to hear the Caribbean leaders speak out so forcefully in favour of political legitimacy derived from elections rather than force. Democracy was an important part of their history and I hoped that they might be a source of light in the developing world, influencing African nations in particular.

In the autumn of 2004, I was in Hungary to attend the "progressive governance summit," originally a Clinton-Blair vehicle established in the 1990s. There, at the margins of the conference, I was able to take aside the South African leader, Thabo Mbeki, and press on him the importance of curbing Aristide, who had taken refuge in his country. From exile, Aristide was egging on his supporters back in Haiti, making it yet more difficult to restore a semblance of order there.

In November, the government invited me to visit Haiti as a means of helping Haitians move toward reconciliation. It gives you some sense of how unstable the country still was that we were warned that my motorcade might be attacked on the way in from the airport. The RCMP and Canadian Forces dispatched a special unit to assure the safety of the corridor. In fact, I was told they eventually made an agreement with the rebel forces to let me through.

I thought it was crucial from the start to underline the necessity of democratic reform, so I made it clear that I would not participate in a formal luncheon put on by the government unless the opposition parties were also present. This happened as I requested, and it was the first time since the rebellion that the various parties had all agreed to come together in one place – a significant event in itself. I wanted to encourage the development of a "loyal opposition" in Haiti, which would not head to the hills with guns every time they found themselves out of power.

One incident during the trip left a particular imprint on me. A few weeks earlier, there had been mudslides in Haiti in which many people had died. As part of my itinerary in Port-au-Prince I was taken to a school and orphanage. The priest who was in charge there said that he wanted to show me something. He took me to the roof of the building, which was several storeys high, and asked me to look across the valley that was pinched on each side by steep hills.

Then he said to me: "Look down and what do you see?"

There were hundreds of tar-paper shacks on the hillsides, so I said that.

"What more do you see?" he asked.

At first, I wasn't sure what he was talking about, and then the chaotic picture below me began to pull into focus. "Good lord, they are building shacks on top of other shacks," I said, suddenly realizing that these tumbledown structures were literally going to collapse one on top of the other in the next serious storm, which would inevitably come.

Aristide's departure left Haiti struggling to re-establish a legitimate governing authority. There continued to be bitter, often bloody clashes between the supporters of various parties and factions. I thought that Canada, as a francophone country with a large Haitian diaspora community, could play a leadership role quite different from that of France, the former imperial power, and the United States, viewed in some quarters as the current one. But I was determined that if we stepped into this difficult place, we would not hit and run. We needed to make a significant long-term commitment in three areas: security, development, and political stability. We contributed RCMP and other Canadian police officers to help restore order in Port-au-Prince and other cities, and provided development assistance to get the economy on its feet and technical assistance for government administration.

I left Haiti determined that Canada would do all it could to ensure that the country would stabilize and grow. But I was under no illusion about the scale of the challenge. Not long after I left my hotel with my retinue of soldiers and policemen, an armed gang rushed in and kidnapped the hotel manager. She was later released, but it was another sign of how far this fractured land had to go. Canada has played an important role in the agonizingly slow process of rehabilitation since then. Life in Haiti is improving, but very slowly and painfully. We will have to be there for a long time. We cannot make the mistake the international community had made time and time again in Haiti and elsewhere, which is to descend in force during a crisis, but then ignore the longer term reconstruction that might prevent further crises.

A few weeks after my visit to Haiti, something like the disaster the priest and I foresaw that day atop the Haitian orphanage occurred half a world away and on an unimaginably larger scale. The Sumatra-Andaman earthquake reverberated under the Indian Ocean just to the west of Indonesia at one minute before 8 a.m. on December 26, 2004. It was still Christmas evening in Canada. The earthquake unleashed what came to be called the Asian Tsunami, claiming the lives of as many as two hundred and thirty thousand people widely dispersed along the shores of Indonesia, Thailand, Sri Lanka, and India, as well as many smaller and more obscure places. It was at its root a geological event. But such a huge human catastrophe could not have happened a hundred years earlier. The population explosion of the twentieth century meant that there were vastly larger numbers of people than ever before living along the shores of the Indian Ocean, many of them poor and poorly sheltered.

The news media beamed pictures of devastation and human horror into our living rooms on a week when many of us in the West were feeling fat and comfortable and uniquely open to the deep feelings of empathy the tragedy evoked. The Biblical scale of the event presented a unique challenge to our preparedness and, I hope, has taught us some lessons. Within minutes of the first reports of the scale of the destruction my foreign policy adviser, Jonathan Fried, phoned me in Morocco where I was on Christmas vacation with my family after my trip to Libya. We spent many hours on the phone that day as I followed the news and ensured that our operations were moving ahead. A few days later, I cut short my vacation and returned home to Canada. I was no more effective operating from Ottawa than I had been by phone from North Africa, but criticisms of the pace of government reaction always flourish as people struggle to cope with the overwhelming, and it was important to demonstrate our commitment visibly.

In these circumstances, the media invariably clamour for the "number" – the exact figure in millions of dollars the government is prepared to commit – before the scale or nature of the needs can possibly be known. They then criticize the government for increasing the amounts as the days pass, saying that it has reacted too slowly and is now only reacting to public pressure. The reality is that this ramping up of commitments as the situation becomes clear is exactly the right way to proceed: announcing an initial amount to galvanize the international effort, and increasing it as better information comes in as to what the needs are. In the first few days after the tsunami hit, the media also got caught up in a sideshow about the Disaster Assistance Response Team (DART), which is designed to provide medical assistance and water purification in the case of an emergency. There was some validity to the criticism. DART is a logistically heavy and expensive system that needs the co-operation of local authorities to deploy and it may not always be the most cost-effective way of delivering emergency relief. Dumping the DART somewhere in Indonesia on short notice might actually have been counter-productive, as the government there struggled to manage the offers of help coming from the international community. But not surprisingly, many people were asking what the point of having a disaster assistance unit was if it was not deployed in this, of all crises. Once we identified a location in Sri Lanka where the DART could usefully be deployed, we made the decision to do so, just one week after the tsunami.

The truth is that we probably could have provided clean water more cheaply and more rapidly than the DART was able to do. At the same time, it was important for Canadians to see tangible evidence of our commitment to the relief effort. In the end, the soldiers we deployed treated thousands of patients in Sri Lanka, produced millions of litres of potable water, and assisted in general relief projects such as setting up temporary shelters and repairing schools. Although it constituted only a fraction of our overall relief effort, it gave

Canadians a human connection with the efforts of their country to help – and that is important too.

More fundamental than the issue of the DART, however, was that as a government we do two things: leverage the enormous goodwill that Canadians felt in a moment of global need and ensure that it not be just another of those international photo ops in which governments make huge promises on which they have little intention of delivering. In the case of the tsunami, Canada did deliver. When we promised to match individual donations made by Canadians to relief organizations, we did not anticipate the scale of individual generosity the crisis would produce. It was a wonderful thing to behold. It did create a problem, however, which was that we quickly had more money than we needed for emergency humanitarian relief, or than the humanitarian organizations could absorb, when some of those funds might have been better directed to longer term recuperation and development. I raise all this for one reason: to point out that environmental disasters appear to be on the increase and that all the world's governments, including Canada's, need to develop a greater capacity to respond quickly and make a greater commitment to staying in place through the process of reconstruction.

In mid-January, at the beginning of a previously planned trip to Asia, Sheila and I went to see some of the scenes of devastation. First, we went to Phuket in Thailand. As it happened, we had considered spending the Christmas holidays in Phuket ourselves that year. Our son Paul was living in Singapore at the time and had recommended it for our family get-together. In the end, we had decided on Morocco instead. It was a sobering thought.

We found it even more sobering when we toured the devastated resort city, where we were met many dedicated Canadian volunteers, and were briefed by the former coroner of Ontario, Dr. James Young, who was assisting in the grisly task of identifying the thousands of unclaimed bodies. On the side of one building there was a poignant picture gallery, mounted by relatives searching for their loved ones. Sheila and I took a walk on one of the beaches. It was a beautiful day – the kind that had once drawn tourists here: cloud-less sky, deep blue sea, gentle breeze. It was difficult to imagine that this peaceful scene had been transformed into one of horror just a few weeks before.

The devastation wrought by the tsunami did not hit us with full emotional force until we visited Sri Lanka the next day. We took a helicopter out to see a fishing village that had taken the brunt of the wave. From the air, you could see the carcasses of fishing boats piled up two kilometres inland. When we landed, we went for a walk along the beach. As we walked, we sometimes would stub our toes in what looked like pristine sand, only to realize that we had just kicked the foundations of a house that had stood there just three weeks earlier. Eventually, we came to an area where the skeletons of former houses were more visible and encountered a man and a little boy. The boy spoke a bit of English, and so I started to ask the man questions that the boy translated. He told me that his house had pre-viously stood right where we were standing and talked about his worries for the future. After we had chatted for a while, I said to the boy directly that his father must be very proud of him for his courage after the destruction of their home. "This is not my father," he replied. "My father disappeared in the wave."

For every catastrophe that humankind suffers at the hands of nature, there is always another that we have brought on ourselves. Of all the world's disasters, crises, and conflicts, none insinuates itself so deeply into every dark crevice of the globe, and with such poisonous results, as that between the Israelis and the Palestinians. The Israeli-Arab con-flict lies at the heart of the turmoil across the broader Middle East. And the travails of that region, some of them rooted in religion, some in the legacy of colonialism, and others in developmental challenges and the struggle for resources, have incubated the dominant global security concern of our time.

It seems obvious that part of the remedy to this contagion must be a direct dialogue between the Israelis and the Palestinians, and between the Israelis and their other Arab neighbours. Tony Blair was absolutely right when he was British prime minister to insist that the Arab-Israeli conflict be addressed directly by the United States and the world community, and not simply as an afterthought to the war in Iraq. Canada is not the lead player in the region, of course, but I was convinced that, given our long-standing connections in the region, and given our large and various diaspora populations, we could play a larger role. Our support for Israel is well known and of long standing. I thought we could also carve out a larger constructive role as friends of the Palestinian people and their aspirations for statehood.

As prime minister, I had frequent contact, sometimes in person, and much more frequently on the phone, with the leaders of Israel, the Palestinians, and the Arab countries. One of my first phone calls as prime minister was with my Israeli counterpart, Ariel Sharon, with whom I subsequently had a lengthy meeting at a UN summit in New York. I was impressed with his willingness, notwithstanding his reputation as an implacable warrior, to make the changes that he hoped would lead to a more peaceful region. Many doubted his readiness, given his history, to withdraw from the Gaza Strip, for example, but he did it. Although subsequent events in Gaza have been tragic, I think that history will judge the Gaza withdrawal alongside other Israeli moves to evacuate conquered territory, from the Sinai and Lebanon, as a necessary precursor to a lasting peace.

Palestinian leader Mahmoud Abbas, or Abu Mazen as he is sometimes known, never enjoyed as much freedom of action as Sharon, though he was surely a committed partisan of a peaceful settlement to the conflict. I hosted a dinner for him at the Pearson Building in Ottawa when he visited in 2005 and was impressed by his gentle but determined manner. His son Yasser Abbas is a Palestinian-Canadian businessman, and I also had two meetings with him during my time as prime minister. After succeeding Yasser Arafat in the fall of 2004, Mahmoud Abbas called elections on the urging of the international community and won handily. He felt, however, that he never received the support he deserved from the international community (including

Israel and the United States), and he was right. A greater effort to improve the lives of ordinary Palestinians in the year after his election might have forestalled the Hamas victory in parliamentary elections a year later, and all the trouble that ensued. The Israeli withdrawal from Gaza in the summer of 2004, while laudable, was essentially conducted unilaterally, without negotiation with Abbas. The result was that Hamas claimed it as a military victory, while Abbas looked on as an apparently impotent bystander.

By the time I became prime minister, my Middle East policy was already well articulated. I had made it clear that I supported the legitimacy not only of the state of Israel, but of Israel as a Jewish state. I also disagreed with the view of the Department of Foreign Affairs that UN resolutions regarding the region were "balanced." There was no doubt in my mind that while Israel might be subject to legitimate criticism, it had been singled out at the United Nations as if it were the world's most egregious miscreant, which it clearly was not. Take the issue of the barrier – or "wall" – that Israel was constructing. I disagreed with the route the Israelis had chosen for it, which clearly cut through Palestinian lands and potentially prejudiced future peace negotiations. On the other hand, the Israelis had a right to defend themselves against the suicide bombings that had reached a terrifying pitch in 2002, and there was at least circumstantial evidence that the wall had reduced the number of such bombings, and therefore saved lives.

At the same time, I felt strongly that Canada and the major powers had to have as a priority the development of a realistic plan for a viable, peaceful Palestinian state. It should be obvious that an impoverished Palestinian territory, whose people are left without hope of normal life, will not be fertile ground for peace. When I spoke to the UN General Assembly in September 2004, I explained why Canada felt it had to change its vote on some of the resolutions there, and in other international bodies. But I also made it clear that Canada would be much more active in support of the Palestinians. As prime minister, I announced a new aid package, which included aid to refugee camps, support for Palestinian parliamentary elections, and a commitment to build a Canadian democracy centre in Ramallah.

At the same time as we did what we could to help the stabilization of the region we also tried to assemble some of the building blocks for a lasting peace. This included using our understanding of border issues, through our experience with both the United States and NAFTA, to help the Palestinians prepare to control their own borders in the future. Our customs service had scanner and transponder technology that might be adaptable to future Palestinian borders with Israel, Jordan, and Egypt. I also believed that Canada should be prepared to contribute to a peacekeeping or a policing force in the case of a settlement of some kind. At one point, in discussions with my old friend Jim Wolfensohn, I thought this might be a possibility, albeit a remote one. Canada had been involved in the region in a peace-keeping role in the Sinai and until very recently also in the Golan Heights. Whereas American troops would be deeply suspect on the Palestinian side, and European troops might have similar problems with the Israelis, Canada would likely be acceptable to everyone.

Prior to the summit of G8 leaders in Gleneagles, Scotland, in July 2005, Jim called to discuss the Middle East. After leaving the World Bank, Jim had been asked by the group known as the "Quartet," consisting of the United States, the European Union, the United Nations, and Russia, which took the lead on Middle East issues, to work out the non-military aspects of the Middle East dilemma. He had developed an ambitious plan that might have contributed to a genuine revival of a path to peace in the region. Jim's idea was that the international community would provide $3 billion (U.S.) each year for three years to economic reconstruction in the Palestinian territories. A third of the money would come from the G8, a third from the Arab League, and a third from the rest of the world. Jim intended to make this proposal at the Gleneagles summit and asked me to jump in a split second after he made it to ensure that the proposal got some momentum from the start, which is what I did. Jim had obviously done his homework with the other leaders as well, because it quickly passed. This is precisely what had to be done. It was exactly what I thought was needed. Palestinians without hope would do what people without hope do. They were entitled to decent lives.

Unfortunately, as so often happens with bold international commitments, this one faded from view soon after the ink was dry. In the months that followed the summit, Jim discovered that the Bush administration was growing cool to his plan, particularly after the election of a Hamas majority in the January 2006 parliamentary elections, held the same week as my last election here in Canada. As a result, Jim resigned in the spring of that year, feeling that he had been undermined and could no longer continue. Still, he was keen to play a role in finding a successor as Middle East envoy. He approached me to see whether I was interested in having my name put forward, after I had found myself involuntarily out of the prime minister's chair. My reaction was that, as fascinating as it might sound, it was a detour from the route I had chosen for a post-prime ministerial career, which pointed to Africa and Canada's Aboriginal peoples.

One of the last issues I dealt with as prime minister relating to the Middle East was the taking of hostages in Iraq. On November 26, just two days before the government fell on a motion of non-confidence, four peace activists were snatched from the streets of Baghdad and held as hostages. James Loney from Toronto and Harmeet Singh Sooden, who had lived in Montreal, were members of the Christian Peacemakers, as were the other two hostages, an American and a Briton. Soon the hostage-takers were demanding the release of all U.S. detainees. I had appointed Dan McTeague as parliamentary secretary to the minister of foreign affairs with special responsibility for Canadians abroad. Although the department wasn't always happy with his energetic advocacy for Canadians caught up with problems in other countries, his appointment made sure that there was a degree of political accountability and pressure on consular matters – a sometimes neglected aspect of our foreign responsibilities. Even as the election campaign was launched, he continued to devote a great deal of time to the cases of Loney and Sooden. Dan and I both spoke with the families on a number of occasions.

At one point Jim Wright, who was handling the file at foreign affairs, notified me that the Americans thought they had located where the hostages were being held. We already had Foreign Affairs, CSIS, and RCMP personnel on the ground in Jordan and in Baghdad. However, they were asking for assistance from the Canadian Armed Forces, to provide intelligence and secure communications. This obviously created a political and diplomatic issue, since the presence of Canadian soldiers on the ground could be misconstrued as participation in the American-led mission in Iraq. Still, there were Canadian lives involved and we decided to deploy the small number of military personnel required, but not in uniform.

The hostages were still in captivity when I left office. In early March 2006, the tortured body of American hostage Tom Fox was found. Eventually, at the end of March, a rescue team, including some Canadians, stormed the house in which they were being held and released the three remaining hostages, including the two Canadians, James Loney and Harmeet Singh Sooden.

CHAPTER TWENTY-FIVE

From Gleneagles to Hong Kong

L ike most prime ministers, I always intended to take a lead role in shaping my government's foreign policy. It is a bit of a puzzle to me why the Foreign Affairs Department, once the intellectual heavyweight of the public service, does not have the capacity it once did to generate ideas and shape public policy, for it still contains many of the brightest people in government. It may be that a combination of globalization and the ease of modern communications allows departments such as Environment, Transport, Agriculture, Finance, and so on to deal directly with their foreign counterparts, leaving Foreign Affairs as something of a bystander. It is also true that policy making in most areas has gradually been centralized in the Privy Council Office – a process that began in earnest under Pierre Trudeau. Probably only Finance, among the most important policy departments, has fully retained its independent capacity through the recent decades.

In any event, so far as Foreign Affairs was concerned, I largely worked through my foreign policy adviser in the PCO, Jonathan Fried, a distinguished Canadian diplomat who had come to assist me on international issues as G7 deputy when I was at Finance. Jonathan was an expert on trade policy, having been deeply involved in the negotiations on NAFTA, but also had a very broad perspective on foreign affairs. I soon learned of his encyclopedic knowledge both of the files he had to deal with and of the key players around the world.

Proof that the policy-making capacity of Foreign Affairs had to be strengthened came after I commissioned the departments with focused international responsibilities – which also included Defence, International Trade, and CIDA – to develop a new overarching policy document that was called the "international policy statement" or IPS. Unfortunately, the process quickly bogged down in internal bureaucratic rivalries. The Department of Foreign Affairs was not able to seize the lead and integrate the work to the degree I would have wished. The drafts that came into the PCO and PMO were so poor that Peter Nicholson has since told me he hesitated to show them to me, and when he did, I was openly frustrated with their quality. Eventually, in desperation, we turned to Jennifer Welsh, a brilliant young Canadian academic teaching at Oxford at the time, to apply a single pen to the IPS, and with her assistance it was much improved. In the end, the IPS was frequently delayed, variable in quality, and only a partial success. However, the process of reflection it encouraged did benefit the government as we shaped policy on the individual challenges Canada confronted. It captured many of the elements I have already outlined here, including the emphasis on a new kind of multilateralism, the Responsibility to Protect, and a revivified, more robustly capable military. It also argued for a more geographically focused approach to international development assistance. And it outlined my desire to concentrate much more trade promotion and development on the emerging giants of the developing world.

In the run-up to the G8 summit at Gleneagles, the anti-poverty campaigner and pop-star Bob Geldof, along with my friend Bono, helped organize a very substantial international campaign to pressure the G8 leaders to allocate 0.7 per cent of GDP to international development assistance by 2015. The campaign involved a string of concerts around the world, including one near Toronto, under the name "Live 8" – an echo of the highly successful Live Aid concerts for Ethiopian relief that Geldof had helped organize in 1985. The Live 8 concerts were just the centrepiece in the campaign, which also involved demonstrations, including one in Edinburgh (as close as they could get to the summit site), which attracted many tens of thousands of people.

I applauded the aims of the concert organizers and demonstrators. As I have said before, I took the lead on the issue of debt relief for impoverished nations during my tenure as finance minister and in 2002, I strongly supported Jean Chrétien's commitment to increase Canada's foreign aid by 8 per cent each year and to double aid to Africa. While the goal of having G8 nations commit to increasing aid to 0.7 per cent of GDP by 2015 was a noble one, I knew that was very unlikely to happen. For Canada reaching the goal of 0.7 per cent by 2020 would have been possible, but it was barely obtainable even on the most optimistic of assumptions by 2015. I preferred setting realistic two-year targets increasing our aid on a track toward 0.7 per cent, building on success as we went. I saw other countries "taking the pledge" – Germany, Italy, and France, for example – that have failed to follow through. This kind of thing is really counterproductive because it is nothing more than a cover for inaction, and as such hurts those who need help most. Poor countries take these commitments seriously. They depend on them and incorporate them into their planning. My recent work at the African Development Bank, which I will discuss later, confirms this absolutely.

From the point of view of the Live 8 campaign organizers, my position was upsetting, and I understand why. Their tactical goal at the G8 was to isolate the United States, which among the major players was the only country that did not have much of a commitment to increasing development assistance. Jeffrey Sachs, the American economist who was one of the leaders of the movement, told Ralph Goodale that the symbolic pressure on the United States was more important that the substance of the 0.7 per cent pledge. Well, it wasn't for me. Bono, Sachs, and others had regarded me as a sympathizer to their cause, which indeed I was. But if I was going to commit to a target it was because I believed we could keep our commitment, not in order to scold the United States. In the end, what the leaders agreed at the Gleneagles summit was to double their aid to Africa. Canada had already committed to a higher target than that: increasing aid to $3.8 billion by 2010.[1] And we would have continued to do even more (since I had already said publicly that we would increase our aid every two years).

During the summit, I had an intense but friendly meeting with Bono to explain my position. We were so engaged in our discussion that Bono was going to be late for another meeting he had scheduled: this one with Tony Blair. Officials from the British Foreign Office came to fish him out, but the RCMP wouldn't let them. Bono got to his meeting with Blair, but only after having left him to cool his heels for a few minutes. Bono had once promised to be a "pain in the butt" for me if I did not agree to 0.7 per cent, which he proved to be. At the time of Gleneagles, he told reporters: "I guess I'm going to kick his butt . . . Canada has lost its chance to lead, but I think he'll come through in time." I certainly don't fault Bono; he is a champion of a great cause. After the summit ended, Sheila and I sat on the patio of the hotel and I had a beer with him, more than one if I remember correctly. I think that he must have understood later that he had lost an ally at subsequent G8 meetings attended by my successor.

The Gleneagles summit, which showed every prospect of being dominated by the issue of aid, was knocked sideways on the morning of July 7. According to a pre-established protocol, the visiting leaders gathered in a courtyard of the Gleneagles Hotel that morning. One by one, we walked out along a sidewalk for a formal greeting by Tony Blair in front of the cameras. As I walked toward him, I realized that

---

[1] Stephen Harper later twisted the facts in this matter in order to wriggle out of Canada's commitments to Africa. Because Canada's spending on Africa turned out to be somewhat lower than anticipated in the base year used to calculate the doubling of spending under the Gleneagles agreement, he lowered his government's commitment to $3.1 billion – double the lower base. The fact is, even before Gleneagles, our government had committed to the $3.8 billion figure, which everyone knowledgeable understood at the time went beyond the Gleneagles commitment.

Tony was not beaming his characteristic smile, which puzzled me. While we shook hands, he told me why. News had just reached him that a series of bombs had been detonated on the London Underground. As we later learned, those bombs, plus another on a London bus, killed more than fifty people and injured seven hundred. When the leaders' meeting began a few minutes later, Tony was very open with us about how torn he felt. Should he remain in Scotland as host of this very important international meeting or rush to London? Of course, the rest of us had no hesitation is saying that he should go immediately and leave the chair in the capable hands of Jack Straw, his foreign minister, which he did.

In the hours that followed, George Bush was regularly updated on the London situation through his national security and intelligence staff. I soon discovered that I was receiving more or less the same information in equally timely fashion from Jonathan Fried, who was getting his from the BBC and CNN.

Sheila and I had planned a few days' private vacation after the summit, travelling around the Scottish Islands. We ditched those plans because of concerns the London attacks might be the start of a wave of similar outrages in other G8 countries, including Canada. Besides, I did not want to have our presence be the cause of diverting even a few British security officers who could be better used elsewhere at the time. It was another sobering reminder of how much our world had changed since September 11.

Besides the shock of 7/7, as the British came to call their own echo of 9/11, and the political theatre surrounding the pledge on development assistance, the Gleneagles summit drove home for me another of my concerns: the exclusion of the major emerging economies from our exclusive club. On the first day of the summit, we had a working lunch with leaders from Brazil, China, India, Mexico, and South Africa; on the second day, we did the same thing with a group of African leaders. (We had met with a larger group of African leaders the year before at the Sea Island summit in Georgia, hosted by President Bush.) It was progress of a sort, I suppose. But the image of

Hu Jintao, the president of China, and Manmohan Singh, the prime minister of India – leaders of the two most populous countries on earth, quite possibly destined to be the largest economies on earth within our lifetimes – waiting outside while we held our G8 meetings, coming in for lunch, and then being ushered from the room so that we could resume our discussions among ourselves, is one that stayed with me. How long will the emerging titans of the developing world be prepared to kowtow to the G8? The answer is: not as long as some people appear to think. Either the developed world will reform its institutions, including the G8, to embrace these new economic giants, or they will go ahead and establish their own institutions, and perhaps one day we will be the ones waiting in the corridor for lunch to begin. The danger for Canada, of course, is that we might not even make the lunch list.

For my part, I was doing everything I could to open doors to new powers such as China and India by promoting the development of multilateral institutions such as the G20 finance ministers and the creation of its counterpart at the leaders level – the L20. At the same time I also sought to augment our trading thrust, turning it east to face Asia and Latin America as well as south toward the United States. As a trading nation, Canada's essential dilemma is that we have a relatively small domestic consumer base: just 33 million people. We are lucky, of course, to have a huge reservoir of consumers nearby in the United States. But we also know, only too well, that even with agreements such as NAFTA, we are sometimes at the mercy of powerful domestic interests in the United States, which can override even the letter of our trade agreements.

I have always believed that the key to economic success in the modern world is the ability to develop a large middle class, or at least access to a large middle-class market, as Canada does with the United States. The economic significance of China and India does not derive from their huge populations. Their populations were huge in the 1960s too, but their economic weight internationally was relatively puny. What has happened in the last two decades is that these countries, and many others in the developing world like them, have reached a stage in their economic development where they have produced significant middle classes. These people are consumers, and they act as an incubator for emerging industries, which can develop a critical mass in their domestic consumer marketplaces before launching onto the international stage. To me, it was self-evident that Canada, with a small population, needed to burrow into these emerging markets without delay. That is why I put a great importance on my trip to India and China and of course Japan, which came right after my visit to the tsunami-affected countries.

India, which I visited first, is a fascinating human experiment. Despite its enormous developmental challenges, it has managed to remain the world's largest democracy since independence in 1947. It has by no means finally resolved the challenges of a uniquely complex society with deep divisions of wealth. In the last decade or so, however, the liberalization of its economy has assisted in the growth of a large middle class. Dr. Manmohan Singh had been a colleague of mine as Indian finance minister for a time in the 1990s. I knew him well, and now as I was returning to India as prime minister, he had become prime minister too. The Indians have managed to leverage their superior tradition of education to create dynamic research and high-tech centres. For this reason I sought and obtained an agreement in which both our countries would co-operate as we built our research infrastructure. As well we have an important Indian population in Canada. We need to build on it to forge links, city to city, university to university, and business to business.

From there, I went to Japan, in part because my old friend Senator Jack Austin felt it was necessary to send a signal to the Japanese that they continue to be important economic and political partners. In the rush to court China, he pointed out, many countries neglect Japan, whose growth may be slower than the emerging Asian economies but whose economy is nonetheless huge. I knew Japan's importance and I didn't need to be told twice. By this time, I already knew Prime

Minister Koizumi; I was very impressed with him as a statesman who was modernizing elements of the Japanese system and we had developed a warm working relationship. I think that Japan lost a great champion when he later passed from the political scene. The focus of our discussions was the automobile industry and Japanese investment in Canada; but we also discussed the issues of overfishing and the L20.

My most memorable experience during my visit – and among the most memorable I had as prime minister – was a meeting with the emperor and empress. I had first come to Japan as a young businessman, and was familiar with the sight of the imperial palace, which is surrounded with walls and a moat – creating both the symbol and substance of the emperor's isolation from the society over which he presides, in a ceremonial and even spiritual sense. I had often gazed at the palace and wondered what it might be like inside. So it was a special privilege to be invited to meet Emperor Akihito there. I have said before that I am not generally impressed by famous people. I have visited many castles, palaces and grand buildings in my career. But this, I have to say, was different. Not because it is lavish, as many such buildings are, but because it is so austere. Inside the palace, there are few decorations. It is the simplicity of the place – the absence of pictures or ornate heraldry – that inspires awe.

Some Japanese foreign ministry officials came with me to the palace, as they had evidently done with many foreign dignitaries before. Yet they had never been allowed to venture in. I insisted that they be added to our party when we crossed the moat and passed through the doors. As stunning as the effect of entering the palace was on us, it was emotionally overwhelming to some of them, who were reduced to tears by the experience.

Before we went, we had received very specific instructions about our comportment. Sheila remembers that she was told not to wear certain colours or open-toed shoes, and that her hem could not be above the knee. When we entered the imperial chambers, we walked a designated number of steps into a long hallway, then paused while the emperor and empress entered from the other end. We bowed, and then, once they were seated, we were led to our chairs, Sheila at the elbow of the empress and me on the other side by the emperor. Empress Michiko speaks good English, so that she and Sheila chatted amiably about music and children's literature without much help from the translator, as she recalls. In my case, there was more of a language barrier so the conversation was cordial but less animated. After a while we rose, the imperial couple walked us back to the door, and we said goodbye with slightly less formality than had accompanied our arrival.

From Tokyo, I went to Beijing. I had been to China many times before, of course. The first time I went was in the 1970s, when China had not yet really opened up. When I applied for my visa, I was told that it had been granted in recognition of my father's early support for China as Canadian foreign minister. I also remember going to China in the 1980s when I was in business and my dad, who had retired by this time, coming with me. There was a large dinner where our hosts introduced us each in turn, after which we were expected to stand and be duly applauded. The fact that we both bear the same name caused some difficulties when introductions were made, perhaps not enhanced by the simultaneous translation. It is bad enough going through your life with your father known as "senior" and you known as "junior," but on this occasion the translator introduced "Paul Martin the Great" – that would be Dad – and me – "Paul Martin the Not-So-Great."

Things went better on this trip, when I met with President Hu Jintao and Premier Wen Jiabao, whom I had first met in Ottawa just before becoming prime minister. I regarded this visit as very important, because we were able to raise the status of the Canada-China relationship to that of "special partnership" – something the United States and the European Union had achieved, but few others. These were not empty words. This partnership would give Canada priority attention through what is a surprisingly decentralized bureaucratic system managing trade in China. We also had Canada designated as a preferred tourist destination for China's burgeoning middle class, something that could prove of growing importance in the years to come. Unfortunately, the Harper government, with its truculent approach to the Chinese, has not been able to take advantage as others have of the special partnership nor to negotiate the details of the tourist designation that would give it effect, and would bring a huge influx of Chinese tourists and their money to Canada.

Just before we arrived in Beijing, Zhao Ziyang died after fifteen years of house arrest. Zhao had been purged from his post as Communist Party chief for opposing the crackdown in Tiananmen Square in 1989. Conservative MP Jason Kenney, who was part of a parliamentary delegation accompanying my mission, went to visit Zhao's widow, despite the fact that the family asked that we not draw greater attention to them during our visit. In fact, Kenney missed a meeting we had arranged to discuss human rights with Chinese officials in order to do so. Unfortunately, it is precisely this kind of grandstanding, to no useful effect, that has become the dominant strain in Canadian foreign policy toward China since Stephen Harper became prime minister, and threatens to disrupt our relationship at a time when it is vital to our national interest. The situation leaves many China experts shaking their heads.

I don't think we can ignore China's failings on human rights. In fact, we have engaged with the Chinese on many levels over many years, helping build rule of law in their justice system and working to improve their universities. I was the first Canadian prime minister ever to meet with the Dalai Lama, for example. And the meeting sent a subtle message to the Chinese over their treatment of the Tibetan people. But the meeting, which took place in Ottawa, was not an official one and took place in a religious venue, at the residence of Ottawa Archbishop Marcel Gervais.

When Hu Jintao later came to Canada, the meetings in Toronto and Ottawa went very well. I was especially glad that he agreed to come to Vancouver, because it gave B.C. premier Gordon Campbell the chance to talk extensively with him about his province's trade with China. Along with Jean Lapierre, who as minister of transport had made it a priority, I had put great importance on establishing the province as this country's – and the continent's – "Pacific Gateway," which involved building up infrastructure as well as strengthening commercial and human ties.

There is no doubt that there is a cultural and political divide with the Chinese that is sometime difficult to bridge. For instance, while the meetings in Vancouver went well, the Chinese were upset with the fact that demonstrators outside his hotel kept President Hu up during the night, and the state luncheon was almost cancelled as a result. The Chinese could not understand how we could treat a guest like that. It was only with great difficulty that I was able to explain to Hu that under our system, the protestors were doing nothing wrong, and that it was certainly not within the powers of the Canadian prime minister to stop them.

This kind of divide affects foreign policy in unexpected areas. I witnessed a similar difference of understanding in Santiago in 2004 at an Asia Pacific Summit. Our hosts, the Chilean government, organized a reception for the attending leaders and made a special request that all bodyguards be left at the door. The Chileans asked this of all leaders, without exception. The United States chose not to comply, and the difference of opinion was felt quite strongly on both sides.

During my time in office, I had the good fortune to visit a number of the scenes of Canadian military heroism around the world, including Juno Beach in Normandy, Appeldoorn in the Netherlands, and the cemetery in Hong Kong where many Canadian servicemen now rest in peace. Many of these were return trips for me. Sheila and I had taken the boys on a European trip years earlier where we visited Canadian battlefields from the two world wars. One of those battlefields had a very personal connection for our family.

Sheila's father, Bill Cowan, had landed in Normandy as a Canadian tank commander a few weeks after D-Day in 1944. He and his crew eventually became part of the battle of Hochwald Gap. His tank was destroyed and one member of his crew was killed, while he was captured and was sent to a prisoner-of-war camp. His family did not know this, however. The first notification that Mrs. Cowan received told her merely that he was "missing in action." Naturally, she feared that he might have been killed. In fact, he was alive and being shuttled from one POW camp to another. At one point, as the war neared its end, and the Nazi regime had nearly exhausted its resources, he found himself being transferred under guard on a public tram! When he was liberated and returned home in 1945, Sheila met her father for the first time. She had been born after he had shipped out four years earlier.

Mr. Cowan accompanied Sheila and me on our trip to commemorate the sixtieth anniversary of the D-Day landing (at his expense – for those who keep tabs on these things). He sat with other veterans at the ceremony, which was attended by Queen Elizabeth and the Allied leaders. What meant most to him was the time he spent with the other vets, while Sheila and I followed the official itinerary. Like many of his generation, Bill Cowan was not in the habit of talking much about his experiences in the war, but the few days in Normandy allowed him to open up his storehouse of memories for the family to share. It was a very moving experience for him, and for all of us accompanying him.

Although building a more capable military had been one of my objectives from the start of my government, prior to becoming prime minister I had not given much thought to the more symbolic element of rebuilding pride in our military tradition among the Canadian public. Indeed, when I appointed Albina Guarnieri to be veterans affairs minister, she might well have taken the attitude that it was a post better suited to sound management than to great vision. Fortunately, she did not. For my part, I did not come into office intending to make 2005 the "Year of the Veteran." I am very glad Albina did. She set herself a goal: to celebrate our veterans during the year that marked the sixtieth anniversary of the end of the Second

World War, a time of great military achievement for Canada as Albina pointed out at cabinet. Remembering and recognizing our fighting men and women from that period when we were preparing to take on new responsibilities internationally in Afghanistan and elsewhere was a fitting reminder that we had a proud military past.

Despite my genuine enthusiasm for rebuilding pride in our military, I was not always the stirring patriotic orator I might have liked to have been. One time at the forces base at Gagetown in New Brunswick, I gave an impassioned speech to some of our troops about Canada's history at arms. It was my intention to invoke the heroics of the Normandy invasion on D-Day in the Second World War. It was only when the speech was over that my assistant, Jim Pimblett, took me aside and informed me that on several occasions I had referred to Canada's invasion of Norway – an event otherwise unrecorded by history.

An important stop in my Asian trip in 2005 was Hong Kong, where there was a gathering of Canadian veterans who had been prisoners of war there – among the most harrowing of Canada's experiences during the Second World War. Albina suggested I attend their annual memorial, and I eagerly accepted. It was a moving ceremony commemorating an episode in Canada's war history that is often overshadowed by the battles to liberate Western Europe. While I was there, I met a veteran in his eighties who told me that when the Japanese first invaded Hong Kong in early December 1940, but before they managed to conquer the territory in its entirety, he was a young soldier stationed there. Hearing that some Canadian nurses had been captured by the Japanese and were being held in a commercial building in another part of the city, he managed to sneak behind the Japanese lines in a truck and find where the nurses were being held. To his astonishment, when he entered the building the Japanese sentries did not react. As he led the nurses out, he stumbled in the dark over what turned out to be a wine bottle. He quickly figured out that this was a wine warehouse and the Japanese soldiers had passed out from drink. He helped himself to what he said were only a few bottles and fled with the nurses to safety (although he was later captured).

The next day I bumped into him again, this time as I was crossing the lobby of my hotel about 10 a.m. He called out to greet me and suggested we have a drink, which I resisted because of the early hour.

"It must be twelve o'clock somewhere," he replied. And so I joined him at the hotel bar.

CHAPTER TWENTY-SIX

Friends and Traders

L ike many prime ministers before me, I came to office hoping to improve relations with the United States. Growing up in Windsor, I had a special window on America from early childhood, with a clear view of all its strengths as well as its warts and imperfections. From Windsor, you could see the bright towers of Detroit and in a few minutes be walking amid the shambles all around them. The automobile manufacturers that dominated their side of the border also dominated ours, and when I was a youngster the same was true of the unions. No one growing up in my hometown could fail to see how enormous our trade (legal and illegal!) as well as our exchange of people and ideas truly was. But understanding how important our relations are, is not the same as slavishly following the American lead. When I was in business, I was very conscious of the fact that the United States was proving itself more successful than we were as Canadians at adapting to a globalized economy, even though as the smaller country it was more important to us. As a political leader, I believed that our relationship was primarily one of ally and trading partner, but I never forgot that our companies were also economic competitors in North America and around the world.

There is a tendency sometimes in analyzing world events to overemphasize the role of personal relationships among leaders as opposed to enduring national interests and values. Obviously, that tendency may be even greater with the leaders themselves, who experience international relations in a very personal way. On the other hand, there are those who go to the other extreme and dismiss the personal element from international relations, and I think that is a mistake too. With the United States, for instance, I believe it is important to get along with the president if you can.

My relationship with George W. Bush was cordial; he is a sociable guy. He was receptive, at least in a general way, to my notion that the United States cannot possibly lead on every issue, that Canada is in some cases better placed to lead, and that others, sometimes including the United States, should see some advantage in this. Eventually, this did happen, for example, on Darfur. President Bush and I got along well, but we also had our differences. The fact that we were able to talk frankly with each other helped produce some progress, although I wouldn't exaggerate this. I ran into the same wall that many others have done with the United States. The truth is that it is extraordinarily difficult to move administration policy at the international level if there are significant domestic forces at play in Congress.

I had met George Bush before, of course, when I was finance minister, but it had never been much more than a handshake. My first meeting with him after I became prime minister was in January 2004, at the Summit of the Americas in Monterrey, Mexico, just a few weeks after I took office. It was a friendly meeting and memorable, at least in the eyes of one person in attendance, for an inimitable George Bush moment. The president's press secretary at the time was Scott McClellan, who, as it happened, was the same age as Scott Reid, who was my friend, adviser, and now once again my communications director – a job he had held once before when I was at Finance.

"You've got a pretty face," the president remarked to Scott Reid when he met him. "You're a good-looking guy. Better looking than my Scott anyway."

"My" Scott, who is blond and boyish-looking, told the media he would have preferred to be described in other terms. "But I'll take what I can, I guess," he said. "When a Texas Republican says you've

got a pretty face, then I guess there is just no way around it."
Needless to say, all of us made Scott's life miserable for at least two
weeks after that.

That first meeting was in any event primarily a get-to-know-you
session rather than a substantive policy discussion. We did talk a
little about U.S.-Canada relations, but mostly it was about baseball,
football, and hockey. The president, who had been an owner of the
Texas Rangers, was obviously very knowledgeable and was quite
interested when I mentioned in passing that the Montreal Expos,
who were on the move to Washington D.C. at the time – much to my
regret – had an excellent farm system. I also talked hockey and football with Condoleezza Rice. She was a hockey fan, having known
many Canadian hockey players in her university days in Denver. She
was also a big Cleveland Browns fan, while as a Windsor boy, I
hoped in vain for the Detroit Lions.

More significant was my first visit to Washington for one-
on-one meetings with the president at the end of April. It was
important to me that this meeting occur in Washington, and not
at Camp David or at President Bush's Texas ranch because having
had the introductory session I wanted to get down to business.
The day before I went to the White House I gave a speech to the
Woodrow Wilson Center in which I raised in public some of
the issues I would discuss in private with President Bush. I addressed
softwood lumber and "mad cow disease" at the beginning of the
speech because I believed it is important in our relationship with
the Americans that the need to resolve our disputes not get lost
in the glow of good relations and warm words, which is always the
danger of high-level meetings.

I also talked in that speech more broadly about how I saw
Canada's relationship with the United States and the world. We share
democratic values, of course. We have a common commitment to
free trade, though it is sometimes honoured more in rhetoric than in
practice on the American side. I emphasized our commitment to
addressing the security issues that preoccupied Americans in the

aftermath of September 11. But I also talked about how Canadians see the issues of development in the poorer parts of the globe being intimately tied with those of security. And specifically, I talked about our efforts in Haiti, Africa, and the Middle East. All of this led directly to one final message I would deliver to the president later in the day: if we were going to undo the gridlock that prevented progress – on issues as various as climate change, global pandemics, and nuclear proliferation – the G8 would have to be reformed by bringing the leaders of the emerging economies to the table. That is what finance ministers had done at their level when they created the G20 following the Asian crises, and it had been a lasting success.

One other set of issues that I raised frequently with the president was our joint responsibility to be stewards of the North American ecosystem. Very early on, I expressed my concern about the plans to divert water from Devils Lake in North Dakota into the Red River system, with potentially serious ecological consequences for Manitoba. This was a clear violation of the spirit under which the International Joint Commission was set up by Canada and the United States to deal with boundary waters. Devils Lake has no natural outlet, and historically only lost water through evaporation, which meant that pollutants such as arsenic, sulphates and phosphorus built up to very high levels. It also contained potentially invasive species, including parasites, which could find their way into the Red River basin for the first time. Every bit as serious was the threat that the lake might be opened up to inflows from the Missouri River, which would introduce further invasive species into the system. Reg Alcock and Manitoba premier Gary Doer spent a great deal of time working with their American counterparts in Congress and in the state government to press Canada's case. In the end, we were successful in persuading the Americans to install a filter on the Devil's Lake outlet, which would limit the harm. This was to be an interim filter, however, with a permanent and more sophisticated one to follow. Unfortunately the second filter has not yet been installed, and the government should be pushing Washington to do so.

An issue on which Bush was dug in hard was the Arctic National Wildlife Refuge in Alaska (ANWR). I knew from my own experience as a young man working in the North how delicate the Arctic tundra was. I was deeply disturbed by the president's desire to bring oil drilling into the refuge, which borders on the Yukon. Drilling in the North is an entirely different proposition from drilling else-where, and what might be a containable environmental issue in southern climes could leave the Arctic landscape and wildlife blighted literally forever. On a number of occasions, I went into this in considerable detail with the president, explaining to him, for example, that the migrating caribou herd that would be affected by drilling in the area was unique – and that disturbing it could destroy the way of life of the Gwitch'in people who live just on the Canadian side of the border.

In March 2005, the NAFTA partners – President Bush, President Fox and myself – met in the morning at Baylor University in Waco, Texas, and then at the Crawford ranch. At one point during our dis-cussions, President Bush said, "Hey, let's hop in my truck and we'll take a look around the property." Besides just being hospitable, I assumed it was also a chance for the three of us to have a few minutes alone without our advisers. So we clambered into the truck, with George Bush at the wheel, me sitting in the front passenger seat, and Vicente Fox, who is a huge man, leaning over from the back of the extended cab. The Secret Service followed behind in their own vehicles, with some of our aides aboard. This seemed to me a perfect opportunity to raise the issue of the Arctic refuge again, especially with only Vicente Fox present. So, I said plainly that this was really a bad way to manage North American relations and set a terrible precedent for cross-border issues that would inevitably arise among us from time to time. I guess, in the informal atmosphere of the truck ride, I was a little blunter and less diplomatic than usual. And President Bush's response was equally blunt and unyielding.

When we got back from our tour, my executive assistant, Jim Pimblett remarked, "Well, you really went at him on the Arctic refuge, eh?" I looked at him, bewildered, wondering how on earth he could have known what we had talked about during the truck-ride. "My God," I said. "Can you read lips from behind a moving truck?" At which point he told me that he had been riding in the Secret Service vehicle, and the entire conversation had been relayed in real time, with everyone listening in. So far as I could tell, this was standard practice – but entirely new to me. In any event, eventually the issue of the Arctic refuge went to Congress and the decision went the way we hoped: sometimes you win, sometimes you lose – but it's better to win!

The purpose of the morning meeting at Baylor was to set in motion the Security and Prosperity Partnership (SPP) between our three countries. The three of us recognized that important as NAFTA was, the pressures and opportunities facing North America required an agenda that went beyond NAFTA and that the three leaders should hold an annual meeting to discuss that wider perspective.

It was President Bush who said that we had to work together more closely if we were to increase North America's competitiveness in light of the rise of China and India. Both Fox and I agreed.

We then asked our ministers to deliver a detailed work plan within ninety days. Anne McLellan headed up the Canadian team, and the work plan she delivered recommended that we ask business leaders from all three countries to meet on an annual basis. We agreed, and this led to the creation of the North American Competitiveness Council in March 2006, under the auspices of the SPP.

The main issue for me was the Canada–United States border, where U.S. national security measures were becoming a severe non-tariff barrier to trade. Unfortunately the problem has become more acute of late, and I believe we must become much more active on the file. Clearly Canada must build the infrastructure required to facilitate border traffic, such as the bridge across the river from my hometown of Windsor to Detroit, for example. But no amount of infrastructure will compensate for a U.S. bureaucracy bent on protectionism under the guise of security.

Our shared borders are becoming stickier and stickier, and we are seeing more and more unilateral decision-making by the United States. Dealing with this requires the forceful intervention of the Canadian government with the administration in Washington and an all-out effort with U.S. importers. The cost to Canada is huge, but it is no less costly to the Americans. Congress should be made to understand this. Who better to make the point than their own business community? Which is why the North American Competitiveness Council can be of great value to Canada.

There is, of course, no politician more powerful than the president of the United States. Ironically, the president is much less powerful within his own political system than most other political leaders, who do not have to operate within the same system of checks and balances as the Americans do. I remember U.S. treasury secretary Rubin's amazement when I told him that a Canadian finance minister's budget normally passes intact within weeks of its introduction; in the United States, there are months of negotiations with Congress, which often leads to a much weaker result. These limits on executive power are especially important when it comes to many of the trade matters and border issues that Canada is most concerned about, where local interests can have a powerful impact on the attitudes of individual members of Congress. That's why I made a point, on one of my early trips to Washington, of meeting with the key Congressional leaders such as Republican Speaker of the House of Representatives Dennis Hastert and his Democratic counterpart, Nancy Pelosi. I also met with the Republicans' leader in the Senate, Dr. Bill Frist, and the ranking members of the Senate's foreign relations committee, Democrat Joe Biden and Republican Richard Lugar. I was surprised how critical Lugar was of Bush's handling of Iraq, and that he did not hesitate to repeat his criticism at the media scrum after our meeting.

In short, the administration was not the only U.S. branch of government important to Canada's trade interests. Congress was as well. This was why I implemented an idea brought to me by ministers Joe Volpe and Joe Comuzzi, to establish a secretariat in the

Canadian embassy in Washington – under the aegis of Scott Brison, who was my new parliamentary secretary – that would support individual MPs and provincial governments in their interactions with Congress on the broad range of American legislative and regulatory issues that directly affect Canadians.

While I believe I am realistic about Canada's relationship with the United States, and have no problem going toe to toe with the United States when I think it is necessary, I have no time for the anti-Americanism that sometimes infects Canadian politics at the margins. It is really just another form of prejudice, and it over-emphasizes the significant differences we have with our neighbours, as opposed to the much richer lode of similarities and common interests. That's part of the reason that I simply could not tolerate the antics of Carolyn Parrish, a Liberal MP from Mississauga.

On one occasion she was overheard on an open mike to say, "Damn Americans; I hate the bastards." She later qualified her remarks saying that she was only talking about the Bush administration – not really a brilliant defence. She continued to mine this vein with rude comments about the U.S. electorate, and eventually went on a TV comedy show and stomped on a voodoo doll of President Bush. In the end, I dumped her from caucus.

We Canadians are generally a civil and patient people. Still, who among us in the first decade of the new century would not have allowed a small sigh of frustration to escape their lips, when they heard the words *softwood lumber* or *mad cow disease*? The issues often grind on for years without a decisive resolution but with multiple negotiations, partial fixes, reversals of fortune and renewed campaigns, diplomatic and judicial.

For example, take the issue of mad cow disease. The Canadian cattle industry is huge, supplying both domestic consumers and exporting large quantities to the United States. The United States placed a ban on Canadian beef after a single case of mad cow turned up in Canada. The same problem existed in the United States, and there was every reason to believe Canadian beef was every bit as safe, if not more so, than American. However unjustified, when the United States closed its market to us, we were in real trouble because we could not absorb the surplus here at home, nor did we have any major alternative export market.

The U.S. departments of Agriculture and Health argued the border should be reopened early on, as did the large-scale American cattle operations. When I told President Bush that unless the U.S. market opened quickly, we would build new slaughter capacity ourselves, and were raising our standards well above theirs – making us a formidable competitor for them in their major export markets, such as Korea and Japan – he agreed the ban should be lifted. Unfortunately neither the president nor the large U.S. producers could prevent a small American cattle association called R-Calf from obtaining an injunction that held matters up for months, then years. Eventually, the issue was resolved, but it should be a lesson to us about over-reliance on the American market.

Similar issues have affected our other great ongoing trade dispute: softwood lumber. The softwood lumber industry in the United States – which competes with our own to supply American builders and homeowners – is powerful partly because it is so widely dispersed and has so many small operators involved. In the congressional system, this reality has a tremendous impact. To strike an analogy, the big car companies in the United States are certainly influential, but nothing like the car dealers, who operate their businesses in every town, city, and suburb in every congressional district in America. The American softwood lumber industry was so influential that it managed to get itself excluded from the provisions of the Free Trade Agreement and eventually NAFTA (though the dispute settlement mechanisms in those agreements do apply). Instead, the cross-border trade was regulated by a separate agreement that ran from 1996–2001 but was not replaced when it expired.

There was certainly a time when the American industry had an argument. Canadian provinces, keen to have a busy lumber industry, sometimes allowed logging on Crown land for less than a fair market

Grey Cup 2003 in Regina, just before I formally took office. (David Chan)

An informal get-together with the provincial premiers that day was my way of starting off on a friendly footing. From the left are Danny Williams, Gordon Campbell, Bernard Lord, Dalton McGuinty, Pat Binns, me, Jean Charest, Lorne Calvert. (David Chan)

In the House, with Stéphane Dion, Ralph Goodale's hands, Ken Dryden, and Scott Brison in evidence. (David Chan)

My second Cabinet.
Back row left to right: Ken Dryden, David Emerson, Raymond Chan, Claudette Bradshaw, John MacCallum, Stephen Owen, Joe McGuire, Joe Commuzzi, Mauril Bélanger, Carolyn Bennet, Jacques Saada, John Godfrey, Tony Ianno
Middle Row: Albina Guarnieri, Reg Alcock, Geoff Regan, Tony Valeri, Aileen Carroll, Irwin Cotler, Judy Sgro, John Efford, Liza Frulla, Joe Volpe, Joe Fontana, Scott Brison, Ujjal Dosanjh
Front Row: Jack Austin, Jean Lapierre, Ralph Goodale, Anne McLellan, Lucienne Robillard, me, Adrienne Clarkson, Stéphane Dion, Pierre Pettigrew, Jim Peterson, Andy Scott, Andy Mitchell, Bill Graham. (Brigitte Bouvier)

Four important women in my life. Terrie O'Leary (top left), Lucie Santoro, Thérèse Horvath, Sheila. (Dave Chan)

At the G8 conference at Sea Island, Georgia, (from left) Bertie Ahern, Romano Prodi, Tony Blair, Jacques Chirac, me, Junchiro Koizumi, George Bush, Silvio Berlusconi (obscured: Gerhand Schroeder, Vladimir Putin). (Dave Chan)

Sheila and me with Bono, whose description of me on CNN would have made a very memorable book title. (Dave Chan)

With China's President Hu Jintao. (Dave Chan)

With George Bush. (Dave Chan)

As prime minister in Saskatchewan at an Aboriginal school – an area where I now spend a great deal of my time. (Dave Chan)

As the 2004 election came down to the wire, I wound up the campaign by going from coast to coast, starting early in the morning in Chester, Nova Scotia near Jim Cowan's cottage. (Dave Chan)

Victory! A minority, but a victory. (Brigitte Bouvier)

Displaying my well-known musical ability on National Aboriginal Day. (Dave Chan)

Behind the scenes, welcoming Belinda Stronach into Cabinet. Ken Dryden to her right, Ethel Blondin Andrew and Claudette Bradshaw to her left. (Dave Chan)

Behind the scenes, conducting a meeting inside the PMO, with (from left,) Tim Murphy, Scott Reid, Alex Himelfarb, Jim Pimblett, Helene Scherrer. (Dave Chan)

With Bill Graham, my Minister of Defence and General Rick Hillier, discussing the Afghan mission. (Dave Chan)

At the United Nations discussing Afghanistan with the President Hamid Karzai, with Allan Rock and Pierre Pettigrew. (Dave Chan)

Visiting Sudan. My affection for Africa continues, and I am still working hard to help its people. (Brigitte Bouvier)

In Sri Lanka in the wake of the tsunami. This was the visit when I met the boy on the beach, an unforgettably moving experience. (Dave Chan)

Meeting the Japanese Emperor at the Imperial Palace. Some of the attendant Japanese officials were so thrilled to be invited inside the Palace that they shed tears. (Dave Chan)

The last campaign, January 2006.
(Dave Chan)

A moment for reflection.
(Dave Chan)

David and Laurence
watch while Sheila
and I hold our
grandsons, Ethan
and Liam.
(Martin family)

price. But that problem had largely resolved by the time I became prime minister. In 2002, the Bush administration imposed tariffs, which were nothing but an attempt to restrain trade and protect their industry against more competitive Canadian producers. Over the years, the Canadian industry had modernized, installing new plants and introducing new technology. The U.S. lumber industry, which consisted largely of many small inefficient timber companies that couldn't compete, fell back on protectionism to stay in the game. Canada repeatedly took its case to the dispute panels set up under NAFTA, as well as to the World Trade Organization. We almost always won because objective observers could see that we were plainly in the right and the Americans in the wrong under anybody's trade rules. Unfortunately, we could win case after case, but that did not stop the Americans from collecting billions of dollars in tariffs in defiance of these decisions. They could lose a thousand times in a thousand tribunals, but we still couldn't send in the army to make them stop. If our producers wanted to sell their lumber in the United States, they had to pay when they crossed the border.

Obviously, we needed to reach an agreement with the United States. The status quo wasn't acceptable and we didn't have the power to change it unilaterally. The problem was this: on the Canadian side, we have an incredibly diverse industry with divergent interests. In the Atlantic provinces, most of the harvestable timber is on private wood-lots (as in the United States). In British Columbia, there is a huge, successful industry, harvesting mostly on Crown land, but suffering from pine beetle disease, forcing the harvest of larger quantities than would otherwise have been the case. In Quebec and Ontario, there is also a sizable industry working mostly on Crown land but more vulnerable financially.

Of course I raised the issue every time I met with George Bush. I cannot truly say how he felt about it. He did not show the same empathy as he had in the case of mad cow disease, and we were told that some senior White House staffers were strong allies of the U.S. lumber interests. Usually, he would shrug and say that Congress was the problem, something I wouldn't deny. Interestingly, in a conversation I had with the head of the U.S. Chamber of Commerce, Tom Donahue, he told me: "You have to understand, Americans are a disputatious people; you have to come down here and argue your case." Part of what he was saying was that not everyone in the United States liked the tariffs; after all, they drove up costs for the consumers of lumber. And so we set about raising the profile of the issue. I gave a speech and answered questions from a very large and influential business crowd at the Economic Club of New York in which I laid out Canada's case, saying that the American position was "nonsense" and a "breach of faith"; it was very well received. I made my case on CNN and in other American media. As ambassador to the United States, Frank McKenna, with his acute political antennae and capacity for pungent language, was able to raise the profile of the issue in the press. Behind the scenes, he and the embassy staff were very successful at building links to domestic American constituencies, such as homebuilders, who had no interest in paying a premium on Canadian lumber to protect the American softwood lumber industry.

That Frank McKenna was prepared to take on the role of Canadian ambassador was a stroke of good fortune. His knowledge of politics and of business made him ideal for the job. It also represented a sacrifice for him and his wife, Julie, for which I was very grateful to both of them.

One of the most effective arguments I was able to make on softwood lumber was around the principle of free trade, which I had always espoused (even, as in 1988, when my party opposed the original Free Trade Agreement). In the fall of 2005, a Summit of the Americas was held in Argentina. It proved to be the scene of a showdown between the United States, which wanted to use the summit to promote hemispheric free trade, and an emerging anti-American movement in Latin America, led by Hugo Chavez, the president of Venezuela. Nestor Kirschner, the president of Argentina, had deliberately set up the event as a venue for Chavez's populist anti-American rhetoric by arranging for Chavez to address a crowd in a soccer stadium in parallel with the leaders summit.

President Bush took all this in good humour. All the leaders drove to the summit meeting through crowded streets, where they either cheered or booed depending on the flag flapping on the hood of the limousine. When Bush arrived, I was talking to a couple of the other leaders. He came over, and I asked him how it had gone. He had received a great reception, he said, "but you know Argentinians wave in a strange way – they only use one finger."

Latin America has always pulsed with conflicting sentiments toward the United States and the developed world. During the 1990s, the economic doctrine of the Chicago School, with its emphasis on market mechanisms and free trade, swept through much of the region. There were many successes, such as Chile. But there was also, inevitably, a great deal of social and economic disruption associated with that change, and many individuals, regions, and even countries suffered from it. Chavez was the leader and the product of the backlash. George Bush knew that he had very little credibility in South America, especially after the invasion of Iraq, which most people in the region viewed as an imperialist war. So when Condoleezza Rice came to Ottawa in her first trip to Canada as secretary of state, just prior to the summit in Argentina, she urged me to take a lead role in defence of free trade in the hemisphere. At it happened, when Anne McLellan and I met her for dinner at 24 Sussex, we sidetracked her when we got into a set-to over what we felt was the U.S. responsibility for the flow of guns, often bought legally in the United States, then smuggled into Canada. But I understood where she was coming from on free trade. Vicente Fox, among others, had also asked me to step up on the issue at the summit.

Soon after the summit began, President Kirschner, as chair of the meeting, gave Chavez the floor. Using the classic rhetoric of anti-imperialism, Chavez spoke at great length of the suffering of the poor, which he laid at the door of the United States. However the other leaders may have felt about the substance of what he said, in many cases they knew that it resonated with large constituencies in their own countries, so Chavez was having a palpable effect in the room.

After he had spoken for more than half an hour, I jumped in with what is sometimes called a "two-handed" intervention – asking Kirschner if I could interrupt Chavez to say a few words of comment. I talked about the social concerns Chavez had raised: poverty, illiteracy, housing, and lack of medical care. I said that I shared those concerns. As rich as Canada is, I said, we had similar issues in our own country, which we were struggling to address. As a developed country, I said we also had a duty to help those in the developing world to find the resources and expertise to address their challenges. I acknowledged some of the mistakes of international institutions such as the International Monetary Fund in pushing developing countries too hard, too fast toward a new economic model, sometimes at the cost of great suffering.

I could see that I was making considerable headway in the room. Some of the leaders who had been nodding approvingly as Chavez spoke were nodding now in agreement with me. And then I said very directly to Chavez that while I agreed with his identification of the social problems the Americas faced, I had to reject utterly his analysis and proposed solutions. The region would never lift itself out of its poverty, I said, by deliberately shutting itself off from the largest and most dynamic market in the world, which also happened to be its geographical neighbour. I said that the challenge was to embrace the opportunities free trade offered to harvest the wealth that was potentially there for them, but to do so in a way that permitted their people to adapt and enrich themselves in the process.

As a leader, at these heavily prepared summits, it is not often that you feel your words have an impact. (It is a bit different among finance ministers as the debates are more free-wheeling.) But on this occasion, I could feel the room move. By the time it came to agree on a closing statement, Chavez was relatively isolated – certainly the leader of no more than a small minority among the nations represented there.

Afterwards, Bush came up to me and thanked me for my remarks. I took the opportunity to make a point. "Lookit, I am out there making the case for free trade – something that you want – and yet you aren't respecting that principle with your NAFTA partner in the face of judgment after judgment against you on softwood at international tribunals. How can you be credible on free trade of the Americas when you won't respect the deals you've already signed?" It was the first time I felt the message really penetrated.

I also raised the issue of Canada's energy resources, which I knew were central to the administration's thinking on energy security for the United States. I never threatened, but I did say that American access was guaranteed through NAFTA and that the Americans had to understand that they could not cherry-pick the agreement, ignoring the clauses they disliked but insisting on our scrupulously following the clauses they did like.

After that conversation, I asked Jonathan Fried to approach Stephen Hadley, the president's national security adviser, to press the point. The result of that conversation was that within a few days, the Americans appointed an interlocutor to mount a serious push on the softwood file. In fact, in very short order, we were tantalizingly close to reaching a deal, even though we were adamant that all of the money the Americans had collected in harassment tariffs – $5 billion by that time – must be returned, and none be diverted as subsidies to U.S. timber companies.

At that juncture, we were forced into the 2005–06 election. When the Harper government picked up the thread of our negotiations in the spring, they yielded on this point, settling for an agreement that returned a billion dollars less than what had been improperly collected, and inexplicably allowing half a billion dollars to flow directly into the pockets of our American competitors.

This was blood money the Americans had won through a policy of harassment. It was a dagger in the heart of NAFTA. The Harper government said there was no alternative. But there was – even if the negotiations fell through. The American policy on softwood lumber did not even conform to domestic American law, and ultimately we could have taken the matter to court in the United States. We would have won, and won in a way no U.S. administration could ignore. The Harper government chose the easier alternative, conceding, in effect, that what Canada won through the disputes settlement mechanism could, with enough bullying, be taken back at the negotiation table.

The Harper government's excuse was that the Canadian companies couldn't hang on any longer. They had to settle quickly. Of course they had to settle, but that was because David Emerson as a Conservative minister accepted a deal he had rejected as a Liberal minister! His new prime minister in essence threatened a very reluctant Canadian industry: "Knuckle under, because you won't get any help from us if you don't," he said. Think of the message this sends not just to the United States but to the other major economies such as Europe, China, or India, whose large populations will always give them a huge advantage over countries such as Canada, with comparatively small populations, and who will always be able to fight a battle of attrition in trade disputes and win, unless Canadians, including their government, stand together. In the lumber dispute with the United States, Canada's companies and their communities said, "We'll hang tough, but you have to support us." My government said, "We will, and we'll win." The Harper government said, "Give up or else!"

This, perhaps more than anything else, defines the difference between Stephen Harper and me on trade. Of course the United States is, and likely always will be, our most important market. But that the Conservatives have turned their backs on China and have ignored India is simply incomprehensible. I believe the time has come, after decades of false starts, for Canada to hammer on the European door, to build on the natural resource investments of Canadian companies in Africa, and to recognize that within our lifetime the Chinese, Indian, and Brazilian markets will be crucial to our economy.

But of course, it is not enough to simply open up foreign markets. Global trade is in many ways a game of muscle. This was important in the context of our NAFTA disputes; it will be even more important in the future when we will be trying to compete in the Chinese and Indian markets against local companies who will not hesitate to use the methods pioneered by the U.S. lumber industry. It is important that the Canadian government stand behind its industries when they are getting the shaft. We need to fight and win trade battles and earn a reputation for doing so, because the problem is not going to go away as we expand our trade worldwide.

CHAPTER TWENTY-SEVEN

Tough Calls

The origins of the American ballistic missile defence (BMD) program lie in a Reagan-era scheme dubbed Star Wars by its critics. It aimed to end, or at least vastly reduce, the possibility of a massive Soviet attack on the continental United States through yet-to-be-developed U.S. technology, some of it based in space, that would shoot down Soviet missiles long before they reached their targets. It was much more ambitious than practical, and it was put on the back burner under Bill Clinton. The second Bush administration revived the idea in more modest form, aiming to develop an Earth-based system that could knock down missiles from rogue states, such as North Korea, or limited volleys, perhaps launched by accident, from Russia or China. Personally, I did not think it was a particularly cost-effective approach to the Americans' genuine security concerns. Realistically, they were more likely to be hit by a ship- or submarine-based missile, or terrorist-style attacks mounted with even more primitive technology, than by a ground-based intercontinental ballistic missile. Like Star Wars, BMD required the United States to modify the old Cold War principle, enshrined in treaties, which held that defence systems designed to stop incoming missiles could be "destabilizing." The idea was that if military planners began to think they could defend against incoming missiles, they might launch a preemptive attack believing they were safe against a return strike.

Of course the 1960s logic of what used to be called "mutually assured destruction" has looked a little stale since the collapse of the

Union of Soviet Socialist Republics. And George W. Bush's version of BMD did not involve the militarization of space, as some of its critics suggested – something to which I am strongly opposed. The most important factor for Canada was this: as a practical matter, the United States did not need Canada's help or co-operation to mount the BMD system. It could and would go ahead without us. At its root, what the Bush administration really wanted was our political and diplomatic support. So, the case for getting on board with BMD was one of diplomatic prudence rather than enthusiastic support for the principle. If the Americans were going ahead with BMD anyway, I thought there might be some virtue in Canada being at the table. (This was not the view of most of my party, as was shown by the introduction of a resolution against BMD at a subsequent Liberal convention.) Interestingly, prior to my administration, every Canadian prime minister had adopted a position of studied ambiguity over the long history of this issue going back to the Reagan era, never giving the U.S. administration a final yes or no.

Gordon Giffin, who had been President Clinton's ambassador to Ottawa, made the case for us supporting BMD in a particularly arresting way. Like many Democrats, Gordon was skeptical of the BMD plan, thought it would be enormously costly, and did not think it would work well enough to add to American security. On the other hand, he said, the United States is Canada's neighbour and closest ally. It has a right to do what it thinks best to defend itself and Canada, as a friend, should accept that. He was right, of course. But that did not mean we had to participate.

In any event, BMD was not our first priority in terms of military co-operation with the United States when I came to office. That was the North American Aerospace Defence Command (NORAD) agreement, to which the Americans had requested some modification. NORAD, in place since 1958, is a cornerstone of Canada's defence of its territory and security. It makes Canada and the United States partners in the detection and interception of airborne threats from outside of North America. It allows us to shape our defence while leveraging the vast American military power to defend North America. The American military took the view that the existing agreement prevented the passing of information about incoming missiles from NORAD to "Northcom," a purely American military organization whose mission is to defend the security of the United States, and which was integral to BMD. We did not agree with that interpretation, and some felt it was just a pressure tactic. That being said, we could understand that, if true, it could potentially make NORAD an impediment to the Americans' defence rather than an important part of it, thereby jeopardizing our entire bilateral military relationship, and ultimately the security of Canadians. So we chose to address this concern rather than contest it. Preserving NORAD was my priority, and I wasted no time after the spring 2004 election in making the necessary changes to the NORAD agreement through an exchange of letters with President Bush. The result of the new arrangement was that NORAD would share access to tracking data on incoming missiles, which the Americans might use on their own for managing the BMD system.

Although support for BMD was not an American condition for the renewal of the NORAD agreement, a decision to spurn it obviously would not have helped. With NORAD secured, we were able to concentrate on the elements of the BMD scheme that were critical to Canadian interests. The first was money. The Bush administration said it was not expecting us to support BMD financially. The Americans would put the thing up themselves, and what they wanted from us was our moral support. That was fine for the moment, but my concern was that down the road the American attitude would change. It would not be the first time. Talk was already beginning to circulate that they might request forward installations on Canadian soil. Or, as costs escalated, as they inevitably would, or as the bidding on contracts was opened to Canadian companies, we were concerned that the Americans would turn around and say, "Wait a minute, you're benefiting from this. Why don't you pony up your fair share?" I wanted a commitment stating plainly that Canada would not be asked to fund the system now or at any later point.

My second concern was even more serious. I was under no illusion that if the Americans spied an inbound missile and had two or three minutes to decide whether to push the button and launch an intercept they would politely pick up the phone and ask Paul Martin or his successor for permission to do so first. But I did not want to have a situation, to put it starkly, in which the Americans sacrificed Edmonton to save Denver. The trajectory of missiles heading for the United States would in many cases take them over Canadian territory. I wanted to make sure that the system was designed with as much concern for Canadian lives and territory as American. To this end, I wanted Canada to be involved in the design of the BMD system and its technical parameters to ensure our interests, and I made it clear if I was not prepared to proceed without this undertaking.

As the weeks passed, I could not get the answer to my questions and it became increasingly obvious that someone, either in the U.S. Defence Department or at our Department of National Defence was stalling on my requests. I was getting increasingly frustrated. At that point, however, George Bush was deep in the final weeks of his re-election campaign against John Kerry. I was becoming more and more doubtful about signing onto BMD, but to have gone public then – and inject the issue into the U.S. campaign – would have been impossible. Indeed the real question is: Why did I have to make an announcement at all? The conventional wisdom at the time was that I was delaying the decision unduly, but a forthcoming book on the subject by Professor James Fergusson of the University of Manitoba will put the issue into better context.

When Professor Fergusson – who doesn't necessarily agree with my decision not to participate – met with me as part of his research, his question to me was not, Why did you take so long to make your decision? It was: Why did you not do as your predecessors as prime ministers had done and continue to put off the decision indefinitely? Given that I had not received an answer to my inquiries, it's a perfectly valid question and I believe it is what future historians will ask. The answer is twofold. First, the anti-American rhetoric in

Parliament and across the land was becoming increasingly shrill, and I felt to delay much longer would only feed this, which would not benefit Canada, the United States, or our relationship. Second, very soon after his re-election in early November, President Bush decided to accept a previous invitation I had extended to visit Canada. I was seriously concerned that the visit might turn into an embarrassment for him. There was the potential of street protests, and who knew what the NDP and the Bloc would say in Parliament. In retrospect, it might have been wiser to declare my intentions on BMD in advance of his visit, but that also ran the risk of embarrassing the president. Instead, our offices arrived at what turned out to be a clumsy compromise: we agreed that the president would not raise the BMD issue in public while he was here.

When he arrived in Ottawa, one of the first things President Bush did was take up the matter directly with me, as he was perfectly entitled to do. It was not a long conversation, but long enough for me to realize he was not aware that we had a host of unanswered questions. I simply said that he should not count on our support for BMD, and reminded him of the agreement not to discuss the matter publicly. And then we moved on. The next day, at a speech in Halifax, however, Bush turned up the pressure, publicly urging us to get on board. That was a clear violation of the agreement worked out between our officials and it infuriated me. Clearly, the issue could not be left dangling much longer. Unless I could get reasonable answers to our concerns, I was going to announce that we would not participate, and the announcement would have to be soon.

In December, I held a meeting at my Parliament Hill office with Bill Graham and Pierre Pettigrew, along with senior officials from their departments. I peppered the officials with questions about the concerns that I had been raising for months. I was still not getting clear answers. I did get the sense, though, that some of the public servants involved in discussions with the Americans on this issue had an exaggerated view of how important it was to the Bush administration. I came to believe, frankly, that their only argument for signing up for

BMD was that the United States would be angry at us if we didn't. But while it was clear to me that President Bush would like us in, I never had the impression that it was crucial to our overall relationship – nor did my officials at the PMO and PCO.

The time had come to make a firm public decision.

Bill Graham gave Donald Rumsfeld a heads-up by phone, and Tim Murphy did the same with his counterpart, White House chief of staff Andy Card. They both took it in stride, as did Condoleezza Rice when Pierre Pettigrew communicated the decision to her. When I saw the president at the NATO summit in Brussels, there was no time for a meeting, though he would have been informed by then. The problem wasn't that we delayed; the problem was there were significant policy considerations that never became part of the public debate. In retrospect, however, we could, and should, have done a better job of managing public expectations and communicating our decision-making process.

Frank McKenna, who favoured participation in BMD, was on his way to become ambassador to the United States at the time. Frank and I had not discussed the matter, and in a scrum on Parliament Hill he told reporters that since we had agreed to have NORAD supply information about incoming missiles to Northcom, we were already effectively involved. This was read by the media as a signal that we were about to sign on formally to BMD, when the fact was that we had already decided the opposite and, a few days later, said so publicly.

When I next saw President Bush at Baylor University during a visit to Texas, I walked him through the reasons behind my decision. I explained my concerns over targeting and financing of the BMD system. He understood, and when it was raised at a press conference, he handled it deftly, saying that he accepted our decision and that we were moving on in our relationship.

One odd footnote to the BMD controversy is worth adding. In the autumn of 2004, while all this was going on behind the scenes, I met with Russian leader Vladimir Putin in his office in the Kremlin. He asked me what we intended to do about BMD, to which I replied that he would know once we made an announcement. He said that BMD would provoke an arms race and I answered very forcefully that the system was not aimed at Russia, and so that there was no need for that to happen. He immediately responded by denouncing NATO and what he saw as its encroachments on Russia's sphere of influence in central Europe and parts of Asia. And then he did something remarkable. He pulled out a piece of paper on which he drew a rough map purportedly showing the location of American anti-ballistic missile installations and the trajectory along which the American weapons were supposed to intercept Russian missiles. Then he said, "But we have developed a low-flying missile that zigzags along a path that the American missiles will never be able to hit."

"That will be hard to do," I said.

"We already have it," he replied.

In the spring of 2007, more than a year after I left office, press reports revealed publicly that Russia was planning to deploy a weapons system specifically designed to flummox the BMD.

In comparison with BMD, a far more important measure of our friendship and alliance with the United States – though I do not think it was always acknowledged as such – is our commitment to the mission in Afghanistan. The principles behind the mission there are simple, though the specifics of our participation are complex.

The attacks of September 11, 2001, were an assault on the very idea of our civilization, as the rhetoric of Osama bin Laden and his imitators and followers subsequently confirmed. They were not related to any particular grievance or any identifiable military, social, political, or economic objective. There was no demand, however outrageous, that could be met. September 11 was simply an attack on our way of life.

It is easy to forget now, given the Iraq quagmire, how deeply all of us were struck by this elemental truth as we watched those images of horror on our television screens. One hundred thousand Canadians gathered on Parliament Hill a few days after the outrage

for a memorial service. The French daily *Le Monde* published a headline that read "We Are All Americans," a deliberate echo of John
Kennedy's famous declaration forty years earlier at the Brandenburg
Gate: "I am a Berliner." It was how we all felt. When the Americans
decided to respond to the attack from al-Qaeda with a mission to
root out its bases in Afghanistan, and its basis of support among the
Taliban, their response was understandable and reasonable. As
members of NATO, which is after all a self-defence pact, we had a
moral if not a legal duty to support them. We also had self-interest in
doing so.

If the transition from the Taliban regime to the government Afghans
later chose has been a disappointment, it must be in part because the
Bush administration became preoccupied with a larger and more
dubious adventure in Iraq, whose relationship to September 11 was
repeatedly suggested without ever being adequately explained.
Interestingly, the Bush administration never applied any pressure on
me for Canada to join the United States in Iraq. I unequivocally supported Prime Minister Chrétien's decision to stay out of Iraq once the
United States decided to go it alone without the United Nations. At
one point when I was prime minister, the U.S. administration asked
that we send forty military trainers to Iraq, which we declined, end of
subject.[1] In these cases, as in others in my experience, the Canadian
officials who deal directly with their American counterparts are often
spooked by the dreadful implications of not falling into line with U.S.
policy. Usually these are not as severe as they have been led to
imagine, and so it was with Iraq.

The tragedy of the Iraq excursion, when we consider Afghanistan,
is that the military and development resources as well as the diplomatic capital that the United States might have applied to great effect
in Afghanistan were diverted elsewhere. But as for Canada, we
were in Afghanistan for the right reasons and, having been part of

---

[1] We were already providing Iraq-related police training in Jordan.

displacing the Taliban regime, we continued to have a duty to help construct something sturdy to replace it. It has been an unfortunate aspect of Canadian foreign policy that we are sometimes happy to sun ourselves in the warm glow of public opinion – domestic and international – when we are in the midst of a crisis but later act as if making a commitment is the same thing as fulfilling it.

My view of the Afghanistan mission was that it needed to fit within our overall foreign and defence priorities. I understood that this was more a peacemaking than a peacekeeping mission, as were many others I expected us to be called upon to perform: in Haiti, and Darfur, and perhaps in the Middle East. That's why I sought and received General Hillier's assurance that our role in Afghanistan would not compromise what I felt could be an increasing role in other theatres, and most certainly in Darfur.

One of the reasons I strongly supported General Hillier's appointment as chief of the defence staff was his view that Canada's Armed Forces had to be capable of responding quickly to new demands. I also strongly believe that you cannot do much good in failed or fragile states with military force alone. You need to engage people's hearts and minds, and the way to do this is rebuild economic infrastructure along with social and political and judicial institutions. One of the lessons of Haiti is that military intervention without this kind of follow-through means that you have to come back time and time again, intervening in crises but never fixing the underlying problems.

All that having been said, the mission in Afghanistan was a collective one, shared by the NATO allies among others. Our responsibilities as Canadians were to play our part, not to shoulder any and all burdens that might come our way. When I came to office, we had nearly two thousand troops in Afghanistan, mostly in Kabul. They were there on the understanding that they would be rotated in for a time and then replaced by troops from other countries. One of the first things I was told as prime minister by NATO secretary-general Jaap de Hoop Scheffer was that he would like Canada to extend its commitment because there was no other country ready to step up to replace us. My reply was straightforward: "We are pulling our troops out according to schedule. You have got to find a replacement. I am not going to negotiate this." The secretary-general came back empty-handed, several times, and repeated his plea. My answer was the same. Finally, he found replacements, and I learned a valuable lesson: whatever commitment we made, we needed to have an end date and an assured rotation out.

It was always clear in my mind, in the instructions I gave to General Hillier and in my interaction with our NATO allies in Brussels, that Canada had a long-term commitment to the Afghanistan mission. We needed to rotate our troops out, yes, but we were prepared to consider sending them back in at a later point. We were not going to get ourselves locked into an open-ended commitment, however, and there were good and precise reasons for that. First of all, the Canadian military had lived with decades of tightening budgets. We did not have the capacity to do everything we wanted to do militarily in the world as a result. I came to office publicly committed to doing something about that, and quickly laid out a plan to rebuild our military, but the necessary reinvestment had barely begun. In the meantime, our troops needed to be relieved and rested. Some of them were even needed to train the new recruits we were going to bring into the military. And it was important that our military commitment in Afghanistan not crowd out every other mission we might choose to undertake.

General Hillier was a key player in the Afghanistan mission during my administration and since. Canada's military spending had been inadequate throughout my adult life, and the cuts I had imposed during the deficit fight hadn't helped. I believed it was time to reverse this, because a robust military is an important element in an effective foreign policy as well as a foundation of national sovereignty. In my time out of office, I had spent a great deal of time thinking about military matters, and consulting with military experts such as Dr. Doug Bland, chair of defence studies at Queen's, and David Pratt, whose expertise made him the obvious choice to be my first defence minister. One of my first acts as prime minister was to go to Defence headquarters overlooking the Rideau Canal in downtown Ottawa and meet with soldiers and staff. It was a signal of the importance I placed on our Armed Forces. My view was that we needed to have a larger military with an ability to deploy rapidly, and with the latest equipment for the men and women we were putting in harm's way. After the election, I needed to replace David Pratt, who had unfortunately lost his seat, and asked Bill Graham, whose experience at foreign affairs would prove invaluable, to take the job.

General Hillier and the senior people at Defence worked out the plans for our future deployment to Kandahar. Some confusion later arose about whether Canada ended up in Kandahar because it was all that was available by the time we made the decision to redeploy. The fact is we could not have deployed earlier because our overstretched troops needed an "operational pause" to recuperate and retrain. Moreover, there were logistical advantages to Kandahar because of its proximity to Kabul, which would allow us to draw on the supply chain we had already set up there. Certainly, General Hillier was enthusiastic about committing to the Kandahar mission, and I supported him in that. It may be, as some have subsequently claimed, that the proposal to go to Kandahar was delayed by wrangling between the departments of Defence and Foreign Affairs. But by the time the issue reached my desk in the late winter of 2005, the decision was a straightforward one and was made within a few weeks.

The move to a more forward deployment in Afghanistan was an absolutely essential part of making progress in the country. Afghanistan's president, Hamid Karzai, had been mocked as the "mayor of Kabul" because the central government was unable to extend its reach much beyond the capital.[2] NATO had developed a

---

[2] On one occasion when I was at the United Nations in New York, an elevator operator there told me that he had once been the actual mayor of Kabul. Such is the fate of politicians out of office – although it can be argued that he is going up in the world.

plan for its troops to move out into the provinces, gradually pacifying them and allowing the incremental extension of areas safe for reconstruction. Interestingly, many of the Canadian non-governmental organizations working in Afghanistan opposed the plan. Their argument was that the increased military activity would expose aid workers to harm from the Taliban. The Canadian military, on the other hand, strongly supported it, arguing that meaningful reconstruction could only take place in close association with the growth of safe areas. I agreed with them.

It is important to understand the strategy as it was originally devised, because as the troops moved into Kandahar and began military operations under the Conservatives, its two principal thrusts were largely abandoned. The plan General Hillier presented to me was based on Provincial Reconstruction Teams, meaning the gradual restoration of order by the military in expanding circles, with reconstruction intimately linked and immediately underway once the area was secured. There was no point in dominating an area militarily if we did not win the fight for "hearts and minds" once we got there. In my time as prime minister, we never envisaged a broad military campaign that would make reconstruction efforts more difficult, if not impossible, as we bit off more than we could chew. In my view, the change in strategy under the subsequent government was unfortunate. I don't think anyone, including me, expected the Taliban resurgence that Canadian troops encountered when they moved to Kandahar. I do believe, however, that the virtual abandonment of reconstruction efforts in the first year or so of the new government was a mistake.

Second, when I was prime minister, I made a one-year commitment to Kandahar. My earlier experience with NATO's secretary-general convinced me that a short-term time limit was necessary if we were going to retain flexibility for our forces and have maximum leverage with NATO. I fully expected that the deployment might be extended for another year as we worked out the details of our being relieved by troops from another country. But the time limit was there to put NATO on notice from the start that our commitment was not open-ended and that all NATO members had to live up to their responsibilities. That isn't "cutting and running"; that's common sense. And that is why it was such a mistake for Stephen Harper, in his first months as prime minister, to make our troop commitments virtually open-ended. This made it harder for Canada to negotiate within NATO to make sure others did their share. The Harper government now says that our NATO partners have to be held to account. The time to do that was at the start, not much later into the deployment.

CHAPTER TWENTY-EIGHT

To Govern Is to Choose

As prime minister, there are issues you choose and there are issues that are thrust upon you. I would not be truthful if I claimed that the issue of same-sex marriage was one that I expected would play a role in my years in office. But so it was to be. And I'm glad.

On Sundays when I am home at the farm in Knowlton, I attend St. Rose de Lima, a small country church nearby. When I was prime minister, one day after mass the parish priest did something unusual. He returned to his pulpit and told us that he had more to say. Frankly, I felt that he had already had his chance when he gave his sermon, and as usual I was a bit impatient to get home. A few days earlier, however, nine women had been ordained in Gananoque as priests in a Catholic ceremony; it goes without saying that this was not approved in Rome. The parish priest said he wanted to talk about this, and I thought, Oh my gosh, here we go. To my astonishment, he said, "I want to tell you that nowhere in the scripture did Jesus say that women couldn't be priests."

After mass, I went up to him and said, "Father, that was terrific."

"Well, Mr. Martin," he replied, "I may be in trouble with the bishop, and I think you are too." He was referring to my position on same-sex marriage.

"You know I'm right," he continued. "And so are you."

I have not spoken much about my Catholic faith in this book for the simple reason that for the most part I do not believe that it is relevant. I am, and have been, a practising Catholic all my life, but I regard that as a personal matter. I believe the question of the role of religious belief – and specifically the Roman Catholic faith in relation to public life – was settled as a practical matter in North America by John Kennedy in the 1960 election when I was in university, and later by Mario Cuomo, the governor of New York, on a more philosophical plane, before I had entered politics. For Kennedy, only the second serious Catholic candidate for the presidency, and the first to win, the issue of his relationship to the church was a significant one. At an important speech to a mainly Protestant audience in 1960, he said that he believed in a politics "where no public official either requests or accepts instructions from the Pope, the National Council of Churches, or any other ecclesial source. . . . Whatever issue may come before me as President – on birth control, divorce, censorship, gambling or any other subject – I will make my decision in accordance with these views, in accordance with what my conscience tells me to be the national interest."

It was in that tradition that Mario Cuomo gave a famous speech to the theology department at the University of Notre Dame in 1984 in which he laid out his view of how to reconcile his Catholic religious beliefs and his responsibilities as a political leader. Remove the specifically American flavour – the Americans are really not as singular as they like to think – and Cuomo's views conform closely to my own:

"The Catholic public official lives the political truth most Catholics, throughout most of American history, have accepted and insisted on: the truth that to assure our freedom we must allow others the same freedom, even if occasionally it produces conduct by them that we would hold to be sinful.

"I protect my right to be a Catholic by preserving your right to believe as a Jew, a Protestant, or nonbeliever, or as anything else you choose. We know that the price of seeking to force our beliefs on others is that they might some day force theirs on us. This freedom is the fundamental strength of our unique experiment in government.

In the complex interplay of forces and considerations that go into the making of our laws and policies, its preservation must be a pervasive and dominant concern."

Of course, the years since Kennedy's election have also been turbulent ones. The Second Vatican Council under Pope John XXIII opened up the church and also exposed it to unprecedented questioning from the faithful. Catholics were suddenly debating birth control and abortion – as were non-Catholics, of course. Catholics also began to discuss whether women should be allowed into the priesthood, and whether priests should be required to be unmarried and celibate. The list goes on. In the case of birth control, most Catholics in North America simply ignored the edicts of the church. Many of us found ourselves "cherry-picking" those parts of the official Catholic teaching we agreed with, often ignoring the rest. This weakening of the hold that the church had on faithful Catholics was very distressing to the church authorities, and I understand that.

I remember some years ago having a conversation with a childhood friend who is a Catholic missionary. He talked about the particular challenges he faced in his work, where the teachings of the church did not always fit sensibly with the real lives of the people he worked with. He had fashioned his own Catholicism, one that he believed kept faith both with the church and with the people to whom he ministered. I think that I have tried to do something similar in my secular profession. There are, of course, some politicians who enter politics very much as a completion of their religious mission. Tommy Douglas and Preston Manning are two examples that spring to mind. That is not my case.

What does all this mean? Two things. First, while I am a practising Catholic, I do not necessarily share the church's view on every moral issue. Second, that even when I share the church's view, I do not think it is necessarily wise to try to impose it on others. On abortion, for example, I am uneasy about it. But I do not believe that I can substitute my own judgment for that of a woman facing a difficult, and very personal, moral decision. I also worry about the back-street abortions that would inevitably occur if we placed legal limitations on the ability to get a safe medical procedure.

It is worth saying here, by the way, that some variation on this point of view was held by Prime Ministers Trudeau, Clark, Turner, Mulroney, and Chrétien – all of whom were Catholics. Abortion was not a major issue in my time as prime minister, as it was in previous decades. However, the issue of same-sex marriage was, and it raised similar questions.

Same-sex marriage first came up in Parliament when Jean Chrétien was prime minister, and like the overwhelming majority of MPs I voted to reaffirm the traditional definition of marriage as a union of a man and woman. It wasn't a difficult decision. It was simply what I had always believed, and I didn't think much more about it. My position changed over the next few years, and some have wondered why. The answer is pretty simple too: like many people, I began thinking about the issue much more deeply.

Something that affected me greatly was a story told to me by a friend. His daughter had been a girl of great energy, enthusiasm, intelligence, fun, and accomplishment up until about the age twelve or thirteen. At that point things began to go wrong in her life, and she got into difficulties at home and at school. At fourteen and fifteen, it just got worse. By the time she was sixteen she was clearly depressed and possibly even suicidal. Her parents could not fathom what had happened to their lovely, happy girl. And then, in her later teen years, she met another young woman and suddenly everyone understood. My friend and his wife said, "This is our daughter; we love our daughter." They supported her. And soon the problems vanished. Today, she has her Ph.D. and lives with her partner on the West Coast.

That story had a profound effect on me. Was I prepared to accept the situation where this young woman, because of nothing but who she was, would not be allowed to find happiness? On reflection, I decided that I was not.

In April 2004, not long after I became prime minister, the bishop of Calgary, Fred Henry, issued a pastoral letter in which he claimed that it was "morally incoherent" to be a Catholic and hold the views I did on same-sex marriage. A priest in my riding announced that if I showed up for mass at his church, he would refuse me communion. But the church in my riding that I attended most frequently was St. John Brébeuf, and the pastor, Father John Walsh, who is my idea of a great parish priest and whose pastoral work makes the Church stronger, was interviewed by *Maclean's*. He said that while he would not perform a same-sex marriage because it was contrary to the directives of the church, he wondered why it was that some elements of the church had so much trouble recognizing the need to love all its members. Indeed.

When the courts ruled that the legal acceptance of same-sex marriage was demanded by the Charter of Rights and Freedoms, there was no doubt in my mind that it was the government's responsibility to uphold and implement those judgments. This was a classic test of the duty to protect minority rights. When Jean Chrétien was prime minister, the government was confronted with the issue of whether to change the definition of marriage to conform with the rulings of a number of provincial courts of appeal. Before acting, he referred several questions to the Supreme Court, including whether it was lawful for religious ministers to decline to marry same-sex couples. When I became prime minister, I added another, which explicitly asked the court whether it was unconstitutional to *exclude* same-sex unions from the definition of marriage. I think it was unfortunate that the Supreme Court chose not to answer the question I added, since it would have made it absolutely clear from the highest court in the land that same-sex marriage was a constitutional right, and would have barred the door to those in the Conservative Party who may still hope some day to take that right away. Once the court rendered its decision, we put forward legislation to change the definition of marriage to be the union of two people to the exclusion of others.

The legislation went to great lengths to ensure that priests, ministers, rabbis, and other clerics would not be required to perform same-sex marriages. I felt very strongly about this. This was about civil, not religious, marriage. It was also about ensuring rights, not imposing obligations on the unwilling. There were many among my caucus who opposed the legislation. I had made it a free vote and spent a great deal of time with individual members who had doubts about what we were doing. I understood how difficult it was for them, but I felt strongly that what we were doing was right. Of course, despite the numerous court rulings on the issue, the Conservatives did everything they could to delay the legislation, in the hopes of preventing it from going through. Eventually, however, Tony Valeri, certainly one of the most gifted House leaders of recent times, managed to do the seemingly impossible. He convinced the Bloc and the NDP to support a motion cutting off debate – something opposition parties are loathe to do – and ended the Tories' delaying tactics. The law passed, and we made an important contribution to the history of human rights in this country.

This was not the first time Tony had managed to do the impossible. We were a minority government, perpetually on the brink of an election, and yet in the two years we were in office, our legislative record compared favourably with that of any previous government in a similar period going back more than thirty years – all of this thanks to Tony Valeri.

My views on the Charter of Rights and Freedoms have evolved over the years. When it was first introduced, I was a supporter of the "notwithstanding clause" in the Constitution that allows Parliament or provincial legislatures to override some features of the charter as interpreted by the courts. That seemed like a reasonable compromise to me between entrenched constitutional rights and the supremacy of Parliament. When you are outside government, it is hard to imagine that the men and women in positions of responsibility would act out of bias.

Once you are on the inside, however, you quickly realize that governments – which are made up of human beings, after all – are subject to the same prejudices or ignorance that afflict us all, and may act in accordance with what they think are the rules or the established practices of government, without thinking through their effects on society as a whole. We are a land of minorities – linguistic, racial, religious, sexual, and so on. Some of these minorities may band together to form an oppressive majority on selective issues from time to time, and so each of us may become susceptible to the arbitrary power of the state at some point in our lives. That is why I came round to the view that the charter and its protection of minority rights and freedoms, especially in the face of a hostile majority, was crucial, that it had become one of the defining characteristics of our nation and that it should not be overridden by Parliament. That is why I believe the "notwithstanding clause" is incompatible with the Charter of Rights and Freedoms and should be abolished.

The issue took on a new form, for me, when the airplanes slammed into the World Trade Center on September 11, 2001. I was keenly aware of the new reality that those attacks created for us in North America. As finance minister, I brought in a "security budget" with nearly $8 billion dedicated to the issue and I supported our government's numerous new security measures, including anti-terrorism legislation, which proved to be controversial with many, but most particularly with the Arab and Muslim communities.

In the weeks following the Liberal leadership convention, as my transition team and I discussed the design and shape of my first cabinet, we decided to bring many of the disparate pieces of public safety, security, and emergency preparedness together in one place. Our goal was to create a strong new department that would include the Solicitor General's department as well as the Canadian Security Intelligence Service (CSIS), the RCMP, Corrections, the newly created Canadian Border Security Agency (CBSA), and a new emergency preparedness agency that would replace an organization previously lodged with DND. The aim of the new department was to provide greater coordination and effectiveness among these various agencies.

In my mind, it was important to have a senior minister in charge of this new portfolio. It is never easy to create new departments from the pieces of others. Often there are fears and resentments on the part of public servants, and this new department would have to function, from the very beginning, under the bright glare of media and public interest. We were well aware of the kind of attention that the creation of the Department of Homeland Security had generated in the United States and we anticipated comparisons, both good and bad. I asked Anne McLellan, a former justice minister and one of the most able people in the government, whom I had also asked to become deputy prime minister, to take over this new portfolio. I wanted to send a message, both inside and outside government, that Canadians' safety and security would be high on my government's priorities, and so would our freedoms.

I firmly believed that as we worked to better prepare our country against the threat of global terrorism we also had a duty to be firm in protecting Canadian rights. We only needed to look south of the border, to some of the experiences of our American neighbour, to see how hard it is to get the balance right.

The most vivid example of what I am talking about was presented to me as soon as I became prime minister in December 2003: the case of Maher Arar. The facts are well known to Canadians now. On his way back from a family vacation in Tunisia, Arar – who holds dual Canadian and Syrian citizenship – was detained at a stopover in New York. The American authorities believed him to be a terrorist suspect, in part due to erroneous information provided by the RCMP. After being detained and questioned by U.S. authorities, Arar was whisked off (via Jordan) to Syria, where he was held in prison from October 2002 until his return to Canada on October 6, 2003.

Throughout the rest of that fall, we all learned more of his harrowing story of arbitrary detention and torture. At the time, I suppose that I was like most other Canadians, including many officials, both elected and unelected: I had no idea whether Arar was guilty of something, or whether he was innocent, as he claimed. After I became prime minister, however, I quickly discovered that I still could not get a clear answer or explanation to my questions from either the RCMP or CSIS. No one would tell me precisely what had happened with Arar, or why. "If you have evidence that the man was engaged in dangerous activities, then show it to me," I said. Instead I got contradictory information about the role our security services had played in Arar's arrest and detention. It was muddy, very muddy.

Nor was I impressed when someone leaked negative information about Arar to Juliet O'Neill, a reporter with the *Ottawa Citizen*. As later determined by Mr. Justice O'Connor, these leaks came from high-level sources, in an orchestrated campaign to smear Arar. There were also a number of other leaks through the fall. The clerk, Alex Himelfarb, and my national security adviser, Rob Wright, ordered an investigation, but as often happens in these cases, the culprits could not be identified.

Through the months of December and January the calls for a public inquiry grew louder, especially from Arar, his wife, and various civil liberties organizations. The last straw for me was when, in the name of investigating the December leak, the RCMP sought and received a search warrant for the home of Juliet O'Neill. I was in Davos at the time, attending the World Economic Forum, and I remember being caught off guard by a question from a reporter about the RCMP raid on O'Neill's home. I was asked whether I thought that she was a criminal, and I gave a candid response, saying "no." I was later criticized for offering my opinion on a matter better left to the courts, but my response was genuine and it reflected my growing frustration with my inability to get answers from anyone, not only about what happened to Mr. Arar but about the leaks. I found the search of O'Neill's personal effects shocking, and I suppose my response in Davos reflected that sense of shock.

I wanted to put the system on notice that no one could play fast and loose with the lives of Canadians. This whole series of events only reinforced my views that in times of crisis you must fight the enemy; but you must also be vigilant to ensure that individual rights continue to be protected, or the enemy wins.

In late January I concluded that a public inquiry was the only way to uncover the facts on these events and reassure Canadians. Anne

McLellan told me that the best person for the job was Mr. Justice Dennis O'Connor of the Ontario Court of Appeal, who had just concluded an inquiry into the tainted water situation in Walkerton, Ontario. He was appointed to head the inquiry on January 28, 2004. I continue to be grateful to Mr. Justice O'Connor for taking up this task, and for reminding us all that the "ends" do not always justify the "means."

There was real confusion around what role, if any, the RCMP, CSIS, or others may have played in the U.S. decision to remove Mr. Arar to Syria. While that question was a key part of the terms of reference for the O'Connor inquiry, I decided that we needed to work with the U.S. administration to ensure that there were no more Arars. Bill Graham, then foreign minister, and his officials, had already begun discussions with their U.S. counterparts, including Secretary of State Colin Powell. These discussions ultimately led to the Monterrey Protocol, signed by President Bush and me at a meeting in Mexico on January 13, 2004. The protocol's main purpose was to protect Canadians detained in the United States who were being "rendered" to a third country. Under the agreement, the United States would advise a designated senior contact in our foreign ministry in such a case, and there would be consultations before any action was taken. The goal obviously was to make it difficult, if not impossible, for the United States to remove any Canadian citizen to a third country unilaterally. Both Bill Graham and I felt that the arrangement to consult could prove crucial in saving some Canadian citizen from meeting Arar's fate in the future.

Mr. Justice O'Connor's Reports on the Arar Affair were issued after I left office in February 2006. His factual inquiry has helped all of us better understand that in the aftermath of tragic events such as 9/11, government agencies might very well overreact or ignore their own operational guidelines, to the detriment of Canadians. Justice O'Connor exonerated Arar and implicated our security officials in providing erroneous information about Arar to the Americans. Meanwhile, the courts ruled that the raid on O'Neill had violated her charter rights, including freedom of the press and freedom of expression.

I am under no illusion as to the dangers that terrorism poses, and I share the view that we must fight terrorists with every legitimate weapon at our disposal. That being said, I also believe that the courts are an important compass, especially when events threaten to make a democratic society lose its bearings with regard to human rights. In the United States, the courts have proved to be the only check on the misconceived policy of detentions at Guantanamo Bay and elsewhere.

And speaking of Guantanamo, with the benefit of hindsight, given the revelations about events there, I must say that I now regret that my government did not intervene in the case of Omar Khadr to bring him back to face Canadian justice.

Of course, the adoption of the charter in 1982 brought with it new responsibilities and new power to the courts. The fact that judges are appointed by the prime minister created an appearance of unaccountability, which allowed the enemies of the charter in the Reform, Canadian Alliance, and Conservative parties to focus their attack on "unelected judges." The truth is that all the prime ministers in the charter era have, without exception, exercised their powers of appointment, particularly with regard to the Supreme Court, with great circumspection, and that court has been peopled with exceptional jurists. Yet the process was not as transparent as it needed to be to give the public complete confidence in their judiciary. As part of my package of democratic parliamentary reforms geared to enhancing the role of Members of Parliament, I wanted to give the parliamentary justice committee the opportunity to review all judicial appointments, including those to the Supreme Court. I did not expect that they would take it on themselves to review every single nomination to the lower courts, but I was confident they would want to hear from Supreme Court nominees.

At the same time, I was not prepared to go the extra step to give Parliament a power of veto over appointments, fearing the kind of politicization of the process that we have seen in the United States.

Ironically, however, the moderate reform I advocated, balancing parliamentary and judicial concerns, fell afoul of parliamentary opinion. Many of the MPs in my own caucus as well as in the NDP and Bloc Québécois opposed the appearance of Supreme Court nominees before the parliamentary committee because they were fearful that the Conservatives, in particular, would embark on a witch hunt and thus bring the judiciary into disrepute. There was also opposition from the chief justice, Beverley McLachlin, and the bar associations. What support my proposals had came mainly from leading legal academics such as Patrick Monahan at Osgoode Hall. But I could hardly force on MPs a reform they rejected in the name of empowering Parliament.

As it happened, I had two vacancies to fill in my time as prime minister, as a result of the resignations of Justices Louise Arbour and Frank Iacobucci. The justice minister, Irwin Cotler, conducted careful consultations before we nominated Rosalie Abella and Louise Charron, both distinguished jurists from Ontario. For many reasons, it was proud moment.

Irwin Cotler is one of the world's leading human rights lawyers. It was Irwin who came up with a proposal to resolve the impasse over how to present the nominations to Parliament. He, rather than the nominees themselves, would appear before the Commons justice committee to explain the appointments and answer questions. We both agreed that this was an interim measure, but one that advanced the cause of greater parliamentary involvement. Stephen Harper struck a different compromise, one that was also reasonable in the circumstances – an ad hoc panel chaired by a non-parliamentarian – when it was his turn to make his first nomination, but clearly we have not yet found a procedure that will fully satisfy the demand of democratic accountability and judicial independence.

There is one other appointment a prime minister has to make, which may be less important in terms of substance than choosing members of the Supreme Court, but may be even more important in the way we see ourselves as Canadians. Shortly after the 2004 election, I began to consider a replacement for Adrienne Clarkson as

Governor General. I did not have anyone in particular in mind for the post, nor did I have any hard and fast criteria. A number of those around me suggested various names. Véronique de Passillé and Hélène Scherrer (who had replaced Francis Fox as my principal secretary after the 2004 election) raised the possibility of Michaëlle Jean. I did not know Madame Jean, but was immediately drawn to the idea. I had seen her on television in both French and English and had been impressed by her charm, intelligence, and poise. I knew very little of her moving personal story: her family had fled the Haitian regime of Papa Doc Duvalier in the 1960s to find refuge here. For a nation of immigrants who had forged a common identity based on the traditions of many peoples from all corners of the earth, I thought she would be a fitting symbol to ourselves and the world. I asked Hélène and Lucienne Robillard to make some informal contact and report back to me. Both were favourably impressed, and so I invited Madame Jean and her husband, Jean-Daniel Lafond, to bring their daughter, Marie-Éden, down to the farm for a visit.

I had it in mind to chat for about an hour. I wanted to hear about Madame Jean's background in Haiti, her experiences as a Montrealer and a Quebecer, and, of course, her feelings about the country. I was immediately taken with her and her love of Canada. Before we knew it, four or five hours had passed. I was completely satisfied by the end of the day of her unequivocal commitment to Canada and her belief that Quebec's future was only within Canada. I also had a chance to speak at length with her husband, and came to understand that his outlook as an accomplished filmmaker was profoundly apolitical. He had come from his birthplace in France to Quebec, in whose culture he had become very much immersed. He had no separatist leanings. After thoroughly exploring the issue with both of them, I was completely satisfied.

I mention this, of course, because the loyalty of Madame Jean and her husband later became an issue, as a result of separatist mischief. Aghast that members of the creative community in Montreal would take such a prominent symbolic role as Canadians, hard-line

separatists tried to shatter the enthusiasm Madame Jean's appointment had received in both Quebec and the rest of Canada. Instead of
recognizing this for what it was – a backhanded tribute from the
most determined enemies of Canada – some of the unreconstructed
Reformers in the Conservative caucus, such as Jason Kenney, chimed
in on cue to question the appointment, which was precisely what the
separatists wanted. Fortunately, when I spoke to Stephen Harper and
told him that I was completely convinced of her love for Canada,
and that the frustration of the separatists proved how important a
role model she could be in Quebec for a stronger Canada, he simply
said, "That's all I want to hear."

In the end we waited out the furore and in time, it became clear
that the allegations against Madame Jean's loyalty, and that of her
husband, were unfounded. As the public got to know her, her charm
and compassion came through. Her appointment was one of the
most important and successful that I made as prime minister.

CHAPTER TWENTY-NINE

Keeping Faith

S oon after I stepped down as leader of the Liberal Party, I began working to fulfill a wish I had put on hold for more than forty years – trying to make a personal difference to the lives of those who need help most: people in Africa and our Aboriginal peoples here at home. I'll talk about this in greater detail later, but the experience of working in these two areas simultaneously has revealed a sad reality. While Canadians continue to have their hearts and consciences tugged by the plight of people in the Third World abroad, the same is not true of those living in Third World conditions here at home. Somehow, we have reached a point of despair, or at least a sense of futility with the problems that confront the First Nations. In our comfort, we would prefer to forget these people, who are our fellow citizens and who have had so much taken away from them to allow us to live our prosperous lives in what we like to think of as the best country in the world. Part of it boils down to apathy. Part of it boils down to a moral blindness. The world may have awakened to the weight of its collective responsibility to those who live in poverty abroad, but if Canadians don't care about their fellow citizens who happen to be of Aboriginal descent, who will?

It is important to understand that Aboriginal Canadians do not want handouts. What they want is that we work with them to reverse the legacy of colonial governments that has carried into this day – a heritage that said, "Assimilation is your only way out, and everything *we* do to achieve that end is justified."

Like a lot of urban Canadian kids growing up in central Canada, I did not have much direct contact with native people in my early years. The places I knew – Windsor, Colchester, Ottawa, and Pembroke – had small native communities, if any at all. My father had a close friend, Buster Ribberdy, who was Métis. He was probably the first Aboriginal person I ever met. I also used to go fishing with my dad occasionally at Walpole Island, not far from Windsor, where some of the guides were Indian. None of this prepared me for what I saw when I went to work on the Mid-Canada Line one summer near Winisk on Hudson Bay. We lived in a workers' camp, but there was a Cree community nearby. For the first time, I saw the shocking conditions typical of reserves. I began to understand that there was another set of Canadians who lived in an utterly different world, in which the comforts we considered normal and the opportunities we saw as a birthright did not exist and perhaps could not even be imagined. I learned that it is one thing to read about a problem but quite another to come face to face with it.

Later, while still a teenager, I happened to be on a station stop at the old CP train station in Winnipeg's North End. Someone told me I shouldn't walk around the area, so of course I did exactly that. I saw with my own eyes that the appalling divide between native people and the rest of us was not just a question of the state of our reserves. This world apart – this Third World slum – existed in the heart of a major Canadian city, in which non-Aboriginal peoples went about their lives a short walk away, unperturbed and perhaps even wilfully unaware.

Subsequently when I entered the business world I developed an interest in Aboriginal entrepreneurship. I invested in a group trying to support Aboriginal business and I backed a bid to create a local Mohawk television station being mounted by a young entrepreneur on the Kanesatake reserve near Montreal. In the end, it couldn't get the requisite licence. Perhaps the most lasting consequence of these efforts was when my friend Murray Koffler of Shopper's Drug Mart fame asked me to become a founding director of what has evolved into the Canadian Council for Aboriginal Business. This was Murray's vision and I was but a bit player, but it's a bit I'm very proud of.

Later on, when I entered political life, I was exposed to Aboriginal issues from a very different perspective. The Liberal Party has long attracted many of the most able and politically active people from the native community, and this is how I met some exceptional leaders, including Donnie Ross, Mark Leclair, and Jim Sinclair, a non-status Indian from Saskatchewan. Jim went to court to have people such as himself represented at constitutional negotiations under Pierre Trudeau and reached an out-of-court settlement that became an important milestone for a growing community that was too easy to overlook.

It was also in these early political years that I met two very influential Métis leaders from Manitoba: Dave Chartrand, now the president of the Manitoba Métis Federation, and Phil Fontaine. Phil would eventually become national chief of the Assembly of First Nations (AFN). I met Phil through his cousin, Jerry Fontaine, who was for a time chief of the Sagkeeng First Nation (formerly Fort Alexander) east of Lake Winnipeg and a supporter of mine in the 1990 leadership race. At the time, Phil was grand chief of the Assembly of Manitoba Chiefs and I was very impressed with him from the start. I have known many First Nations leaders over the years – Ovide Mercredi, Matthew Coon Come, and George Erasmus, just to mention some of the grand chiefs of the AFN – all of them people of great passion and ability, just as there are in bands throughout the land.

Even a brief glance at the history of our country shows how much of the civilization we have built here in the northern half of North America was erected in partnership with Aboriginal peoples. From the start, we needed native knowhow even to survive the first winters. The fur trade, which was the source of so much wealth in the early centuries, was built along well-established native trading routes and based on the work of Aboriginal trappers and traders. In the wars fought to defend Canada from the encroachments of the American Revolution and the "manifest destiny" of the United States, Aboriginal warriors were an indispensable element to our military success. We signed treaties with many First Nations because their co-operation and their lands were essential to the growth and success of our communities. And then, when our economic and military needs changed, and the peoples with whom we had contracted solemn oaths had been enfeebled by us, we simply abandoned our honour, ignored our agreements, and did what we damned well pleased. It is our national disgrace.

Of course, it was not just about breaking our promises to native peoples. It was also about attempts to break their societies. We tried to strip them of their languages and traditions, we attacked not only their system of government but their religion. We systematically ripped children from the bosom of their families to cut them off from their heritage, and than subjected many of these children to degra-dation and abuse. Yet, for all the fearsome efforts we have made over the centuries, we have failed to destroy them.

At the same time as we adopted policies calculated to dismantle their traditional societies, we were not exactly welcoming Aboriginal peoples into our own. Tommy Prince, born on a Ojibwa reserve in Manitoba, was decorated eleven times for his heroism in the Second World War, including one medal bestowed personally by King George VI. He re-enlisted for the Korean War and was decorated several times again. But when he returned to Canada – unbelievable as it may seem – as a so-called "status Indian" he was not entitled to vote. When I was a young student, preparing for university, the rule for Aboriginals was that they had to forfeit their treaty status under the Indian Act if they wanted to pursue a university education. Incredibly, this government policy was only abandoned in 1953.

As minister of finance, I spared Indian Affairs from the absolute cuts in the 1995 budget – alone among the departments of govern-ment. I did, however, impose a spending cap, which made things difficult for growing Aboriginal communities. In the years after that, as the government began to have greater flexibility, we also began to reinvest. For instance, in 1998, the government created the Aboriginal Healing Fund and contributed $350 million, which represented a turning point in acknowledging the profound hurt that had been caused by the residential school system, its physical and sexual abuse as well as family dislocation. I don't think anyone could have remained unmoved by National Chief Phil Fontaine's very obvious emotion at the time we made the announcement, springing not only from the suffering of his communities but also from his own childhood experiences.

That being said, we had three hundred years of history to make up for and clearly a long way to go. So when I became prime minister I was not prepared to brook any delay. Initially I asked Andy Mitchell, who had a deep understanding of these issues, to be minister of Indian and northern affairs. After the 2004 election when Mitchell moved over to Agriculture (where he was required after Bob Speller's unfortunate defeat at the polls), I asked Andy Scott to assume the portfolio.

I had been struck by Andy's passionate interventions as Solicitor General under Jean Chrétien, when he often argued at the cabinet table that the over-representation of Aboriginal peoples in our correctional institutions was mainly a social and economic rather than a justice issue. He was perfect for the job. He told me later that he quickly realized that he was the first Maritimer to hold the position since Joseph Howe, one of Nova Scotia's greatest statesmen, who had fiercely opposed Confederation but later joined the federal cabinet. When a reporter asked him how he knew about all this, Andy replied, "I have a couple of files on my desk with his name on them because that's the department of Indian Affairs: some of those files are more than a hundred years old, and still open."

Because Andy was going to be asked to break a lot of new ground and would need the full support of all the federal government machinery, and to make sure that I could make my presence felt wherever it was needed, I also appointed John Watson, a former senior public servant at Indian Affairs, as head of the newly created Aboriginal Affairs Secretariat in the PCO, and Jeff Copenace as special adviser in the PMO.

Andy came at the job very much from the perspective that Aboriginal policy had to be grounded not on rules but on a relationship of respect and trust. Part of his challenge, as for any Indian Affairs minister, was that the federal government is not solely concerned with so-called status Indians living on reserve. There is a large and growing off-reserve population, and then there are the Inuit and Métis peoples, each of whom has different concerns and are affected by different laws and policies. To complicate all this further, the federal Department of Finance was always particularly wary of any financial commitment we might make to the Métis, whom they regarded as a provincial responsibility. From my point of view, I have always believed Louis Riel was a true Canadian hero, whose defence of his people continues to have relevance today. Even when I was in Finance, I had begun referring to the "Métis nation," which my officials regarded as a threat to the federal purse.

Indeed, from the time we came into government in 1993, Ralph Goodale argued very strongly that the federal government had a responsibility to the Métis – notwithstanding the objections at Finance. To be sure, over the years there had been moments when Ottawa had shown some concern for the Métis, but typically this interest was short-term, episodic, and inconsistent. Ralph's view was that this was a deeply unsatisfactory half-policy. In 1997, Jean Chrétien appointed Ralph to become the federal interlocutor for Métis and non-status Indians, a responsibility that he continued to hold until I appointed him finance minister in 2004. He became convinced that the constitutional tradition that divided status Indians, to whom we had treaty and legal obligations, from the non-status Indians and Métis, to whom we didn't, was a neat, legalistic distinction that failed to match the reality of Canadian life. Andy shared this view, as I did.

I had carved out the residential schools issue from Andy's responsibilities, and asked Anne McLellan to take the lead on this file. There was a huge wound there; even where the wound had partially healed, there remained a terrible scar and I wanted to deal with this in parallel to moving on the health, education, and other issues to be raised in what ultimately became known as the Kelowna Accord.

We cannot underestimate the trauma brought on by the residential schools tragedy and its effect on successive generations. This was driven home to me again in 2008, two years after I left office, when I went to the University of Alberta to speak with graduate students at the school of native studies. Two of the students had had grandparents who attended residential schools but whose parents, unlike most, had not. I remarked that "This issue must be far removed from your own consciousness, since residential schools was not an issue for either you or your parents." The passion of their reaction took me aback. Their grandparents had been terribly scarred by their experience in the residential schools, and that had shaped their parents, who raised them. The corrosive effect passes from generation to generation, and it has not stopped to this day.

In May 2005, Anne McLellan appointed Frank Iacobucci, the former Supreme Court justice, to lead the discussion on residential schools, and on November 23, 2005, Anne, Irwin Cotler, the minister of justice, and Andy Scott announced an agreement in principle with the Assembly of First Nations, representatives of former students, and the involved churches. The agreement provided for a compensation payment of close to $2 billion, measures to support healing, including continuing investigation and education, which became the Truth and Reconciliation Commission, and as a government we announced our intention to apologize for past abuses, which we all saw as a crucial step in the healing process.

I am glad to say that this is one of the few areas in Aboriginal affairs in which the Conservative government had the wisdom to carry through with what we had done, although it is inexplicable that it still fails to understand that, as important as it was to apologize for yesterday's residential schools, it is equally important to adequately fund today's Aboriginal schools.

In addition to his responsibilities running his department Andy was given two overriding objectives: to bring about the Northern

Agreement described elsewhere, and to guide the process that would lead to a comprehensive agreement on the future of Aboriginal peoples in this country, among the federal government, provincial and territorial governments, and the Aboriginal leaders. That process began when we held a meeting of all the pertinent members of cabinet with the Aboriginal leadership of the country. It continued when the Aboriginal leadership met with me and the provincial and territorial premiers to conclude a groundbreaking agreement on Aboriginal health.

This was all part of building a relationship of trust in preparation for what came to be called the Kelowna Accord. My goal was quite simply to redress the history of centuries of broken promises. It was clear to me that no comprehensive approach was going to succeed without the full support of native peoples themselves and their leaders.

Andy created a series of discussion tables, including all the parties, on health, lifelong learning, housing, economic opportunities, negotiations, and accountability for results. In each of these areas we came to important conclusions, but what was equally important was how we got there. It was crucial to our success that everyone be involved in the process – Aboriginal leaders, the provinces and the territories, and our own bureaucrats.

The heavy historical legacy and the scale of the current challenges facing Canada's Aboriginal peoples are obviously inseparably intertwined, and sometimes there is a tension between them. Even the most well-intentioned and well-constructed reforms can collapse because of what may appear to be a lack of respect or sensitivity. Worse yet is to launch into a program of change without full consultation and without developing the capacity to implement the change. The trick must be to address historic grievances in a way that will promote the future prospects of young Aboriginal peoples. We shouldn't make the same mistakes we have been making for 250 years. This is at the root of my approach. I support the inherent right to self-government. Aboriginal peoples need to be given the levers to determine their own destiny. They governed themselves for thousands of years before

Europeans arrived here. What we did was bring a halt to the evolution of their systems of government. It is worth remembering that in an increasingly globalized world, most societies – both Aboriginal and non-Aboriginal – seek some balance in their lives by emphasizing their traditions.

At the same time as we worked to build trust with our Aboriginal peoples, we had a job to do with the provinces as well. The reality of the challenges we faced did not fit in the neat little boxes some would make of our Constitution. Two of the most important areas in which we have failed our Aboriginal peoples – education and health – are really handled by the provinces rather than the federal government. Yet, legally, it is Ottawa's responsibility to ensure these services on reserve, which far too often we did badly. Moreover, many Aboriginal peoples no longer live on reserve, so they fall into provincial jurisdiction for most social services. Yet these "urban Aboriginal" peoples continued to have close personal, economic, and cultural ties with their extended families on the reserves. Many of them move back and forth between the city and the reserve several times during their lives.

It was clear to me that we could not effectively address the issues confronting our Aboriginal peoples except in partnership with the provinces. But, understandably, the provinces were wary of a federal government dumping new responsibilities on them without the resources they needed to shoulder them. I was lucky while I was prime minister that Gordon Campbell was the premier of British Columbia, and was prepared to take a leadership role. This was important because any prime minister, if he or she is to succeed in a negotiation involving the provinces, has to have a champion among the premiers.

As the date for the meeting in Kelowna approached, it was clear that goodwill – indeed a will to succeed – had emerged on all sides. However, the deal had not yet been done. At one point I sat down with Campbell and he told me that the money Ottawa had put on the table so far was not enough. He said that $5 billion was going to be required to close the deal, a conclusion I had already reached myself. But I was not going to agree until I knew that all the negotiating tables had concluded their work. Soon this happened. Ralph Goodale then agreed to the $5 billion and Andy, Ethel Blondin, and the other involved ministers and I left Ottawa and headed for Kelowna.

The meeting began with a prayer and a traditional ceremony. The large room was packed with Aboriginal leaders who had come from every part of the country. I was presented with a beautiful Métis buckskin jacket, which I wore throughout the time I was there, and many times since.

In addition to the thirteen premiers and territorial leaders and me, arrayed around the table was a group of exceptional Aboriginal leaders. Phil Fontaine, of course, whose leadership was key to our success. Dwight Dorey, of the Congress of Aboriginal People, who was able to set aside his organization's differences with Phil's to make sure that everyone made progress. The Métis leaders, Clem Chartier and David Chartrand, who were exceptionally constructive. And Jose Kusugak, leader of the Inuit Tapiriit Kanatami, who was in many ways the individual star of the meeting with his infectious humour.

At one point in our discussions, Jose told a story to illustrate some of the difficulties Aboriginal peoples faced with the policies imposed on them from Ottawa. He said that when he was young, the government moved his family and their community from the land where they were living, in traditional dwellings, including igloos in the winter, to often poorly constructed houses that had been built for them by the federal government. He said that Southerners sometimes come up and ask why the Inuit didn't take proper care of these houses. But they had never had houses before, he said, and no one told them how to maintain these buildings when they were forced into them. In your culture, he said to the premiers and me, when your wife is tired of your house she tells you to move the couch and you do it. And if she wants you to move it back again the next day, you do that too. But in our culture, he said, when your wife tells you she's tired of the igloo, you build her a new one. He had everyone in stitches. Of course he was also making a serious point: even well-intentioned policies dropped on communities without consultation are likely to go awry.

Another participant in the meeting was Beverly Jacobs of the Native Women's Association, whom I had invited. At Kelowna, she told us that we were not giving women's issues – such as violence in the home and civic equality on the reserves – the priority they deserve, and she was right. For that reason, we agreed to hold another conference specifically to focus on the issues Aboriginal women were raising.

The Kelowna meeting formalized an agreement that we had already worked out through many painstaking months of negotiation. Every single provincial premier and every territorial leader in the country and every Aboriginal leader at the table endorsed the accord. All of us felt the historic significance of the occasion. Incredibly, never before had the prime minister sat with his provincial and territorial counterparts and the country's Aboriginal leadership to deal with the issues that lay before us. Not only that, but we came to an agreement on what had to be done and how.

Despite this, the Conservative government reneged on Kelowna, and in so doing broke the word of the Canadian government to the provinces and territories and to Canada's Aboriginal peoples. They did this despite the fact that during the election campaign they said, through Jim Prentice, their Aboriginal affairs critic, that they would honour it. Did they renege for purely partisan reasons, on orders from the new PMO? Or did they do it because they do not believe that Aboriginal Canadians are entitled to the same quality of education and health care as other Canadians? I don't have the answer but it must be one of the two, as they presented no other option. In either case, it's beyond the pale.

One thing, however, is immutable. This government may have walked away from the Kelowna Accord, but sooner or later the Kelowna approach will be the law of the land. Sooner or later a future government will have to come back to the Kelowna principles: the goals we set for Canada must be no less than the educational, health, economic, civic, and social equality of Aboriginal peoples with their fellow citizens; that progress toward those ends must be made by providing adequate funding and by setting specific, measurable targets along the way; and that all of this can only be done with the consensus and collaboration of Canada's Aboriginal peoples.

Under the agreement, the federal government was committed to an initial contribution of $5 billion in the first five years of a ten-year plan. Our objective was to bring the high school graduation rate for Aboriginal peoples to the Canadian norm by 2016 and to close the gap in post-secondary education by 50 per cent over that same period. In health care, we set targets to reduce infant mortality, youth suicide, childhood obesity, and diabetes by 20 per cent in five years, and 50 per cent in ten years, and to double the number of health professionals. On housing, we agreed to specific targets to reduce the shortage on reserves, for urban Aboriginal peoples, and for the Inuit (where the housing shortage was perhaps the most acute). We committed to reducing the income gap between Aboriginal and other Canadians, and to cut unemployment by 30 per cent over five years and 50 per cent over ten.

Some commentators have said that the Kelowna process did not deal with the issue of accountability. That is nonsense.

Accountability is a critical issue. It is for me, and when you examine what the vast majority of Aboriginal leaders have said, it is clear that they are aware of the need. It is for Phil Fontaine, who called for a First Nations ombudsperson and it is for his office, which initiated work with the federal Auditor General seeking to create the office of a First Nations Auditor General. Yes, there have been problems of accountability in Aboriginal governance, just as there have been in all governments in Canada, not to mention other well-established institutions, from school boards to some of North America's largest corporations.

Some years earlier, in an effort to address the issue Bob Nault (who was minister of Indian affairs before I became prime minister) tried to apply a legislated system of accountability. He was right to want to act. The problem was that his initiative was open to constitutional challenge, and it was going to be challenged. This would have meant years of litigation, with no better than a fifty-fifty prospect of success. I wasn't prepared to wait a decade to see what would happen, while the whole process of increased accountability was hobbled.

I chose to adopt a different approach in part because of Roberta Jamieson and Herb George. Jamieson is the first Aboriginal woman to earn a law degree, a former ombudsperson of Ontario, and the first woman to become chief of the Six Nations of the Grand River. Herb George is an expert in Aboriginal public administration who has taught in Canada and abroad and is now the chairman of the National Centre for First Nations Governance. Their argument was that the Aboriginal leadership fully supports the need for strong accountability, but there is a problem of a lack of capacity, which has to be developed and cannot be imposed. They argued forcefully that part of the solution to the riddle we confronted was the development of strong institutions of accountability within Aboriginal communities, coupled with a First Nations ombudsman and a First Nations Auditor General as Phil Fontaine has proposed.

To address the issue of accountability, the Kelowna Accord set aside $120 million, and a joint work plan detailed the agreement on principles and objectives. Ten specific project areas were identified, including the development of processes for financial certification, data measurement, improved reporting, and the development of management capacity. What is the situation today? When the Conservatives walked away from Kelowna, they cancelled the whole process. What is more incredible is that they even cancelled the funding requested by those chiefs who wanted to pursue the accountability initiatives on their own.

It is important to understand that Kelowna was not only a plan of action, with specific financial commitments from the federal government; it was also a framework for continued co-operation among governments and Aboriginal peoples, right down to the band level. Everyone at Kelowna understood that each province is different and each band is different. The needs of the Haida of British Columbia and the Cree of northern Ontario are not the same. As the Kelowna Accord came into effect, there would be negotiations at every level in the context of a firm federal fiscal commitment. Gordon Campbell and British Columbia's native leaders signed an agreement right then and there at Kelowna that set the stage for the other provinces in negotiations with their Aboriginal peoples that still lay ahead. To my mind, these successful examples of collaboration, consensus, and joint planning – given the doleful history of government relations with Aboriginal peoples – were almost as important as the goals themselves. But the goals were not just airy good intentions. I had set measurable targets as finance minister to eliminate the financial deficit. Similar targets were set in Kelowna to eliminate the social deficit borne by Canada's Aboriginal people.

Furthermore we laid out a plan for subsequent federal-provincial-territorial governmental-Aboriginal meetings every few years, to assess our progress against the specific targets we had laid out for outcomes in terms of the numbers of Aboriginal kids in school, the number of housing units built, the number of health professionals in Aboriginal communities, and right through the piece.

There was a time when native peoples in this country signed treaties relying on the name of a monarch, half a world away, believing that they would not be betrayed. Time and time again, they were proven wrong, and we dishonoured ourselves. I believe that if the Harper government had carried through with the solemn commitment that we made at Kelowna, the next decade would be one of real progress in every Aboriginal community in the land. It would mean the restoration of some damaged lives and the avoidance of much suffering and frustration in others. It would mean that many young children who did not have much reason for hope, and turned to alcohol and other intoxicants for solace, would see another, better way opening up. It would not mean an erasure of the hundreds of years of bitter interaction between Aboriginal peoples and the rest of us, but it would be the foundation of a new relationship of collaboration and trust.

Instead the government has gone back to the old ways of trying to impose solutions: something that scores of years and dozens of discarded policies have proven will not work. And because it will not work, I believe the approach that we – the provinces, territories, and Canada's Aboriginal leadership – adopted at Kelowna will once again see the light of day: working together instead of confrontation, better education instead of more high school dropouts, better health care instead of higher infant mortality, measurable results instead of malignant neglect. Call it what you will, I believe the Kelowna approach if not the Kelowna Accord is inevitable. In the meantime, however, so much opportunity has been lost.

How can the federal government justify spending substantially less per capita on the high school education of a young Aboriginal Canadian in its jurisdiction than the provinces do for a similar student in their jurisdiction. It's wrong, and it cannot last.

That the Conservatives reneged on Kelowna, and in so doing condemned another generation to the same compromised lives to which their parents were condemned, is my deepest regret at losing the election of 2006.

CHAPTER THIRTY

Flying in Turbulence

Transition. Cabinet selection. Sponsorship cancellation. Budget #1. Auditor General's report. Mad as Hell. Whistleblowers Legislation. Gagliano. Health care. Child care. Cities. Kyoto. Ontario health premium. Election call. Darfur. Haiti. Afghanistan. Debt-relief. L-20. Mexico. Russia. India. Japan. Hong Kong. China. Sudan. Libya. Thailand. Sri Lanka. Middle East. Responsibility to Protect. Tsunami. DART. NORAD. BMD. DND. CIDA. International Policy Statement. Second cabinet. Budget #2. Sea Island. Gleneagles. Bush visit. Parrish. Kilgour. Stronach. Grewal. Cadman. Gomery. Fisheries. Mad cow. Softwood. Devils Lake. Health accord. Atlantic accords. NDP budget accord. Kelowna Accord. Equalization. Pacific Gateway. Safe Borders. Maher Arar. The North. The West. The East. Quebec and Ontario.

Have I left something out? Of course I have. Many things. It was that kind of time, and we had a minority government. I have tried in this book to separate out many of these moments, places, issues, and challenges, and put them in their proper context. But my time as prime minister was concentrated into just a couple of years and if, for some people looking in from outside, it all seemed like something of a blur, they may be forgiven. The truth is that all governments deal with many different files, each of which demands urgent action and not all of which can be delegated elsewhere. You probably have to be inside the eye of the storm to see the connections and continuities.

We won 135 seats in the 2004 election, much better than many pundits and pollsters had predicted in the waning days of the campaign. In fact, our victory came as a surprise to many of the so-called "experts." Still, it was well short of a majority. The Conservatives had 99 seats; the Bloc Québécois 54; the NDP 19; and to begin with there was one independent, the former Reformer and Canadian Alliance MP Chuck Cadman. Initially, that appeared to mean that we could get our legislation through with the support of any one of the opposition parties – just barely in the case of the NDP. It did not take long however for us to lose our first MP (Carolyn Parrish). Then in December 2004, Lawrence O'Brien, an MP from Labrador, passed away after a long struggle with cancer at the untimely age of fifty-three.

Whenever these things happen, they help put political life in better perspective. Lawrence had been a wonderful representative for his constituents as well as a friend and supporter of mine, and his brother Leo was one of my RCMP bodyguards. I flew out to Happy Valley-Goose Bay for the funeral. I had been to his riding of Labrador with him many times before. We had worked together to save the Canadian Forces Base at Goose Bay, and had toured some of Labrador's reserves together. One visit with Lawrence that I will never forget was to Charlottetown, a beautiful small fishing village on the Labrador Coast where virtually the only access was by air. Sitting in the school gymnasium talking to the children, it became clear that they knew as much about Toronto, Vancouver, or Montreal as any other Canadian, but I wondered how many Canadians know about their home on the Labrador Coast.

Lawrence had been an educator, a public servant, a town councillor, and eventually a four-time MP. He was a champion, among other things, of the constitutional amendment to change the name of Newfoundland to "Newfoundland and Labrador." He fought and won a tough election after his diagnosis with cancer, which in itself was a tribute to his dedication to public service.

In the House, we were now in a tough position. To get our legislation through we needed the support of either one of the larger opposition parties or the NDP and the independents. From the moment the Gomery inquiry began its public hearings in September, it was clear that both the Conservatives and the Bloc Québécois would be spoiling to have an election at the first opportunity. Although we might be able to win their support on specific pieces of legislation that spoke directly to their constituencies or platforms, we felt it was only a matter of time before they would gang up to try to force an election. The NDP were the exception on the Opposition benches. They had performed relatively well in 2004, after a dismal decade, and probably would have done even better if many of their potential supporters had not come to us for fear of Stephen Harper. The minority offered them a special opportunity to capitalize on their success; another election might snuff that out by electing a majority government of one stripe or another. At the same time, many New Democrats were wary of co-operating too closely with us, fearing that their hard-core base would treat that as a betrayal, and their softer supporters might come to see it as a reason to vote for us.

The first real crunch we faced (though there were plenty of phony crises through the fall) was over our 2005 budget. Not long after Ralph Goodale introduced it, Jack Layton came looking for a negotiation. We met at the Royal York Hotel in Toronto. It was pretty clear that he wanted a deal, for the reasons I've explained above. Initially, he presented a long list of demands that was not very well thought out – or even coherent, to be frank. However, when Tim Murphy sat down with Layton's advisers afterwards, the core demands boiled down to a delay in enacting corporate tax cuts, which we had already delayed in the actual budget announcement itself, so that was no problem, and an acceleration of some other plans we had for housing and student aid by one year. Compromise is not a dirty word in a minority Parliament; it is the way you get things done. And this was a compromise on timing, not substance: an easy deal to make. The Conservatives and the Bloc, who had formed an increasingly close parliamentary alliance, seized on these amendments to set non-confidence motions in play that they hoped would topple the government.

It was clear that the public had no interest in an election so soon after the last. I mentioned in an earlier chapter that I had pledged in a televised address to call an election within thirty days of the final report from the Gomery inquiry, which was intended to make clear to the public that they would eventually get their chance to pass judgment on the sponsorship affair at the ballot box in an orderly way. But we had no illusions that if the opposition succeeded in forcing an earlier election that this would hurt them beyond the first week of the campaign. Jean Chrétien had twice called elections earlier than tradition would dictate. In the spring of 1997, he called an election while southern Manitoba was in the midst of an unprecedented flood, and our candidates there spent as much time in boats on flood relief as they did on the hustings. In both 1997 and 2000, the government was criticized in the media, by the Opposition, and to a degree by the public for going to the polls early. But in the end no one chooses a government on the basis of when the election is called, and the issue of election timing always quickly subsides.

By April 2005, between the NDP and ourselves, we had 151 seats in total; the Conservatives and Bloc Québécois had 153; and there were three independents. With such a delicate balance, every vote counted. In this context, we couldn't help but be intrigued when we got hints and soundings from Conservative MPs, which had begun almost as soon as the 2004 election count had finished, that they might be willing to leave their party. Word would reach us that so-and-so might be willing to "retire" if this or that attractive job opened up in his or her home province, or to cross the floor if there was a cabinet post. We weren't dealing, and those wisps usually disappeared in the next puff of wind.

On Friday of the second week of May, however, I received some startling news. Tim Murphy told me that he had received a phone call late the previous night from former Ontario premier David Peterson. David had been at an event that night and had been speaking to Belinda Stronach, who was a Conservative MP. David had tracked Tim down through the PMO switchboard long after even my burn-the-candle-at-both-ends staff had left their desks. Belinda had told David that she was unhappy with the direction in which Stephen Harper was taking the party, as well as his dismissive attitude toward those with other ideas, such as herself and Peter MacKay. She told him that Harper consulted only his personal inner circle and that members of caucus and other party leaders had almost no role to play. David told Tim he thought she might be open to crossing the floor. Tim suggested that David keep the conversation alive, but he was skeptical. So skeptical that he did not inform me of the conversation.

The next day, however, David phoned Tim and said that Belinda was serious. David felt strongly she was an able individual who would bring a great deal to the government. Then Tim phoned me. My first reaction was that there wasn't a snowball's chance she would actually cross the floor. Still, Belinda Stronach would be a stunning political catch. She represented an important socially progressive strain within the conservative movement in Canada. She was, in a sense, the embodiment of a significant slice of the "progressive conservative" electorate, representing many women who were troubled by Harper's leadership. She had been a leader of industry and a recent candidate for the leadership of the Conservative Party. Although she was a virtual rookie in politics, she had quickly established herself as a high-impact player, both here in Canada and abroad. And she carried with her one badly needed vote in the House of Commons.

David reported from his conversation that she was considering three options: quitting politics, sitting as an independent, or crossing the floor to us. She did not feel the government should be defeated on the budget vote, and she was very much interested in continuing to play a political role. It seemed obvious to me that if she did cross the floor, it would be sensible to have her in cabinet, given her business and political background, her stature in the country, and her symbolic importance in the contest with the Conservatives. Tim remained skeptical, but both of us were getting interested. With more trepidation than hope, we gave David Peterson our okay to pursue the discussion.

Among ourselves, we began discussing the possibility of appointing Belinda minister of human resources. Some time earlier, I had asked the indefatigable and supremely competent Lucienne Robillard to occupy that job temporarily, in addition to her ongoing responsibility for intergovernmental affairs. Belinda's business background gave her experience with issues of skills training that were central to the portfolio. We decided that neither Tim nor I would speak directly to her or even send signals indirectly about entering cabinet, until she had declared her firm intention to cross the floor. Tim arranged through David to meet Belinda at the Château Laurier on Monday afternoon at 4 p.m., on the condition that she would make that commitment. Tim, David, and Scott Reid attended for our part, and Belinda came with her adviser, Mark Entwistle. Once she said she was prepared to join the Liberal caucus, Tim told her I wanted to appoint her minister of human resources with responsibilities for democratic renewal, and would do so when her decision would be made public the next day. Scott and Mark Entwistle were there to work out the details of the press conference. Tim was very insistent that Belinda not talk with Harper, Brian Mulroney, or Bill Davis, as she wanted to do that day. He was concerned that the news would leak out, and also that they might succeed in dissuading her. Tim extended my invitation to Belinda (and to David) to dine with me at 24 Sussex that evening.

Over dinner, Belinda talked at length about her frustrations with Harper's leadership, both on specific issues such a same-sex marriage and more generally on his narrowly ideological approach to politics. When I asked her whether she had spoken directly to Harper about her intention to cross the floor, she said that she had not. She planned to tell him shortly before the announcement the next morning. No problem with that, I thought.

Then I asked her whether she had discussed this with Peter MacKay, with whom she was personally involved at the time. "Well, I am going now to tell Peter," she said. And at that point, I said to myself, Uh-oh.

As we dined at 24 Sussex, Karl Littler was having dinner with Martha Hall Findlay, the Liberal candidate who had lost to Belinda in 2004 by the narrowest of margins, and who hoped to run again in the riding. Karl was under instructions not to say anything to her until he got the word from Tim that the deal had been sealed, leaving Martha a bit mystified, no doubt, why Karl had been so anxious to dine with her that night and yet seemingly had nothing much of substance to say. Finally, as their dinner was nearing its end, he got a call from Tim, and had the tough task of breaking the news. As she has subsequently shown in many ways, Martha is a woman of great quality, with a real future in the party. She was taken aback, as anyone would be by this very difficult news, but she accepted it with dignity.

The arrangement for the next morning was that Tim and Scott would meet with Belinda and Mark Entwistle at 7 a.m. at the Château Laurier to iron out last-minute details. I would pick Belinda up at the side door of the hotel fifteen minutes before the press conference. When Tim and Scott arrived for their meeting, only Mark was there. According to him, Belinda was having second thoughts. Understandably, perhaps, after having worked out all the logistics, she was beginning to deal with the emotional weight of her decision. Tim sent a BlackBerry message to John Webster, one of the few others who knew what was happening, saying, "She has cold feet." Webster's reply was brief: "Rub them." Mark Entwistle disappeared for a time and returned with the news that it was back on.

Still, when I got to the side door of the Château at the appointed time, Belinda was not there waiting for me. Five minutes passed. Then ten minutes. Long enough for me to wonder whether Peter MacKay had succeeded in dissuading her after all. In my mind's eye, I could see the media gathering at the national press theatre a few blocks away, and I began to think about how to explain the fact that I was a no-show, if that turned out to be the case. And then Belinda appeared. She and Peter MacKay had had a long talk, but she had made up her mind. Harper, on the other hand, had received the news without emotion when she called him, and had made no attempt to dissuade her.

It was such a stunner, stepping out of the car and walking into the national press theatre with Belinda Stronach at my side, I cannot deny feeling a childlike delight in the sheer element of surprise. At the news conference, I overplayed my hand a bit, saying that the significance of Belinda's defection was not the vote she carried with her from the Tory benches, which triggered a wave of laughter from reporters, and I couldn't help joining in just a little. What I guess I meant to say was that Belinda was much more than just an ordinary Tory MP – she was a political star. And something else that should have been obvious to the media: even with Belinda on board, we still did not have the numbers to win the confidence vote.

Of course, Belinda Stronach was accused of cynicism for her decision to cross the floor. This is nonsense, if you think seriously about her situation. The political as well as personal differences she had with Harper were well known. Moreover, she might have set herself up for the shortest-ever period in government, since at the time she made her decision, no one knew whether the government would survive even a matter of days. Winning re-election in her riding in these circumstances – with a Liberal riding association that had just run a campaign against her the year before – was by no means a forgone conclusion. As for the sexist and often sexual slurs she suffered at the hands of some of her former colleagues and some people in the press, they did not deserve to be dignified with a reply, and Belinda did not do so. But they must have hurt. The decision she made was a courageous one.

Even with Belinda on board, we needed several more votes to survive the confidence motion. Carolyn Parrish had stated publicly that she had not been elected to bring the government down, and would vote with us. Kilgour was against us. So the fate of the government hinged on Chuck Cadman.

Although we had sat across the aisle from each other in the House of Commons since 1993, I barely knew him. Cadman was a unique character in Parliament. He was a former professional musician and electronic technician who had been propelled into politics by the murder of his sixteen-year-old son in 1992 and his determination to change the criminal laws. He was elected from Surrey, British Columbia, in 1993 as a Reformer, and later sat as a member of the Canadian Alliance, but he was unlike his colleagues in many respects. He often wore his hair in a long ponytail – a reminder of the days when he was a professional guitarist, sometimes backing up the Guess Who. Because he came to politics very briefly before entering Parliament, he did not necessarily share every element of the Reform/Alliance ideology. He was his own man and someone you had to respect. In 2004 he lost the Conservative Party nomination to a well-organized opponent, but ran as an independent and won. About the same time he was diagnosed with a fatal form of skin cancer, and was often absent from the House of Commons to receive therapy.

Ujjal Dosanjh, who was minister of health at the time, knew Cadman well, and arranged for the three of us to meet. Cadman decided to come to Ottawa a few days before the confidence vote so that he would be well rested on the critical day. We met with him and his wife, Dona, at their apartment. He never asked for anything, and I never offered anything.

Visibly frail, he was at a stage of his life when it took some physical courage even to show up for the vote. Everyone would have understood had he stayed home. Still, he was also under enormous pressure from his erstwhile colleagues and friends in the Conservative caucus – some elements of which have only begun to dribble out over time. He told me his personal view was that the government should not be defeated, but that he felt bound to respect the wishes of his constituents, whatever they were. There were a number of straw polls in the riding suggesting that people there did not want an election, and then a more scientific poll that reinforced that impression. Still, Chuck Cadman kept his own counsel and so, on the day of the non-confidence motion, May 19, 2005, we were hopeful but uncertain about how he would vote.

When he rose in the House, a little unsteadily, to support the government, it was a moment of great drama and dignity – and more than a little relief for us. With Cadman's vote, it was a tie, broken by the vote of the Speaker, Peter Milliken, according to tradition, in the government's favour. Cadman later explained that he supported the budget because his constituents felt an election was unnecessary at the time. Less than two months later, he passed away at home with his family.

In the context of these dramatic events, I should say something about the Gurmant Grewal farce. Ujjal Dosanjh phoned me to say that Grewal, a Conservative MP from British Columbia, was making noises about doing something, and I asked Tim to connect with Ujjal directly. We might have been willing to take Grewal into our caucus, but when word came back that he was making demands, later reported as a diplomatic post for him and a Senate seat for his wife, our position was a flat "no" – a reiteration of the position that Ujjal, Tim, and I had reached without debate when Grewal made his initial approach. When his "negotiation" failed to lead anywhere, Grewal publicly released an ineptly edited version of his secretly taped conversations with Tim and Ujjal – an act intended to embarrass us. That kicked off Grewal's slow-motion descent into political oblivion as his hoax was revealed, and under pressure he discovered progressively more complete versions of the tapes, each one more embarrassing to him than the last. Still, some of the first clod of mud he threw at us stuck.

Another result of Grewal's hijinks was that Tim came under tremendous attack from the Opposition for his role in the discussions. It is one of the drawbacks of public and political life that you expose yourself to this kind of attack. Given the delicate political situation and the embarrassment the Conservatives must have felt at having Grewal as one of their own, it is understandable, in a way, that they tried to deflect the controversy by attacking Tim. The truth is that Grewal was asking, and Tim was refusing, which is why Grewal never left the Tory side of the House. But the Tory attack was furious enough that Tim considered resigning – something I refused to contemplate.

In fact I'd like to take a bit of time right now to say why I reacted that way. Tim is a tireless worker, someone who is fascinated with public policy as well as gifted with a shrewd political mind. Before joining me at Finance, Tim served for several years in the Ontario legislature, where he distinguished himself as a defender of human rights, in particular those of same-sex couples. It is a shame that he is not still in public life. He was a huge asset for the government, whether it was negotiating the special agreement with Ontario signed by Dalton McGuinty and myself, the invaluable and close relationship he formed with the White House staff, or his deep understanding of political calculus. I don't know what I would have done without him. It pains me that Tim, like some others close to me, have had to pass through such harrowing periods out of commitment to the public good, as well to me personally.

By the fall of 2005, Jack Layton's situation had changed from the previous spring, when he had made an agreement with us to support the budget. He had come to the conclusion that the best way to ensure his party's future was to get rid of us and help Stephen Harper get elected. His far-fetched plan was then to have the NDP displace the Liberal Party as the natural alternative to the Conservatives. The fact that it also meant doing away with many policies his supporters favoured – such as the Kelowna Accord, the national child-care plan, and the cities agenda – did not appear to me to concern him.

On the other hand, Layton obviously was concerned about preserving the veneer of a politician who wanted Parliament to work rather than one always itching for the next election, as Harper and Duceppe so plainly were. He approached us again for a negotiation, but in a much different spirit than earlier in the year. It was clear that there was going to be an election, sooner or later. The only issue was when. At the time of the budget the previous winter, Layton wanted to make something work. This time, it seemed to me that he wanted our discussions to fail, with us taking the blame. When we met at 24 Sussex, he had a long list of demands, as before, but wanted to speak only about health care. I said that we were willing to give his proposals serious consideration and that we would get back to him after we had analyzed them. But he was not interested.

After a meeting of less than half an hour, he up and left, telling the media, as he had evidently planned all along, that we were not interested in addressing his concerns about health care.

After that meeting, it was obvious that Layton had an election in his sights. It was only because we publicly embarrassed him over the fact that an early election would strangle the Kelowna process, on which NDP provincial governments had worked hard alongside others, that his caucus was able to stay his hand until the late fall.

Intellectually, I had prepared myself for the coming election campaign. Over the summer of 2005, I decided that I needed to set out as clearly as I could the objectives of my government amid all the clutter of the Gomery inquiry and noise of the minority government. In my mind this was not to be a narrowly political exercise, but a roadmap for the public service. It was a plan for governing after an election I believed we could win. The people who worked with me most closely in fleshing out my ideas were Alex Himelfarb on the public service side and Peter Nicholson from the PMO. I brought in my principal speechwriter, Scott Feschuk, whose eloquent pen so often fashioned my ideas into words so much better than I could alone. Along with Scott Reid, we crafted what was in my view one of my most important speeches as prime minister. I gave the speech in September to a meeting of senior public servants in Gatineau, just across the river from Ottawa.

Domestically, I talked about the demographic change Canada was experiencing as the baby boomers aged and new populations of immigrants moved here to enrich our society. Getting the health-care system right, which we were on the road to doing, was an important part of preparing for the retirement of the baby boomers beginning in 2011. But we also needed to lift up the youngest and fastest growing segment of our population – the Aboriginal peoples – not only as a matter of justice but also as a matter of economic and social growth.

Internationally, I spoke about the rise of China and India, and the effects this would have not only on our trading relationships but also the international political system in which we needed to secure a role fitting to our interests and ideals. Preparing ourselves for the economic challenges and opportunities, I said, meant building up our cities, the engines of growth in the globalized world, as well as the research, innovation and skills of our population. At the same time, I argued, government needed to transform itself because the international dimension of our national life was no longer the sole property of the Department of Foreign Affairs. We needed to show international leadership on the environment, on human rights, on conservation, on trade, and capital flows. That meant that departments such as Environment, Justice, Agriculture, Fisheries, and Finance were increasingly operating in a world that stretched well beyond our borders. Nowhere was this globalization of government more in evidence than in the area of security, whether it was the threat of terrorism or of SARS (severe acute respiratory syndrome). I also talked about rebuilding our Defence forces and refocusing our international development assistance.

This speech, which also addressed many other issues close to my heart, including Arctic sovereignty, and education, for example, became the spine of my platform in the election, when it was fleshed out to more than eighty pages of concrete proposals. It prepared us for the election campaign I wanted to fight – but not the one I eventually did.

CHAPTER THIRTY-ONE

Last Election

It is a little difficult in retrospect to recreate the atmosphere in which we entered the 2005–06 campaign, when it was triggered by the NDP on a Tory non-confidence motion in the last days of November 2005. The polls at the time had all the parties at pretty much the same level of support as the 2004 election. We had recruited some "star" candidates, for example Marc Garneau, the former astronaut, and Michael Ignatieff, the high-profile professor and writer. Our campaign organization was reasonably well financed and in good shape, ready to go. The opposition parties were champing at the bit for an election because they hoped to explode from the box on the strength of Mr. Justice Gomery's preliminary report, which laid out the details of the sponsorship mess at the beginning of November. They preferred this to going to the polls after the final report as I had promised, just a few months later, because they knew from the evidence that it was likely to state clearly that neither I nor any of my ministers were involved in any way.

As I went to Rideau Hall on the morning of November 29 to ask Governor General Michaëlle Jean to call the election, I hoped that I could shape the election around the future of the country. Our plan was not to lay out the platform in depth before Christmas, before the public had fully tuned in. Until then, there was plenty to talk about in terms of our record on the economy, on health care, child care, and Aboriginal affairs – and to contrast it with Stephen Harper's record and plans. There was also the United Nations' conference on climate change starting in Montreal, with Environment Minister Stéphane Dion at the helm. Our plan was to lay out the details of our platform for our next government in January, after the holiday season, when we hoped the public would begin to pay more attention.

It was the 180-degree opposite of the Conservatives' strategy, which was to roll out their long list of promises before Christmas – many of which we can now see they had no intention of keeping – backed up by extensive advertising. We were husbanding our ad money for when it would count most. We could see that they were shooting their bolt and wondered how they hoped to compete in the home stretch. Of course, we could not have anticipated the "in-and-out" scheme later unearthed by Elections Canada, who have accused the Conservatives of shuffling money around between constituency organizations and the national party, giving themselves about a million dollars more for advertising than the law allows. As I write, the commissioner of elections has only recently directed investigators to raid Conservative offices with the assistance of the RCMP to obtain documentation of the scheme, so there may be more to come. What we could see during the campaign in terms of their sustained advertising campaign – continuing to buy ad-time long after we thought they should be out of cash – certainly defied the laws of political gravity as we understood them.

The United Nations' climate change conference, which we hosted in Montreal from the end of November until December 10, turned out to be my government's last hurrah on the international stage. Of course, we had not planned for this to occur in the middle of a campaign since these events don't happen at the drop of a hat. I had been enthusiastic about bringing the conference to Montreal, and we had made a significant diplomatic push to host it. The purpose of the conference was to lay the groundwork for the next stage of global efforts to reduce greenhouse gas emissions, beyond the term of the Kyoto agreement.

Some of my officials did not take to the idea of hosting the conference, feeling quite justifiably that it would highlight our poor record
on limiting emissions. I was very much aware that our performance,
even as signatories to Kyoto, had not been impressive. But I drew
the opposite lesson from this. By hosting the conference, I hoped to
signal to Canadians and the world that while we had not yet lived up
to our obligations, we were now determined to do so. I wanted to
acknowledge our failures openly, and to use the conference to build
public support for getting this country back on plan and to stop
blowing hot air on the subject.

As the conference approached, we found ourselves in a game of
chicken with the Americans (and to a degree with the Russians), who
preferred that the conference fail to create a robust process to set
targets for after 2012, when the first phase of Kyoto would end. As
my adviser Brian Guest remarked, they wanted to keep Kyoto's face
under the water until it stopped moving. The Americans were trying
to subvert the conference despite a commitment at the Gleneagles
summit that they would re-engage and try to make it work. Later,
some critics said that by taking on the United States at the Montreal
conference, I had been deliberately provocative. The provocation
came from the Bush administration's attempt to blow up this important conference on our soil.

Stéphane held the gavel at the conference and did a superb job,
both before and during the formal deliberations, of negotiating the
diplomatic shoals and leading the international community toward
a productive outcome. It was his day in the sun, and no one could
have been better suited or better prepared for it.

Long before the election was called, or was foreseen for that time,
I had committed to delivering the opening speech for the key negotiating session. I wanted to convey my belief that we were facing a
global challenge in climate change, and to ask whether we wanted to
look back on this moment and say that we had failed humanity by
not stepping up to the challenge.

In my speech, I acknowledged before an international audience what I had already said to people here at home: that we were laggards in reducing our emissions and that the laggards had to catch up and become leaders.

I wanted to raise the bar in terms of what we had to do as a global community. The speech received an enthusiastic response from delegates who had come to expect more cautious, bureaucratic interventions. Many countries began to redraft their remarks in response, and Elizabeth May has said that it was the first time in all her years attending these conferences that she saw someone receiving a spontaneous standing ovation.

I did not criticize the United States directly from the podium, but in the press conference afterwards, I said that there is such a thing as a "global conscience" and that it was time for all of us, including the United States, to listen to that conscience. I had for some considerable time been talking about the need for a "New Multilateralism," including the United States. However, that term was too dry to capture the moral dimension of what I was advocating. In the context of the press conference, I used the more evocative term, and I am not sorry that I did.

Inside the negotiating halls, the American delegation was becoming increasingly obstructionist, walking out of meetings, for example. It was in this context that news first circulated that Bill Clinton was going to attend the conference as the guest of the Sierra Club, whose leader, Elizabeth May, was an old friend. The conference organizers decided to ask Bill Clinton to speak in the main conference hall. It was a way of raising the profile of the conference in the United States, and sending a message to the Bush administration that we understood that there was a large domestic constituency south of the border that did not want our efforts to fail.

I learned that when the American delegation discovered this, they reacted with anger and a fair degree of panic. They actually offered to change their position and allow some of the previously disputed resolutions to pass if President Clinton was prevented from speaking.

That was their negotiating posture: "Ban Bill Clinton and we'll allow these critical negotiations to take a step forward."

But no one on our side blinked. There really was no separating out the domestic and international politics in this situation. We knew that to make the conference a success we had to rally opinion inside the United States. I also knew that with an election under way, a photo op at an environmental conference with Clinton wasn't going to do me any harm. But I would have done the same thing even if there hadn't been an election. Behind the scenes, the Americans were furious, but within forty-eight hours they bent to the will of the world and allowed progress to be made. Thus the conference not only demonstrated our commitment to the environment, but it was a major international success and served Canada well.

Another element of our pre-Christmas campaign had been longer in the works, however. My relationship with Buzz Hargrove, the leader of the Canadian Auto Workers (CAW), surfaced in the public's mind early in the election campaign when Buzz invited me to a meeting of the union and gave a strong recommendation to his followers that they vote Liberal in seats where we were best positioned to defeat the Conservative candidate. Unlike the NDP, who seemed to relish the prospect of a Conservative government, Buzz, along with many other less outspoken labour leaders, recognized that our health-care and child-care policies were important to his members, as was the Kelowna Accord. His stance created some controversy and led to his eventual divorce from the NDP.

What many people did not understand was that my relationship with Buzz and with the CAW was not just a made-in-campaign marriage of convenience. As I have said, my father had deep relationships with the labour movement in Windsor where the Canadian auto industry was originally based, despite the fact that the NDP was an increasingly strong challenger in his riding. I believed, like him, that organized labour was capable of making a profound contribution to economic growth. What many people overlook in Buzz's case, because of his often gruff, confrontational rhetoric, is that he has helped make the CAW one of the most progressive and innovative unions in North America. The CAW evolved when unions south of the border – and the NDP up here – failed to do so, in the face of a changing world economy.

After the 2004 election, I appointed Joe Fontana as labour minister, and he proved to be a tremendous asset to the government. Joe, who represented a riding in London, Ontario, is as affable as he is politically astute. Joe already had a good relationship with the labour movement prior to joining the cabinet; he also had a social activist bent and had been active as an MP on matters such as poverty and housing. In fact, I first got to know Joe many years before when we were still in opposition and we co-chaired a Liberal task force on housing. Joe was the point man in nurturing the relationship between the government and the labour movement. Both of us developed a good working relationship with Ken Georgetti, head of the Canadian Labour Congress, and Secretary Treasurer Hassan Yussuf. It was through Joe that the CAW was heard at the cabinet table on the issue of reciprocity in the auto sector as we negotiated trade agreements with Korea. Buzz met with us on many occasions concerning other issues, and we saved a lot of jobs in the industry through strategies that were worked out together. When the election campaign came, Buzz shared my conviction, and that of many progressive voters, that the greatest danger to our ideals was a Conservative victory, and that the NDP had become their accomplices. I think subsequent history bears that out.

Not everything went well in the pre-Christmas campaign. Scott Reid, who was my director of communications, a long-time aide, and a great friend, has been an invaluable asset to me for nearly two decades. But he would be the first to admit that his quick tongue sometimes betrays him, as it did in a CBC interview in mid-December when he was commenting on the Tory plan to replace the national child-care program we had put in place with a direct subsidy to parents – cutting them a cheque, in essence. "Don't give people twenty-five bucks a week to blow on beer and popcorn," Scott said. "Give them child-care spaces that work. Stephen Harper's plan has nothing to do with child care." I certainly wouldn't dispute the underlying point: that the proposed cash subsidy was trivial compared with the significance of the system we were building. But the choice of words was poor as he was the first to admit. "It was dumb," Scott said, soon after, when he made a public apology. I don't remember him getting much argument from the rest of us.

Still, this was hardly a turning point. There were more ups than downs in the pre-Christmas campaign, and although the Conservatives were putting out their "Gainesburgers" as the media calls them – the daily ration of pre-packaged announcements – including their promise to cut the GST, they were not getting much traction with the voters in the short-term, although these promises probably helped lay the groundwork for their later success. For my part, I strongly believed from all my years at Finance that cutting the GST, rather than taxes on income, was unwise policy – something with which virtually all the economists agreed. Perhaps for that reason, we tended to discount the impact of the Conservatives' pledge. As I headed back to the farm with the family for Christmas, I was happy with the campaign so far, and was looking forward with relish to January, when we would start laying out our platform, of which I was very proud, and which I believed was going to prove compelling to voters – and we were already in the lead. But if I went to bed on Christmas night with sugar plums dancing in my head, I was soon to have a rude awakening.

The decisive moment in the campaign came three days after Christmas. I was in a hotel room in Halifax when Alex Himelfarb reached me by phone with the news. I realized the significance right away. What had happened was unbelievable and built on a falsehood, as subsequent events have proven. It was nonetheless devastating.

Guiliano Zaccardelli, the then still-respected commissioner of the RCMP, had written a letter before Christmas to the NDP's finance critic, Judy Wasylycia-Leis, saying that the RCMP had launched a criminal investigation into the possible leak of a planned change on the taxation of income trusts announced by Ralph Goodale the previous month. As I understand it, when they did not hear back from Wasylycia-Leis, the RCMP actually phoned her office to make sure she had received the letter. The letter was found and a breathless Wasylycia-Leis revealed it to the world – as Zaccardelli surely knew she would.

The announcement that an investigation had been launched, which the RCMP soon directly confirmed to the media in the form of a press release, was utterly unprecedented and not consistent with the previous practices of the RCMP, as later confirmed by the official report from the public complaints commissioner for the RCMP, Paul Kennedy, who noted "the absence of a rational and justifiable basis for such disclosure." His report also established that the RCMP's press release was specifically amended by Zaccardelli himself to add Ralph's name, despite the fact that there was not a shred of evidence at the time or since that he had done anything wrong. Any reporter will tell you that in normal circumstances, the RCMP would refuse to answer the kind of questions that they happily briefed on that day.

There is no doubt in my mind that what Zaccardelli did was improper. The only question there can be about the incident is whether it was an act of ineptitude or of malice aforethought. My own view is that no one can be that inept.

I hope that some day the truth will come out. Was it payback for my decision to call the Arar inquiry? Was it an attempt to curry favour with the Tories, who had been quite critical of Zaccardelli to that point but later backed him up strongly for as long as they could bear when they took office – even in the teeth of public outrage at his questionable testimony before the Arar inquiry? I don't suppose anyone knows but him. Astonishingly, Zaccardelli refused to co-operate with the public complaints commissioner, refusing to be interviewed, *or to provide a statement*. The commissioner noted that his excuses for not doing so were logically incoherent.

In my view, Zaccardelli should have known that the release of this information in the midst of an election campaign – a release that was made in a deliberately political way, creating inevitable insinuations of political wrongdoing and inciting the opposition parties to run those insinuations through a particle accelerator at the public – would have a huge political effect. And it did. Here is what Commissioner Kennedy said in his report:

> It is impossible to state with certainty that the RCMP disclosure was the sole factor contributing to this dramatic shift in voter support. It is not unknown for the fortunes of contending political parties to rise and fall drastically even during the relatively short duration of a federal election. It is equally clear that members of the general public, media and those involved in the political process believed that the RCMP disclosures of December 23rd and 28th had an influence and, in the absence of a rational and justifiable basis for such disclosure, questioned the motives of the RCMP and its Commissioner in making such disclosure.
>
> It is clear that acts or omissions by the police may intentionally or otherwise have an influence upon the electoral process, which would subvert democracy. Any such real or perceived negative influence could also break the trust between citizens and the police that is essential to maintaining the rule of law in a civilized society.

That this calumny fell on the head of Ralph Goodale, a man whose absolute integrity over a long political career is unimpeachable, even legendary, only added to the injustice. Ralph immediately offered me his resignation, not because he had any responsibility to do so, but because he did not want to become a millstone around the neck of the campaign. I immediately rejected the suggestion. But I also knew from the moment the story hit that this could turn the campaign on its head and cost us the election. The absolutely vacuous and malignant suggestion that Ralph, the minister of finance, might have done something improper destroyed our attempts to distance ourselves from the scandals of the previous government. After all, this was coming from the Mounties!

We know now that the RCMP investigation, completed long after the election, absolutely cleared Ralph, as well as other ministers of any wrongdoing. Only one low-ranking public servant was ever charged, and the allegation against him was not that he had leaked sensitive information but that he may have personally profited from advance knowledge of the income trust announcement with a small personal trade, which couldn't possibly have affected the market.

Before I pass from this appalling affair, let me say as clearly as I can that I do not think that Zaccardelli's behaviour reflects in any way on the professionalism of the women and men of the RCMP. As prime minister I had especially close contact with RCMP officers who looked after Sheila and me twenty-four hours a day. We got to know them personally. Believe it or not, when we tried to organize a Christmas party for them and their families at 24 Sussex, Zaccardelli forbade it as improper fraternizing. We held it anyway, but not at our home the first year. The second Christmas, we said to heck with Zaccardelli, and had them round to 24 Sussex, as we wished to do.

My deepest feeling about the rank and file of the RCMP were captured in my brief address to the memorial service after the tragic deaths of four officers at Mayerthorpe, Alberta, in the late winter of 2005:

> We use the word debt to remind us of something owed. The people of Canada owe an untold debt to these four officers and to their families. We owe a debt to each and every woman and man who chooses to put on the uniform, to submit to risk, to face harm, to uphold the law. The presence here of so many police officers, from cities and communities across the continent, is a testament to the camaraderie and the devotion that thrives within the law enforcement community. The bonds forged by dangers shared are strong and they are everlasting.

That memorial was one of the most moving occasions I experienced in public office, and I would never want failures of leadership to undermine the reverence we Canadian have for our Mounties.

In terms of the election, in the case of Ralph's own riding – among the people who knew him best – the Zaccardelli-inspired announcement actually created a backlash among voters in his favour. Unfortunately, in the rest of the country that was not the case. Not by a long shot. For the most part, polling organizations had suspended their calls over the New Year's weekend, but a few days into January, the news hit that we were lagging the Tories for the first time in the campaign. With that, the media had a new and more exciting narrative. Instead of a boring story about an election headed to producing a carbon copy of the last one, they had an exciting new tale to tell: "Tories on their way to government." Our carefully crafted strategy of saving our detailed platform for after the Christmas break now came undone.

Let me just say a few words here about the media. The brilliant, erratic, and controversial British politician Enoch Powell once remarked that a politician complaining about the media is like a sailor complaining about the sea. I have tried to keep that idea in mind while writing this book. The truth is that I have had several distinct periods in my relationship with the media. After the 1995 budget, and then again after I "got quit" from Jean Chrétien's cabinet, I enjoyed very favourable media coverage. At the time, naturally enough, I was inclined to think that it was a tribute to the sagacity of the media that they saw things so clearly. Of course, I knew, as did those around me who dealt with communications, that this would not last forever. Indeed, the favourable coverage in the period when I was out of government, I fully understood, raised expectations for when I became prime minister, which would be difficult, if not impossible, to meet.

Still, in the last weeks of the campaign I found it frustrating that we could not generate any interest in the ideas I had hoped the election would be about. I had insisted that we go into this election with a detailed list of commitments that were carefully costed. They included, for example, commitments to pay half of every university student's tuition in his or her first and graduating years; to add one thousand family doctors to our health-care system, and establish a national cancer strategy; to double spending on child care; to continue with sensible tax relief that would emphasize the needs of low-income families; to provide action and leadership, domestically and internationally, toward achieving the Kyoto targets on greenhouse gas emissions, and then beyond. I could go on.

As I said before, we had deliberately left our detailed policy announcements until the New Year. We had also reserved much of our advertising budget for that period, intending to talk most specifically to Canadians at a time in the election campaign when we expected they would be listening most carefully. The income trust story, however, obliterated any interest in what we had to say. Moreover, our platform was leaked – some claimed by hostile elements within the Liberal Party – so that the dominant news story became one about internal disarray in the Liberal organization, instead of what we intended to do if we were re-elected – a matter that in theory, at least, should be of at least equal importance to the voters.

Finally, some of the choices the media made during the leadership debates were truly puzzling. There were four debates among the party leaders, two in English and two in French. In each of these debates, we were told ahead of time that the moderator asking the questions would select four issues from the following list, the economy, governance, national unity, the environment, social policy, and foreign affairs. When the first debate passed without foreign affairs, or the environment, coming up, I was certain that they were holding them for the second debate or later. We were just moving our troops into more forward positions in Afghanistan, and this was obviously going to be a major challenge for the next government, whoever won. I was also keen to talk about the role we were playing in Darfur. Meanwhile, the environment was one of the issues about which voters were most concerned, and we had just sponsored a major international conference on the subject.

When there were no questions about foreign affairs or the environment in the second debate, which occurred before Christmas, who would have believed that these issues would not have been front and centre in the final two debates to come in the new year? They were also issues where we had a clear advantage over the opposition parties, as opposed to the sponsorship issue, which had been the main focus of the debate organizers before Christmas. Thus you can imagine my puzzlement when the issues raised in the last two were exactly the same as the first round, and there was not a single question on Canada's role in the world or the environment, both issues which were of prime concern to Canadians. Not one, in four debates.

Just after the New Year, I made a commitment in one of the debates that I had been thinking about for a long time, which was to repeal Ottawa's ability to use the notwithstanding clause in the Canadian Constitution. Tom Axworthy and Serge Joyal helped me craft my proposal. The notwithstanding clause allows Ottawa and the provinces to add language to legislation overriding the Charter of Rights and Freedoms. As I discussed earlier, initially I had supported the clause, believing that it protected the supremacy of Parliament and the legislatures – a prized value in a democracy. But respect for human rights is also an important value, and I came to the view that a parliamentary majority overriding the rights of a minority, which the courts had ruled were entrenched in the charter, was wrong. Later on I became increasingly concerned that the Conservatives were planning to use the notwithstanding clause to remove rights that the courts had adjudicated to exist. In retrospect, trying to launch this debate in the midst of an election campaign, as I did, was not very effective and the idea sank like a stone. The communication may have been faulty but I truly believe the principle is right.

The deeper we slogged into January, the gloomier my organizers got about our hopes of turning the election around. But we kept trying. We had succeeded under similar circumstances in the 2004 campaign. As often happens with candidates, I was more hopeful than many of those around me, if only because I had to be. Having Sheila by my side kept my spirits up and the campaign in perspective. Strategic Counsel had published polls that suggested we were headed to a disaster on a scale the party had not seen since 1984. I was convinced the situation was better than that. However, I was not surprised, when midafternoon of election day, David Herle came to see me in our suite at the Queen Elizabeth Hotel in Montreal with his last analysis. "Look," he said, "we aren't going to win; we aren't going to pull it off." He was very matter of fact. David thought we would come in around a hundred seats (which proved to be almost dead-on), with a worst-case scenario of eighty seats.

I spoke first to Sheila and said that I was going to have to make a decision. I was determined that if I decided to go, I would do it quickly: that night. It was one of her many gifts of love over a lifetime that she, who never chose politics, took this moment to make certain I was making the right decision. "Are you sure?" she asked. "We'll move to Stornoway. We can take our time." Paul and David were with their mother. Jamie, who never had much enthusiasm for politics, was the most adamant that I go right away. "Now you can do what you want," he said.

Clearly the country was going to be in other hands. The issue was what would be best for the party. I chatted with Elly Alboim, Mike Robinson, Tim Murphy, Scott Reid, Jim Pimblett, David Herle, Michele Cadario, and Terrie. As often happened, David and Terrie were on opposite sides, with Terrie arguing that I should make a clean break and go. David, arguing for himself and the campaign team – John Webster, Lucienne Robillard and Karl Littler – made the case for staying on. I also consulted Mike Eizenga, our very able party president, who had been with me for the last couple of weeks of the campaign and who contributed the party perspective. But in the end, advisers can't make a decision for you – especially on a matter like this. It was up to me. I felt that the best way for the party to start fresh was with a new leader, unencumbered with the legacy of the split between me and Jean Chrétien, free of the deadweight of sponsorship, and able to present a fresh face in a way that I had wanted to.

As difficult as that day was in many respects, I did not find the decision a hard one to make. And as it happened, it was that very day that Sheila and I also received some of the most joyful news of our lives: David and Laurence were going to give us our first grandchild!

There was also another silver lining for me personally. I would dearly have loved another three or four years to see through what I had started. But I had been in politics for eighteen years, and in government for most of that. There are wonderful rewards in public life: accomplishments unattainable anywhere else. But after a while, you wonder about seeing life at thirty thousand feet. It's sort of nice to see it from the ground. It was time to move on.

CHAPTER THIRTY-TWO

Fast Forward

I had been scheduled to attend the World Summit on Progressive Governance in South Africa, just a few days after the election, along with other government leaders including Britain's Tony Blair, Brazil's Lula da Silva, South Africa's Thabo Mbeki, and Sweden's Goran Persson. As a former prime minister now, I sent my regrets. But both Blair, who was one of the founders of the group, and Mbeki, who was host, phoned and insisted I come. And I thought, Why not?

The summit was held at the Didimala Game Lodge in lovely countryside about an hour's drive from Pretoria. The conference centre has an unusual organic design, made from brick and straw bales. I knew most of the leaders at the meeting reasonably well, and the discussion, which was on familiar topics including African development and the stalled Doha round of international trade negotiations, went quite well. There was one man at the table whom I did not know, and who didn't say very much, so as we left one of the sessions I went over to introduce myself and we ended up having lunch together.

His name was Joachim Chissano, and he was the former president of Mozambique. He had quite a story. Chissano was the first black student to attend the high school in Maputo, the capital of what was then a Portuguese colony. He travelled to Portugal to study medicine, but his studies were ended abruptly because of his political activities. He became an activist for the Liberation Front of Mozambique

(Frelimo), the Mozambique independence movement, and later a diplomat and a prominent moderating influence on the organization. He returned to Mozambique and lived many years in the bush as a commander in the liberation struggle, rising to the rank of major general. He played a key role in negotiating independence from Portugal in 1975 and became the country's first foreign minister. When he became president in 1986, the country was in the middle of a civil war, which he was able to bring to an end in 1992 after sixteen years of fighting. He created a multi-party system in Mozambique, won two elections as president, and then did a very unusual thing in African history: he voluntarily stepped aside, even though the Constitution would have allowed him to run again. He later received the first-ever African award for achievement in government: a $5-million prize bestowed by the Mo Ibrahim Foundation to encourage good governance in a continent that has often suffered from its absence.

He had done more in each year of his existence than many people do in a lifetime. Just let me say that I don't think I'd volunteer to take to the stage beside him on Career Day. But as it would happen, our post-political lives would soon bring us together in an unexpected way.

From South Africa, Sheila and I headed to Turkey. On the second last day of that short trip, we ended up in Izmir (formerly Smyrna) on the Aegean Coast. During this visit, we had been assigned two Turkish police bodyguards.

After we checked into the hotel about four in the afternoon and went to our room, the bellboy brought up our luggage. I tipped him, he said thank you, and I was a bit surprised when he hesitated to leave the room.

Then he said, "Can I ask you something?"

"Of course," I said.

"I'm a graduate student in international relations at the university here in Izmir," he said. "I wonder whether you could come and speak at the university."

I told him that we were leaving at eleven the next morning, but he said that was okay. He would organize something for eight. I found it hard to believe he could arrange much at such short notice, but he assured me it would be no problem.

When I came downstairs the next morning, instead of two body-guards there were a dozen. When I got to the university, where I had expected perhaps twenty students, there were more like three hundred, rounded up no doubt through a network of text-message exchanges. And more police.

This was at the height of the controversy about the cartoons of Muhammad published in a Danish newspaper, and it turned out there was a huge interest in hearing from an ex-prime minister of a Western country – however distant you might imagine Canada must have seemed to them.

I spoke for twenty minutes about foreign affairs, and then we went to a question-and-answer session that went on for an hour and a half. We covered all kinds of topics, but primarily they drilled me on the cartoons. What frustrated many of the students was the failure of people in the West to understand the anguish the publication of the cartoons had caused even to secular people such as themselves. Surprisingly, some others believed that the whole cartoon contro-versy had been deliberately provoked to stir up anti-Muslim feeling and to prejudice Turkey's bid to enter the European Union.

I told them that I thought the publication had been more than dis-courteous and showed a profound lack of sensitivity to Muslim feeling. But I also said that they needed to understand that Western traditions included the right to say and even publish things that might offend some people in the deepest way.

In the end, what impressed me the most was that the students really tried to understand both sides of the controversy, while their professors seemed reluctant to do so. One observation I have made over the years is that the biggest challenge in international relations is often not simply reconciling different points of view. Often the biggest difficulty is getting people to understand the origins of those points of view that are different than their own, something that is often an essential first step in coming to agreement. For cultural or ideological reasons people of influence who ought to know better often appear incapable of understanding where the other side are coming from – and even more to the point, they lack the desire to do so. This was the attitude manifested by the professors, but not the students. It may be that as my generation passes from the scene, things will improve.

By the time I returned home from this trip (which also included a few days in Portugal to golf), I had confirmed this much about my "third career." After business and politics there was a lot I still wanted to do, and it didn't include professional golf.

I have said before that I have a tendency not to look back but rather to throw myself into each stage of my life, whatever it is, and let what has passed drop very much into the background. In this case, it is not as if I did not have regrets about leaving the job as prime minister. I did. Those regrets included the fact that some terrific people didn't return to Parliament because we didn't win. And clearly I was – and am – deeply disappointed that I wasn't able to conclude the agenda I had laid out for myself in government. As time has passed, I have been aghast at what the Harper government has done in walking away from the Kelowna Accord, our child-care agreements, and our role in the world. I have also been deeply troubled by the degree to which this government has been willing to put at risk the fiscal achievements of the previous decade.

One reason for Canada's success over our 150 years has been the ability of successive governments to build on the achievements of their predecessors, regardless of political stripe. The Harper government has not only walked away from what my government built, it has turned the clock far back. It is not only Liberals who should be upset, but Conservatives as well.

Of all the projects I have taken on since leaving the Prime Minister's Office, writing this book has in some ways been the toughest, because it has meant looking back rather than going forward.

The chief archivist of Canada, Ian Wilson, contacted me within a few days of the election to organize an oral history of my political career. Within a few weeks, he had recruited Sean Conway, the former provincial Ontario minister and academic, to lead the project. Along with former journalist Paul Adams, Sean conducted literally hundreds of hours of interviews with me, and also with many of the people who worked most closely with me in politics, the public service, and Parliament. The transcripts of those conversations make up the spine of this book. By the time you are reading this, I can guarantee you that any desire for retrospection on all those past glories and goof-ups will be pretty much completely out of my system.

What was of much more interest to me in the weeks after the 2006 election was what I might do next. I wanted to concentrate my efforts in my new life on the places where poverty was the greatest. To my mind, that meant Africa from a worldwide perspective, and our Aboriginal peoples from the Canadian point of view. If you think about it, there are real parallels. Both have fast-growing populations, which means that their populations are skewed heavily toward the young. And both are living a reality shaped by the depredations of colonialism. In Africa, traditional societies were disrupted or decapitated, and an arbitrary set of new borders imposed on them as the colonial powers started exiting the continent a half-century ago. I have already written about what has happened to Canada's Aboriginal peoples, whose land has been taken and whose cultures and societies have been subjected to merciless pressures. In both cases, these experiences have been hugely damaging to their self-confidence and identity, as well as to their political, social, and economic structures.

Not long after the election, I received a phone call from Kofi Annan, who was at that time still secretary-general of the United Nations. He asked me to come to New York to discuss the African Development Bank, the largest African-run financial institution on the continent. In the 1990s it became seriously overextended and was forced to spend roughly a dozen years getting its house in order, largely by becoming less ambitious than it had been. The new president of the bank, Donald Kaberuka, had decided that the time had come for it to move from this era of retrenchment back into being a leading force for African development. He approached Kofi Annan to help him assemble a high-level advisory panel that could help set a strategic direction for the bank. Kofi asked whether I would be willing to co-chair the panel along with Joachim Chissano, whom I had met just weeks earlier in South Africa. It did not take long for me to say yes.

For the next year and a half, during many trips to Africa, many hours of meetings with experts in international capitals including Washington, Paris, and Beijing, and many hours of reading, I plunged into the issues facing Africa and its economic development. Africa comprises fifty-three states – the greatest number of countries per square kilometre of any continent. The average GDP of these countries is only about $4 billion. Africa's share of international trade is shockingly small – just 1 per cent of the world's trade – and it is falling. The small, fragmented internal African markets offer no economies of scale, and the infrastructure is so poor that intracontinental trade is almost inconsequential.

What Chissano and I – and the panel we led – concluded was that there needed to be a massive effort in Africa directed to building up infrastructure, ensuring capable governments, promoting the local business sector, and upgrading skills – and that the guiding star for all these efforts needs to be the creation of a single African common market that would create economies of scale and open up markets to build prosperity. This may not be a sufficient condition to alleviate poverty on the continent, but it certainly is a necessary one.

When I was a young man, I worked for a while as an intern in the legal department of the European Coal and Steel Community (ECSC) – the forerunner of the European Union (EU). Our job was to start developing competition law for a common market that did not even exist yet. There were only six member-countries in the ECSC, but the interns I worked with were drawn from across Europe, including countries that did not join the EU until decades later. The farsighted planners behind the European project were already thinking about building up a European public service, and part of the purpose of the internship program was to develop those skills. This is just one example of the institutional foundation that was laid down for the European Union, long before it became a reality.

The same kind of preparation in a wide range of areas is crucial now in Africa. Without it, the task of building regional common markets on the way to the creation of the Pan African Economic Union – something contemplated by the charter of the African Union – will be impossible. Right now, if a smaller or poorer African country seeks to create an economic union with a larger or richer neighbour and the two co-exist behind high common tariff walls or customs duties, the smaller country will lose its industrial base to the larger country. This is what happened when Kenya, Uganda, and Tanzania created a single market for a time: Kenya's better-developed economy quickly became a threat to the health of its partners. The European Community avoided this problem by planning long in advance, committing itself to building up vital infrastructure such as roads and rail, and by creating transitional funds that allowed poorer members to adjust. Joining the European Union was scary for Spain, and Ireland too, but look at them now. This approach is what Africa needs, though, unlike Europe, it does not have enough wealth to manage the planning and sustain the transitional funding. The panel therefore recommended that the African Development Bank should become the focal point for these efforts, and I believe that the rich nations must participate. Having made the argument for the African common market, I have been asked by the bank to follow up in the years to come and to work with others who share this important goal. I intend to do so.

Not long ago, just before he became prime minister of the United Kingdom, I got a phone call from Gordon Brown. He said he had a favour to ask. Gordon had been approached by Dr. Wangari Maathai – a Kenyan scientist who formed a grassroots environmental movement in Africa in 1977. She is also a leader on women's issues and has served in the Kenyan parliament and cabinet. In 2004, she won the Nobel Peace Prize for her environmental work, the first African woman to have done so.

Wangari had approached Gordon Brown to discuss the Congo rain forest. Though it is not well known in the West, the Congo rain forest is the second largest on Earth, after the Amazon. Some people nowadays call it the "world's second lung." The Congo rain forest is twice the size of France, and it sprawls across the borders of ten[1] countries, though it is concentrated in six of them, particularly the Democratic Republic of Congo (DRC). Earlier in this decade a treaty was signed to manage the rain forest because its continuing deforestation threatens both the global climate and the economic sustainability of the people who live in it. But very little had been done, and that's why Wangari had come knocking on Gordon's Brown's door. Convinced that this was an important project for the future of the world as well as for Africa, he decided to allocate £50 million in his upcoming budget (his last before becoming prime minister) to a fund to sustain the rain forest. The Norwegian government has now joined the fund, which has doubled to £100 million, or roughly $200 million.

The favour Gordon was asking was for me to co-chair the fund. There would have to be a lot of planning, a lot of local diplomacy, and a lot of international politicking to make sure the fund got up and running and started getting the job done. There would also be tremendous opportunities. At the moment, for example, the countries of the Congo basin – some of the poorest in the world – do not get carbon credits under the Kyoto protocols for preventing deforestation. That could change in 2012, when deforestation will be on the agenda for the next round, which could create an important opening for those working to save the rainforest. But it will take a great deal of negotiation to ensure the right result.

So I signed on.

---

[1] The ten countries touched by the rain forest are Rwanda, Burundi, Cameroon, Democratic Republic of Congo, Gabon, Equatorial Guineau, Central African Republic, Sao Tomé and Principé, Chad, and Angola.

Not so long afterwards, I found myself in a place called Mbalmayo in Cameroon, one of the Congo Basin countries. Sheila, Jim Pimblett, and I had ridden in a truck over some very rough jungle roads to get there. A worker from a NGO who was acting as our guide took us to an empty field. On the map, he showed us, it was marked as rain forest.

I asked a villager what had happened.

"There was a forest here three months ago," he told me. "But it was cut down."

"Why didn't you stop it?" I asked him.

"It happened too quickly," he replied.

"Why haven't you informed the government?" I asked.

He shrugged and indicated a forestry official who was standing nearby. It didn't take a lot of imagination to guess why nobody had done anything. Later we went to the local sawmill, where the head of the mill shook his head in disapproval when we told him about the clear-cut field. But as we left, our NGO guide produced a photo for us of that very same mill operator standing and watching as the logging had taken place.

As our experience in Mbalmayo showed, no one really knows the extent of the rain forest's degradation. The maps aren't always accurate. One of the first things our fund is devoting itself to is fixing that. We will do this with a combination of satellite technology and community projects that will engage local people, not only in identifying the contours of the forest but also in understanding how they see and use it in their daily lives.

Ultimately, alleviating poverty and saving the rain forest are closely linked, and this is the nexus our fund will explore. Poor people need the rain forest for their survival and their long-term well-being. But this is not true of others who exploit the forest. Moreover, logging may generate desperately needed, if short-lived, cash for local people. Our fund will work to find ways for local people to make a living from the rain forest without destroying it. And we need to make sure that they and their governments are compensated, perhaps through an international regime, for the losses they may suffer from curtailing logging for the benefit of humankind. In essence, what we need to do is to make these forests more valuable standing than they are cut down – not only for the world, but for the people who live in and around them.

One day in Northern Ontario, an Aboriginal boy about fifteen years old came up and said that he had read a bit about me on the Internet.

"It says you were a lawyer but became the head of a shipping company," he said. "How did you do that? How did you learn to run a shipping company?"

"Well," I said, "I went to work for Canada Steamship Lines when I was young, and I learned the business from the people who worked there. That's what they call mentoring."

Then he said, "I read you bought the company. You must have had a lot of money."

"No, not at all," I said. "I borrowed a lot of money."

"Do you think when I grow up someone will mentor me?"

I said, "Yes." But of course I wasn't sure it was true.

"Do you think that someone would lend me money to buy a company?"

Once again, I said, "Yes." But I wasn't sure of that either.

That conversation captured what I believe to be a huge problem with the way we approach the advancement of Canada's Aboriginal peoples. Mentoring is an enormously important part of our informal educational system. A student who graduates from engineering school doesn't really become an engineer until he or she gets a job and learns the business. An accounting graduate doesn't become an accountant until he or she has some working experience under the belt.

And if you don't have that work experience – if you don't learn a business, as I did shipping, at the side of people who have been at it long before you – then no one will ever lend you money to buy a company or start up a new one. It is a vicious circle, and I wondered whether there might be a way to help break it.

That gave my son David and me the idea for one of the projects we are most immersed in here in Canada. Its purpose is to create a private-sector equity fund that would invest in Aboriginal ventures and ensure the mentoring and transmission of entrepreneurial skills to a rising generation of Aboriginal Canadians. Our goals are to bridge the Aboriginal entrepreneurial gap and to demonstrate to Canadian investors that there are opportunities that are passing them by. We hope to have the fund underway in the very near future.

One complication we encountered as we raised money for the fund is that it is neither fish nor fowl. That is, when I asked investors to join in, they would often ask, "Will I get a charitable deduction?" And I would say no. The whole idea is to invest in profit-making businesses, not to create a charitable institution.

Then they ask, "Will I get a market rate of return?" And I would have to say no to that too. It would be unreasonable to expect each of these businesses to make a profit similar to other enterprises, at least in the early years.

We will succeed because those who have invested in the fund have done so recognizing that there is a growing body of Aboriginal business people who seek a hand up, not a handout. But I do believe that if there was a change in the tax laws and regulations recognizing hybrid proposals such as ours we could do so much more. This is not a new idea. It's well advanced in the United Kingdom and the United States. It's called social enterprise, and I believe its time has come in Canada.

We recognize the essential role that business entrepreneurs play in filling gaps in the economy. Why wouldn't we recognize that social entrepreneurs can play the same role in filling gaps in society?

This may shake conventional wisdom a bit, but so did Donald K. Johnson. Johnson was the man who convinced me, and through me the Department of Finance, that if we reduced by half the capital gains tax on securities donated to charities, it would open the doors to a huge influx of funding for our universities, hospitals, and other worthy and important causes. He later convinced Ralph Goodale to eliminate the tax completely, and the new government carried this through after the election.

As a result, gifts and donations are being made in amounts that would have been impossible to imagine a decade ago. All because Don Johnson challenged the status quo.

Well, I believe that the time has come to challenge the status quo again, and to give social entrepreneurs the same opportunities that business entrepreneurs have of realizing their dreams for a better Canada.

The other big project we have underway is much further advanced because I didn't have to raise the money to get it up and running. The high school dropout rate among Aboriginal Canadians is much worse than it is for non-Aboriginals. Forty-three per cent of Aboriginals between the ages of twenty and twenty-four have not graduated from high school compared to 16 per cent for the non-Aboriginal population. The issue is what can we do about it? Some years ago, I heard about a program that began back in 1987 in the South Bronx in New York with a single teacher, Steve Mariotti, who had a business background. It occurred to him that many of the low-income "at risk" kids he was teaching had street smarts, and perhaps they could be converted to academic and business smarts. He started a high school program that emphasized entrepreneurial skills, connecting schoolwork to practical business skills, and exposing the students to businesses and business people, all as a means of keeping kids in school. The program has been a phenomenal success, and has spread to fourteen countries (including the United Kingdom, Ireland, Austria, Israel), with more than one hundred and fifty thousand students going through the program.

I'm not an educator so I asked Sean Conway, who used to be minister of education in Ontario, whether he could connect me with an educator with an expertise in Aboriginal education who could help me think this through. He found Dr. Carlana Lindeman, who is based in Thunder Bay. I asked her to go to New York and take a look at the program, and to go to UCLA to sit in on a teacher-training session for the program. She came back saying it was one of the most exciting things she had ever seen in all her years in education.

One issue remained, however. Could the program be adapted to Aboriginal students and their cultural needs? Furthermore, would a program that worked in inner-city New York or inner-city Dublin be transferable to a reserve school in northern Saskatchewan or northern Ontario? To find out, we decided to do a pilot project. We worked with a teacher, Judy Flett, who spent eight months adapting the curriculum and enrolled thirteen students in a pilot program at Dennis Franklin Cromarty School in Thunder Bay. This is an Aboriginal high school that services many fly-in reserves in northwestern Ontario. We've had a few kids drop out – no surprise, considering all that they have going on in their lives – but most of them have stuck with it, and are succeeding.

One of the amazing things to me was that the first time I met with the students, they were intensely shy. It was very difficult for me to get them engaged in a conversation. A few months later, when I was back, these young women and men were standing in front of a gymnasium with a hundred people and pitching their business plans with full voices and a clear gaze.

Once I saw the potential in the program, I started contacting the premiers of the Western provinces and Nunavut, and told them I wanted to connect with their ministers of education. Each of the ministries has now sent teams to look at the program, and this pilot is about to become part of a network across the West and North. What I discovered is that the provinces really want to be involved. I expect that in the very near future we will have projects going in northern British Columbia, Alberta, Saskatchewan, Manitoba, and Nunavut, with others to follow in other parts of the country.

Lakehead University agreed to monitor and evaluate the program, which they have now done. The evaluation was very positive. We are also going to commission a new textbook, specifically adapted to the needs of Aboriginal Canadian students.

Unlike my entrepreneurship fund, I am doing this on my own, so

I can keep the momentum going. But over time I plan to bring in partners, and I issue fair warning to all my friends – I'll be calling you! And you thought buying this book would get you off the hook.

As I've delved more deeply into the subject of Aboriginal education, one of the discoveries I have made is how isolated Aboriginal educators are. When a schoolteacher or principal in Toronto or Montreal or Vancouver has a special issue – dealing with kids with disabilities, say – he or she can call on support from the resources of their school board. That isn't true for those educating Aboriginal kids, who are often on isolated reserves, without even a system for sharing experiences with their colleagues.

To help fix this I have consulted more than twenty universities with large Aboriginal enrolments or interests, along with much of the country's Aboriginal education leadership, about setting up a centre of best practices and eventually a centre of excellence focusing on Aboriginal primary and secondary school education. The idea, which is still in the conceptual stages, is to have a network across the country, with an administrative office in Montreal and a "node" located in a university in each province. I am fortunate that Carlana Lindeman has agreed to join what we now call the Martin Aboriginal Initiative as education director, and Lucie Santoro has come on board full-time as administrative director. Lucie has been with me for thirty years. She joined CSL when she was sixteen, worked her way through school, and followed me into politics serving in my office when I was minister of finance and in the PMO. Her ability to manage several complex projects at once, get along with everyone, and always produce top-notch results will go a long way toward ensuring we achieve our goals. Education is undoubtedly the key to any society's success. It certainly is the key for the next generation of Aboriginal Canadians. I hope this initiative, with the help of Canada's educational and Aboriginal leaders, can play a role.

I have also been drawn into another set of issues even though they were not on my original agenda for life after politics. As you may remember from earlier chapters I spent a lot of energy in public life seeking to reform certain of the world's multilateral institutions, and in particular the G8. It now seems that the pebble that we dropped in the water with the establishment of the G20 at the level of finance ministers has continued to produce a ripple, and the idea behind it has been seized upon by governments and thinkers in Africa, Europe, North America, Latin America, and Asia. President Sarkozy of France and Prime Minister Brown of the United Kingdom have both spoken out in favour of increasing the G8 to include the so-called "Outreach 5" (namely: China, India, Brazil, South Africa, and Mexico). On the other hand, another school of thought has suggested ejecting Russia from the G8 and including India and Brazil but not China. Some have called this the "concert of democracies."

I am agnostic on the notion of a "concert of democracies." Whoever wants to get together can get together. But this cannot be the replacement for the G8. Excluding countries such as China or Russia would be a throwback to the era of strategic and antagonistic alliances. The consequences would be international gridlock at best, war at worst. What the world needs is a steering committee, a caucus made up of the great powers and the major regional powers including China and Russia. I believe that this steering committee will be created. It is needed; indeed, I believe it's inevitable. It should be based around the G8, either as an extension of it or as a parallel organization to it, just at the G20 finance ministers group parallels the G7 finance ministers.

At the moment, Canada is absent from this debate. This makes no sense. The debate is no longer unilateralism versus multilateralism, where our support for the latter is well known. The debate is about what kind of multilateral structure will the world's great powers adopt, and how things play out will be a determining factor in the role Canada plays internationally in the future. As finance minister and later as prime minister, I helped create the G20 at the finance ministers level, and promoted the concept at the leaders level. I continue to believe that this structure, or something close to it, is what we need. The G8 is no longer sufficiently representative to play the role it did prior to the rise of China and India. The G8 should be augmented to at least fifteen (the current G8 members, plus China, India, Brazil, South Africa, Mexico, Indonesia, and either Nigeria or Egypt), or, failing that, such an organization should be established to exist alongside a continuing G8. Either option, by the way, should assure Canada of a place at the table. But that is not inevitable. If we drag our feet, there is a risk we will be left out. That's why we should not be afraid to take the lead.

I thought I had left this issue behind when I stepped down from office, but it has taken on a life of its own. Thanks to governments in both the G8 and the G20, but also thanks to the efforts of a number of think-tanks in Canada and abroad – the Centre for International Governance Innovation in Kitchener, the Centre for Global Studies in Victoria, the Brookings Institution in Washington, the OECD in Europe, and others in Germany, Mexico, the United Kingdom, and China – I have been asked to continue to participate, and I intend to do just that.

I am very excited by where my third career has taken me, as I hope comes through in this chapter. One place, you might notice, where it has not led is back to business. Been there, done that! And besides, as my sons were quick to point out when I stepped down, things worked out well at CSL in my absence – why tempt fate? At least that's the polite version of what they said.

I'm busy, but I don't want you to think it has been all work and no play, though I have to say that according to Sheila, having me around the house more is not always an unalloyed joy. My grandson Ethan, on the other hand, thinks it's great. The farm at Brome Lake, nestled in a beautiful little valley along a dirt road, long ago displaced the cottage at Colchester as my sentimental home. It has now, for the first time, become my actual home as well. Many days when I'm there, I ignore the newspapers on the kitchen table, head out to the porch, put my feet up, and watch the sheep graze and the birds fly by. And then I get itchy feet.

With so much of what I have started since leaving government, I am back to a place similar to the fall of 1993, after I had agreed to become finance minister and was staring at the deficit for the first time as a problem that had become mine. I knew what had to be done. I was certain that I was ready to do it. But I could not know all the obstacles I would face, how truly difficult it would be, or with certainty whether I would reach my goal. As I look at my life today, I cannot say for sure whether my aspirations for an African common market will come to fruition, whether the Congo rain forest can be saved to the extent it must, whether my ideas and plans for Aboriginal education, mentoring, and entrepreneurship will be as successful as I hope, or whether the G8 will expand in the way it should. I am going to give them all the energy I have, and I have found some very interesting and determined travelling companions for the trip. I imagine there are going to be some surprises along the way, some disappointments, and some unanticipated joys. I am looking forward to it.

Acknowledgements

There are two ways to write a memoir.

The first is to wait a while. This has the advantage of permitting you to see which of your projects matured and bloomed, and which withered on the vine. And it allows passions to cool – both your own and those of other actors in your drama.

The second is to launch into the project right away. This is the option I have chosen. I knew that if I did not put pen to paper – or, more graphically, my backside on a chair in front of a desk – now, it would never happen. Even more important for me, however, is that by writing soon after the events described in this book I hoped to stimulate further discussion of the issues that were of my greatest concern, discussion that might help others finish the job.

I have had a full business career and a full political career. In the course of these lives, I have been blessed with the most extraordinary support and friendship from literally thousands of people without whom none of it would have been possible. If you are one of these people and I have not told of our story together, please forgive me, the limitations of space and time are unrelenting – but I know the story, and I will never forget you.

When I first entered the business world, I knew little of its excitement. In the book, I mention some of those who let me learn from them, but there were so many more.

Canada Steamship Lines has gone on to fulfill all the hopes I had for it. But I was away for most of that period and the credit goes to others.

When I first entered government, I had much to learn. When I left government, I still had a long way to go. But where I succeeded I did so by working alongside many outstanding public servants, from whom I learned more than I can say. Where the narrative called for it I was able to name some of them. Let me just say here how fortunate we are that so many of Canada's finest men and women have dedicated themselves to serving their fellow citizens; I believe we should say that more often.

My father used to say that it was to the people of Essex East that he owed his political career. I know what he meant, and I feel what he felt. Whether it was walking in Montreal's St. Patrick's Day Parade, serving spaghetti at Le Parc Terrasse des Rapides by the St. Lawrence River on Canada Day, or commemorating Armistice Day at Branch 212 of the Canadian Legion, I was and am very proud to have represented the people of LaSalle-Émard, and am privileged that they elected and re-elected me six times in a row. Would this have happened without a strong riding association or without a dedicated riding executive and an election team made up of hundreds and hundreds of volunteers? No, of course not.

The Liberal Party is like family to me. I have run in two leadership races. I think of those in every riding across the country who were part of that ragtag but determined band that formed my 1990 campaign. I think of those same people augmented by so many others who were described as the Juggernaut of 2003. I think of the tens of thousands of Canadians who joined the Liberal Party to support my leadership. I think of my devoted, selfless, and long-suffering political staffs at Finance and in the PMO, all of whom had unlimited options before them, all of who chose the public service. I think of those who put their careers at risk for me in 2002.

I think of my caucus colleagues who informed so much of what we did, in Opposition, when I was in Finance, and when I led our country. I think of those who voluntarily entwined their fortunes with mine and stood as candidates under my prime ministership in two election campaigns.

Each and every one of those who recognize themselves in what I have just written cannot be recognized individually in this book. As I sit here, and the names and faces roll through my mind, I know that would be impossible, for how can I mention one without mentioning everyone. Every one of you played a unique and critical role in the story played out here. We both know what it was; you must know how grateful I am.

When I first conceived of this book, a few weeks after stepping down as prime minister, I thought I might be able to write it in a year. My publisher and editor, Doug Gibson (he of the merciless edit, graceful pen, and lack of tolerance for last-minute changes), wisely suggested I take two. I am glad I took his advice. Even two years, it turns out, is not such a long time for a project of this size. I thank him for his experience and his understanding. I forgive him for his insistence on meeting deadlines.

The core of the research was the oral history suggested by Canada's chief archivist, Ian Wilson. He recruited Sean Conway, the distinguished former Ontario MPP and minister, now at Queen's University, to lead and manage the project. Sean is extraordinarily well read, particularly with regard to Canadian history and politics, of which of course he was a successful practitioner. Not only has he devoured almost everything ever written on these subjects, but he remembers most of it in amazing detail. Add that to a voluminous personal memory of many of the political figures and events of recent decades, a very acute mind, a wicked sense of humour, and you have a man with a lot of sharp and well-informed questions. On the other hand, the modern tape recorder would appear not to be an instrument with which Sean has much familiarity. My sons allege that I was born before the quill pen was invented. Let me say that compared to Sean Conway, I am the inventor of the BlackBerry.

Sean led an interview process assisted by Ryan Zade and Nigel Smith that soon sprawled to hundreds of hours over the summer and fall of 2006, and continued through 2007. Along with Paul Adams, the former journalist now teaching at Carleton University, they took me through every phase of my life and career – often refusing to accept my first response, always digging for more. On the tapes, the contents of which become public after my passing, I am allowed to let fly. In this book, Paul Adams forced on me an unwelcome but necessary objectivity. His is a wonderful pen. His ability to take the most complex subject and make it intelligible is something to behold. He is not the most patient person I have worked with. He might say the same about me, but that would be unfair. Over many drafts he helped me shape my words, and although he inexplicably lost his composure at times, he kept coming back for more. Quite simply, his hand touched every element of the final product. I thank him for the time, effort, and soul he put into my life. Paul also has the ability to cut to the heart of the matter. If at times the book seems to wander off into back yards and back alleys that is because I could not bear to deprive the reader of the trip.

At my suggestion, Sean organized a series of roundtables with many of the political and bureaucratic figures who played a major role in my career. These discussions were organized by themes: the early budgets, pension reform, international finance, the environment, the North, foreign affairs, federalism, and Aboriginal issues, to pick a few examples.

Along with many other documents, the transcripts provided the basis for this book. In addition, Dr. James Fergusson of the University of Manitoba described to me a portion of his forthcoming book dealing with ballistic missile defense. Separate discussions with John McCallum on defence and Bill Graham and Gene Lang on Afghanistan were very helpful.

I usually began the roundtable discussions with Sean and Paul by giving a resumé of my memory of events, and then invited the others around the table to challenge and correct me, which they did with gusto. Among those who participated in these roundtables were: Terrie O'Leary, whose memory extended back to before I entered politics, through my political and government careers; Elly Alboim, who contributed to many phases of my career after I took ministerial office; Tim Murphy, who had been part of my first leadership bid and then led my staff in the latter part of the Finance years and at the PMO; and Peter Nicholson, whose intellect contributed to my career as well as to this book.

Others who shared their recollections, particularly from the Finance years, included: David Dodge, Scott Clark, Ian Bennett, Pete DeVries, and Don Drummond, who played key roles in many of my budgets; and Susan Peterson, Réal Bouchard, and Charlie Seeto, who were a crucial part of the process of pension reform. Gordon Thiessen, who became a great friend despite being a central bank governor, also contributed greatly to this book.

Ruth Thorkelson contributed her knowledge of social issues, both in the Finance and ministerial years, particularly with regard to child care, as did Yaprak Baltacioglu. Brian Guest lent his enthusiasm and knowledge on the cities file and the environment. Johanna Leffler most certainly brought passion and expertise to the issue of the environment.

Many of my parliamentary colleagues participated in this process. They included Ralph Goodale, Dennis Dawson, John English, Francis Fox, John Godfrey, Jean Lapierre, Anne McLennan, Allan Rock, Andy Mitchell, Jim Peterson, Lucienne Robillard, Andy Scott, Reg Alcock, Ethel Blondin-Andrew, Nancy Karetak Lindell, and Doug Young. Some of them even had similar memories of the unfolding of similar events.

In addition to those I have already mentioned, David Herle and Scott Reid – each of whom played pivotal roles in my political and governmental careers – contributed many memories and corrected some of mine.

Alex Himelfarb and Jonathan Fried, who were the public servants with whom I worked most closely in my time as prime minister, and who now both have demanding posts abroad, nonetheless gave generously of their time. Simon Kennedy, who was at the Privy Council Office when I was prime minister, also contributed his recollections, as did Louis Lévesque. Barbara Anderson on equalization and Janice Charette on health care were invaluable.

I want to thank Jim Pimblett, who in between trips to the Congo, to North Africa, and places in between was not only the final fact checker of record but also read the manuscript so many times looking for errors, omissions, and the occasional bit of exaggeration that if he ever wants to teach ancient history I am sure he has a solid base.

I want to thank the indefatigable Thérèse Horvath, who organized Sean's round tables, sifted through thousands of pictures, including those provided to me by my cousin Michael Maloney (for which I am most appreciative), and did this while at the same time ensuring that I got to wherever I was supposed to get to on time.

I want to thank Veronique de Passillé, who worked hard to ensure that the French and English versions of the text provided an accurate reflection of each other.

I want to thank Diane Johnson, who eased my return to normal life, and Lucie Santoro, who did the same while plunging headlong into the world of Aboriginal education.

I want to thank Ann Luu, Cheryl Mayhew, and Kaylann Knickle, who made sure my parliamentary office continued to run smoothly through all the distractions, and Suzanne Ranger, Lorraine Poissant, and Sylvain Savard, who did the same in my riding office.

There are many others who contributed in various ways to the preparation of this book, helping check a fact, find a document, or remind me of a forgotten incident. Please accept my thanks – and my apologies if I have not mentioned you here.

To my family and the next generation, you have made it all worthwhile.

To Sheila, who contributed her memories and looked over my shoulder as I changed each word for the hundredth time, nothing I could say here would express the gratitude I owe you over a lifetime of companionship, love, and support. Much of this was your life too, and mine would have been utterly incomplete without you.

This book has been the labour of many minds, but the text is mine, and I take full responsibility for everything here.

Paul Martin
At the farm
July 2008

Index